Facing Fascism

The Threat to American Democracy in the 21st Century

Jerry Sorlucco

Bloomington, IN Milton Keynes, UK

authorHOUSE®

AuthorHouse™
1663 Liberty Drive, Suite 200
Bloomington, IN 47403
www.authorhouse.com
Phone: 1-800-839-8640

AuthorHouse™ UK Ltd.
500 Avebury Boulevard
Central Milton Keynes, MK9 2BE
www.authorhouse.co.uk
Phone: 08001974150

First published by AuthorHouse 8/10/2006

ISBN: 1-4259-4980-0 (e)
ISBN: 1-4259-4895-2 (sc)
ISBN: 1-4259-4894-4 (dj)

Library of Congress Control Number: 2006907044

Printed in the United States of America
Bloomington, Indiana

This book is printed on acid-free paper.

Contents

Part One
The 2004 Election

Part Two
Worldview

Part Three
The Issues

Part Four
Taking Back America

Preface

It is with a great deal of humility that I invite you to join me on this journey into contemporary politics from my perspective as a progressive Democrat living in Littleton, New Hampshire, the "North Country." As this is written in early 2005, many authoritative national analysts are trying to make sense of the 2004 election in which President George W. Bush won a second term, and Democrats yet again lost seats in both houses of Congress. My perspective is far from that lofty perch; it's from the grassroots, the trenches of political warfare.

As in all wars it is the foot soldiers who win or lose the battles. In politics that means the activist who feels so strongly and passionately about the election that he or she is willing not only to stand and be counted, but also to ring doorbells, distribute literature, make countless telephone calls, attend rallies, march in parades, make and distribute signs, and conspicuously dance and wave to people on busy street corners. That's the grassroots campaign, and despite the unprecedented amount of money spent in the 2004 election by both major political parties, by so-called 527 advocacy groups, and by the candidates themselves, at the grassroots level most of the campaigns were as flat as stale beer. In the following pages we'll investigate why, and why the lack of informed passion that motivates people to actively participate in politics is threatening the very foundation of our democracy.

The book is divided into four parts: Part 1 deals with the 2004 national and New Hampshire state election; the candidates, leadership, the parties, the lobbyists and advocates, the money, and more. Part 2 offers a worldview. It examines the fundamental concepts and ideas that we need to intelligently participate in the elective process. Part 3 focuses those concepts and ideas on the major contemporary issues facing our nation and state. Part 4 faces toward the future. The United States is in a political crisis; it is in danger of becoming a one-party country. Unless we bring people and passion back into politics, progressive thought in America could be dealt a deathblow as the Republican far right manipulates us back into the political and economic dark ages.

The opinions and statements made in this book are mine and mine alone, and in no way do they represent those of the Democratic Party or any other group of which I am a member or an officer.

Part One

The 2004 Election

One

Politics on Parade

———◆•◆•◆———

When the telephone rang at 1:30 in the morning on November 3, I knew exactly who was calling: Barbara Tetreault, the senior reporter for the *Berlin Daily Sun,* looking for election results for the morning paper. She'd said she'd call for any early returns I might have access to through the New Hampshire Democratic Party. Besides running for the State Senate District 1, as chairman of the North Country Democratic Committee I had some contacts. She shared the news that John Gallus, my opponent, was ahead by several thousand votes and was the likely winner. Would I like to concede?

I like Barbara; she's a good and fair reporter. Frankly, what I would like to have told her was that if the voters were stupid enough to reelect Gallus they'd get what they deserved. Of course I didn't say that, nor do I actually mean that, but it was certainly the way I felt at the time. What I said was that I had been out all day visiting the polls (mostly in a cold, drizzling rain), had only very preliminary results when I went to bed, and would wait until the morning for an official count.

Trying to get back to sleep was all but impossible. My mind kept replaying the campaigns going back to the first run in 2002. How could all my work and effort, and that of the many people who supported me, not win? Why had I failed to deliver for the thousands of people who voted for me? We had worked hard, bringing lessons learned from the first campaign I mounted in 2002 into the second. One of the lessons was the need to be visible, and that still brings a smile.

The family Jeep Grand Cherokee was plastered with bright yellow decals and towed a billboard trailer, equally as gaudy, in every parade and public event we could find. Art Tighe, the proprietor of the Foto Factory in Littleton, decorated the vehicles. We had supporters marching with us wear bright yellow caps labeled "Jerry Sorlucco State Senate" in blue, and proudly we marched. For the first time in the North Country (where Democratic business owners sometimes do not reveal their political affiliation for fear of losing customers), Democrats were highly visible in broad daylight and in large numbers. Before, we would simply conceded the turf to the Republicans, who had been in control for what seemed like forever.

Many who joined us were older. Some walked with canes, others brought their grandchildren or dogs. Altogether, we were a splendid bunch. And every sign, every banner, and every flyer the Sorlucco campaign put out proudly identified me as a Democrat. Sadly, I was the only Democratic candidate who did. Most didn't want to offend the Republicans or appear too liberal for Independents to vote for them. I'm convinced they got it wrong. If Democrats hope to regain their status as the party of the people, that attitude must change. We must learn to play as a team and sell our brand.

As it worked out, the final numbers were Gallus 15,838, Sorlucco 10,749. Hardly a close race at a 3:2 ratio; however, historically for a Democrat in the North Country it wasn't a bad showing. In 2002, I got only 5,733 votes to Gallus' 12,140, a 2:1 ratio.

Why did I, a reasonably sane and intelligent person, run a second time against such odds, in a place where running as a Democrat is usually akin to fishing for marlin in Arizona? I was well aware that Gallus would have the financial support of special interests—the power of incumbency is huge. The answer is both complex and simple. I am not a quitter and I did think there was a chance of winning if my campaign could tie into a broad Democratic victory, which I thought was a possibility. I also felt a responsibility to stand for the ideals that my supporters and I value, and they are not John Gallus' ideals. Democracy requires a citizenry that participates in the electoral process and I am proud that I did, both as a candidate and as a party leader. But, trust me, that doesn't make it any easier to lose. Like most of our Democratic candidates, I had put my heart and soul, and a considerable amount of money, into the campaign and lost. Our loss to George Bush was particularly disheartening. But nationally we also lost four seats in the Senate and four in the House, solidifying Republican rule in the United States.

On the bright side, New Hampshire went blue for John Kerry, albeit by a very small margin of one percent. We were the only so called "swing state" to do so. Unfortunately, Kerry's victory in New Hampshire didn't have coattails for the rest of the Democratic slate. All the support and money that came into the state in the form of manpower and media advertising was either focused for John Kerry, attack ads against G.W. Bush, or on the Get Out The Vote (GOTV) effort. The GOTV was the particular focus of the well-financed 527 organizations such as Move On and America Coming Together (ACT). McCain/Feingold campaign finance reforms allow 527s to GOTV and attack candidates or issues, but prohibit them from advocating for candidates or political parties. Consequently, many towns with a large base of Democratic voters, such as Berlin and Gorham, carried for John Kerry but then reverted to the Republican incumbents. The reforms sponsored by Senators John McCain (R-AZ) and Russ Feingold (D-WI) and promulgated in 2002, also greatly restricted contributions of so-called "soft" money to political parties—money contributed for party building that was used to advertise generically and not for a specific candidate. In 2004, Democrats failed to work effectively within the new rules, and as a result failed to elect a slate of candidates. The Republicans did a much better job.

All three Democratic candidates running for Congress from New Hampshire lost to the Republican incumbents. Doris "Granny D" Haddock lost to Sen. Judd Gregg, Paul Hodes to Rep. Charlie Bass, and Justin Nadeau to Rep. Jeb Bradley. On average, 98 percent of incumbents in the House and 85 percent in the Senate win reelection. Speaking to that issue, Nathaniel Persily, an election law expert at the University of Pennsylvania, said, "The turnover in the United States House of Representatives is lower than it was in the Soviet Politburo."

There were 11 gubernatorial elections in 2004 and six Democrats won, including John Lynch in New Hampshire, who ousted one-term Republican Craig Benson by a small one-percent margin. Lynch ran on the Democratic ticket but carefully distanced himself from Democrats, choosing instead to focus on Benson's unethical behavior and courting Republican and Independent voters. It worked for him but did little to help the ticket. In 2005, the national gubernatorial partisan lineup is 27 Republican governors and 23 Democrats. Between 1972 and 1994, Democratic governors at times greatly outnumbered Republican governors. Since 1996, however, Republican governors have outnumbered Democrats.

In 2004, a total of 5,805 legislative seats (79 percent of the 7,382 state legislative seats) in 46 states were up for election. In 2005, Democrats control both chambers of the legislature in 17 states, and the Republicans in 21 states. Eleven states will have split chambers (Nebraska has a unicameral legislature). In New Hampshire, Republicans continue to control both chambers of the legislature by a large margin, although Democrats gained two seats in the Senate and about 25 in the House; the breakdown in the House is **253r/147d** and in the Senate **16r/8d**. The Republicans have had control of the New Hampshire House since the Civil War.

The 2004 election, while not a landslide for the Republican Party, reinforced its control of government in America; and clearly, the leadership of the Republican Party intends to leave no holds barred to retain and increase that majority to advance its far-right agenda. President Bush, in a 2005 speech in Brussels appealing for support for his global campaign for democracy, expressed his concerns that President Vladimir Putin has chosen an increasingly authoritarian path. Bush said, "We recognize that reform will not happen overnight. We must always remind Russia, however, that our (NATO) alliance stands for a free press, a vital opposition, the sharing of power and the rule of law." Many of us think that, given the oppressive measures the Bush administration has taken since 9/11, 2001, the United States needs to practice what it preaches.

Politically, New Hampshire is a strange state. We have the first in the nation presidential primary, although, being overwhelmingly white and conservative, we hardly represent a cross section of the diverse people in this country. Being "first in the nation" is great for business, and New Hampshire's politicians from both parties ardently protect that position. Somehow we seem to offer a venue that lets presidential hopefuls test the water by rubbing elbows with "the people," and of course trips to the wilds of the North Country are a must for all the candidates. It's a state where it is possible for activists and reporters to actually meet the presidential candidates face-to-face, giving credence to the old story of the codger who, when asked if he was going to vote for a certain candidate, said, "I haven't made up my mind yet. I've only met him a few times."

It's fun and an honor to meet those running for our country's highest office. I got to meet all the Democrats who ran in 2004, to hear them speak, and in some instances to share the podium with them as a state Senate candidate. When President Bush visits, on the other hand, those with different opinions are not welcome; we are carefully weeded out. Democrats and other protesters are only allowed to wave their signs from distant, unseen corrals.

I was closest to Howard Dean, the former governor of our neighboring state of Vermont. The first time I got to meet Gov. Dean was in 2001, when he was still a governor testing the waters for his run in 2004. It was my job to squire him around to *The Courier* (a Littleton weekly newspaper), WLTN (a local radio station), and to the popular Village Book Store to speak to a small group. I was, and remain extremely impressed with the depth of his understanding of the issues and his vision for America. I went on to work for his presidential bid as a Dean campaign captain for Littleton. He in turn not only endorsed my Senate run, but was also in a TV campaign commercial we produced.

As the world knows, Dean lost in the Democratic primary to Sen. John Kerry from Massachusetts, and we "Deaniacs" shifted gears and did our absolute best for Kerry and his vice presidential running mate, Sen. John Edwards. My only regret is that the Iowa caucus Dean "scream" (for which the media crucified him) couldn't be bottled and given to other Democrats. Lord knows we can certainly use more of his passion. Evidently, a majority of delegates to the Democratic National Committee (DNC) meeting felt the same way. Dean was elected chairman of the DNC in February of 2005.

Running for the presidency is an unbelievably demanding challenge. We've had governors, senators, generals, political leaders, businessmen, and even a few comedians throw their hats in the ring. Running for public office at any level is noble.

Unfortunately, running for election in America now is usually closely linked to the candidate's ability to raise huge amounts of money in order to run a credible campaign. And it certainly helps if he or she brings personal wealth to the effort. There is no limit under the campaign finance laws to the amount of money a candidate can personally spend—it has been judged protected by the constitution as freedom of speech. And spend they do; we will discuss that more in subsequent chapters.

New Hampshire makes running for office even tougher than other states in several ways: We pay state legislators, in both the House and Senate the grand sum of $100 a year (plus gas money). Supporters of the system have the audacity to proudly call it a "citizen" legislature. In fact, it discourages citizens from serving, especially those who need to earn a living. This is further exacerbated by the size of the House, 400 members (one member for about every 3,000 people), of which about half turn over every two-year term, leaving control easily in the hands of the leadership. As I said, the Republicans have dominated the New Hampshire House since the Civil War and, by refusing to change this system, they clearly hope to keep it that way.

In contrast, the Senate, with only 24 members, is one of the smallest in the country. NH Senate districts are determined by population (about 52,000), with no consideration given to geography or county lines. Consequently, sparsely populated Senate District 1, where I contended, is huge. It encompasses all of Coos County and the northern parts of Carroll and Grafton Counties—over 52 communities. By contrast, in the densely populated southern districts a brisk walk can get you from one end of the district to the other.

The term of office for the governor and both houses of the legislature is two years. The only other state that has a two-year term for the governor is Vermont; the 48 other states have four-year terms. While all the New

England states have two-year terms for the Senate, 39 states have four-year terms.

The 22nd Amendment to the United States Constitution, ratified in 1951, limits presidents to two terms in office. There are no term limits for Congress, which contributes to the low rollover rate. Nineteen states, including our neighboring State of Maine, have limited the terms of their state legislators.

Given all this, how in the world do we get people to run? As a party officer, I can tell you it's a challenge. But it is a challenge we have to meet in facing the threat to American democracy.

Two

Nourishing the Grassroots

———◆•◆•◆———

My two state senate campaigns alone form a tale worth telling. Here I'll just share some of the people and events related to the campaigns that I experienced over that four-year period.

I began to consider a run in the summer of 2001. After retiring from US Airways in 1997 (I was a captain for the airline and its predecessors for over thirty-seven years), I became increasingly active in our community. It was merely a continuation of a lifetime of service. My life has been blessed and I have always felt the obligation to pay back. During my airline career, I was an officer in the Airline Pilots Association, an AFL-CIO union, and a founder and vice president of the Professional Pilots Federation, an organization that advocates for airline pilots. I was an activist, a fighter, and as a representative, no stranger to negotiation or confrontation.

After years of vacationing in the area, my wife Sue and I settled in Littleton in the late 1970s. The year before I retired we moved into a new home we'd built on a peak a few hundred yards within the Littleton town line. The New Hampshire Electric Cooperative supported by the Rural Electrification Administration (REA) had electrified our local area years before. President Franklin D. Roosevelt's 1935 executive order created the REA to offset the prohibitive cost of running power to farms and homes away from town centers. Downtown Littleton, on the other hand, had a privately held company. The Littleton Water Works provided electric power as far back as 1887. In 1903, the state allowed the Town of Littleton to buy the company and it became Littleton Water & Light (LW&L). Because of some costs related to the closing of the Seabrook nuclear power plant in 1996, the co-op's rates were twice those of LW&L.

For whatever reason, my new neighbors asked me to investigate the possibility of getting onto the LW&L's grid. After conversations with members of select board, I was certain they weren't going to move in that direction. The town would have to buy the power lines and that would affect the town's property tax rate. To encourage the select board's deliberation, I appeared with quite a few of my friends and neighbors at a board meeting and we filled the room.

While our unexpected and unprecedented demonstration got quite a bit of press and notoriety, it didn't move the select board to solve our problem. But it was my first taste of the destructive nature of New Hampshire's dysfunctional tax structure. Our state relies more on the property tax, which is a regressive tax, than any other state in the nation. New Hampshire has neither an income tax nor a broad-based sales tax so it has been struggling with a structural deficit in its budget for a decade and a half. Understandably, voters will not tax themselves out of their homes, so school budgets and vital town improvements are voted down time after time at town meetings.

However, our efforts did help the co-op get relief from New Hampshire when the state passed a deregulation bill that allowed the power company to buy power on the open market. Of course, deregulation of the nation's electric power and the rise and fall of Enron is in itself a compelling issue that we'll touch upon later in the book. In any case, my leadership was noticed.

A short time after the notable select board meeting, my next-door neighbor, Everett Chambers, a retired Air Force colonel, and I were asked to meet with two members of the town planning board, Paul McGoldrick and Katharine Terrie. They had a problem and wanted our help. The hundred-year-old Littleton Regional Hospital was building a new multi-million dollar facility two miles from our homes at the base of Walker

Hill on Route 18.Their dilemma was that it was sited in a area zoned rural, which provided few safeguards either for the hospital or the surrounding community. Could our band of newly found activists help? Our first question was why? We would quickly learn the reason.

It was the start of an extensive education on land use and zoning. One of my teachers would be Jason Hoch, a newly hired assistant town manager and director of planning. (Jason eventually became town manager.) The fly in the ointment (the why) was a very militant, far-right citizens group in town called Citizens for Growth with Common Sense. They had formed half a dozen years earlier for the specific purpose of opposing the site plan review provision of the town's zoning ordinance. It was in response to a town zoning officer, who, perhaps overzealously, tried to enforce the town's sign regulations. He was ostracized and fired for his effort and any form of site plan review was removed from the zoning ordinance.

Common Sense was, and to some extent remains, well financed by a wealthy old guard and local real-estate interests who share a 19th-century worldview. They also have worked hard and successfully at getting teachers' contracts and other progressive issues voted down at town meetings; anything that could possibly increase property tax is opposed. Although not in lockstep on all issues, their support of the Republican far right is unflagging. In step with that tradition, Littleton voted a one hundred percent Republican ticket in the 2004 election.

Falling back on my experience in negotiating union contracts, my first thought in trying to help the planning board was to reach out and try to find common ground. A good deal is almost always a good deal for all concerned. So I went to Eddy Moore, an officer of Common Sense, and also (oddly enough) chairman of the Littleton Zoning Board of Adjustment (ZBA). Eddy, a short, portly man who always talks in a low voice, sort of whispered in my ear that there were "very powerful people with deep pockets" who would never allow a change in the zoning, nor permit any form of site plan review. Site plan review is the mechanism that allows a town to enforce its regulations. There would be no negotiating with Common Sense. Frank Porfido, Jr., their chairman, quickly held a meeting and the group publicly took a threatening posture.

So our little band of activists went to work, caucused and formed a competitive progressive citizens group called Littleton Citizens for Responsible Growth Route 18. We chipped in our money and hired Jerry Coogan, a professional land-use expert, and petitioned the planning board to rezone the entire corridor surrounding the new hospital into a much more compatible mixed-use zone—with restrictions.

And then the shit hit the fan. All winter long, in the months preceding town meeting and the vote, huge four-foot by eight-foot plywood signs appeared all over town (it's allowed in Littleton), attacking me and the Route 18 Article that was on the ballot. Common Sense was in a red rage. On top of Route 18, I'd also had the audacity to run for an open seat on the select board! Me, a flatlander (the local pejorative for a person from "away")! I was called that repeatedly.

To make a long story short, I lost my bid for the select board, and the Route 18 Article failed. However, Common Sense, having spent their energy on Route 18, and me, allowed other important articles to pass, including a teachers' contract that had failed twice before.

But our band didn't go away. The group caucused again, changed its name to the Littleton Alliance, and broadened its mission based upon what I had come to see as the interrelationship of all the major issues—land use, education, health care, taxation, and the environment. I was again elected the group's chairman. The next year the Littleton Alliance spearheaded a second drive for compatible land use on Route 18 that succeeded. The ordinance created a smaller mixed-use district that has become the model for contemporary zoning issues.

In 2000, there were two events that wetted my interest in partisan politics. Katharine Terrie, with whom I'd worked on Route 18, invited me to a house party for three Democratic candidates in the November 2nd election: Barney Brannen, who was running for Congress; Wayne Presby, who was running for the State Senate District 1, and Jon Edick, who was running for the state House. Katharine, an old hand in Democratic politics, had worked for President Lyndon Johnson and West Virginia Senator Jay Rockefeller. Shortly after her party, I had another invitation, this one from Catherine Menninger, a well-known liberal in Franconia, who was hosting a house party for state Senator Mark Fernald. Fernald was running in the Democratic primary for governor against the incumbent, Jeanne Shaheen. All of the candidates at the two house parties lost, but it was my first experience with partisan state politics and I was hooked.

Some have said that politics is addictive and, you know, I've grown to think that's true. It is the prospect of actually being able to do something, to have that power. By the summer of 2001, I'd grown extremely frustrated as the progressive leader of the Littleton Alliance trying to influence the major issues in conservative Littleton. It had become abundantly clear that the state and federal governments set the agenda and towns, at the bottom of the pecking order, were more or less left holding the bag. If I wanted to make a difference it would have to be in the New Hampshire Legislature and, always one to set my mark high, it would be in the Senate. Mark Fernald was running again in the Democratic primary, but this time Gov. Jeanne Shaheen wasn't running for reelection. She was running for the U.S. Senate. Fernald stood a chance. The centerpiece of his platform was a state income tax for education. I had got to know Mark and I supported his income tax proposal, even though it was hard to explain. The plan would have given badly needed aid to education and, most important, reduced property taxes.

Republican Harold Burns, who had beaten Presby in 2000, wasn't expected to run for a second term in the Senate District 1 seat. Two Littleton Republicans, Brien Ward and Ralph Doolan, were both exploring a run. If elected, Ward, a Littleton lawyer with close ties to Common Sense, or Doolan would perpetuate the far-right's control over the North Country. Ward had spent a couple of terms in the New Hampshire House, was chair of the Littleton Chamber of Commerce and was highly active on the Littleton Economic Development Council. He was definitely an insider with aspirations to be governor, or so I was told. His mother, Kay Ward, had served multiple terms in the House, earning a reputation for being farther to the right than Attila the Hun. A third Republican from Berlin, John Gallus, a well-known realtor and two-term House representative also threw his hat in the ring. In the House, Gallus supported every off-the-wall, far-right piece of legislation to come down the pike. Against this potential three-way Republican primary, I, a progressive Italian immigrant's son from Brooklyn, New York—a flatlander—announced my candidacy on the Democratic ticket.

Mark Fernald was very helpful in getting my campaign started. At his suggestion I contacted the New Hampshire Senate Democratic Caucus in Concord, told them I was considering a run, and eventually had a meeting with state Sen. Lou D'Allesandro and the caucus' executive director. This was actually my first contact with an officer of the Democratic Party. Democrats were pretty rare in Littleton and for all I knew they met at night in secret covens to which I had never been invited. Lou was very nice, although I didn't hit it off with the executive director, an attractive young woman who was new to the job. Lou and I talked briefly about different issues but the major focus was that I'd have to beat the bushes to raise money; I was told it would take fifty thousand dollars to run a campaign, which proved to be true.

There was also another potential Democratic candidate in the wings who apparently had the support of Gov. Shaheen; he was a well-liked manager at the paper mills in Berlin and Gorham who had been helpful in getting the mills reopened after they'd been closed in bankruptcy. I made it clear from the beginning that my only interest in running was to give people an option to the Republicans. If there was another, stronger candidate I'd gladly defer to him, but I needed to know soon. I was an unknown in partisan politics and would need time to get my name out.

Next I had to find out where the rest of the North Country's Democratic Party was hiding. I learned that there actually was a Littleton town committee shown on the state books, but apparently they hadn't met since sometime during the Great Depression. The chair emeritus was Don Merrill, a local merchant, who confirmed that the committee was pretty much dormant and needed leadership to crank it up. Next was the Grafton County committee. Here I also found that the group hadn't met in recent history and had an acting chair, Arnold Shields. I found Arnold and we agreed to try and crank things up at a county caucus during the New Hampshire Democratic Party convention in the fall. In Carroll and Coos counties, all part of Senate District 1, I had better luck.

Paul Robitaille, the chair of the Coos County Democrats, had monthly meetings in Gorham, and Dorothy Solomon, the chair of Carroll County party, had regular meetings in the North Conway area. I started going to both meetings regularly.

Paul is barrel-chested guy of French Canadian descent who is dedicated to his union work. When I met him in 2001, he was waiting to be recalled by the paper mill where he had worked as a mechanic before the bankruptcy. He was doing union social work to help other laid-off workers. Paul would eventually give up the wait and go back to college to finish his degree. The Coos County Committee was fairly small and centered on a group of activists in Berlin, Gorham and the surrounding area. Historically, Berlin and Gorham, both mill towns, had been staunchly Democratic, and at one point even had a strong Socialist party. Along with changing demographics, allegiances in recent years have shifted farther to the right. I would learn a lot about the heritage of these towns, but I sure wish I had taken my high school French a whole lot more seriously. It's the second and sometimes first language of that region.

Dorothy Solomon and her husband Stan are former schoolteachers from New York, now retired in the town of Albany. I grew up in a Jewish community in the Flatbush section of Brooklyn and I loved those guys at first sight. We kind of had the same roots, and were liberal, progressive people dropped into one of the most conservative, regressive regions in the country—and we weren't taking it lying down. The Carroll County Democrats were also small in number but feisty as hell.

Both Dorothy and Paul knew they had a political neophyte in me as a Senate candidate, but they took me under their wings and as time went on I've grown to think of them as dear friends. We also came together to do quite a lot of Democratic Party building in the North Country; more on that in the next chapter.

When a potential candidate says that he or she is forming an exploratory committee or exploring the possibility of running, it really means that the person would like to run and is going to reach out to his or her network of supporters and others to learn if there are sufficient financial resources, and a chance in hell of winning. My network was the Littleton Alliance, which although nonpartisan by charter, had a very progressive membership of mostly registered Democrats and Independents. The feedback was extremely positive but realistically the support was limited to the Littleton area, about one-fifth of the population of the Senate district. Plus it was unlikely that I could carry the Republican stronghold of Littleton; Wayne Presby didn't in 2000, and he was a native son and far better known than I. At best I could only do well in my hometown; to win the election I'd have to carry Berlin and Gorham.

The same analysis was true in both the 2002 and 2004 elections but the situations were different.

In 2002, Gov. Jeanne Shaheen, a Democrat, was largely responsible for getting the Berlin and Gorham paper mills reopened and hundreds of employees back to work. They loved her, and rightly so. She'd earned it and she would need that support for her run for the U.S. Senate. In deciding to run, I banked on her popularity having coattails for the rest of the Democratic slate, but I was dead wrong.

The mid-term Congressional elections were hotly contested with control of Congress in the balance. The New Hampshire seat that Shaheen was running for could decide which party controlled the U.S. Senate. In 2002, campaign finance laws still allowed "soft money" contributions to political parties and both the Democratic National Committee and the Republican National Committee poured millions into New Hampshire; the DNC in support of Shaheen for the U.S. Senate, and Katrina Swett and Martha Fuller Clark for Congress. And there it stopped; the DNC and the New Hampshire Democratic Party ignored the state races. Politically, Shaheen totally distanced herself from Mark Fernald (who had won the Democratic gubernatorial primary), and the state slate of Democratic candidates. Mark and many others were advocating for an income tax, the third rail of New Hampshire politics, and the governor wasn't about to get sapped. Consequently, even though there was a tremendous amount of money spent on the media, there was no team effort. We were left to run our own races.

At the state level there were three Republican candidates in the gubernatorial primary, Craig Benson, Bruce Keough, and former U.S. Senator, Gordon Humphrey. Between them they spent over $13 million

(Benson $6 million), breaking all NH records. My three Republican opponents in their primary spent over $100 thousand, again breaking all records for the Senate district. New Hampshire and Boston TV broadcast stations, cable TV, radio, and print media made a fortune in 2002.

Republicans from top to bottom passionately pumped out the far-right's collection of beliefs, feelings and ideas that reflected their collective conservative worldview. Democrats didn't; we pounded individual Republican candidates and reached for the mythical "middle." There was no passion in the Democratic message for our progressive worldview; quite the contrary, we were collectively afraid of the party label. In 2002 we lost our collective ass. It was a bloodletting.

In chapter 1, I discussed the results of the 2004 election. As a presidential election, 2004 was different, but the Democratic Party's failure was much the same as in 2002; we failed to passionately present in a compelling way our beliefs, feelings and ideas, as they relate to the important issues of our day. We wanted to be all things to all people. While we did somewhat better in New Hampshire, particularly up north (for which I freely take some credit), it was far from good enough. And let me tell you, there was no lack of passion or team effort in my campaign in the North Country. It works.

The subject of worldview is extremely well covered by the Grassroots Policy Project based in Washington, D.C. I urge any serious progressive activist to attend one of their training sessions; they're doing great work. Part Two of this book is devoted to examining the major issues of our day from a progressive worldview.

I waited and waited and, when the mill manager never materialized as a candidate, I announced my candidacy at the end of January 2002. While I certainly hadn't lined up any deep pockets, I knew that one way or the other I could finance the campaign. I had the personal assets to do that if needed, and it was needed to a large extent in both campaigns. Unlike Democrats in affluent areas of the state, average people up north just don't have the money, while it flows to flood stage in Republican circles, particularly to incumbents.

A Senate campaign requires professional help and volunteers; you can't do it alone. You need a knowledgeable confidant whose opinions you trust and value, someone to travel around with you to events, and if you're lucky someone with a knack for raising money. I was lucky to have some wonderful people help me on the campaigns, and most have remained active working to build the Democratic Party. Here are just a few.

Linda Warden, a friend and neighbor, volunteered to be my fiscal agent and stayed with it throughout both campaigns. She also serves as secretary of the Littleton Alliance. A fiscal agent is the campaign's banker and responsible for filing numerous financial reports to the New Hampshire Secretary of State.

Tim McCarthy came to me from the Salmon Press. They fired him as editor of *The Courier,* Littleton's weekly newspaper, shortly after I announced my candidacy. Salmon Press never owned up to the real reason he was terminated, but everyone knows it was because of his liberal editorial policy, especially his warnings against the Bush administration's rush to war after 9/11. He published my progressive op-eds, but was always fair, giving equal ink to opposing views. I knew him casually but deliberately shied away from personal conversation, which I thought inappropriate. I firmly believe in the autonomy of the press. I offered him a poorly paid job as my campaign manager, which he took. He's been my confidant and close friend ever since. The only thing he can't do worth a darn is fundraising; like me, he's more prone to give money away than to ask for it.

This is the second book that Tim has collaborated on with me. He is an excellent published writer, journalist, editor and teacher. The first book is a memoir called *A Good Stick*, published by Author House. He encouraged me to write the memoir because of all the airline stories I'd told him while driving countless campaign hours throughout the North Country.

John Graham, a ski buddy, retired teacher and Democratic activist was also always there to make the long drives; to put up signs, come with me to debates and meetings, canvas, make telephone calls, dance and wave on the sidewalks, the works.

Jeff Davis and his wife Karen joined us in the second campaign, and boy did we need them. Jeff's a semi-retired marketing guy with an extensive background. He'd say that selling a candidate wasn't much different than selling cars or soft drinks. He's right, and following his advice I doubled my vote count the second time around. Karen did a radio ad playing a constituent voicing her heart-felt concerns that was absolutely convincing. Gallus, on the other hand, ran a crummy campaign, said nothing, did less, and won. Apparently the slim majority of the voters that voted for John Kerry, or against the ethics of Craig Benson, are still drawn to the Republican worldview. The Democratic Party didn't frame the issues in a compelling way, and I alone couldn't overcome that disadvantage.

Paul Robitaille and Robert Theberge were extremely helpful by introducing me to people in Berlin and Gorham. We knocked on doors and walked the streets. They know everybody and patiently instructed me on how to pronounce their French Canadian names; some of those names don't roll off this old tongue easily. We are also fortunate to have Robert serving a second term in the New Hampshire House.

I learned the parade business from Dorothy and Stan Solomon, and their wonder dog Sir Gal (a Collie). In some I marched proudly holding the Carroll County Democrat's banner with Dorothy, in others walking with the Sorluccomobile. Stan would work the crowd with Sir Gal, the dog dressed to the nines in a campaign bonnet and allowing children to pet him. It sounds foolishly superficial, but it is not. You become likeable and understandable and people are drawn into your worldview. They love dogs, you love dogs, you're for social justice, and then maybe they should be also.

The Internet and e-mail are indispensable to a modern political campaign. Veronica Francis and crew at Notchnet.com were an integral part of both campaigns for the Senate and continue to be part of the team. Frequently, their technical ability and art help those of us technologically challenged to maintain our sanity.

Direct mail and campaign flyers are essential to getting the message out. Doug Garfield's Sherwin Dodge Printers offered help beyond measure.[1]

To be a serious candidate today is a 24/7 job, and quite a challenge both to your health and safety. The house parties, meetings and appearances are endless, with most requiring two hours or more driving time. While I won't bore you by rehearsing a lot of them, I will share a couple.

I had made it a goal to address as many town select boards as I possibly could. Berlin is large enough to be classified as a city. Early in 2002 I asked to be on the agenda of a city council meeting. In 2002, Robert Theberge was the Berlin city manager and I had no problem getting on the agenda.

That would change in 2004; Robert had resigned as city manager and ran for mayor in 2003, losing to the incumbent, Bob Danderson. Danderson is a great buddy of John Gallus' and in 2004, when I requested an appearance before the city council, Danderson told me that he would only allow me to address them if Gallus were present to rebut my remarks. On that basis I could only refuse; I don't do public arguments. I would have been delighted for an opportunity to do a debate or forum with a moderator. Needless to say, Danderson is no fan of mine, nor I of his. For many reasons, I think the City of Berlin would do well to be rid of him.

In any case, one afternoon Tim McCarthy and I drove to Berlin for the city council meeting. Just minutes before my appearance I discovered that my hemorrhoids, which had been irritated from all the rubber chicken dinners and long periods sitting in the car, had bled profusely enough to stain the seat of my chinos. My God, what was I to do? Well we entered the chamber with my back to the wall and Tim to the rear and promptly got seated. The meeting itself was kind of fun. At the time the council was split about evenly between Democrats and Republicans. I was astonished to hear them all speaking French until the meeting was called to order, and then they switched to English.

After I made my pitch and answered questions from the council, the trick was to get the hell out of there with the embarrassing bloodstain. Well I went out as I had come in, with my back to the wall. Thinking back on it is good for a laugh, but I've often imagined that those people must have thought I was the most awkward man they'd ever seen because I always walked with my back to the wall!

But the dangers to health and personal safety are very real; you're always on the move with little time to take care of yourself. Incidentally, after the 2002 campaign I underwent surgery to correct the hemorrhoid problem and now enjoy the posterior of an eighteen-year-old.

Driving or flying in the mountains of the North Country can be extremely dangerous, winter or summer. Snowstorms, icy roads and thunderstorms all enliven our world, and moose encounters on dark country roads kill people every year. Moose have no natural predators (except man) and fearlessly cross or walk the roads, standing so tall drivers fail to see them in their headlights until it's too late. Stan and Dorothy Solomon hit one returning home from a late meeting, as did Susan Bruce, a friend who ran for the New Hampshire House and is an organizer for the New Hampshire Citizens Alliance. Fortunately, they suffered only minor injuries and wrecked automobiles. They were lucky. I've been lucky too. Although I've seen many moose, and had a couple of close calls, I've never hit one.

Campaign flying is another story with a deadly history. As an airline captain I flew many candidates, including presidential candidates, on scheduled and chartered flights. Aside from the frequency of politicians flying, which increases their exposure, the odds of being in an accident on a major airline are statistically miniscule. That's not the case with small, chartered aircraft used in stump-stop campaigning on tight schedules.

A high profile example was the tragic death of Minnesota Senator Paul Wellstone. The senator, five other passengers, and the crew of two were killed on October 26, 2002, when their small twin-engine aircraft, a Beech A100, crashed in freezing rain outside of the Eveleth-Virginia Municipal Airport, about 175 miles north of Minneapolis. Weather was a dominant factor.

Earlier, in 2000, Missouri Governor Mel Carnahan was killed in the crash of a small aircraft just before the November election while campaigning against John Ashcroft for Ashcroft's Senate seat. Carnahan won anyway and was probably the only dead person ever elected to the U.S. Senate. George W. Bush consoled Ashcroft by making him attorney general, an appointment that came to cost Americans a great deal in terms of their civil liberties.

Another high profile tragedy was the death of Senator John Heinz. He was killed when his small twin-engine aircraft collided with a helicopter over Merion, Pennsylvania in 1991. His widow Teresa would become Teresa Heinz Kerry and well known to us all in John Kerry's 2004 presidential campaign.

In the closing days of the 2002 campaign, a few days after Wellstone was killed, I was stumping with Katrina Swett, who was running for Congress. I was to pick Katrina up at the Whitefield Airport and escort her to Littleton to do a visibility appearance on Main Street, and then run her back to the airport and send her off to some other stops, meeting her later to stump in Berlin.

The trouble was that the weather was crummy, threatening snow or freezing rain. We made it into Whitefield all right, but I was concerned about the rest of the day. When we got to the airport, I took Katrina aside and explained that, aside from being a crackerjack politician, I was also a highly experienced retired airline captain who was going to speak to the pilot of her aircraft. I was going to tell him that there was absolutely nothing she had scheduled that day that was worth risking her life for, and that I was concerned about the flight later in the day to Berlin because I thought the weather was going to deteriorate further. The weather did deteriorate and thank God Katrina never showed up in Berlin, although I made it there by car. That was a smart pilot who made a good decision.

Three

Party Politics

————•◆•◆•————

Political parties are as old as humanity's attempts at representative
government. They flourished throughout Europe and the United States
in the 19th and 20th centuries as new governments emerged from revolution
or regional unification into nation-states. In Europe in the 1920s and 1930s
some were to become infamous single-party dictatorships.

In America, much to President George Washington's chagrin, political
parties were developing by the end of his first term in office. They polarized
around the Federalists (Alexander Hamilton, James Madison and John
Jay), those who favored a strong centralized government, and Democratic-
Republicans (Thomas Jefferson), who championed the rights of states. A
disappointed President Washington (1789-1797), urged his countrymen, "to
forswear excessive party spirit and geographic distinctions." I wonder how
he would have viewed the blatant hostility of the 2004 election.

It was Thomas Jefferson who founded the Democratic Party in 1792
as a Congressional caucus to fight for the Bill of Rights. He would be the
first Democratic President of the United States in 1800 (it was officially
named the Democratic-Republican Party in 1798).

The seventh president, Andrew Jackson (1829-1837), is also considered
one of the founders of the Democratic Party. The Jacksonian Democrats

created the national convention process, the party platform, and unified the Democratic Party. In 1844, the National Convention simplified the party's name to the Democratic Party.

The Republican Party was born in the early 1850s by anti-slavery activists and individuals who believed that government should grant western lands to settlers free of charge. The name Republican was chosen because it alluded to equality and reminded people of Thomas Jefferson's Democratic-Republican Party. At the time the new Republican Party was considered a "third" party; the Democrats and the Whigs, which had come out of the Federalist Party, represented the two-party system. That would change when Abraham Lincoln, a former Whig, was elected the first Republican President in 1861.

Although both the Democratic and Republican Parties would change greatly over the years, they remain the major parties of the "two-party system" in the United States. In 2004, there were no less than fifty-three so-called "third parties" registered with the Federal Election Commission. A few have gained some stature: the Reform Party formed by Ross Perot after his unsuccessful run for the presidency as an Independent in 1992; the Green Party, which nominated Ralph Nader for president in 2000; and the Libertarian Party, founded in 1971. The Libertarians, without false modesty, call themselves America's third party, and are neither left nor right. They just don't like government, period (they're pretty popular in New Hampshire). In Vermont the Progressive Party has been somewhat successful in state and local government.

Other "third" parties run the gamut: American Nazi Party, Communist Party USA, Independence Party (Pat Buchanan), Labor Party, Socialist Party USA, and there's even the U.S. Marijuana Party and many more.

The two-party system evolved in the United States because it is compatible with our form of government, which, while separating powers between three branches, focused power on the winning party. The president, the executive branch, and Congress, the legislative branch, are elected. The president with the consent of Congress appoints the justices of the Supreme Court and subordinate federal judges—the judicial branch.

The parliamentary systems used in most representative democracies work differently. The members of Parliament are elected in local districts, and then the party with the majority of members (or a coalition of parties if no single party holds the majority) selects a prime minister and forms a government. Unlike the United States, in a parliamentary system multiple parties have power because they can form coalitions to govern.

The president of the United States, with the consent of Congress, also appoints the Cabinet, which holds executive power in the United States Government. In the U.S. Congress and in most state legislatures, the majority party has a leadership role, forms the bodies' committees (usually within a seniority system), and selects the committee chairmen (or women), a powerful advantage in the legislative process. The vast majority of all introduced bills never get out of committee.

Consequently, political parties have an important traditional and fundamental role in the government of the United States; they also nominate candidates, establish values and platforms, advocate for or against legislation, and support the campaigns of candidates.

Across the world there are and have been many single-party states. Single-party states allow no opposition parties (or only token opposition) and are generally viewed as dictatorships. Here are a few severely condensed and simplified history lessons worth remembering:

Fascism and communism reared their ideological heads in many parts of the world in the early 20th century (presaged by the 19th century's international workers' movement and, in 1871, by the ill-fated Paris Commune, the first workers' government ever formed). Dominant national parties built on those worldviews sprang up in Germany, Italy, Spain, and the Soviet Union. They were international movements rising from political oppression, senseless wars, the extreme poverty suffered by working people, the worldwide depression, and the great inequality of the distribution of wealth. The champions of both ideologies were highly active in Great Britain and the United States. Fortunately, neither party gained more than a foothold because the governments acted to moderate fiscal policies and allowed the budding labor union movement to provide alternatives. Great Britain turned heavily socialistic during that period. The United States turned the corner toward social consciousness with

President Franklin Roosevelt's New Deal legislation—the same social safety net that the Bush administration is trying to unravel.

Strong national parties in Europe would evolve into single-party state dictatorships embroiling Spain in the bloody Spanish Civil War, and the world in WWII. It is important to note that they didn't start out as dictatorships. They started out as political parties.

The Spanish Civil War (1936-1939) pitted an exiled right-wing army general, Francisco Franco, against the democratically elected government of the Popular Front (a coalition of left-wing parties). It was an especially brutal war that became a weapons testing ground for fascist regimes in Germany and Italy. Hitler and Mussolini supported Franco's Nationalist rebellion while the United States and Britain refused to sell arms to the republican government. But that did not stop thousands of British and American volunteers from flocking to Spain in support of troops loyal to the republic. Among them were journalists Ernest Hemingway and George Orwell, a Brit. Hemingway's novel *For Whom the Bell Tolls* and Orwell's *Homage to Catalonia* are two of the best books in English to come directly out of the war. (Hemingway's book was a romanticized account; Orwell's report was not.)

It is estimated that between 500,000 and 1,000,0000 people were killed, many the result of brutal mass executions perpetrated by both sides. Jose Antonio Primo de Rivera, founder of the fascist Falange Espanola party, was one of those executed after the republicans captured him in 1936. By April 1937 Franco had put together a Falange coalition, which he headed. Following his 1939 military victory, the party established him as the country's dictator and he ruled ruthlessly until his death 35 years later. He repaid his former Axis allies by keeping Spain neutral during WWII.

The Russian Revolution is thought to have started with "Bloody Sunday" in January1905, when Tsarist troops opened fire on a peaceful demonstration of workers in St. Petersburg. It was followed by strikes and civil unrest that ended with the outbreak of the First World War in 1914. After the start of WWI, things worsened for Tsar Nicholas II. He was forced to abdicate in March 1917 and was later executed with his wife and children by a squad of Bolshevik secret police in July 1918.

While the rise and fall of Marxism-Leninism and Stalinism, the Union of Soviet Socialist Republics (USSR), and the Communist Party of the Soviet Union (CPSU) are major studies in themselves, for the purposes of this narrative it is sufficient to understand that the USSR, one of the world's two superpowers to emerge after WWII—along with the USA—was governed by a single political party for 74 consecutive years (1917-1991), despite an early challenge from Socialist Alexander Kerensky and a counterrevolutionary civil war that lasted from 1918 to 1920. After Joseph Stalin emerged victorious from a power struggle with Leon Trotsky in the 1920s, he established a deadly dictatorship that lasted until his death in 1953. One of his successors, Nikita Khrushev, loosened things up a bit (as Mikhail Gorbachev did to a far greater extent in the 1980s), but power rested solely with the CPSU until the collapse of the Soviet Union in 1991.

Italy is another example of one-party rule. After Italy's unification in 1870, the country had a constitutional monarchy like that of Great Britain. The Italian Parliament, failing on every front, became a symbol of decadence and corruption, neither trusted nor respected by the people. Following WWI, after Italy lost 600,000 men fighting Germany, the Paris Peace Conference, as something of a slap in the face, granted Italy only minor territorial spoils, further branding the government as weak.

By 1919, Italy remained a poor, backward country; a ripe target for the so-called "Red Menace." Many people turned to the Socialist Party and the Catholic Popular Party; there were strikes and civil unrest as people sought new leadership to improve their lives. Alarmed, industrialists, landlords and other property holders turned to the fascists, led by Benito Mussolini. In 1921, Mussolini formed the National Fascist Party and won 35 out of 355 seats in Parliament. After that the fascists and their goon squads called the Black Shirts carried out systematic terror campaigns against the socialist and communist groups. Fearing civil war, King Victor Emmanuel refused to oppose the fascists and asked Mussolini to form a new government. Mussolini became prime minister.

Il Duce, as he was called, remained in power until 1943, when a royal coup forced him to resign, and he was subsequently publicly hanged with his mistress from a lamppost, as the Allies fought their way up the Italian boot. Although certainly unpopular at the end, El Duce enjoyed great popularity during his reign. To this day you'll hear that he brought order, public education and reliable railroads. Fascism is, if nothing else, efficient.

Hitler's fascist regime also sprang up under the guise of a legitimate political party in 1919. It was called the German Workers' Party, changing its name to the National Socialist German Workers' Party when Adolf Hitler became leader in1920-21. The nickname Nazi was taken from the first word of its full name, Nationalsozialistische Deutsche Arbeiterpartei. The German people, vanquished by WWI, the Treaty of Versailles and the Great Depression, were easy prey for the Nazis. By 1932 the Nazi Party, aided by strong-armed groups called the Brown Shirts (later to become the SA), had become the largest elected bloc in the Reichstag (Parliament). After Hitler was named chancellor in 1933, he obtained passage of the Enabling Act, and his government declared the Nazi Party to be the only political party in Germany and required all bureaucrats to become members. Thus was the start of the Third Reich, which ended with Hitler's death in a bunker under the ruins of Berlin in 1945.

The Nazi ideological theory of the supremacy of the Aryan race and hatred of the Jews (anti-Semitism), whom they blamed for all the world's woes, culminated in the Holocaust, and the involuntary euthanasia of those not thought pure enough for the Aryan race. The driving force was unrelenting propaganda. Here again, make no mistake, Hitler and the Nazis were popular. One cannot help but equate the Nazi propaganda machine under Joseph Goebbels with the Bush White House—they seem to be using the same playbook.

It is also interesting, if not disheartening, to know that the fascist, totalitarian governments of Italy, Germany and Vichy France during WWII got along very well with the Catholic Church in Rome, as did Franco's Spain. Some argue the church had no choice; I think they chose wrong. They also chose wrong in supporting fascist governments in Austria, Slovakia, and Croatia, to name a few. Again, it is hard not to find similarities from the past with today's religious far right.

Wikipedia online free encyclopedia lists 64 examples of past and present single-party states as of 2004. Here is just a notable handful—something to think about when considering President Bush's plan to bring democracy to the world: Burma, Peoples Republic of China, Cuba, North Korea, Laos, Vietnam, Syria, Pakistan, Turkmenistan, and Sudan. Then there are the oil-producing monarchies: Saudi Arabia and Kuwait. Iran is a constitutional Islamic Republic—non-Moslems need not bother running for office.

In the dominant-party system, the ruling party tolerates other parties, but those parties never receive enough votes to stand a chance of winning. There can be official harassment, unfair electoral systems and outright electoral fraud. In the United States we can add to those dangers the extremely high cost of running for office, the financial advantage of incumbency, and the marginalization of the strength of political parties brought about by the Bipartisan Campaign Reform Act (McCain-Feingold) of 2002.

Dominant-party systems govern dozens of countries around the world, including many in Africa. The results can be mixed as in Egypt, relatively benign as in Singapore, or downright pernicious as in Zimbabwe.

I believe the United States is in danger of losing its vibrant two-party system; all the historical warning signs are there. One of them is particularly startling; people are opting out of participating in political parties and identifying themselves as "Independents."

Poll after poll in the past two decades have shown that voters in America, when asked to identify themselves politically, divide about one-third Democrat, one-third Republican and one-third Independent. The small percentages of those who claim a third party are considered statistically to be Independent.

A paper released by Rhodes Cook, co-author of *America Votes,* reports that in the 27 states (plus the District of Columbia) that have been registering voters by party since 1987, the Democratic share has plummeted from a total of 51 percent to 43 percent. The Republican share has stayed steady at

33 percent. But the proportion of voters who have not identified themselves with either of the major parties has jumped from 16 to 24 percent. Plus, it is more than likely that many voters in the reporting states opted for one major party or the other because that was the only way they could vote in a party primary.

Since 1987, the proportion of unaffiliated voters has grown in every region and in every party-registration state except Colorado and Kansas. Those "other" voters are now a plurality in Connecticut, Maine, Massachusetts, New Hampshire, New Jersey, Iowa and Alaska.

New Hampshire currently allows its registered Independents (42 percent), to vote in the party primary of their choice, and then to immediately reregister at the polls as an Independent—no loyalty required.

What in the world is going on? Many high-powered political pundits think it is a trend toward an increased comity or friendlier middle that will elect candidates of either major party, or even of one of the many third parties. Listening to the advice of these pundits, Democratic candidates, certainly in conservative New Hampshire, fall all over themselves courting "the center." Already, the same seers are cautioning the Democratic Party to rally behind a "centrist" presidential candidate for 2008. They assume that a Democrat can no longer win an election based upon the traditional Democratic values of social and economic justice.

I am convinced that if the Democratic Party follows their advice the ruling Republican Party will continue to dominate the United States for decades, or until the ever-increasing schism between the haves and have nots forces change.

Those same pundits suggest that the 2004 presidential election was close and that the pendulum will simply swing back. I strongly disagree. I think their perspective is dangerously sanguine given the methods the Republicans used to gain and keep power, the disengagement of Independent voters, the 40 to 50 percent of eligible voters who don't vote, the enormous power of incumbency, and campaign finance laws that favor the very rich and marginalize populist parties.

The far right controlling the Republican Party has a long-range plan. The seeds of conservative dominance over the Republican Party were planted in 1964, with the nomination of conservative Barry Goldwater over liberal Nelson Rockefeller as their presidential candidate. President Ronald Reagan's administration (1981-89) gave ultraconservatism a new look. He busted the Air Traffic Controller's strike, gave tax breaks to the rich—sugar coating it as trickle-down economics to create jobs—was tough on the Soviet Union—calling it the Evil Empire—and people loved him.

The movers, shakers and spin doctors more than noticed, they conspired, poured money into conservative think tanks, and easily gained the collaboration of the Rev. Pat Robertson's Christian Coalition, and the Rev Jerry Falwell's Moral Majority. Rev. Falwell is quoted as having said, "get them saved, get them baptized, and get them registered."

George Bush the elder followed Reagan into the White House for one term (1989-1993), then lost to President Bill Clinton, who would win a second term and keep the White House under Democratic control from 1994 until 2000. They were tough years. The far right had a bone in its craw and proved capable of going to any extreme to compromise Clinton's presidency (no matter what the result for the country), and to discredit the Democratic Congressional leadership.

They embroiled President Clinton in lawsuit after lawsuit, engaging special prosecutors to hound him, resulting finally in impeachment in the House over comments made concerning a sexual impropriety with Monica Lewinsky, who had been a White House intern. Clinton survived the impeachment and served out his full term, but the damage was done, both to him and to the country. Not quite the strong-arm tactics of the Brown Shirts or the Black Shirts, but no less treacherous or effective.

Rep. Newt Gingrich led the conservative movement to take over Congress. He used confrontational tactics to challenge the Democrats' longtime control of the House, forcing Speaker Jim Wright to resign in 1989 by questioning his financial dealings. Then the Republicans gained a majority in the House and elected Gingrich Speaker in 1995. After being reprimanded for campaign funding violations, Gingrich resigned in 1998. Democrats held a slim majority in the Senate for a while but the tide had turned and Republicans now rule both houses of Congress by a large majority.

In 2000, George W. Bush won back the White House for the Republicans in an election hotly contested in the courts over voter fraud—the infamous Florida hanging chads. Bush lost the national popular vote but won the election by a 5 to 4 victory in the U.S. Supreme Court, which swung the Electoral College vote in his favor. The whole world knows the antics of Bush's campaign/propaganda manager Karl Rove. Outright lies and spin bombarded American voters in 2004. Bush wrapped himself in the flag—America was at war. A preemptive war in Iraq that he started and a war on terrorism that many think will never end so long as it keeps the far right in power. Fascist regimes have always found that fear works to control people.

Yes, I am afraid for our country and you should be, too. Fear can also be a positive tool. In fact, I hope that the Democratic Party and progressive groups of all stripes get so afraid that they act with passion. People don't need politicians with poop in their mouths; they need passionate leaders willing to stand up for what's right. If we continue to yield passion to the Republican and religious far right, it will be our fault, not theirs, if we fail.

Four

Lobbyists and Stealth Parties

————◆●◆●◆————

In the last chapter we discussed some of the history of political parties and their importance; identified the Democratic and Republican Party as the two majors, and mentioned some of the so-called "third" parties. The next question that begs consideration is who else advocates for or against candidates and issues in the United States? And that's where it gets terribly confusing because their number is enormous, their identities clouded, and their combined effect on our political system profound.

Lobbyists, like parties, have been around from the beginning. It wouldn't stretch the imagination to believe that when the founding fathers gathered at their taverns after a hard day's work on our Constitution, there were lobbyists waiting to buy them a cup so as to have their ear to advance one perspective or another.

Concerning lobbyists, then Senate Majority Leader Robert C. Byrd delivered an enlightening essay on September 28, 1987, as part of a unique historical project on the Senate's history and operations. Here are a few pertinent and eloquent excerpts:

"Mr. President, in 1869, a newspaper correspondent published this vivid description of a monster in the Capitol building: 'Winding in and out through the long, devious basement passage, crawling through the corridors, trailing its slimy length from gallery to committee room, at last it lies stretched at full length on the floor of Congress—this dazzling reptile, this huge, scaly serpent of the lobby.' What was this awful creature? It was intended as the embodiment of lobbyists, who were proliferating in the years after the civil war and who, many believed, were corrupting the Congress.

"Citizens of the United States, whether as individuals or in organizations, have both direct and indirect interests in legislation considered by Congress. They make their interests known by electing sympathetic senators and representatives and by petitioning for or against legislation. This is a right guaranteed them by the First Amendment to the Constitution.

"The past fifteen years have witnessed a political phenomenon: the development and proliferation of political action committees (PACs). These PACs are formed by special interest groups for the purpose of funneling contributions to the political campaigns of members of Congress and other office seekers, and they constitute a subtle but sophisticated form of lobbying. Spiraling campaign costs in this electronic age have made members of Congress increasingly dependent upon PAC contributions. Incumbents and challengers alike, unless they are inordinately wealthy, besiege scores of PACs in every election for money to finance their ravenous advertising and other political expenditures. The demand for funds to wage a successful political campaign has now become so excessive that the average cost of winning a Senate seat in the 1988 election was roughly four million dollars. This means that a senator is forced to raise an average of more than twelve thousand dollars every week over a six-year term in order to remain in public service. And this is just the average! [Eighteen years later, in the 2004 election, the average incumbent senator raised $8,613,793—challengers only $969,505.]

"It should be clear from my remarks that Congress has always had, and always will have, lobbyists and lobbying. We could not adequately consider our workload without them. We listen to representatives from the broadest number of groups; large and small; single-issue and multi-purposed; citizens groups; corporate and labor representatives; the public spirited and the privately inspired. They all have a service to fulfill. At the same time, the history of this institution demonstrates the need for eternal vigilance to ensure that lobbyists do not abuse their role, that lobbying is carried on publicly with full publicity, and that the interests of all citizens are heard without giving special ear to the best organized and most lavishly funded."

I had the honor to meet and hear Sen. Byrd speak in 1992 at luncheon in Washington. Our lobbyists, Sparkman and Cole, got us a front-row table. Sen. Byrd spoke about issues that were before the Federal Aviation Administration, and our advocacy group, the Professional Pilots Federation. I was the PPF vice president. At the luncheon there were key people in the FAA whom we wanted to meet. We were lobbying Congress to change the regulation that forces airline pilots to retire at age 60. Unfortunately, that fight still continues but I spent a lot of time in Washington lobbying.

Most of the time I worked with Tim Cole, an astute Congressional lobbyist and a former deputy administrator of the FAA. "Remember these guys (the senators, congressmen and staff members) don't know anything at all about your issue. You have fifteen minutes or so to educate them, that's your job," Cole told us. And he was right. There are countless issues brought before Congress and the advocacy of those interested is essential to the process. Bitterly, I would also learn that successful advocacy has a price. Senators and representatives, including one unmentionable attorney representing the Clinton White House, reminded us that the Airline Pilots Association and the AFL-CIO didn't want the age-60 rule changed, and those organizations made substantial campaign contributions and carried a lot of votes. The PPF couldn't do either, never mind the morality or ethics of an important civil rights issue. Consequently, we got nowhere.

Disgraceful? Yes I think so, and probably one of the reasons why so many people have grown distrustful of their government. Unlawful? How could you ever prove that the largess of a lobbyist swayed an elected representative's vote? You simply cannot. But Congress requires that lobbyists register, and the Federal Election Commission (FEC) requires that their PACs (the mechanisms used to funnel money to candidates) report all political expenditures and campaign contributions. From that information, impropriety can be publicly noticed and our ethics committees can take action, if they are doing their job.

There are ethics committees in both houses of Congress to investigate and censure violations by members. Former House Majority Leader Tom DeLay—an evangelistic far-right zealot—stood accused as this was written of violating House rules by accepting an expense free trip to South Korea in 2001 from a group that was registered as a foreign agent. House rules forbid members from taking gifts from such groups. DeLay had already been admonished three times in the past for official misconduct. What did the Republican leadership of the House do about the allegations? Investigate? Not by a long shot. They circled the wagons to protect DeLay by replacing members of the ethics committee with legislators more loyal to the party leadership.

DeLay also stands accused of misconduct concerning Leadership PAC contributions to Texas state legislators, who in turn gerrymandered Congressional districts to the Republicans' advantage: quite a guy, Tom DeLay. Eventually, his colleagues could no longer protect him. He dropped out of his 2006 reelection bid and resigned from the House.

The Bush administration's willingness to sell out America is obvious if you look at the laws currently being fast tracked through by the big business lobby.

On March 27, 2005, Jim VandeHei, Washington Post staff writer, ran a piece titled "Business Sees Gains In GOP Takeover." Here are some excerpts:

"Fortune 500 companies that invested millions of dollars in electing Republicans are emerging as the earliest beneficiaries of a government controlled by President Bush and the largest GOP House and Senate majority in a half century.

"MBNA Corp., the credit card behemoth and fifth-largest contributor to Bush's two presidential campaigns, is among those on the verge of prevailing in an eight-year fight to curtail personal bankruptcies. [The measure passed.] Exxon Mobil Corp. and others are close to winning the right to drill for oil in Alaska's wildlife refuge, which they have tried to pass for better than a decade. Wal-Mart Stores Inc., another big contributor to Bush and the GOP, and other big companies recently won long-sought protection from class-action lawsuits.

"Bush and his Congressional allies are looking to pass legal protection for drug companies, doctors, gun manufacturers and asbestos makers, as well as tax breaks for all companies and energy-related assistance sought by the oil and gas industry.

"With 232 House seats, Republicans have their largest majority since 1949. This is the first time since the Calvin Coolidge administration in 1929 that the GOP has simultaneously held 55 or more Senate seats and the presidency. Senate Republicans are only five votes shy of the 60 needed to break the most powerful tool the minority holds in Congress—the filibuster."

Companies, labor unions and other organizations spend big money lobbying Washington—there are thousands registered with Congress. Following is the Lobbyist spending by sector in 2000, as reported by The Center For Responsive Politics. [2]

Sector	(in millions)
Agribusiness	$78
Communications/Electronics	$204
Construction	$23
Defense	$60
Energy & Natural Resources	$159
Finance, Insurance & Real Estate	$229
Health	$209
Lawyers & Lobbyists	$16
Misc. Business	$224
Transportation	$138
Ideological/Single-Issue	$85
Labor	$27
Other	$103
Grand total:	$1.55 billion

The last report was for year 2000 because the Center For Responsible Politics ran out of funding to continue the project.

Lobbyists also work at the state level. In 2004 there were 510 registered lobbyists in New Hampshire. It costs $50 to register as a lobbyist with the NH Secretary of State. There is no research data available for total or sector amounts spent by New Hampshire state lobbyists or their associated PACs. Required reports for campaign contributions by candidates indicate that it is a substantial amount of money. Unfortunately, in my Senate race, as a challenger rather than an incumbent, precious little came to my campaign.

Other types of advocacy groups are Political Action Committees (PACs), and 501(c) and 527 groups. 501(c) and 527 groups are identified by the section of the tax-exempt federal tax code they fall under. The United States has a profoundly confusing system that intertwines regulations by Congress, the FEC, the IRS, and state regulators. Add to that the Bipartisan Campaign Reform Act of 2002 (BCRA) and you can rest assured that only the most informed professionals have any real understanding—and they'll be fighting in court into the foreseeable future.

PACs have been around since 1944, when the Congress of Industrial Organizations (CIO) formed the first one to raise money for the reelection of President Franklin D. Roosevelt. The PAC's money came from voluntary contributions from union members rather than union treasuries, so it did not violate the Smith Connally Act of 1943, which forbade unions from contributing to federal candidates. Although commonly called PACs, federal election law refers to these accounts as "separate segregated funds" because money contributed to a PAC is kept in a bank account separated from the general corporate or union treasury. Most PACs represent business, labor or ideological interests, although some raise money for a specific candidate, or so-called Leadership PACs to help fund other candidates' campaigns.

501(c)3 groups are nonprofit, tax-exempt organizations that can engage in religious, charitable, scientific or educational pursuits. They can lobby for issues but cannot engage in partisan campaign activities. 501(c)4s are commonly called "social welfare" organizations that may engage in political activities, as long as these activities do not become their primary purpose. Similar restrictions apply to section 501(c)5 labor and agriculture groups, and section 501(c)6 business leagues, chambers of commerce, real estate boards and boards of trade.

527 groups: Prior to 1975, the Internal Revenue Code (IRC) was silent as to the tax treatment of organizations whose primary purpose is influencing elections. The IRS treated contributions as gifts, which meant that the organizations did not have taxable income and were not required to file tax returns. P.L. 93-635, enacted in 1975, added section 527 to address the tax treatment of political organizations.

Following is the pertinent part of a Summary concerning the Code, released by the Congressional Research Service of The Library of Congress on January 11, 2005:

"Political organizations have the primary purpose of influencing federal, state, or local elections and conducting similar activities. Those that qualify under section 527 of the Internal Revenue Code are taxed only on certain income. Under the Code, 527 organizations are subject to reporting requirements that involve registration, the periodic disclosure of contributions and expenditures, and the annual filing of tax returns. Section 527 organizations must also comply with applicable campaign finance laws."

Now here's the kicker with 527 organizations: There are two kinds. This built-in dichotomy changed the political landscape in the 2004 elections when the Bipartisan Campaign Reform Act of 2002 eliminated "soft money" contributions to political parties and their committees—the committees that technically engage in federal election campaign activities. They must register with the FEC, file regular reports, and are subject to strict limitations on how much money they can accept and spend, as well as many other restrictions.

The other so-called "issues" 527s, such as America Coming Together (ACT), The Media Fund, MoveOn.org, The Leadership Forum, and Swift Boat Veterans for Truth (there are many and the list is growing) claim that they do not engage in federal election activity, but merely address issues and perform voter drives to Get Out The Vote (GOTV). Some of these take the position that they are not required to register or file reports with the FEC, nor does federal campaign finance law restrict them; others did file with the FEC but take the position that 98 percent of their activity is for voter drives and is not restricted. Some also have PACs, which must registration and report to the FEC. All must file tax returns under section 527 to the IRS.

Collectively, hundreds of millions of dollars were funneled though such organizations in the 2004 election, breaking all records for soft money. The Republican Party, Common Cause, Democracy 21, the Campaign Legal Center and the Center for Responsive Politics (and perhaps others) have filed complaints with the FEC claiming that those nonregulated 527s are illegally attempting to replace the political parties as new conduits for injecting soft money into federal campaigns. To date, none of those complaints has been acted upon.

On February 2, 2005, Senators John McCain (R-AZ) and Russell Feingold (D-WI)—the sponsors of the McCain-Feingold Bill, which was enacted as the BCRA—-Representative Christopher Shays (R-CT) and Marty Meehan (D-MA), and two key Senators, Republican Trent Lott (MS) and Democrat Charles Schumer (NY) re-introduced legislation in Congress to stop section 527 organizations from illegally spending millions of soft dollars to influence elections.

Prior to BCRA, "soft money" was the term used for unrestricted amounts of money that wealthy individuals and others could contribute to political parties for the purpose of party building or advancing that party's worldview and values to increase party membership—and of course encourage them to vote for that party's candidates in whatever elections were taking place. BCRA eliminated soft money contributions to political parties. But it did not restrict unlimited contributions or expenditures to 527s that did not engage in federal campaign election activities, i.e. advocating for the election of a candidate.

If the goal of the McCain/Feingold Bill that created BCRA was to cut down on the money spent on campaigns, it has failed miserably. More money was spent in the 2004 elections than ever before. The money was simply diverted into stealth parties allowed under section 527 of the IRC and within the guidelines allowed by the FEC.

No matter now well-intentioned, I believe these stealth parties are deleterious to our two-party system, particularly to the Democratic Party, which has roots as a populist party.

Five

Following the Money

———————◆•◆•◆———————

W hat helped sink President Richard M. Nixon ("Tricky Dick") after the Watergate break-in was when "Deep Throat" (identified in 2005 as Mark Felt, who was assistant director of the FBI at the time) advised Washington Post reporters Bob Woodward and Carl Bernstein to "follow the money." The scandal, involving illegal campaign activities and corruption, resulted in the impeachment proceedings that led to Nixon's forced resignation on August 8, 1974.

In an unrelated development in 1973, Nixon's vice president, Spiro T. Agnew, was also forced to resign because he was facing corruption charges related to taking kickbacks as governor of Maryland in 1967. Particularly newsworthy was testimony by a contractor that he made payments to Agnew, always in cash delivered in a plain envelope prior to receiving the contract. After Agnew's resignation, Nixon nominated and Congress approved House Minority Leader Gerald R. Ford to be vice president. The following year Ford replaced Nixon. What a time in American history!

As a result of Watergate, campaign finance laws changed dramatically as an outraged citizenry demanded safeguards and accountability in federal elections. Congress passed the Federal Election Campaign Act (FECA) of 1975, the statute that regulates the financing of federal elections, and created the Federal Election Commission (FEC) to enforce them. The FECA tightened things up considerably, setting campaign donation limits and reporting requirements. In conjunction with the FECA, the IRS added section 527 to the Internal Revenue Tax Code. One reason was to divert some of the more politically active 501(c) groups, which reported to no one, into 527s that would be accountable to the FEC.

The Federal Election Commission is made up of six members, who are appointed by the president and confirmed by the Senate. Each member serves a six-year term; two seats are subject to appointment every two years. By law, no more than three commissioners can be members of the same political party, and at least four votes are required for any official commission action. This structure was created to encourage nonpartisan decisions. The chair of the commission rotates among the members each year, with no member serving as chairperson more than once during his or her term.

Critics of the FEC, such as major campaign finance reform supporters like Common Cause and Democracy 21, have objected to this feature of the FEC, claiming that it renders the agency toothless. [3]

Besides trying to prevent corruption, the prime motivation for campaign finance reform was to reduce the vast amount of money that is funneled into federal campaigns. However, neither the Federal Election Campaign Act of 1975 nor the Bipartisan Campaign Reform Act of 2002 (BCRA) reduced that amount of money at all. The amount spent continues to grow with each election cycle.

Another observation is that campaign finance limitations increased the power of incumbency and diminished the chances of challengers to be elected. [4] Researcher John Lott said, "Take the issue of donation limits: prior to 1976, when such limits were first introduced, House members lost 12 percent of their races (according to data since World War II). After 1976, it was just 6 percent.

"My own research on donation limits on primary and general election races for state senators—with data covering 1984 through the 2002 primaries—analyzed the impact of state regulations similar to those in McCain-Feingold. These regulations increased the incumbents' winning vote margin by at least 4 percentage points, and the number of state Senate candidates running for office fell by an average of about 20 percent."

Lott goes on to say, "Every round of federal and state campaign finance regulation has been preceded by high-minded rhetoric decrying corruption of the political process. Every round of regulation has succeeded only in protecting incumbents and divorcing voters further from the political process."

The Bipartisan Campaign Reform Act of 2002, which came from the McCain-Feingold bill, is the latest attempt at campaign finance reform. Its main provisions prohibit political parties from raising so-called "soft money," while increasing the donation limits on hard money, and limiting the timeframe for so-called attack ads. The resulting campaign law compiled by the FEC is hundreds of pages long with extensive updates. In federal court challenges, there is a Federal Appeals Court Decision of a record-breaking 1,600 pages, and a sharply divided Supreme Court Decision of 298 pages—none of it light reading.

And, as indicated in the last chapter, Senators McCain and Feingold, along with other co-sponsors, reintroduced legislation on February 5, 2005: S. 271, "The 527 Reform Act of 2005." Their apparent goal is to plug the loopholes that are allowing some 527s to make an end run around the FEC.

Here's my take. The reformers are barking up the wrong tree. America cannot legislate good government; it can only elect good men and women to govern. In 1975 there was ample reason to reform the way federal elections were conducted. Who needed another Watergate? The law they promulgated pretty much left state and local elections alone, leaving those limitations up to the states. In the bitterly contested 2000 presidential election (Bush-Gore) so called "stealth PACs[5]," and allegations of election fraud once again forced Congress to consider reform. And once again the reformers focused on attempting to limit the flow of money into the system, only this time they got it dead wrong.

Election fraud was indeed a real issue—and still is—extending well beyond the good old days of dead people voting, voting more than once, or even vote buying schemes. These days the disenfranchisement of voters through voting systems, errors, mismanagement of registration databases and intimidation or harassment is a far bigger problem.[6]

Money from 527 organizations, political parties and candidates wasn't funding stealth PACs, all those have strict FEC reporting requirements; it was unlimited money flowing into 501(c)s from unnamed donors; 501(c)s don't report to the FEC.

In eliminating soft money[7] contributions to political parties, Congress created a problem rather than solving one. Transparency is needed to rein in stealth organizations that are propagandizing American. We can't forbid people or groups from publicly expressing their views on issues; it's their First Amendment right. Nor can we prevent them from lying or distorting the truth, short of outright slander. What we can do is require that those pulling the strings be identified—and, most important, if those 527 or 501(c) organizations are not in compliance with the Internal Revenue Code, we can take away their tax-exempt status. Congressional ethics committees and voters can also take the appropriate actions.

The crisis that America faces today has little to do with election law in any case; it's a crisis from within. Never before has the combined industrial, financial, health, high-tech, media, and service international complex of business interests had so much power in the United States. With few exceptions, someone joined at the hip with big business occupies every top-level position in the Bush administration. The raw financial and political power of this embedded complex dwarfs any amount of soft money that can be raised by any political campaign in opposition. That complex is the dangerous true base of the current Republican Party, and it plans to use that power and have the enormous additional power of incumbency to continue to rule. President Bush is merely the easily replaceable top piece of that power pyramid.[8] The base of the pyramid—the complex—plans to reign indefinitely.

The solution for America is to elect candidates who represent the people, not big business, and that can only be achieved if America has a strong opposition party, in a strong two-party system.

BCRA is lousy law because it encourages the opposite; it marginalizes political parties by prohibiting legitimate sources of revenue. Soft money was mostly populist money from wealthy, progressive individuals, men like George Soros and Peter Bing, who have no problem with being identified. Their values are well known and respected. And it was soft money that was used for building a party's strength, which is essential because the use of federal hard money is greatly restricted. The law also raises enormous obstacles to state and local political committees in supporting state candidates.

It's not surprising that progressive 527 organizations have found a way to be heard. Unfortunately, there is a downside. They are draining revenue and volunteers away from the Democratic Party and in some ways appearing as shadowy substitutes for the party. And ultraconservatives, not to be outdone, have jumped on the 527 bandwagon, creating a confusing mess that is enriching the broadcast media.

Will The 527 Reform Act of 2005 help? Frankly, I don't think so, unless Congress shifts gears and focuses on the real issues: They can reign in the 501(c)s and noncomplying 527s, including religious organizations; repeal the soft money restriction; allow parties to once again easily move money between committees; and they can get off the backs of state and local committees. It is unreasonable to delineate between federal and state campaigns as required by BCRA.

The United States needs to strengthen its two-party system not weaken it. Within a strong party system, candidates must be afforded the resources to wage creditable campaigns, and there definitely are things that can be done to level that playing field:

1. Reign in the K-Street lobbyists. Strengthen the House and Senate ethics committees, make it open public knowledge of who's giving what to whom, and lengthen the waiting time from office holder to lobbyist from one-year to two-years.

2. Provide partial public funding for all federal and state elections. There are several plans for federal elections being floated, including "Just 6 Dollars." Some states already partially fund elections.

3. Restrict the length of time candidates can campaign. Campaigns in America have become ridiculously long. And during the allotted time afford candidates a degree of free access to the nation's airwaves. Europeans do all of this with great success.

4. Require the U.S. Postal Service to issue special low political rates for candidate direct mailings. Direct mail is one of the biggest costs to a campaign.

Let's Follow the Money

The following data is all public information gleaned from three sources: The Center for Responsive Politics (opensecrets.org), the Federal Election Commission, and the New Hampshire Secretary of State.

President 2004 Election

Party	No. of Candidates	Total Raised	Total Spent	Total Cash On Hand	Total From PACs
All	15	$867,450,185	$827,826,017	$37,448,675	$3,701,629
Dems	10	$493,374,788	$475,827,300	$18,044,804	$782,112
Repubs	1	$367,228,801	$345,259,155	$19,291,231	$2,917,017

George W. Bush (R)

Individual contributions	$271,814,020	74%
PAC contributions	$2,917,017	1%
Candidate self-financing	$0	0%
Federal Funds	$74,620,000	20%
Other	$17,877,764	5%

John Kerry (D)

Individual contributions	$224,906,601	69%
PAC contributions	$141,918	0%
Candidate self-financing	$0	0%
Federal Funds	$74,620,000	23%
Other	$26,190,541	8%

As the nominees of their party, Bush and Kerry each received $74.6 million in government funding for the general election, but in return were prohibited from raising or spending private funds after accepting their party's nomination.

Past year total contributions to Presidential Candidates

2000	$528.9 million
1996	$425.7 million

Senate 2004 Election

Party	No. of Candidates	Total Raised	Total Spent	Total Cash On Hand	Total From PACs
All	189	$489,933,781	$490,522,922	$57,875,238	$68,561,869
Dems	77	$248,080,103	$252,332,909	$30,681,237	$30,747,426
Repubs	93	$240,317,114	$237,321,445	$26,530,753	$37,798,891

House 2004 Election

Party	No. of Candidates	Total Raised	Total Spent	Total Cash On Hand	Total From PACs
All	1213	$695,827,825	$643,754,030	$174,974,786	$233,979,757
Dems	556	$301,685,071	$280,678,278	$75,942,993	$103,348,707
Repubs	606	$392,356,139	$361,332,258	$98,394,165	$130,460,893

Incumbent Advantage – All Candidates 2004 Election

Senate

Type of Candidate	Total Raised	No. of Candidates	Avg Raised
Incumbent	$223,958,619	26	$8,613,793
Challenger	$80,468,919	83	$969,505
Open Seat	$239,971,128	80	$2,999,639
Grand Total	$544,398,666	189	$2,880,416

House

Type of Candidate	Total Raised	No. of Candidates	Avg Raised
Incumbent	$546,818,434	407	$1,122,404
Challenger	$112,111,384	582	$192,631
Open Seat	$126,786,858	223	$586,551
Grand Total	$695,716,677	1,212	$574,024

Democratic Party
2003-2004 Election Cycle

	Total	Hard money	Soft money
Raised:	$816,976,491	$816,976,491 (100%)	$0 (0%)
Spent:	$809,132,697	$809,132,697 (100%)	$0 (0%)
Cash on Hand:	$18,096,339	$18,096,339 (100%)	$0 (0%)

Democratic Party
2001-2002 Election Cycle

	Total	Hard money	Soft money
Raised:	$463,312,470	$217,251,321 (47%)	$246,061,149 (53%)
Spent:	$459,331,677	$208,665,194 (45%)	$250,666,483 (55%)
Cash on Hand:	$17,247,244	$17,200,443 (100%)	$47,001 (0%)
Debt:	$15,423,407		

Republican Party
2003-2004 Election Cycle

	Total	Hard money	Soft money
Raised:	$889,752,453	$889,752,453 (100%)	$0 (0%)
Spent:	$871,253,566	$871,253,566 (100%)	$0 (0%)
Cash on Hand:	$32,805,691	$32,805,691 (100%)	$0 (0%)

Republican Party
2001-2002 Election

	Total	Hard money	Soft money
Raised:	$691,646,873	$441,614,253 (64%)	$250,032,620 (36%)
Spent:	$685,951,827	$427,031,256 (62%)	$258,920,571 (38%)
Cash on Hand:	$12,552,486	$12,529,796 (100%)	$22,690 (0%)
Debt:	$10,798,532		

Top 527 Organizations 2004

Committee	Total Receipts	Total Expenditures	Federal PAC	Major Player
America Coming Together	$79,795,487	$78,040,480	X	X
Joint Victory Campaign	$71,811,666	$72,588,053		
Media Fund	$59,404,183	$54,494,698		X
Service Employees International Union	$48,426,867	$47,730,761	X	
Progress for America	$44,929,1788	$35,631,378		X
American Fedn of St/Cnty/Munci Employees	$25,144,915	$25,808,816	X	
Swift Vets & POWs	$17,008,090	$22,565,360		X
New Democratic Network	$12,726,158	$12,524,063	X	X
MoveOn.org	$12,558,215	$21,346,380	X	X
Sierra Club	$8,727,127	$6,261,811	X	X
Emily's List	$7,739,946	$6,261,811	X	
Club for Growth	$7,490,544	$9,647,958	X	X
IBEW Union	$6,740,936	$9,986,770	X	
AFL-CIO	$6,585,072	$6,541,896	X	

In the 2004 election the top (50) 527 organizations spent $513, 080,510.

The Top 10 Individual Contributors to 527 Organizations 2004 Election Cycle

George Soros	$23,450,000
Peter Lewis	$22,997,220
Steven Bing	$13,852,031
Herb & Marion Sandler	$13,008,459
Bob Perry	$8,085,199
Alex Spanos	$5,000,000
Ted Waitt	$5,000,000
Dawn Arnall	$5,000,000
T. Boone Pickens	$4,600,000
Andrew & Deborah Rappaport	$4,268,400

New Hampshire Races 2004

US Senate

Senator Judd Gregg (R) * winner

Individual contributions	$1,317,306	(39.6%)
PAC contribution	$1,760,341	(53.0%)
Candidates self-financing	$0	
Other	$246,882	(7.4%)
Cash on Hand	$1,453,454	

Doris R. Haddock (D)

Individual contributions	$222,135	(100%)

Congress NH District 1

Jeb Bradley (R) *winner

Individual contributions	$560,116	(53%)
PACs	$478,997	(46%)
Candidate	$0	
Other	$10,719	(1%)
Cash on Hand	$22,540	

Justin Nadeau (D)

Individuals	$227,670	(68%)
PACs	$75,081	(22%)
Candidate	$29,320	(9%)
Other	$2,595	(1%)
Cash on Hand	($695)	

Congress NH District 2

Charles Bass (R) *winner

Individual contributions	$371,550	(50%)
PACs	$363,551	(49%)
Candidate	$0	
Other	$5,198	(1%)
Cash on Hand	$59,513	

Paul W. Hodes (D)

Individual contributions	$303,779	(65%)
PACs	$59,700	(13%)
Candidate	$100,000	(21%)
Other	$3,685	(1%)

New Hampshire Democratic Party
Expenditures $1,728,471
Includes $840,500 from the Democratic Governors Association-New Hampshire

New Hampshire Republican State Committee
Expenditures $396,275

Republican Governors Association-New Hampshire
Expenditures $1,249,394

Gubernatorial Election

John Lynch (D) *winner
Combined contributions $2,977,713
Candidate $2,100,000

Craig Benson (R)
Combined contributions $3,886,421
Candidate $3,199,495

Record Breaking Self-Financed Campaigns

2000 Sen. John S. Corzine (D) New Jersey - Senate Race
$60,200,967

2001 Mayor Michael Bloomberg (R) City of New York – Mayoral Race
$74,000,000

2002 & 2004 Gov. Craig Benson (R) New Hampshire – Gubernatorial Race
$6,000,000 & $3,199,495, over $9.2 million

Money in politics has become the great American dilemma. Freedom of speech and access to government have lost ground against a government for sale. One thing is for sure, without truly significant reform it will only get worse, with each succeeding election cycle costing more than the last, ultimately resulting in a government of either the independently wealthy or those beholding to special interests, which is pretty much where we are at now. Are there solutions? Sure, I have mentioned a few that could help. The problem is finding a Congress (and state legislatures) willing to sacrifice its own claim to incumbency for the greater common good.

Six

Tuning Out on Democracy

——•◆•◆•◆•——

What surprised me the most in running for the New Hampshire Senate was how terribly uninformed or disinterested so many people are about their government. Aside from activists—most with gray hair—I found relatively few working adults able to engage me in a serious conversation; they didn't know the issues and many didn't even know what a state senator did—was it an important job? (yes), did I get paid? (no). It was a shocking revelation. Many of the people I approached on the stump wouldn't even take a few minutes to talk to me, even though I was running for high office to represent them. They were completely disinterested and tuned out. And far too many others had closed minds, brainwashed by the simplistic propaganda of the far right. At candidates' forums in 2004, which sponsors went to a lot of trouble to present, I found that more often than not the candidates outnumbered the audience.

What in the world is going on? Something is not right. Those who founded this nation recognized that a democracy requires an educated, informed citizenry. The First Amendment to the Constitution, which guarantees a free press, is evidence of that. I fear that the future of American democracy is in peril. Not from terrorism or the emergence of another hostile superpower, but by apathy, propaganda, an educational system that has not kept pace with the needs of our society, and several generations of young adults who do not see it as their duty to keep abreast of the news. If the trend continues, power in the United States will rest in fewer and fewer hands, and the democratic process will begin to break down. This chapter will discuss those aspects of democracy in America.

Here is a deeply disturbing fact: Percentagewise, fewer Americans exercise their right to vote than the citizens of most of the world's democracies. We rank a sorry 139th out of the 172 countries for which figures are available. Ironically, voter registration in the United States is at an all-time high, while voter participation is nearing an all-time low. In the 1964 presidential election (Johnson-Goldwater), 61.92 percent of the voting age population (VAP) cast a ballot.[9] The war in Vietnam was the major issue. In 2000 (Bush-Gore), that number dropped to 51 percent. In the 2004 presidential election (Bush-Kerry), it was 60 percent—not record breaking by percentage of VAP, but a record in number of votes cast. The war in Iraq was the major issue. American participation compares embarrassingly with routine turnouts in Italy of 90 percent, Germany 80 percent, France and Canada 76, Britain 75 percent and Japan 71 percent.

Midterm elections in the United States are much worse; turnout averages a measly 36 percent.

In New Hampshire we rang the bell in 2004 with what seems to be a 70 percent turnout of registered voters (VAP data isn't available). The larger turnout helped New Hampshire to be the only so-called swing state to go blue for John Kerry.

Was 2004 the start of a trend toward greater participation? I don't think so. It was the result of the massive amount of money spent on registration drives and the Get-Out-The-Vote effort. Contributing to that flow of cash (about $1.5 billion) were the presidential candidates, the two major political parties, and the 501(c) and 527 advocacy groups—the 527s being the new gorilla in TV attack advertising. Unfortunately, only the candidates' campaigns could focus on why they were most qualified to lead the country. As we have seen, the other advocates were restricted for the first time (by The Bipartisan Campaign Reform Act of 2002) from outwardly campaigning for a candidate. Instead, using the basic propaganda techniques of fear, half-truths and outright lies (which are allowed), they attacked the opposition. Which leads one to ask, how many of us voted in 2004 in response to that propaganda? It's only a guess, but I guess way, way too many for the good of our country.

Interestingly, some 37 countries have compulsory voting. In some, mandatory voting laws are on the books but not enforced, nor do they need to be, since voter turnout is excellent. However, Argentina, Australia, Austria, Belgium, Brazil, Singapore, Switzerland, Uruguay and others have the laws on the books—and enforce them. Penalties range from fines to disfranchisement for repeat offenders.

The first country to insist that its citizens vote was Belgium, which introduced mandatory voting laws in 1892. It is interesting to note that Australia, a nation that is often compared in frontier spirit to the United States, has had compulsory voting since 1924.[10]

Will the United States ever consider compulsory voting? I doubt it. This is America, many would say, and no one is ever going to tell us we have to vote. On the contrary, this country makes it unnecessarily difficult for people to vote. Registration and poll procedures are irregular and often confusing and elections are held on Tuesday, when most people have to work, rather than on the weekend, as they are in Europe. Compulsory voting doesn't solve the problem anyway. Dictatorships traditionally have close to 100 percent voter turnout. You vote for the big guy or else.

Nonetheless, citizens have an obligation in a democracy to vote, because government, as Thomas Jefferson set forth in the Declaration of Independence, derives its authority from the consent of the governed. That consent must constantly be renewed—through voting. If citizens don't vote, the government loses its legitimacy.[11]

What is really tragic is the great demographic disparity in who isn't voting. Those under age 40, and those on the bottom rung of income and education, are voting at half the rates of their wealthier, better-educated counterparts. Why don't they vote? Who knows? One can speculate about feelings of powerlessness, cynicism, and hopelessness. Or it could be that they are being disenfranchised by illiteracy or racial bias at the polls. But one thing is for sure: The people who need a responsive government the most stand little chance of getting one until they vote.

In trying to get our arms around what constitutes an educated and informed citizenry we have to consider those concepts somewhat separately. We get both education and information from a myriad of different sources and they are unquestionably interrelated. Education is a process by which we use information and other stimuli to learn. As an example, my brother-in-law, Bill Hampt, has an excellent voice and loves to play the guitar and sing country music. One of his favorite ditties is, "I got my education out behind the barn." Now we know the education the songwriter was expressing wasn't just an exchange of information behind the barn; it was a memorable and stimulating experience.

From birth, the family or other caregivers are our first source of education. From them we not only learn a lot of stuff, but we also develop lifelong prejudices. Perhaps we embrace our parents' religion, which was taught to us from childhood. Or maybe we consider ourselves to be a Democrat or a Republican because they are. We may even be a racist or bigot like they are, unless further education expands our mind. And if we're lucky and work at it, we will continue to expand our minds for a lifetime.

Most of us start with a free public school education (K-12), which is provided for every child in the United States. Such provisions are contained, in one form or another, in all 50 of our state constitutions. The U.S. Constitution, however, is silent on public education, although it guards against discrimination under its equal protection clause.

The New Hampshire Constitution provides under Article 3. [Encouragement of Literature, etc...] ... "it shall be the duty of the legislators and magistrates, in all future periods of this government, to cherish the interest of literature and the sciences"... June 2, 1784.

Smooth sailing? Not on your life. Education is the top budget item for most communities (property tax) and the second highest item in state budgets (Medicaid ranks No. 1). The federal government does make major contributions to the states for education but falls miserably short of fully funding programs required by federal law. Special Education (The Individuals with Disabilities Education Act) passed in 1975, and the No Child Left Behind Act, signed into law by President Bush on January 8, 2002, are two notorious examples. The Bush administration's budget proposals in 2005, and projections, show no relief in sight. The federal mandates for education will remain largely underfunded—sacrificed, unfortunately, for tax breaks for the rich and what many feel is an imperialistic foreign policy. The United States has become a nation deeply in debt.

When federal mandates go unfunded, the burden is foisted onto the states. New Hampshire has been playing a shell game with education funding for years, and now must comply with a state Supreme Court ruling that directs the state to fund an adequate education for its children. In response, in every session of the legislature since that ruling right-wing legislators have proposed a constitutional amendment to get them out from under it. So far they have all been voted down. The latest attempt wanted to remove the word "cherish" from the NH Constitution. But the crunch is coming. Somebody is going to have to come up with the money or public education is going to suffer the consequences, not only in New Hampshire but also in just about every state in the union.

The compelling question asks if the United States is providing a quality education for its children equal to the needs of the 21st century. Will they be able to understand the complexities of our government, vote intelligently, and be able to find and hold a good job? Many, including Bill Gates[12], the CEO of Microsoft, think not. Nor do I. Here are a few of the prepared remarks delivered by Mr. Gates to 45 of the nation's governors on February 26, 2005 at a National Education Summit on High Schools[13]:

"Yet – the more we looked at the data, the more we came to see that there is more than one barrier to college. There's the barrier of being able to pay for college; and there's the barrier of being prepared for it."

"When we looked at the millions of students that our high schools are not preparing for higher education – and we looked at the damaging impact that has on their lives – we came to a painful conclusion:

America's high schools are obsolete."

"Our high schools were designed fifty years ago to meet the needs of another age. Until we design them to meet the needs of the 21st century, we will keep limiting – even ruining – the lives of millions of Americans every year."

"Today, only one-third of our students graduate from high school ready for college, work, and citizenship.

"The other two-thirds, most of them low-income and minority students, are tracked into courses that won't ever get them ready for college or prepare them for a family-wage job – no matter how well the students learn or the teachers teach."

Good morning America!

Can you imagine living in a land where you couldn't understand the language—weren't able to read a menu, a road sign or even use the telephone? According to the National Institute for Literacy (NIFL),[14] between 21 and 23 percent of the adult population of America, approximately 44 million people, fall into that category. Another 25-28 percent of the adult population, or between 45 and 50 million people, lack the reading skills to read a newspaper, fill out an application, or read a simple story to a child. Literacy experts believe that adults with skills at Levels 1 and 2 (skill Levels assigned to the above two groups) lack a sufficient foundation of basic skills to function successfully in our society.

Quoting NIFL: "Many factors help to explain the relatively large number of adults in Level 1. Twenty-five percent of adults in Level 1 were immigrants who may have just been learning to speak English. More than 60 percent didn't complete high school. More than 30 percent were over 65. More than 25 percent had physical or mental conditions that kept them from fully participating in work, school, housework, or other activities, and almost 20 percent had vision problems that affected their ability to read print."

How does the United States stack up with other countries? The International Adult Literacy Survey (IALS) conducted in 1997, compared the literacy skills of adults in Australia, Belgium, Canada, Germany, Ireland, the Netherlands, New Zealand, Poland, Sweden, Switzerland, and the United Kingdom. The results show that the United States has more adults in Level 1 and 2 (functionally illiterate) than any of the other countries except Poland.

In the State of New Hampshire, those ranked Level 1 and 2 are 36 percent; in the North Country: Carroll County 37 percent, Coos County 52 percent and Grafton County 37 percent. The City of Berlin, the largest community in the North Country, has 60 percent—the majority—ranked Level 1 and 2. No doubt the fact that English is at best a second language for many of Berlin's French-Canadian residents is a factor.

It is a grim statistic: over 40 percent of the adults in the United States are functionally illiterate. Are they allowed to vote? Yes, and they should be, thanks to the wonderful work of Dr. Martin Luther King and the powerful civil rights movement in the 1960s and 70s. The federal Voting Rights Act of 1965 banned literacy tests and provided federal enforcement of voting registration and other rights in several southern states and Alaska. Literacy testing was nothing more than a scam to prevent African-Americans from voting.

Five years later, the Voter Rights Act of 1970 provided language assistance to minority voters who did not speak English fluently. Asian Americans and Latinos were major beneficiaries of this legislation.

As with education, the United States Constitution is silent on the right to vote; it was left to the states to set the standards. When the country was founded, only white men with property were routinely permitted to vote. Working men, all women, and all other people of color were denied the franchise. And don't think for a minute that some of the lunatic fringe on the far right wouldn't like to go back to those times.

No, we need all our adult citizens to vote and we mustn't disenfranchise anyone. But, make no mistake: Literacy is a factor in the ability of voters to make sound choices. If voters cannot read the unbiased news, in depth, in newspapers and periodicals, they're vulnerable to media hype and outright propaganda.

Propaganda is a specific type of message presentation aimed at serving an agenda. At its root, the denotation of propaganda is "to propagate (actively spread) a philosophy or point of view. The most common use of the term (historically) is in political context: in particular to refer to certain efforts sponsored by government or political groups."[15]

I think Americans are being subjected to a daily deluge of more propaganda than ever before in the history of our country. Hardly a day goes by without President Bush appearing on TV, addressing a carefully selected "friendly," managed group and espousing the administration's agenda. President Bush has given more infomercials and fewer open press conferences than any president since the advent of the modern media.

On April 1, 2005, journalist Helen Thomas, who has covered the White House for decades, noted in part, "Every administration tries to manage the message that the news media convey to the public about presidential policies, problems and successes. But the Bush White House is pioneering new methods that steer message management into outright government propaganda.

"The New York Times on March 13 published an in-depth report on how the administration is cranking up its public relations campaign to manipulate broadcast news by distributing pre-packaged videos prepared by several federal agencies, including the Pentagon.

"These videos use phony reporters to tout the administration's position on major issues. Thinly staffed TV stations are only too happy to receive the free videos, which they then pass along to viewers without any acknowledgement that the images and messages are government issued.

"Spokespersons for the major TV networks say they would never disseminate government-prepared videos for their news broadcasts. But some financially strapped affiliates apparently are willing to air them without identifying the source.

"The government agencies say it is up to the broadcast stations to attribute the origin of the report, if they want to do so.

"The practice is far over the ethical line. Shame on both the government agencies and those TV stations."[16]

My first exposure to propaganda was as a child at the movies during WWII. I watched guys like John Wayne and Ronald Reagan beat up on the "Japs" and Germans—in wartime propaganda is a mighty weapon. Its aim is to dehumanize and create hatred toward the enemy. Of course we didn't see the anti-Semitic hate films Adolf Hitler and his henchman Joseph Goebbels were pumping out in Germany through the Ministry for Public Enlightenment.

The movies and radio were great news and propaganda tools during WWII. Who can forget Edward R. Murrow's radio broadcasts from London during the blitz, with bomb explosions heard in the background? Or the Movietone Newsreels that brought frontline war footage into our movie theaters. Movietone Newsreels, along with still photography, were our only visual news until the early 1950s, when TV brought the movies right into our homes. In the 1960s the Vietnam War was the main feature on our TV evening news. We watched people being napalmed while eating our dinner.

Many hawks blame the Vietnam network news coverage for the anti-war demonstrations that eventually led to the United States pulling out of Vietnam. By contrast, during the invasion of Iraq the media were 'embedded' with the military, and the news seemed more and more to cross the line into propaganda.

Propaganda loves visual stuff. Seeing a baby's dead body leaves a far greater impression than reading about it. And it feeds best on fear, lies and distortion. Mind, the total truth can also be considered propaganda if it crosses the line between disseminating information and trying to influence people. You might call that white propaganda. Should the 527 and 501(c) advocacy ads that sprang up during the 2004 campaign, and have continued both for and against Bush's agenda, be called advertising or propaganda? You be the judge.

Does the broadcast media cross that line? Many think it's a serious issue. The major ownership of the media in the United States, which includes TV broadcast and cable networks, radio, movie production and distribution, theme parks, publishing houses, music production and distribution (and who knows what else) is now in the hands of four giant media corporations: AOL Time Warner, Viacom, Walt Disney, and News Corp. General Electric owns NBC.

News Corp., Australian Rupert Murdock's outfit, owns the FOX News Channel that has earned the reputation of being the far-right news channel. The other big news networks—CNN (AOL Time Warner), CBS (Viacom), ABC (Walt Disney) and NBC—seem to respect the line. Their problem is that broadcasting the news has become less and less profitable with diminishing audience shares. Consequently, the trend is to make the news more entertaining, which can only diminish the news as a valuable source of unfiltered information.

Then there is the National Religious Broadcasters,[17] which boasts over 1,700 member organizations representing millions of viewers, listeners, and readers. No one has ever accused the religious far-right televangelists of not trying to influence people—they are probably the largest group of propagandists in the country. If they save a few souls along the way, God bless them.

One afternoon, while on the treadmill trying to keep body and soul together and shake off some of my negative feelings on the state of our nation, I tuned in to a book review presentation on the Public Broadcasting System. It featured Professor David Mindich talking about his book, *Tuned Out: Why Americans Under 40 Don't Follow the News.*[18] I couldn't believe what I was hearing; Professor Mindich was talking about my experience and frustrations.

He went on to say, "Our democracy is on the brink of a crisis, as more and more young people turn their backs on political news. America is seeing the greatest decline in informed citizenship in its history. The implications for overall civic engagement are also enormous."

Mindich's book is far from anecdotal. He traveled the country interviewing young adults, and did extensive research—much of which, not wishing to be a propagandist in my work, I confirmed from a second source. *Tuned Out* is a great book. If you've gotten this far in *Facing Fascism*, you're tuned in and you've got to read it.

In response to his survey questions Mindich writes, "If the measures I used to assess the young people's political awareness could be compared to a heart monitor, most of the respondents (but certainly not all) would be flatliners. Few had ever heard of Tom Daschle, the Senate majority leader at the time of the interviews. Few could name even their own state's U.S. senators. Few could name John Ashcroft, the most high-profile and newsworthy U.S. attorney general since the Nixon administration. Few could name any of the countries listed by Bush as part of the 'axis of evil,' a formulation that was defining America's foreign policy during the time of the study."

On newspaper readership: In 2002, only 18.7 percent of 23-27-year-olds read a newspaper every day, and 35.1 percent of 33-37-year-olds. In 1972 the percentages respectively were 47.1 and 74.4.

Television news: From 1993 to 2000, regular viewership of TV network news of all ages dropped from 60 percent to 30 percent. Fifty percent of the 65-plus crowd still watch the networks' evening news regularly; only 17 percent of the under-30 crowd do. At CNN's main station, the typical viewer is between 59 and 64. Perhaps that explains why the biggest advertisers on CNN are the pharmaceuticals. Cialis for erectile dysfunction buys a lot of airtime.

Very few of under-40-set are listening to National Public Radio, a leading source of radio news, because they don't like the music.

You would think the Internet would be their medium. It is, but they rarely use it to follow public events or the news. They use it at work, for entertainment, and for e-mail.

Part Two

Worldview

Seven

Righting the Democratic Pyramid

---◆---

I met Richard Healy, the president of the Grassroots Policy Project,[19] when he came to Concord from DC to conduct a training workshop for the New Hampshire Citizens Alliance.[20] I am a member of the NHCA board. The session was called "Power for Social Change."

Healy had us fill in what he termed a "Power Matrix" of what groups we thought had power in America, and then ran the discussion to "The 3 Faces of Power," which he defines as:

Immediate Political Gains - The First Face: direct political decision making and involvement (candidates, political parties, PACs, lobbyists and advocates);

Infrastructure - The Second Face: building organizations (corporations, trade unions, think tanks, media, religious groups and other organizations in civil society that try to influence what is on the political agenda);

Ideology - The Third Face: In his presentation on ideology, Healy notes that "most people in the United States probably believe in some version of the American Dream: this is the land of opportunity; if you work hard, you can get ahead. If you believe in the American Dream and you are a good, hard-working and responsible person, then it is plausible that you too can really make it. It is reasonable to believe that people are individually responsible for their own economic and social fate, which justifies the inequality around us. From there, it is easy to believe that the wealthy deserve what they have and shouldn't be taxed more than others, why unions reward the undeserving and stop others from getting ahead, and so on."

Healy goes on to say that the "American Dream is a central theme in the dominant worldview in this country. By *worldview*, we mean 'ideas that guide social action,' and more generally the concepts and images that shape how people understand the world about them. If people believe in this theme and the corollaries to it noted above, then they may not want to get issues about progressive taxation or labor law reform on the agenda."

Defining "ideology" as a "coherent and systematic version of worldview, aligned with a set of political, social and economic goals," Healy concludes that shaping how people understand the world (including their own self-interests)—their *ideology*—is the third face of power. A few key themes such as "limiting government; privatizing more of the services that government provides; deregulating business" and a "pull-yourself-up-by-your-own-bootstraps individualism" form the base of the right wing's ideology, Healy says. The result is an American social Darwinism in which the strongest (read "wealthiest") prevail and both the winners and the losers get what they deserve. Moreover, Healy adds, "the Right regularly links these themes to race. Think about how much of the attack on government has been fueled by stories about our tax dollars going to *those people*."

One is reminded of the bleak, fascistic world in the novels of the pseudo-philosopher Ayn Rand.

Healy concludes that progressives no longer have such an ideological base and they need to develop one that points "in the direction of democracy and effective government, of community and cooperation, of a healthy individualism as part of a larger society..."

And Richard Healy is right: Progressives are not presenting a clear and unified ideology. In postmortems after the 2004 election, political pundits suggested that until the Democratic Party gets its values in order it is never going to win elections. It's not that Democrats and other progressives don't have values. They do. And they are the values America needs for the 21st century. But they are not presenting them in a coherent way. In contrast, although the far right's ideology is deplorable, everyone knows what it is, and for those with a limited worldview who are easily misled it has become a unifying message.

In this part of the book, I will share some of what forms a progressive worldview and how the resulting ideology, with its political, social and economic goals, is so greatly different from those of the radical far right now ruling America. It will be a free ranging mental exercise that I hope you, the reader, can get into. You may not agree with some of the conclusions, but I think you'll find when it gets down to a fundamental ideology based upon knowledge, as opposed to the distorted vision of the world that American conservatives are shoving down our throats, progressives have a lot of common ground.

The term "worldview" comes from its German equivalent, *Weltanschauung.* It was an important cognitive philosophical concept that emerged in Germany in the mid-19th century.

At all times, religious and political teachings were the basis for forming worldviews. To cite only a few examples, Christianity, Islam, Socialism, Marxism and Scientology are all ways of seeing the world, although those worldviews are open to many interpretations.

The Third Reich used the term *Weltanschauung* to designate the instinctive understanding of complex geopolitical problems, which allowed the Nazis to see themselves as a super race with the right to invade other countries, twist facts, ignore human rights and even eradicate "lesser" beings—all in the name of a higher ideal and in accordance with their view of the world.

The religious and political far right in America are up to their clavicles in preaching the same fundamentalist—"don't bother me with the facts"—message.

Well we have a message for them. Freethinking men and women are not going to permit them to install an evangelistic, Taliban-type government in the United States; nor are we going to allow them to turn America into a fascist state that only looks after the interests of the very rich. They can distort the facts all they like, but there will always be those of us around who will confront them with the truth.

There's an old English proverb that says, "In the land of the blind, the one-eyed man is King."[21] With that in mind—and at the risk of reading too much like an almanac—here are some reminders that may help put this world we are struggling to view in perspective:

◆ As an airline pilot who has used maps and charts of all description, I think one of the biggest myths we foist upon our children is in the wide use of the Mercator projection in school, at least in my day. That map projection draws the meridians parallel to each other and the parallels of latitudes are straight lines whose distance from each other increases with their distance from the equator, thereby projecting a global planet onto a flat surface. More realistic projections are available now, but the Mercator is a visual lie that makes the United States look huge. We are a big country, but when viewed on a globe we're shrunk back down to size.

◆ The land area of the United States (the 50 states and District of Columbia) is 3,717,792 square miles. That's about half the size of Russia and only slightly larger than China and Brazil.[22] Canada, reaching north to the Arctic Ocean, is larger than the United States, encompassing 3,855,081 square miles.

◆ At 13:59 GMT on April 18, 2005, the U.S. and World Population Clocks calculated the world population at 6,431,380,816, the United States at 295,911,625.[23]

The population of United States is 4.6 percent of the world population.

◆ Comparative national populations: China 1,306,313,812 (over 4 times the U.S.); India 1,080,264,388 (over 3 times the U.S.); Russia 143,420,309 (about half the U.S.); Japan 127,417,244 (slightly less than half the U.S.); United Kingdom 60,441,457 (about one-fifth the U.S.); Canada 32,805,041 (about one-tenth the U.S.); Mexico 106,202,903 (over one-third the U.S.); European Union 456,285,839 (over one-and-a- half times the U.S.)

♦ World population by geographic region: Asia 3,271,000,000 or 55.9 percent; Africa 750,000,000 or 12.8 percent; Europe 508,000,000 or 8.7 percent; Latin America and Caribbean 496,000,000 or 8.5 percent; North America (U.S. and Canada) 297,000,000 or 5.1 percent; Near East 160,000,000 or 2.7 percent; Oceania (Pacific Islands) 29,000,000 or .5 percent

♦ By the year 2050 the population of the world and the United States is expected to grow by about 5 percent to 9,190,252,532 and 419,854,000 respectively.[24]

The growth in the United States contrasts sharply with that predicted for most European nations, where populations are expected to decline.

♦ The U.S. Census Bureau predicts that the nation's Hispanic and Asian populations will triple over the next half century, and non-Hispanic whites will represent about one-half of the total population by 2050, down from about 75 percent now.

The black population is projected to rise from 35.8 million to 61.4 million in 2050, an increase of about 26 million or 71 percent.

The population is also expected to become older. By 2030, about 1-in-5 Americans will be 65 or over.

♦ Oceans cover about 70 percent of the Earth's surface and contain roughly 97 percent of the Earth's water supply. However, the scarcity of fresh water needed for human consumption and agriculture is a looming crisis. A third of the world's population lives in water-stressed countries now. By 2025, this is expected to rise to two-thirds.[25]

♦ In the spring of 2006, the cost of crude oil on the world market was hovered around $70 a barrel, driving the cost of a gallon of gasoline at the pump to nearly $3.00 and sometimes more in most parts of the United States. This country imports over 60 percent of its oil, making it the world's largest importer of oil by a factor of over two. Although the population of the United States is less than 5 percent of the world's, we consume 25 percent of the oil produced and burn a whopping 45 percent of the gasoline produced worldwide.

♦ The nation's worst power blackout occurred on August 14, 2003. The *Final Report of the U.S.- Canada Power System Outage Task Force* released on April 5, 2004 stated, "It is not the history of a one-time event but a call to action." "The Task Force found that the conditions that led to the most massive blackout in North America were not unique, were preventable, and could occur again."

From *New York Times* columnist Nicholas D. Kristof: "Global energy demands will rise 60 percent over the next 25 years, according to the International Energy Agency, and nuclear power is the cleanest and best bet to fill that gap. Nuclear energy already makes up to 20 percent of America's power, not to mention 75 percent of France's."

And "… the world now has a half-century of experience with nuclear power plants, 440 of them around the world, and they have proved safer so far than the alternatives. America's biggest power source is now coal, which kills about 25,000 people a year through soot in the air. To put it another way, nuclear energy seems much safer than our dependency on coal, which kills more than 60 people every day."[26]

♦ The Earth's atmosphere extends 1,500 miles above the surface but the greatest bulk of the gases (about 75 percent) reside within ten miles of the Earth's surface, merely an orange skin that sustains life. Most life on Earth exists at elevations less than a few thousand feet above sea level. Pilots who fly over 10,000 feet require supplemental oxygen.

There is no other known planet that has an atmosphere that can sustain life as we know it on Earth.

♦ In the world there are about 216 countries and 61 territories, colonies, and dependencies. Under United States jurisdiction there are 14 territories or dependencies.[27]

♦ The International Monetary Fund (IMF)[28] estimated that in 2000, 23 percent of the world's population existed on $1 a day or less.

In 2005, a UNICEF report shows half the world's children are devastated by poverty, conflict and AIDS.[29]

♦ 640 million children do not have adequate shelter
♦ 500 million children have no access to sanitation
♦ 400 million children do not have access to safe water
♦ 300 million children lack access to information
♦ 270 million children have no access to health care services
♦ 140 million children have never been to school
♦ 90 million children are severely food-deprived

♦ In the United States, the Office of Management and Budget (OMB) defined the poverty threshold in 2003 as $18,810 for a family of four; $14,680 for a family of three; $12,015 for a family of two; and for unrelated individuals $9,393.

The U.S. Census Bureau reports that the nation's poverty rate rose from 12.1 percent in 2002 to 12.5 percent in 2003.[30] The number of people without health insurance rose to 45 million or 15.6 percent.

Just those few facts cover a lot of ground when thinking of a worldview. The far right avoids this sort of information like the plague, and substitutes its ideology: America is huge; we're militarily so strong we can whip the world if we need to; the Caucasian (white) race dominates the world. The other races are effective minorities. Cheap prices are more important than overpaid union workers; people on welfare are lazy; seniors shouldn't take jobs from the young—if they had planned better they wouldn't be bleeding the system; there's plenty of oil, why worry about the future; deregulation will take care of our electric power needs; environmental concerns are for tree-hugging liberals. Why worry about the environment when the second coming of Jesus is at hand and all those who have been "saved" (i.e. born again) will be snatched up to Heaven in what Protestant fundamentalists call the Rapture? And this is only a sampling of what a substantial portion of President Bush's political base believes.

A progressive ideology that everyday people could rally behind might emphasize that the major religions of the world encourage charity and tolerance; that in a world full of hunger and need, it is in America's self-interest to be recognized as a positive force for progress; that the alternative cost in blood and treasure is unacceptable; that a nation dependant upon consumerism eventually consumes itself; that conservation of our natural resources is good business; that the heroes of American individualism traditionally stood up to the fat cats; that a nation can be judged on how it treats the least of its citizens. This, too, is only a sampling of course.

Perhaps the best reasoning I've read as to why the Democratic Party has allowed the Republicans to claim the ideological high ground was in an op-ed column written by former senator and presidential candidate (ran in the 2000 Democratic primary against Al Gore) Bill Bradley.[31]

After rehearsing how the Republican Party carefully built a power pyramid over the past forty years, Bradley writes, "To understand how the Democratic Party works, invert the pyramid. Imagine a pyramid balancing precariously on its point, which is the presidential candidate. Democrats who run for president have to build their own pyramids all by themselves. There is no coherent, larger structure that they can rely on. Unlike Republicans, they don't simply have to assemble a campaign apparatus—they have to formulate ideas and a vision, too. Many Democratic fundraisers join a campaign only after assessing how well it has done in assembling its pyramid of political, media and idea people."

In the Republican model, the base is so strong that top of the pyramid can be replaced at will, leaving an effective structure so resilient that almost any idiot could be elected president. Some see George W. Bush as ample proof of that.

Bradley goes on to say that Democrats lack a clearly identifiable funding base. In the crush of a campaign "there is no time for patient, long-term development of new ideas or of new ways to sell old ideas." Consequently, Bradley asserts, the election year is half over before Democrats start thinking about a party brand and building a consistent message. The result is no more than a catchy slogan rather than a real Democratic brand that voters can identify with.

Bradley believes this approach is the political legacy of John Kennedy, who inspired the Democrats' belief in "the promise of a charismatic leader who can change America by the strength and style of his personality." But, Bradley points out, primary races between several Democratic candidates exaggerate the differences between them and leave voters confused about what Democrats really believe.

Tactics end up trumping strategy in such a system, Bradley says. Big, poorly tested ideas become too risky to debate, so candidates usually focus on minor issues, with none of the deep conviction that inspires voters. Worse yet, some candidates adopt "Republican lite" platforms, which allow the Republicans to define the terms of the debate.

No, Bradley concludes, "A party based on charisma has no long-term impact." He cites Bill Clinton as an example. Clinton, the first Democrat to be reelected since Franklin Roosevelt, was smart and a skilled politician, a charismatic leader. Yet during his tenure Democrats lost ground across the board—from Congress to governorships to state legislators. And the national party was mired in debt. "The president did well. The party did not. Charisma didn't translate into structure."

Later I will explore much of what Bradley has to say. For now, it may be enough to point out that Democrats at all levels of the party's shaky structure should be paying attention to his ideas. There are signs, here in the spring of 2006, that some Democrats, under the national leadership of Howard Dean, are beginning to do that. This book is in part an attempt to push that process along.

Bradley and I were together during the 2002 campaign. I first met him at a fundraiser for Mark Fernald, who was running for NH governor. Bradley endorsed Fernald and gave an inspiring speech on his behalf.

Eight

Fascism: 'wrapped in the flag and carrying the cross'

———————•◆•———————

A s Democrats search for ways to express a progressive ideology that resonates with 21st century Americans, the Republican far right is expanding its dangerous ideological coalition with the Christian evangelical movement. The evangelicals[32] have become the cutting edge of the religious far right. They make no bones about what they want: Their goal is a government in the United States that shares their view of the infallibility of the Bible and the authority of God over the will of humankind. That is quite a contrast with progressive thought, which values truth over dogma, and stands for the rights of individuals as required by our Constitution.[33] One of the cornerstones of the Constitution is separation of church and state.

President Bush and the far-right leadership of the Republican Party have found common cause with the evangelicals because both ideologies are based upon absolute power and authority. From the time of Charlemagne (771-814), until the emergence of democratic forms of governments in the eighteenth and nineteenth centuries, the church held varying degrees of political power. Indeed, the Holy Roman Empire (which was neither holy nor Roman), although never a nation-state, eventually ruled what would become Germany, France, Bohemia and Moravia (now the Czech Republic), Austria, present-day Belgium and beyond.

The emperors were all Roman Catholic (which became a problem after the Reformation), yet their relations with the papacy were usually dicey at best. The pope crowned the emperors, but they were usually chosen through heredity or elected by the German princes. Papal attempts to claim the right to name the emperors met with only limited success. The emperors saw the pope as the spiritual Vicar of Christ on Earth while they were the temporal vicars, so the two were at loggerheads more often than not. In fact, Pope Gregory IX proclaimed a crusade against the Emperor Frederick II in 1228 and drove the empire out of Italy and out of papal affairs. (The empire retaliated in 1527, when its troops attacked Rome, imprisoned Pope Clement VII, and effectively ended the Italian Renaissance.)

During much of this time, the church was launching crusades against Islam in the Middle East and against "heretics" in Europe off and on from 1095 until the 17th century. The first Crusade was an attempt to recapture the Holy Land from Islam. It was a military success but not before it had degenerated—like most of the failed crusades that followed it—into a mercenary excuse to ravage, rape, and sack. Even the long-term positive outcomes of the crusades, such as increased trade, were far more material than spiritual. Put another way, the church's "Holy Wars" became far more imperialistic than religious. There are lessons to be drawn here on both sides of the so-called war on terror.

In 1231, Pope Gregory IX established the Inquisition to combat heresy. The Medieval Inquisition, as it is called, eventually resorted to torture and execution, usually by burning at the stake. But the more common punishments were penance, imprisonment and the forfeiture of all property. Individuals were powerless in the hands of the Inquisition. They were isolated, without counsel, and were not allowed to face their accusers. (No doubt their plight would ring painfully familiar to hundreds of terror suspects the United States imprisoned without charges and usually without counsel.) Many, as in the famous case of Galileo (1633), recanted their beliefs. The Inquisition survived as an office until the early 1960s, when, during Vatican Council II, it became the Congregation for the Doctrine of the Faith, which Cardinal Joseph Ratzinger was heading when he became Pope Benedict XVI in 2005.

The Spanish Inquisition, on the other hand, was another far bloodier matter. Instituted by the Spanish monarchs Ferdinand and Isabella in 1478, with the reluctant approval of Pope Sixtus IV, it was aimed primarily at Jews and Muslims and the death penalty was much more common. After the Reformation, Protestants were burned as well. The Spanish Inquisition was not abolished until 1834.

In the United States today the Catholic Church continues to be a political force, joining the religious far right in opposition to expanded stem cell research, contraception, a woman's right to abortion, and in influencing elections. During the 2004 election, then-Cardinal Ratzinger issued a directive to American Catholic bishops not to allow the sacrament of Holy Communion to be given to Catholic candidates who did not oppose legalized abortion. This targeted John Kerry, who is a Catholic, and was a factor in his failed presidential campaign.

That said, the Catholic Church isn't part of the evangelical movement in the United States (although many individual Catholics call themselves Charismatics and are "reborn" into the gifts of the Holy Spirit, including prophesy and speaking in tongues). The heart of the American evangelical movement is in the Bible belt. Those who consider themselves evangelicals are mostly fundamentalist Baptists such as televangelist Pat Robertson, head of the Christian Coalition and founder of the Christian Broadcasting Network; the Rev. Jerry Falwell, founder of the Moral Majority; and James Dobson, Gary Bauer,[34] Ken Connor and Tony Perkins, who are leaders of the Family Research Council. There is a long list.

The point is that America's wave of evangelical activism isn't breaking new ground; organized religions, including the Catholic Church, have exercised, fought and made war over political power throughout history. Israel is a Jewish state. Iran is a Muslim theocracy (the clergy rules the state); before the United States invaded Afghanistan the Taliban (Muslim fundamentalists) ruled it; Osama bin Laden's Al Qaeda is an Islamic terrorist group; and the Shiite Islamic clergy have great influence in the government being cobbled together in Iraq in 2006.

The German term *Reich* describes an imperial cross between a state and a religious confederation, at least in the case of the Holy Roman Empire, which is thought of as the First Reich. The period between 1871 (when Germany became a nation-state) to 1918 is often called the Second Reich. Adolf Hitler called Nazi Germany the Third Reich.

By the spring of 2005, it was clear that the wall between church and state, guaranteed by our Constitution, was in danger of being torn down, much to the dismay of many mainstream religious leaders. Then House Majority Leader Tom Delay threatened "liberal" judges for not following the social agenda he shared with the religious far right; and Senate Majority Leader Bill Frist participated in a telecast organized by the Family Research Council (FRC), an ultraconservative Christian group, to attack Democrats as enemies of "people of faith." Besides hearing Frist's videotaped speech, an estimated 35 million viewers heard speakers call the Supreme Court a despotic oligarchy and the congressional tactic of delaying debate, or blocking legislation, "judicial tyranny to people of faith."

In regard to the FRC telecast a *The New York Times* editorial on April 26, 2005 titled "The Disappearing Wall" said, "Apart from confirming an unwholesome disrespect for traditional values like checks and balances, the assault on judges is part of a wide-ranging and successful Republican campaign to breach the wall between church and state to advance a particular brand of religion. No theoretical exercise, the program is having a corrosive effect on policymaking and the lives of Americans."

Frist told the viewers he was willing to use the Republican majority to change Senate rules to prevent filibusters of judicial nominees, the so-called "nuclear" option. Democrats had used the filibuster threat to block 10 of Bush's 205 picks for district and appellate court positions, a mere 5 percent. They object to the nominees in question as too conservative to serve in an unbiased fashion on the bench as required by law.

A three-fifths vote in the Senate (60) is needed to end a filibuster. But if the filibuster were eliminated, only 51 votes would be needed to confirm a judicial nominee. Republicans hold 55 seats and Democrats 44, with one independent (Sen. Jim Jeffords of Vermont).

Speaking about the nuclear option in a letter to supporters, Sen. Hillary Clinton (D-NY) said, "the Republican attempt to change the Senate rules by breaking them, in order to eliminate checks and balances and gain more power, if invoked, the 'nuclear option' would be, in my view, one of the most egregious abuses of power that the United States has experienced in its history...President Bush has nominated a few people to serve on our federal courts for life that I and many of my colleagues believe would not abide by the rule of law, which is why some of these nominees were not confirmed. Now, to stack the courts with these nominees and other extreme judges, the majority is attempting to violate long-established and agreed to Senate rules in order to do away with a constitutional check on the power of the President to pick any judicial nominees he pleases. This is wrong and inconsistent with American values...I will do all that I can to ensure that this does not happen."

There is a lot at stake. With two conservative Supreme Court appointments notching his gun belt (Chief Justice John Roberts and Justice Samuel Alito), Bush is well on his way toward swinging the court far to the right for what could be decades. It happened in the 19th century and was a major setback for social justice in America. So it is crucial for the Democrats to regain at least one house of Congress in 2006 and the presidency in 2008.

A federal judiciary weighted with judges who share the ideology and goals of the evangelical movement could well undo many of the civil rights gained in the 20th century. On the chopping block would be a woman's right to abortion, the rights of gays and lesbians, voting rights, racial discrimination, gender discrimination, affirmative action, workers rights, voting rights. The erosion of civil liberties that set in after 9/11, 2001 will almost certainly continue and an ultraconservative judiciary would likely uphold it. All told, it would be a major blow to America.

At one of his infrequent press conferences Bush was asked if he ever asked his father (former President George Herbert Walker Bush), for advice; he replied that he gets his guidance from God the father. I know many people of faith who try to do God's work, but it is disturbing to me to think our president feels he has a direct line to God and needs no mortal advice.

And he now says, claiming that America has brought democracy to Iraq, which is still highly questionable, that America's goal is to bring democracy to the rest of the world. A noble notion, perhaps, but given the diversity of governments in the world it is an incredibly ambitious vision that sounds an awful lot like the Crusades of old to me. Only this time the crusaders are bound to be the same National Guard soldiers and Reservists who have been pressed into repeated tours of duty in Iraq. Our regular military is spread so thin one already wonders how the United States would handle a real threat to our national security, to say nothing of remaking the world in our image.

While Bush talks about spreading democracy, he seems determined to turn America's democracy over to corporations, the very rich, and religious ideologues. One has to wonder if he knows what the term "democracy" means, or for that matter what the term fascism stands for, because the latter is what he is promoting. Or perhaps he takes quite a bit of worldly advice from those that know all-too well what is in their special interests.

For example, consider Bush's so-called faith-based initiative, which blatantly disregards First Amendment and civil rights protections. The program has given billions of dollars to churches and religious organizations under questionable rules that allow a religious test on hiring and providing services, with little or no accountability. Is he trying to do the right thing or is he buying political support from the religious far right? Bush's opposition to expanded stem-cell research; birth control and AIDS prevention programs are all extreme positions that fly in the face of sound public policy. Again, whom is he trying to please?

Am I just an alarmist in warning that the stench of fascism is in the air? No, I don't think so; as a student of history I know the danger signs. Oh, you won't find characters like Hitler or Mussolini. Bush may like to play dress-up in a Navy flight suit but he's not going to be seen strutting around in a field marshal's uniform. And, to give them their due, Vice President Cheney, Secretary of State Rice, and Defense Secretary Rumsfeld are articulate masters of spin who can paint an innocuous face on an ideology that is far from harmless. The similarities with earlier fascist regimes are not in comic appearances or gestures; they are in the actions and goals of those now ruling our country. But you are the judge. Here are a few of the historical characteristics of a fascist state and a brief synopsis of the Bush administration's record. You decide which way the United States is leaning.

The use of fear: At his war crimes trial, Hermann Goring (Hitler's right-hand man) was asked how he and his fellow Nazis managed to hijack Germany's democratic government. He replied, "The people can always be brought to the bidding of the leaders. That is easy. All you have to do is tell them they are being attacked and denounce the pacifists for lack of patriotism and exposing the country to danger. It works the same way in any country."

How right he was. Since the attack on the World Trade Center on 9/11, Bush and his war cabinet have told us daily that we are in a state of war—a global war on terrorism. Therefore we must expect our government to spend huge amounts of money on the military (even while running up record-breaking deficits), and allow the government to trample on civil rights and the rule of law (the Patriot Act, Abu Ghraib, confinement without due process as at Guantanamo Bay, "extraordinary rendition" of prisoners to other countries, where they are often tortured) because, after all, we are at war. The problem is that terrorism has existed in its many forms and on all sides throughout the history of humankind. (The United States has used it and abetted it everywhere from Central and South America to Southeast Asia.) So it is a war we can never totally win, which makes it perpetual, and those who lead may never be held accountable.

Bush and his team are great denouncers. They viciously attacked John Kerry during the campaign, calling him a "flip-flopper," claiming that he lacks conviction, and implying (through the Swift Boat Veterans for Truth) that he lied about his record in Vietnam. The underlying message was that if Kerry were elected he would expose the country to danger. The truth is that Kerry is a decorated war hero who volunteered to serve in Vietnam and later opposed the war because he saw that it was wrong, and is now serving his fourth term in the U.S. Senate. Kerry stands for a strong defense *and diplomacy*—a basic difference with the unilateralism of the Bush administration. Yet Republican lies and character assassination probably cost him the election.

Supremacy of the military: Fascists have always spent heavily on armaments and overall military might, believing that they are necessary to remain in power, a way to fatten industrial coffers, and indispensable to imperialistic ambitions. President Dwight D. Eisenhower spoke of the potential dangers of the relationship between the military and industry in a famous speech he made in 1961. He said, "In the councils of government, we must guard against the acquisition of unwarranted influence, whether sought or unsought, by the military-industrial complex. The potential for the disastrous rise of misplaced power exits and will persist."

I think Ike would turn over in his grave if he saw the growth and influence of the U.S. military-industrial complex today. The military budget for 2006 is about $500 billion, if you include the "special appropriation" of over $80 billion to finance the occupation and rebuilding of Afghanistan and Iraq. To put that in perspective, the U.S. military budget is about equal to that of all the rest of the world's put together, and more than eight times that of either China or Russia, the world's second highest spenders. A significant amount of the defense budget is being spent on high-tech, outlandishly expensive weapons (many, such as Reagan's ill-fated missile defense system, of questionable value), and on contract services to support the military in the field and to rebuild Iraq and Afghanistan. Of particular concern are billions in no-bid contracts given to Kellogg, Brown and Root, a subsidiary of Halliburton Corp. Vice President Dick Cheney was the CEO of Halliburton from 1995 to 2000, the year he was elected vice president.

Wars of aggression: Bush and his War Cabinet misled Congress and the American people into believing that the preemptive war on Iraq was justified because Iraq was a serious threat to our national security in that Saddam Hussein had weapons of mass destruction (WMD) stockpiled and would use them against us and our allies if we didn't act. And, to add icing to the cake, that Saddam in some way had a hand in the 9/11 attacks on the World Trade Center. They have always tried to link the "war on terrorism" with Iraq.

Yet neither pretext was true. No connection has ever been made between Saddam and Al Qaeda or Osama bin Laden, although now, under the U.S. occupation, operatives of Al Qaeda and other terrorist groups seem to be operating freely in that country. And, as United Nations inspectors had reported before the war, Iraq had no WMD, absolutely none has been found. Some die-hard administration supporters clung to the notion that Saddam had spirited the weapons to Syria to avoid capture. In April 2005 the Iraq Survey Group, commissioned to investigate that possibility, declared any mass transfer of illicit weapons improbable.

The Bush White House claims it wasn't its intent to deceive Congress or the American people. Faulty intelligence was to blame and, regardless, the war was justified to rid the world of Saddam and bring democracy to Iraq. But then, amazingly, instead of disciplining or firing those who had provided the faulty intelligence, Bush decorated and promoted many of them. On the other hand, those who spoke up while it was happening were labeled as malcontents and fired.

The unrelenting use of propaganda: In a previous chapter I spoke of the fine line between informational political advertising and what we think of as government propaganda. There is no question in my mind that, since Bush came into power in 2000, the government of the United States has crossed over that line. Hardly a day goes by when Bush doesn't use the public airways to advance his agenda. The media covers all of his staged events. He's the president. That daily exposure of a president is new in America. In the past, presidents held press conferences and answered questions, with few orchestrated sales pitches to sway public opinion. There is a big difference. The Bush administration has also spent hundreds of millions of the public's money on deceptive infomercials, paid media personalities under the table, and has yet to denounce 527 groups that outright lie.

Unknown to many, last year the Department of Defense opened up the Pentagon Channel on cable television. The on-air staffers "aren't reporters," says Ralph J. Begleiter, professor of communications at the University of Delaware. "That's a hugely important distinction," he said. "They're not journalists. They're salesmen." Pentagon Channel senior producer Scott Howe, a veteran of military journalism, puts it another way: "We are an advocate of the Department of Defense and its voice," he said, "We obviously don't air speculation out in the civilian media that questions what the department is doing or its motives."[35] In other words, they engage in propaganda.

Cronyism, the shifting of national priorities: The Bush administration has pushed through unprecedented tax breaks for the rich while slashing essential domestic programs and running up the largest deficits in history. The 2006 budget passed by Congress gives $106 billion in tax cuts to the rich over the next five years, trims the growth of Medicaid (an important part of our social safety net) by $10 billion and freezes all other domestic programs. Meanwhile, the deficit is on track to hit a record $427 billion in 2005. In this session of Congress, the Republican majority, in step with Bush's agenda, has:

- Again refused to raise the minimum wage (it has been $5.15 per hour since 1997);
- Relieved employers of the obligation to pay overtime to many classes of workers;
- Changed the bankruptcy law to force middle income people to pay debt over a long term, instead of relieving them of often unavoidable debt and giving them a fresh start (a boon for the credit card industry);
- Rewritten the rules for class-action lawsuits, to the advantage of industry.

The Medicare, Prescription Drug, Modernization and Improvement Act that Congress passed in December 2003 will cost taxpayers at least $540 billion over the next 10 years and provide little relief to seniors. Drug companies, on the other hand, stand to clean up. Shamefully, many Democrats went along with all of these measures.

The centerpiece of Bush's second term agenda is to privatize and revamp Social Security, which is the cornerstone of America's social safety net given to us under President Franklin Delano Roosevelt. What Bush and the far right really want to do is to kill Social Security altogether. That has been the far-right's goal ever since FDR made Social Security happen in 1935.

Prophetically, also in 1935, Nobel Prize winning author Sinclair Lewis wrote in his novel *It Can't happen Here:* "When fascism comes to America, it will be wrapped in the flag and carrying the cross."

Nine

The Roots of the Republic

---◆◆◆---

In the last chapter we took a look at the far right's cozy relationship with the Christian evangelical movement. The evangelicals are the religious far right's strike force that wants to overturn the First Amendment and install a government in the United States that rules on the basis of the infallibility of the Bible. In this chapter, we will examine how the Republican Party's ultraconservative think tanks[36] and well paid spin-doctors twist and distort our heritage to conform to their ideology. Interestingly, they also claim the infallibility of a piece of paper—the U.S. Constitution—after all, what could be more patriotic? Of course they want to stick their version of it down our proverbial throats. Before we allow these clowns to hijack our heritage, it behooves us to know it better.

To understand the work of our founders we have to go back in time and view the world as it existed for them. If you haven't had the experience, I urge you to visit Colonial Williamsburg in Virginia;[37] it is the closest you can get to witnessing life in that period. I have been there several times and look forward to visiting again. For eighty-one years, 1699 to 1780, Williamsburg was the political, cultural, and educational center of what was then the largest, most populated and influential of the American colonies, Virginia. The restoration of an old section of Williamsburg began in 1926 with the support of philanthropist John D. Rockefeller Jr. It's a great place to soak up the era and to study. There are plenty of lectures, books and tours.

It always impresses me to note how much we take for granted that didn't exist in the 1700s. Life was tough and short. The average life span was only about thirty-five years; twenty-five percent of the children died before their first birthday, and women frequently died in childbirth. Modern contraception didn't exist and large families were prevalent, with sons needed on the farm. Poor sanitation, malnutrition and disease took their toll in colonial life, and people on average were a few inches shorter. A visit to the apothecary in colonial Williamsburg indicates the era's level of health care—a few leaches and bottled remedies (mostly alcohol), not much more. The wigmaker's shop is interesting. Men and women wore powdered wigs because they bathed infrequently. The wigs were the period's deodorant. And they also provided a defense against lice.

A stop at one of the restored inns will give you some idea of what America's early politicians had to deal with when on the road. They didn't rent a room at the inn; they rented a space on a bed that was shared. For those who could afford it, travel was by horseback or horse-drawn carriage; for most it was by foot.

American history is the story of a struggle for progress. Glamorizing the "good old days" is crazy. Only a fool would revive them as our far-right fools are suggesting. Our forefathers founded a nation. They could not and did not hand posterity a finished product. The fledgling United States, and the Constitution that established its framework, was a work in progress, and unfortunately we haven't been doing our share of the work.

So let's take off the rose-colored glasses and have a reality check. There is a dark side to American history, in the way the nation was founded and the way we did many things in our brief two-hundred-thirty-year history. As the famous quotation from Spanish-born philosopher George Santayana has it, "Those who cannot remember the past are condemned to repeat it."

For the three centuries (1500-1800) after the discovery of the Americas, Portugal, Great Britain, France and Spain took land in the New World by simply raising a flag and claiming the place. The land wasn't given to them, nor did they buy it. They stole it and used brutal force to subdue the original inhabitants. (Manhattan was an exception. The Dutch bought it from the Indians in 1626 for 60 guilders, about $24 worth of trade goods.) The Indians fought back with equal brutality, but they stood no chance against a white tide that eventually engulfed everything in its path. Genocidal warfare and foreign diseases such as measles and smallpox devastated the Indian nations. The survivors were eventually herded onto reservations.

The American Indian retained citizenship in the various tribal nations but wouldn't be granted U.S. citizenship until Calvin Coolidge signed the Indian Citizenship Act in 1924! Proof of tribal citizenship can be quite valuable in today's world, if a gambling casino pops up in the right place.

Though most of the founders were born in the colonies, their worldviews were shaped by conditions in Europe. That was their heritage. Their ancestors weren't merely seeking opportunity in the New World; they were fleeing economic oppression, indentured servitude, outright slavery, and religious intolerance in England, France and Spain. As we have seen, in the 1600s and 1700s Holy Roman emperors and despotic kings still ruled the British Isles and Europe. Our evangelist friends and their far-right cohorts are actually no more than ghosts from the past coming back to haunt us.

For a brief time (1649-60), following what's referred to as the British Civil War,[38] Britain was a republic. In 1660 the monarchy was restored and Charles II proclaimed King of England, but a precedent had been set that the king could not govern without the consent of Parliament. That would be challenged when Charles II tried to assure religious tolerance in Britain (partly because of his attraction to Roman Catholicism), but in the end Parliament won out and Anglicanism was rooted as the state religion.

Before and during the American Revolution, it was Parliament's heavy hand that forced the war, and it was Parliament that demanded that George III end the war (largely due to its expense). Today, the United Kingdom is the oldest (constitutional) monarchy on Earth, although its role is now largely ceremonial and, for some, a form of entertainment because of the royal family's antics. Incidentally, the UK doesn't have a written constitution—they consider theirs a "living constitution" based upon common law, statutes and convention.[39]

Oliver Cromwell's victory over the English monarchy (1651) marked the end of Britain's feudal system. In the Middle Ages, feudalism was the military, social, and economic system that prevailed (in varying forms) throughout Europe and much of the world. Here's how it worked: The king granted land to the warrior nobility in return for military obligations; the noble or lord, in turn gave land to a "vassal" in exchange for military service. The land was called a fief; and "serfs" or "peasants" were the names given to those who lived and worked on the fief. Everything they had, their food, homes, and animals belonged to the lord. While Cromwell changed the military allegiances of the feudal system in England, nothing much changed for the peasants; they still lived under the heel of the nobility.

Typically, when most Americans think of "slavery," they don't think of it in a widely historic or global sense; they think of the American Civil War and Abraham Lincoln and that whole era. Actually, slavery is as old as humankind, mentioned frequently in the Bible, and still exists today in countries such as Sudan and globally under the guise of "human trafficking."

(Commenting on the State Department's 2005 "Trafficking in Persons" report, Secretary of State Condoleezza Rice called trafficking in human beings "nothing less than a modern form of slavery." Nearly every country is affected, but some of the worst offenders are our close allies such as Saudi Arabia and Kuwait. The report estimates that up to 800,000 people a year, most of them women and girls forced into sexual servitude, are transported across international borders. Up to 17,500 of them are trafficked in the United States, according to the report.)

Slavery was accepted throughout Europe during the colonial period in America. Therefore it is not surprising that in the late 1660s, colonists in the Chesapeake colonies of Maryland and Virginia began to import thousands of slaves directly from Africa—transported on British slave ships under unspeakably inhumane conditions. Slavery would expand exponentially with the agricultural south's need for cheap labor, and continue for over 60 years after independence. The Brits moved to end slavery before we did. In 1833, Parliament passed a law that quickly phased out slavery in Britain and its colonies, including Canada. In the United States, although Abraham Lincoln issued the *Emancipation Proclamation* on January 1,

1863, slaves in the Confederacy wouldn't be freed until the end of the Civil War in 1865. All told, legal slavery existed in America for over 200 years. Slavery in Russia ended in 1862. Brazil was the last country in the Western Hemisphere to abolish slavery in 1888.

Many Christians cited Genesis 9:25-27 as a justification for slavery: "Accursed be Canaan./He shall be his brothers'/meanest slave." Choosing that passage is tenuous at best. That was not God pronouncing a dictum for all of humankind through the ages. That was Noah, waking from a drunken stupor (probably with a raging hangover) and cursing his son Ham because Ham had seen him passed out naked in his tent. Anyone who would accept that as a justification for slavery must also believe that Noah lived for nine hundred and fifty years, as that same chapter in Genesis asserts. There are scores of more reliable references to slavery in both the Old and New Testaments, many of them well documented. Surely they must still be stumbling blocks for evangelicals and others who insist on interpreting scripture literally.

In 1866, just a year after the Civil War ended, the Vatican issued a statement in support of slavery. The document stated: "Slavery itself...is not at all contrary to the natural and divine law...The purchaser [of the slave] should carefully examine whether the slave who is put up for sale has been justly or unjustly deprived of liberty, and that the vendor should do nothing which might endanger the life, virtue, or Catholic faith of the slave."

The church didn't make a general public pronouncement against slavery until the Second Vatican Council issued the *Pastoral Constitution on the Church in the Modern World* in 1965, although the church did expand its Code of Canon Law to criminalize "selling a human being into slavery" in 1917.

It should be said, however, that committed Christians of many denominations were in the forefront of the abolitionist movement.

That high note aside, how did humanity ever climb out of such dark times and achieve any degree of social and economic justice? No matter how you look at it, the climb was difficult and slow and the struggle is ongoing in America and around the world. If you recall, our focus in this part of the book is on worldview and ideology. From that perspective, there was a major leap forward when philosophers, scientists, and other visionaries emerged to change the way people viewed the world.

Standing on the shoulders of earlier rationalists such as Rene Descartes (1596-1650), Benedict de Spinoza (1632-1677) and Sir Isaac Newton (1642-1727), the 18th century Enlightenment was truly an age of reason. It was a movement of intellectuals who viewed themselves as reasoning the world toward progress, and out of the "Dark Ages" of irrationality, superstition, and tyranny. This movement provided a framework for the American and French Revolutions, as well the rise of capitalism and the birth of socialism. Philosophers such as Voltaire and Jean-Jacques Rousseau in France, and John Locke and David Hume in Great Britain led the way. Their influence upon many of our own revolutionary thinkers, especially Thomas Paine and Thomas Jefferson, is unmistakable.

The Creator invoked in Jefferson's Declaration if Independence, for example, is Rousseau's deist God, not the omnipresent deity of traditional Christianity. This is a Creator who set the universe in motion then stepped back and had nothing more to do with it. Our founders put far more stock in natural law and physical science than they did in the Bible. Theirs was a worldview far more material than spiritual. Those Bible-thumping evangelicals who claim this country was founded upon some sort of fundamentalist Christianity would do well to remember that.

Let's take a look at those formative years of the American Revolution. During the 1700s, the first wave of the industrial revolution was washing over England (and its colonies), increasing the potential for manufacturing and trading goods. The American colonies were a major market. Technology was the driving force, as it is today. Things like the seed drill and iron plow increased food production and improved people's diets and health, which contributed to rapid population growth.[40] A series of inventions such as the flying shuttle, spinning jenny, and water-powered loom, speeded up spinning and weaving the wool and cotton. The new machines (initially powered hydraulically from rivers and streams) led to a factory system; the invention of the steam engine to power them would move factories closer to cities and available labor. The southern American colonies provided the majority of the cotton those textile factories needed to run, and the South needed slave labor to farm the cotton.

The big cities grew around the large northern seaports: Baltimore, Philadelphia, New York, and Boston. Whether it was officially encouraged, as in New York and New Jersey, or not, as in Pennsylvania, the slave trade flourished in colonial ports. New England was by far the leading slave merchant of the American colonies.[41] On the eve of the revolution, the slave trade formed the very basis of the economic life of New England. It gave work to coopers, tanners, sail-makers, and rope-makers. Countless agents, insurers, lawyers, clerks, and scriveners handled the paperwork. Upper New England loggers, Grand Banks fishermen, and livestock farmers provided the raw materials shipped to the West Indies on that leg of the slave trade. Colonial newspapers drew income from advertisements of slaves for sale or hire. New England–made rum, trinkets, and iron bars were exchanged for slaves.

So it would be a mistake to romanticize the revolutionary period. The founders may have been enlightened men, but many of the colonists were every bit as wicked as the old guard in England. They shared the same changing economic dynamics. The collapse of the feudal economic systems eventually gave rise to the bourgeois class, which was the birth of capitalism. Karl Marx and Friedrich Engels, in their *Communist Manifesto* (1848), saw capitalism as a class struggle between the bourgeoisie (the class of capitalists, owners of the means of production and employers of labor), and the proletariat (the class of wage earners who, having no means of production of their own, are reduced to selling their time and labor to live). Marx and Engels rightly saw the industrial revolution as the engine that would drive the ongoing search for New World markets, lower prices, and cheaper labor.[42] They thought that nation-states would ultimately prove dispensable and there would be a worldwide communist revolution.

Many historians believe the American and French Revolutions were both part of and the result of the convergence of the Enlightenment and the industrial revolution. The former changed people's worldview, which promoted religious and intellectual freedom. The latter greatly increased the demand for capital, and open markets. We got that economic development in spades as America moved west, and technology created industry after industry in the 19th century. Napoleon's push to become emperor of Europe didn't work out nearly as well. Instead, other nation-states were formed largely on our example. But this is certain: The inherent conflict that Marx predicted between workers and industrial wealth inspires the chief balancing act that nations must perform, and it is at the core of the political crisis in the United States today.

We'll delve further into the conflicting economic worldviews of progressives and ultraconservatives in the next chapter.

Back now to how the founders managed to pull it off. Before the revolution many of them were already leading figures in their respective colonial governments. Those governments sprang up at the pleasure of the British Crown and changed over the time of colonization.

In the run-up to the revolution, only two of the 13 colonies could be considered anything like self-governing—the two chartered colonies of Rhode Island and Connecticut. The other proprietary or royal colonial governments basically were in the same form: The governor, appointed by the Crown, the council, also appointed by the Crown, and the assembly or house of representatives, elected by the people. These three corresponded to the king and the two houses of Parliament resembled the British government—with one striking difference. The governor had total power and was responsible to the Crown, from which he had explicit instructions. He could convene, prorogue, or dissolve the legislature, or veto any of its laws. He commanded the militia, and appointed many officials, such as judges, justices of the peace and sheriffs. And, especially in the early period, he had industrial, commercial, and ecclesiastical as well as political duties. But in one respect he was held in check: He had no power over the public purse.[43] Nonetheless, the colonies were far from being independent nations.

Britain's interest in the colonies was in their raw materials and trade, not the welfare of their people. The problem was that the American colonies were far across the sea and difficult to guard against other imperialistic powers, specifically France and Spain—both of which were active in North America.

As the British colonies grew in the early 18th century, the people began to look west toward the rich lands across the Appalachian Mountains for opportunities for settlement and growth. The French, however, claimed the entire watersheds of the Mississippi and St. Lawrence Rivers, which included the Great Lakes and the Ohio River valley. It was an enormous area inhabited mostly by Native Americans (Indians) and some trappers and woodsmen. To prevent British encroachments, the French began to set up an extensive series of forts, and granted lands to the Ohio Company and traders to establish bases.[44]

In 1752, the Marquis Duquesne was made governor-general of "New France" and instructed to take possession of the Ohio Valley. At the same time, Robert Dinwiddlie, the lieutenant governor of Virginia, was granting land to the citizens of Virginia, setting in motion the train of events that led to the French and Indian War. A young Virginian officer named George Washington would serve in the war. By 1754 hostilities broke out and war was officially declared between the French and the British in 1756.

The British triumphed in 1760. Signed in 1763, the Treaty of Paris turned over all of North America east of the Mississippi, other than New Orleans, to the British. Indian hostilities lasted until the end of 1764 and began anew with the revolution.

The French and Indian War is important to our narrative because it opened up a vast area for the future United States and because the British spent a large amount of money on the war—and then tried to recover it by bleeding the colonies with taxation. Britain imposed a series of taxes and trade restrictions that raised the issue of "taxation without representation." In 1767, the parliament passed the Townshend Revenue Acts, imposing a new series of taxes on the colonies to offset the costs of administering and protecting the American colonies. One of those taxes was a three-penny per pound import tax on tea.

The Boston Tea Party (1773), of every schoolchild's memory, was in response to the Tea Act of 1773. It gave Britain's East India Company (which was on the verge of bankruptcy[45]) a virtual monopoly by allowing it to sell directly to colonial agents, and it eliminated all of the other taxes imposed on the colonial merchants who traditionally served as middlemen in such transactions (except the three-penny Townshend tax). By eliminating the middlemen (and the smugglers who had taken over the trade), the company could sell cheaper tea than the local wholesale merchants.[46] After failed attempts to turn back three ships loaded with tea, local patriots staged an event. On the evening of December 16, 1773, three companies of men masquerading as Mohawk Indians, passed through a crowd of about 8,000 Bostonians, boarded the three ships, broke open the tea chests, and heaved them into the harbor. As news of the Boston "tea party" spread, other seaports followed their example and staged similar acts of resistance. Thus marked the beginning of open violence in the dispute between mother country and colonies.

In March of 1774, an angry Parliament passed the first of a series of Coercive Acts (the Americans called them the Intolerable Acts) in response to the rebellion in Massachusetts. In May, Parliament enacted a second series of Coercive Acts, which included the Massachusetts Regulating Act and the Government Act, ending self-rule in the colony. They also passed the Quebec Act that established a centralized government in Canada controlled by the Crown and English Parliament; it extended the southern boundary of Canada into territories claimed by Massachusetts, Connecticut and Virginia. The die was cast for war.

The First Continental Congress convened in Philadelphia's Carpenters Hall on September 5, 1774. It was the first joint colonial meeting in history. Benjamin Franklin had proposed it a year earlier but the idea failed to gain any traction until the Crown closed Boston Harbor. Twelve of the 13 colonies sent representatives; Georgia did not. It was facing attacks from the Creek Indians and needed the help of the regular British army. Some of the most prominent figures of the era were among the 56 delegates in attendance, including George Washington, Samuel Adams, John Adams, Patrick Henry, Richard Henry Lee, John Jay and John Dickinson.

The Congress, which continued in session until October, didn't advocate independence, but rather sought to right the wrongs inflicted on the colonies by raising a unified voice the delegates hoped would be heard in London. A Declaration of Resolves declared opposition to the Coercive Acts, saying they are "not to be obeyed;" and promoted the formation of local militia units. The Congress also formed the Continental Association, which established a boycott on British imports and discontinued the British slave trade. They composed a statement of complaints, *The Declaration of Rights and Grievances* that was addressed to King George III, to whom the delegates remained loyal, and pointedly snubbed Parliament.[47] They further agreed to convene the following spring if colonial complaints had not been properly addressed. In the wake of the battles of Lexington and Concord, that meeting of the Second Continental Congress was called into session in May 1775.

Both the public and the delegates considered the First Continental Congress a success. It was America's first attempt at a confederated government, and the delegates formed friendships that would ease the way for the tasks ahead.

It is hard to imagine the difficulties of governing in the 1700s. We live in an age of instant worldwide communications: fiber-optic connectivity, satellites, the Internet, e-mail, telephones, cell/video phones, video-conferencing, television, and radio. Everyday people can afford and use PCs, and copying and fax machines. There are automobiles, trucks, and trains, jet aircraft that can take us to the farthest reaches of the world in a matter of hours. The only way our founders could communicate with London or Paris was by a roundtrip ocean crossing under sail, which took weeks in either direction. They worked with quill and ink by candlelight and exchanged information by mail carried on horseback. It's quite a contrast, and I can't help but feel that they would think of us as blockheads for not doing a better job given all our tools.

The Second Congress established an armed force, commanded by Virginian George Washington, established trade regulations and authorized the issuance of money. It also established ambassadors to be sent forth to other nations to garner support, and urged the colonies to set up organized local governments. It tried to reconcile with Britain, but when the king sent Hessian mercenaries to the colonies, it was clear that independence was the only solution.[48] The colonialists formed a committee to write the document, which in turn used the English Magna Carta (1215) as a framework.

The primary author of the Declaration of Independence was a young 33- year-old Thomas Jefferson (in consultation with Benjamin Franklin and John Adams). On the tombstone he designed for himself is the inscription he wrote. It makes no mention of the prestigious public offices that he held, but says simply: "author of the Declaration of American Independence, of the Statute of Virginia for religious freedom, and Father of the University of Virginia."

The Second Congress signed the Declaration on July 4, 1776 and adjourned on December 12, 1776.

The Third Continental Congress convened within days on December 20, 1776. Participants would prosecute the war and, important to our narrative, they would modify and finalized the Articles of Confederation, creating the United States of America (a confederation). Because of the war and disagreements between the colonies, it took three and half years to get final ratification of the articles, which had to be ratified by every state.[49] The war ended two years after ratification, in April 1783.[50]

Almost every American knows when the Declaration of Independence was signed. Less well known, but no less important, is the date of the signing of the U.S. Constitution, which replaced the Articles of Confederation. It was signed by the Constitutional Convention on September 17, 1787, and ratified by the required nine states on July 2, 1788.

For over a decade the United States was not a nation-state; it was a confederation. In a confederation, the individual political units, states in this case, maintain their sovereignty (each is its own nation), but join together in a coordinated way to deal with certain issues, such as security.

In any case, the confederation was deeply flawed and unworkable. The federal government had no independent power of taxation, and merely relied upon the good faith of the states to pay bills sent to them for maintenance of the national treasury. In some instances those bills were ignored and, with no federal power of enforcement, they were left unpaid.[51]

Nor was the new nation able to repel encroachments on its borders by the British and Spanish; the states wouldn't pay the requested taxes needed to finance a defense. The federal government also had no power to regulate commerce between the states, which lead to bitter tariff wars. The infighting did little to alleviate the deep postwar economic depression that had set in.

One event at the end of 1786 would stir the confederation into action—Shays' Rebellion. Captain Daniel Shays was a veteran of the revolution and a farmer from Pelham, a town in western Massachusetts. Hard hit by the depression, Shays and other farmers who were unable to pay their debts faced court, and then jail. There was no federal law under the confederation and the state courts, following the precedents of the colonies, were harsh on debtors.[52] After petitions for paper currency, lower taxes, and judicial reform failed, Shays and about 1,500 followers staged a popular rebellion.[53] For six months Shays and his rebels terrorized the Massachusetts countryside and the United States found it had little power to put it down. Shays' forces were finally broken up when they marched on a federal weapons depot.

In January 1786, Virginia called for a meeting of the states at Annapolis to discuss modification of the articles. Only five states sent delegates. Amid calls for a stronger central government, due partly to Shays' Rebellion, Congress endorsed Alexander Hamilton's resolution calling for a constitutional convention to be held in Philadelphia, beginning in May.

The Constitutional Convention began on May 25, 1787 at Independence Hall in Philadelphia. Of the 73 delegates chosen by the states, only 55 actually attended. There were 21 veterans of the Revolutionary War and eight signers of the Declaration of Independence. The delegates were farmers, merchants, lawyers and bankers, with an average age of 42. James Madison, a brilliant 36-year-old, was a central figure at the convention, as was 81-year-old Ben Franklin. Thomas Jefferson was serving abroad as ambassador to France and did not attend.[54]

Alexander Hamilton, a young New York lawyer, was one of the three delegates from his state. He had long advocated a strong federal government to replace the confederation and would play a leading role in getting the new constitution ratified.

The delegates' first vote was to keep the proceedings absolutely secret. They then nominated George Washington as president of the constitutional convention. On June 19, the convention voted to scrap the Articles of Confederation and create an entirely new form of national government. It would be separated into branches, the legislative, executive and judicial, thus dispersing power with checks and balances, and competing factions, as a measure of protection against tyranny by a controlling majority. By the end of July a rough draft was drawn. It included a proposed 20-year ban on any Congressional action concerning slavery, which was obviously a deal breaker among the delegates. On September 17, 1787, four months after they had convened, the final draft of the constitution was approved and signed by the convention.

What courage. They were proposing a totally new form of government! It shocked the public when printed copies of the text were distributed; people had only expected a revised version of the Articles of Confederation. It was a brilliant concept—balance of powers, checks and balances, a work of genius and vision, and something all Americans should be proud of. But it certainly wasn't perfect, and it opened up a political donnybrook in Massachusetts and Virginia, which demanded the guaranteed protection of civil liberties. Before it would be ratified by the required nine states and become the Constitution of the United States on July 2, 1788, there would be 20 changes and a proposed Bill of Rights.[55]

Here is the form of government that was proposed and ratified:

◆ The Legislative Branch will consist of two houses. The upper house (Senate) to be composed of nominees selected by state assemblies for six year terms; the lower house (House of Representatives) to be elected every two years by popular vote.

◆ The Executive Branch is to be headed by a chief executive (president) elected every four years by presidential electors from the states. The president is granted sweeping powers including: veto power over Congress, which can be overridden by a two-thirds vote in each house; commander in chief of the armies; power to make treaties with the advice and consent of two-thirds of the Senate; power to appoint judges, diplomats and other officers with the consent of the Senate; power to recommend legislation and responsibility for execution of the laws.

◆ The president is required to report each year to the legislative branch on the state of the union. The legislative branch has the power to remove the president from office. The House can impeach the president for treason, bribery or other high crimes and misdemeanors with the actual removal from office occurring by a two-thirds vote of the Senate.

◆ The Judicial Branch consists of a Supreme Court headed by a chief justice. The court has the implied power to review laws that conflict with the Constitution.

It is amazing isn't it? The basic form of our government can be condensed into a little over 200 words. The whole constitution and its 27 amendments can easily be read at one sitting. I urge you to do so. It can be downloaded at: www.house.gov/Constitution/Constitution.html

Hamilton didn't think the constitution was strong enough in terms of federal power but, writing in collaboration with Madison and John Jay in what became known as *The Federalist Papers*, he was a strong advocate for its ratification.

So let's take a look at this 200-plus-year-old document and compare it to the Republican far-right neocon worldview and its attempts to mold the nation to its ideology.

President Bush told us after the people of Iraq risked life and limb to vote in January 2005 that the delegates elected would have a constitution and a functioning government within six months. Our founders had colonial governments in place, and from the time we declared independence until we had a barely functioning federal government it had taken a decade and a half. Did Bush really think Iraq, badly divided along religious and ethnic lines, was going was going to pull it off in a matter of months? Many think it will take over a decade for Iraq to have any degree of internal security. Does he have a plan to pull our military out of Iraq? By mid-2006, the answer to that question was still not clear.

Bush has also said that it is our national priority to spread "democracy" throughout the world. Democracy is not a precise term. What form of governance is he talking about? In 1933, with the help of the "Brown Shirts," Hitler was elected with the largest minority vote. The Soviet Union, under the Communist Party, used to hold elections before its collapse in 1991. Fascists states, dictatorships, theocracies and single party nation-states have frequently called themselves democracies because of meaningless elections. Such was the case in Iraq under Saddam Hussein.

The word "democracy" doesn't appear in the Constitution.[56] The framers were scared to death of the "tyranny of the majority," as we all should be. Here are two famous viewpoints:

Winston Churchill said, "Many forms of Government have been tried in this world of sin and woe. No one pretends that democracy is perfect or all wise. Indeed, it has been said that democracy is the worst form of government except all those other forms that have been tried from time to time." Churchill was talking about a "representative democracy," such as exists in the UK, which today has a vigorous three-party system.

Edmund Burke: "I cannot help concurring (with Aristotle) that an absolute democracy, no more than an absolute monarchy, is not to be reckoned among the legitimate forms of government. They think it rather the corruption and degeneracy than the sound constitution of a republic."

I think the framers carefully avoided creating a "direct democracy" as existed on a very small scale in ancient Greece, and gave us a representative democracy with a constitution, or perhaps what could more validly be called a Republic. Neocons and Libertarians always try to frame the Constitution in the former, which is entirely incorrect.

One of the major criticisms of the framers is that the government they created was in many ways undemocratic. There is little doubt that's true. The Electoral College is one example; the presidential appointment of federal judges is another. Until the 17th Amendment (1913), the people didn't choose U.S. Senators. They were nominated by the state assemblies and selected by the U.S. Senate itself; it was an abortion of a process fraught with corruption.

In 2000, Bush was elected without the majority of the popular vote. Al Gore won that. The Electoral College elected him after the Supreme Court voted five to four not to force a valid recount in Florida. Never mind that Bush's brother Jeb was governor of Florida and Florida's electoral votes were likely stolen by poll keepers and local party hacks.

In 1998, when President Bill Clinton needed the support of Congress to deal with the looming terrorism threat, his administration was totally sidetracked by impeachment proceedings brought by Newt Gingrich's Republican controlled House of Representatives. As I said, the Constitution provides that the House can impeach the president for treason, bribery or other high crimes and misdemeanors, with the actual removal from office occurring by a two-thirds vote of the Senate. Clinton must have really done something bad (like Nixon, who was forced to resign or face impeachment) right? No. It involved an inappropriate sexual act in the Oval Office, which he lied about. He was impeached after months of a televised spectacle, but the Senate allowed him to finish his term. How many lives were lost as a result? Many think 9/11 (2001) and the whole train of events that happened after may have been prevented if the Clinton administration had not been sidetracked.

So my friends, we're dealing with two documents—the Bible, interpreted by some as God's voice governing the life of the nation, and the United States Constitution, a work of mere mortals who sought to guarantee our freedoms and dignity. I suggest that if the mere mortals could be heard now they would be crying out, "Beware America, your democracy is in mortal peril."

Ten

The Power of Prejudice

———————•◆•———————

To discriminate is to make a distinction. There are several meanings of the word... the colloquial sense of the word is *invidious* discrimination— the irrational social, racial, religious, sexual, disability, ethnic and age-related discrimination of people

- Wikipedia

Segregation in the United States is the legal or social practice of separating people on the basis of their race or ethnicity. Segregation by law, or *de jure* segregation, occurred when local, state, or national laws require racial separation, or where the laws explicitly allow segregation. De jure segregation has been prohibited in the United States since the mid-1960s. *De facto* segregation, or segregation in fact, occurs when social practice, political acts, economic circumstances, or public policy result in the separation of people by race or ethnicity even though no laws require or authorize racial separation. De facto segregation has continued even when state and federal civil rights laws have explicitly prohibited racial segregation.

"Segregation in the United States,"
Microsoft® Encarta® Inline Encyclopedia 2005

L et's do a reality check on our own worldview. If you haven't burned this book yet, it's likely that you think of yourself as an open-minded, informed, progressive person—a discriminating person in a positive sense, one who makes sound decisions and not one who engages in *invidious* discrimination as defined above, which means you may see yourself as a person not easily swayed by the prejudices of the far right. But the fact is that as sophisticated as we may think we are, and as well meaning as we may be, we've all been influenced by prejudices that are the insidious undercurrent of our society. In the 21st century, prejudices and supportive myths continue to undermine the body politic and greatly influence public policy in America. The far-right think tanks and spin masters use them against us and feed on them like bacteria in a cesspool.

Perhaps the worst blight on America is racial discrimination. It has been part of our culture from the beginning. I was born in Brooklyn, New York in 1937. My parents were Italian immigrants and I'm proud to say I never once heard the word "nigger" used in our home. Perhaps you are sensitive to demeaning slurs when you yourself could be called a wop, a guinea, a dago or a grease ball. Yet the Brooklyn neighborhood I grew up in during the 1940s and early 1950s had very few people of color; there were other Italians, Norwegians and, when my family moved a short distance away, Jews from various origins in Europe, but very few children of color went to my public schools. At the time, despite the fact that New York City had a model, progressive public school system, my schools were essential racially segregated, not because it was the law, but because people of color were effectively barred from living in white neighborhoods.[57] However, the law in 17 southern states and the District of Columbia *required* that all public schools be racially segregated; a few northern and western states *permitted* them to be segregated.

As a young adult, racial discrimination continued to surround me with lily-white fellow college students and coworkers. When I landed my job as an airline pilot in 1959, there wasn't a single black pilot (or female pilot) employed by a United States airline. Many wouldn't hire Italians or Jews either.

I remember many of the major events of the civil rights struggle—the NAACP's school desegregation victory in *Brown v. Board of Education*; the founding in 1957 of the Southern Christian Leadership Conference, with the Rev. Martin Luther King as its first president; the Congress of Racial Equality's use of student volunteers to challenge segregation laws; the 1963 murder of Medgar Evers, the NAACP field secretary in Mississippi; the Student Nonviolent Coordinating Committee and the advent of "black power," and much more. I remember TV coverage of the race riots in the 1960s, and being shocked at the assassinations of civil rights advocates Robert Kennedy and Martin Luther King, following the assassination of JFK. I happened to be in Boston when violence broke out in South Boston over school busing, which the Supreme Court had deemed one of the acceptable solutions to desegregate the schools. You could feel the hate and animosity in the air. Yet for all of that, as I look back, I didn't have a clue—politically or socially—of the significance of what was going on around me.

When the U.S. Supreme Court ruled miscegenation laws (laws against interracial marriage) unconstitutional in the case of *Loving v. Virginia* (1967), I was thirty years old.[58] The Warren Court ruled on the basis of the equal protection clause of the 14th Amendment. It's embarrassing to say that the first I learned about this historic, extremely important decision was in researching this book. The same ignorance was essentially true for the Civil Rights Act of 1964 and the Voting Rights Act of 1965—and for the landmark Supreme Court case *Plessy v. Ferguson* (1896), which established the "separate but equal" doctrine, further legitimizing the Jim Crow laws[59] in the south (*Brown v. Board of Education* overturned it in 1954).

I'm not proud of having been "tuned out" during the 1960s civil rights struggle. My education was lacking; but let me tell you, after months of researching this chapter I'm convinced that more than a limited understanding of the racial division of America, Civil War Reconstruction (1866-76), and the civil rights movement is essential to understanding American politics in the 21st century.

Oh, I have the standard excuses for having been tuned out. I was busy pursuing my airline career, doing union business, raising a young family, and of course the war in Vietnam overshadowed everything. In my own defense, I don't think either the media or the politicians ever focused on the political significance of the civil rights movement. I think the politicians on both sides were afraid of the citizenry knowing too much about the history of racial segregation and discrimination in America. It is an ugly story. In that same vein, my public school teachers carefully avoided criticizing the government and the textbooks of my memory characterized Reconstruction as the South being abused by Northern "carpetbaggers," rather than as an attempted historic—if failed—effort to bring social and economic equality to the freed slaves.[60]

I have also come to understand from my work with the New Hampshire Citizens Alliance and Richard Healy's grassroots organization that deeply ingrained prejudices are subliminal, part of our subconscious that influence our actions. Had my passive empathy been impassioned by simply having people of color as friends, or neighbors, or co-workers, I might have joined James Meredith and Martin Luther King in making the 220-mile "March Against Fear" in 1966, or other public demonstrations, rather than sitting on my dead ass and shaking my head sympathetically at the TV. I was a white, affluent male under the age of forty; to me those tragedies were happening to other people in other places. I was much like many Americans catching the infrequent news blurbs about the genocide in Sudan today. I am that no longer.

Needless to say, I was not alone in my ignorance. My government had turned a blind eye to America's racist rule in the South for over 80 years. As this is written in June 2005, the U.S. Senate has finally got around to apologizing for failing to enact federal anti-lynching legislation during the heyday of mob law. It is claimed that 4,743 people were killed between 1882 and 1968, three out of four of them black.[61] Other minorities were also attacked. On March 14, 1891, in New Orleans, 11 Italian immigrants were killed by a lynch mob of 6,000 after a court found them not guilty in the murder of a police superintendent. Following the event, the Ku Klux Klan began a collateral campaign of terror against Italians.[62] Although the House passed three anti-lynching bills between 1920 and 1940, the Senate refused to act and passed none. Southern Democratic senators filibustered anti-lynching measures for a total of six weeks. Some, I think rightly, have called this dark period the "American Holocaust."

In this the United States was not unique. Racial and ethnic segregation and discrimination have occurred in many parts of the world. India still maintains a caste system relating to its Hindu tradition. In the past, laws mandated racial segregation in Rhodesia (now Zimbabwe) and South Africa. After much bloodshed, South Africa's system of segregation, known as apartheid, was dismantled in the early 1990s. Ethnic segregation, leading to the murder or deportation of ethnic groups, was the major driving force of genocide in the 20th century: Armenians in Turkey (1915-18), 1,500,000 deaths; Nazi Holocaust (1938-45), 6,000,000 deaths; Rwanda (1994), 800,000 deaths; and Bosnia-Herzegovina (1992-95), 200,000 deaths (there they called it "ethnic cleansing").

By spring 2006, it was conservatively estimated that more than 200,000 black inhabitants in the Darfur region of Sudan had died at the hands of Arab "janjaweed" militias; another two million were categorized as displaced from their homes and the violence had followed some of those refugees into neighboring Chad. A peace agreement was signed in May and the Sudanese government appeared ready to accept a UN peacekeeping force. But only one rebel group signed the agreement and the crisis seemed far from over.

While de jure (legal) racial segregation was abolished by 1968 by a U.S. Supreme Court that at long last recognized the Constitution's intent for equality in America, and LBJ's Great Society legislative achievements, it came at a price. And, despite the progress, de facto segregation still polarizes America. That is why the far right uses racial stereotyping in much of what it does. Because it works. For the sake of our narrative, it is also important to point out that racial equality is not an isolated objective: It is a fundamental requirement for social and economic justice for everyone.

This is a book about politics. When I say LBJ's Great Society achievements came at a price, my meaning emerges from a long and interesting story. You will have to keep your eye on the ball, because it's quite a shell game to follow.

As I mentioned earlier, President Lincoln's Emancipation Proclamation (January 1, 1863) didn't free a single slave. Lincoln issued it in his capacity as commander-in-chief as a "necessary war measure," and it applied only to those parts of North America under the control of the armed forces of the Confederate States of America. It didn't apply to those slave states that remained in the union—Delaware, Kentucky, Maryland and Missouri—nor did it apply to those parts of the Confederacy that were under the control of U.S. forces—parts of Virginia (which would later become West Virginia) and Florida. In any case, neither the president nor Congress could simply abolish slavery because of the U.S. Supreme Court's 1857 *Dred Scott* decision, which held that slavery was constitutional. To abolish it required a constitutional amendment.[63]

Prior to the end of the war, Congress, in support of Lincoln's initiative, passed legislation and proposed the 13th Amendment to abolish slavery to state legislatures on January 31, 1865. It was ratified on December 6, 1865, eight months after Lincoln's assassination. At the time of his death, Lincoln, our first Republican president, was only a few months into his second term. His vice president, who ascended to the presidency, was Andrew Johnson, a southern, old-fashioned Jacksonian Democrat. Whoa, wait a minute, a southern Democrat? Yes, and it created a donnybrook that led to Johnson's impeachment in the House of Representatives and near removal from office in the Senate. The only other president to endure such a misfortune was Bill Clinton. Richard Nixon resigned before the House could impeach him.[64]

To understand why that happened, let's back up a few years. The Republican Party was formed in 1854 as a coalition of former members of the Whig, Free-Soil, and Know-Nothing parties. The early Republicans were drawn together because of their opposition to extended slavery in the West and to foreign immigration. Lincoln's first vice president was Hannibal Hamlin, a Democrat until 1856, when he broke with the party over the Kansas-Nebraska Act.[65] During the secession crisis, Senator Andrew Johnson, a Democrat, remained in the Senate even when his home state, Tennessee, seceded. That made him something of a hero to the northern Democrats and Republicans. In 1862, Lincoln appointed him military governor of Tennessee. Johnson in turn used the state as a laboratory for reconstruction, which undoubtedly helped shape his ideas for reconstruction when he became president. Passing Hamlin over, Lincoln selected Johnson for his second-term running mate.

It is interesting to note that in the beginning the Republican Party was, on the issue of slavery, the more progressive party; it also supported a proactive federal government. After Reconstruction ended in 1877, that would change as America entered the Gilded Age, the industrial revolution took off, and the Republican Party became more like the party of big business and laissez-faire capitalism that we know today.

On the other hand, the Democratic Party that emerged in the mid-1800s from its Jeffersonian roots retained the characteristics of cautious use of federal power in foreign affairs and limited interference with state and local government. In the south, Democrats considered slavery their economic and social right. The party's supporters in this period were diverse, including southern plantation owners and immigrant workers in northern cities (which created strong city and state Democratic committees). They all shared a common dislike of government intervention in their lives.

When the southern states seceded from the union, the Democratic Party in Congress was severely fractured as members went home to their Confederate states, leaving the Republicans in a large majority. The Republicans continued to control Congress until 1874, when the Democrats won a majority in the House. The Democrats didn't win the presidency again until 1884.

The remaining Democrats in Congress refused to support increased government power to fight the war. They opposed the draft, social changes, and strongly resisted Republican tariff and taxation policies to finance the war. This was politically great for the Republicans, who denounced the Democrats as traitors. It was an effective campaign tactic called "Waving the bloody shirt," much like the Bush administration's tactic of using of the invasion of Iraq and the war on terror as a patriotic imperative.

During the closing months of the war, it was obvious that the Confederacy was vanquished. Looking ahead, the Lincoln government had begun discussing how to deal with the aftermath. The month before Lee surrendered to Grant at Appomattox, the War Department, headed by Secretary Edwin McMasters Stanton, had established the Bureau of Refugees, Freedmen, and Abandoned Lands, commonly called the

"Freedmen's Bureau." The bureau furnished food and medical supplies to former slaves as the Confederacy was occupied. It also established schools and helped former slaves negotiate fair wages and working conditions. It has been asserted that Lincoln never took a step without consulting the secretary of war because he had such great confidence in him. A few days before the president's death, Stanton tendered his resignation because he felt his task was completed, but Lincoln persuaded him to stay on.[66]

There's an interesting correlation between the assassinations of Lincoln and JFK: Had either lived the outcome for America could well have been quite different. Had Lincoln lived, the post Civil War period may well have evolved with a more popular plan for reuniting the nation; had JFK lived, the war in Vietnam might never have happened or, if it did, with a more popular president the outcome might have been different.

In any case, at the time of Lincoln's death no one had decided on how best to unite the country. There was no plan for the peace. Some, including Andrew Johnson, advocated leniency and felt that the South could be reconciled with the Union by simply acknowledging the abolition of slavery. Others were convinced that the region's social, economic, and political systems would have to be thoroughly reconstructed.

Consequently, when Johnson ascended to the presidency in April 1865 he had a blank check for the reconstruction of the South. Amazingly, Congress was not in session and wouldn't meet again until December, eight months later.[67] In May, Johnson issued a series of proclamations that inaugurated the period of what's called Presidential Reconstruction (1865-1867). He granted amnesty freely to Southern whites, appointed provisional governors, and outlined the steps whereby new state governments would be created. Apart from the requirements that they abolish slavery, repudiate secession, and abrogate the Confederate debt, these governments had a free hand. Johnson offered blacks no role whatever in the politics of Reconstruction.[68]

The southern planters, who maintained much of their political power, seized the initiative and legislated "black codes" into state law. Those black codes varied slightly from state to state, but all negated the rights of the freed black slaves to full citizenship, and prohibited them from living in white residential towns and cities. This effectively segregated them into rural areas, forcing them into farm labor. Further, the southern Democrats disenfranchised the blacks from voting. They imposed poll taxes that the blacks couldn't afford, and literacy tests for blacks who had been forced to remain illiterate (educating a black person was against the law).

The ease with which southern planters reestablished dominance over the freed slaves inflamed people in the North and pitted the majority Republican Party in Congress against President Johnson. That majority was increased when the Democratic Party suffered a major defeat in the elections of 1866. With that, the Republican Party took charge of Reconstruction, pursuing a much more radical course that would continue for a decade until 1876. Stanton sided with the radical Republicans, and as secretary of war played a large role in implementing the will of Congress over that of President Johnson.

Congress acted quickly. To overturn the southern states' black codes it passed the Civil Rights Act of 1866: The act entitled African Americans to citizenship and gave the federal government the power to protect their civil rights. This led to the drafting of the 14th Amendment, guaranteeing those civil rights. The 14th Amendment was ratified by the states in 1868. It is the only constitutional amendment ever passed by Congress over a presidential veto (it survived by a single vote). The act specifically excludes "Indians not taxed"; Native Americans wouldn't be granted the rights of born citizenship until the Indian Citizenship Act of 1924.[69]

In March 1867, Congress followed up with the Reconstruction Act, which was strengthened by three supplemental acts. What they did was incredible! They divided the former 10 Confederate states into five military districts, each headed by a federal military commander. This effectively created a federal military occupation of the former Confederate states. (Tennessee was exempt because it had ratified the 14th Amendment.) Before applying for readmission to the union, the southern states were required to ratify the 14th Amendment and revise their constitutions to ensure that blacks had citizenship rights, including the right to vote.[70]

At this point Stanton, as secretary of war, had enormous power over reconstruction—so much power that Johnson wanted rid of him and demanded his resignation. The donnybrook that followed included a Senate resolution declaring that the president didn't have the power to remove the secretary. The president fired him anyhow and Congress impeached

Johnson. The Senate failed to find Johnson guilty by only one vote (35 guilty to 19). Forced out of office, Stanton went back to the practice of law and was later nominated by President Grant as a justice of the Supreme Court in December 1869. The Senate quickly confirmed the nomination, but Stanton died five days later.

On February 17, 1870, the states ratified the 15th Amendment, which prohibited the denial of the right to vote based on race. Interestingly, even though women's suffrage had been an issue for years, it wasn't brought to the forefront of the discussions on the racial right to vote. The 19th Amendment guaranteeing a woman's right to vote wouldn't come until 1920—fifty years later.

Congress made one more move before Reconstruction ended with a whimper. It passed the Civil Rights Act of 1875, which forbade racial discrimination in "Inns, public conveyances on land or water, theaters, and other places of amusement." The act amounted to nothing. By 1876 the will of the northern social activists had died out and the Republicans struck a deal with the southern Democrats to get the electoral votes needed to elect Republican presidential candidate Rutherford Hayes. In return, the Republicans recognized Democratic claims to contested state offices won in 1874 in South Carolina, Florida, and Louisiana. They also pulled the last of the U.S. Army out of the South. Reconstruction was over.

In 1883 the Supreme Court declared the Civil Rights Act of 1875 unconstitutional and in a series of cases drastically undermined the 14th Amendment's protection of black citizenship rights and narrowed federal protection of the right to vote guaranteed by the 15th Amendment. Finally, in 1896, the Supreme Court ruled in *Plessy v. Ferguson* that racial segregation was legal.

For a short period of time federal occupation assured the former slaves the vote, enabling them to elect black and Republican leaders. In all, 20 blacks from southern states served in the U.S. House of Representatives and two in the U.S. Senate during Reconstruction. In addition, hundred of blacks were elected to state and local offices.

But it was a false hope. To regain power southern Democrats used violence to keep blacks away from the polls. Throughout Reconstruction the Democratic Party in the South was indistinguishable from the Ku Klux Klan. The Klan was the major element of a terrorist insurgency that included remnants of irregular Confederate units such as Quantrill's Raiders, and Klan-like groups such as the Knights of the White Camelia, the White Brotherhood, the White League, and the Men of Peace.[71] Klansmen beat, maimed, intimidated and killed Republicans of both colors who challenged them at the polls, or anyone who tested the bounds of white supremacy by providing education or relief to the black freedmen. Congress has documented over a thousand Klan-committed killings in the South during Reconstruction.

After federal forces were withdrawn, the Democrats once again had complete control in the South and the Klan fell back into the shadows as the southern states legislated Jim Crow laws that enforced the legal separation of blacks and whites and disenfranchised the blacks.

In speaking to a group of Pentagon officials at a conference at Gettysburg on May 4, 2005, noted historian James McPherson compared the intriguing parallels between postwar Iraq and the postwar South. Here are some insightful excepts as reported by David Ignatius, a columnist for the *Washington Post*.[72]

The Civil War, like the invasion of Iraq, was a war of transformation in which the victors hoped to reshape the political culture of the vanquished. But as McPherson tells the story, reconstruction posed severe and unexpected tests: The occupying Union army was harassed by an insurgency that fused die-hard remnants of the old plantation power structure with irregular guerrillas. The Union was as unprepared for the struggle as the Coalition Provisional Authority was in Baghdad in 2003. The army of occupation was too small, and its local allies were often corrupt and disorganized.

By 1877, says McPherson, the North essentially gave up. Demoralized by the economic depression of 1873, Northern investors pulled back from projects in the South and turned their attentions to the West. The troops occupying the South were withdrawn. The Southerners, defeated in war, had won the peace. The South slipped into more than 80 years of racism, isolation and economic backwardness.

What lessons does this dismal history convey for U.S. forces in Iraq? First, what you do immediately after the end of hostilities is crucial, and mistakes made then may be impossible to undo. Don't attempt a wholesale transformation of another society unless you have the troops and political will to impose it. Above all, don't let racial or religious hatred destroy democratic political institutions as in the post-bellum South. Giving up on reconstruction led to a social and economic disaster that lasted nearly a century. That's a history nobody should want to repeat, least of all the Iraqi insurgents.

In the first decade of the 20th century blacks started migrating north en masse. Conditions in the South were terrible. A boll weevil infestation had diminished cotton production, cutting back the need for farm labor, and increased racial violence encouraged blacks to leave the South. Soon after, in 1914, World War I broke out in Europe. Though America didn't enter the war until 1917, northern manufacturers supplied the combatants and needed labor, which European immigration could no longer supply because of the war. Consequently, there were jobs and blacks were recruited. After the United States entered the war, the military drained manpower from industry and there were even more jobs. Also, approximately 400,000 black soldiers served in the armed forces in segregated units. From 1910 to 1930 between 1.5 million and 2 million African Americans left the South for the industrial cities of the North. More than 200,000 blacks moved to New York, 180,000 to Chicago, and more than 130,000 to Philadelphia.

It was a time of enormous cultural change replete with anti-black race riots and whites attempting to enforce racial dominance in the North. It also, in places such as Harlem, created a black renaissance.

But post war euphoria, the Jazz Age, and the Roaring Twenties came to a crushing halt with the stock market crash and the start of the Great Depression in 1929. Until that time most blacks voted for the Republican Party of Abraham Lincoln, but many in the North had become affiliated with labor unions that on the whole supported the Democratic Party. Plus, North or South, blacks were the first to lose their jobs and suffered the most as the depression deepened. In a dramatic change, blacks deserted the Republican Party and voted for the Democratic Party, sweeping FDR and a Democratic Congress into office.

In the South, the Democratic Party establishment also bought into the New Deal, forging a rather strange coalition of racial segregationists and Northern social progressives. FDR's success in bringing the nation out of the depression and World War II laid the base for the Democrats to control

Congress in all but four of the 48 years between 1933 and 1981. To maintain the coalition, Roosevelt was careful in the New Deal programs to maintain racial segregation, particularly in the South. Consequently, by the end of his second term, black unemployment was still extremely high.

President Truman was challenged by a group of southern Democrats who bolted the party in 1948 because as commander-and-chief he had desegregated the armed forces and taken other civil rights initiatives. The so-called "Dixiecrats" formed the States Rights' Democratic Party and nominated South Carolina Governor Strom Thurmond as their candidate for president. Their slogan was "Segregation Forever!" Truman won the election in any event.

(On December 5, 2002, Senator Trent Lott of Mississippi, and at the time Senate majority leader, said in paying tribute to Senator Strom Thurmond's 100th birthday party, "I want to say this about my state: When Strom Thurmond ran for president, we voted for him. We're proud of it. And if the rest of the country had of followed our lead, we wouldn't have had all these problems over all these years, either." That slip into candor cost Lott dearly. He lost his job as majority leader.)

Much to his chagrin, President Dwight Eisenhower (1952-60) would have to deal with the fallout from the *Brown* decision to desegregate the schools. He had appointed Chief Justice Earl Warren to the Supreme Court in 1953, expecting a fellow conservative, and wound up with one of the great liberal jurists in American history. Eisenhower did not support a strong federal role in enforcing desegregation, thus encouraging southern resistance. For example, in a "Southern Manifesto," 101 congressmen vowed to resist integration (1956).

After three years of negotiation, the black community had reached an agreement with the school board in Little Rock, Arkansas to enroll nine black students at Central High School. Governor Orval Faubus used the National Guard to block the black students from entering the school. In response to a public outcry, Eisenhower put the National Guard under federal orders, and sent federal troops to enforce the *Brown* decision and protect the students from white mobs. Nonetheless, the following year, Faubus closed all of Little Rock's high schools rather than integrate them.

Ten years after the *Brown* decision, less than two percent of southern black children attended integrated schools.[73]

When the Democrats regained the White House with John F. Kennedy in 1960, they initiated a firestorm of progressive legislation, starting with the New Frontier programs of JFK and culminating in the Great Society policies and programs of President Lyndon Johnson (1963-69). These expanded the New Deal's social commitments to include civil rights and aid to minorities. Here's a litany of what was achieved:

Kennedy persuaded Congress to pass measures that established the Peace Corps, raised the minimum wage, and expanded Social Security benefits. After his assassination, capitalizing on the nation's grief, Johnson pushed the remainder of Kennedy's agenda through Congress, winning passage of the Civil Rights Act of 1964 and the Voting Rights Act of 1965. Then he turned his attention to pushing through his own Great Society programs, which included Medicare and Medicaid, the creation of the Department of Housing and Urban Development (HUD) and the Department of Transportation (DOT), food stamps, Head Start, Legal Services, and many other reforms.[74]

Affirmative Action programs that gave minorities and women special considerations in employment were bitterly contested by employers, labor unions, universities, colleges, and the like.[75] School busing to achieve racial integration also met with bitter opposition.

As a result of all this, the Democratic Party solidified its support with black voters, but created a conservative backlash among southern whites and northern labor and ethnic voters. FDR's New Deal coalition was dealt a mortal blow, and the winds of change began to blow unfavorably from the South for the party.

The balance of power in the United States would from then on drift to the far right, with the Republican Party increasingly controlled by its radically far-right elements. This would get a great push during the Reagan years, 1981 to 1989. Reagan was expert at speaking to the racial and gender stereotypes of ultraconservative white Americans when criticizing those on welfare for taking advantage of taxpayers' money. Envisioned, and actually used in political propaganda, were pictures of young, poverty-stricken black mothers, sitting on broken-down steps with dirty children.

Thus Reagan combined deeply held racial prejudices, avarice, and greed all in one message as he expounded on his commitment to a smaller federal government and fewer federal resources for the poor.

Much of this was reconfirmed in a July 18, 2005 *New York Times* column by Bob Herbert. He called a recent Republican Party apology to the NAACP for the party's decades-long Southern strategy "insulting," because the "G.O.P.'s Southern strategy, racist at its core, still lives."

"The Southern strategy meant much, much more than some members of the G.O.P. simply giving up on African-American votes," Herbert went on. "Put into play by Barry Goldwater and Richard Nixon in the mid – to late 1960's, it fed like a starving beast on the resentment of whites who were scornful of blacks and furious about the demise of segregation and other civil rights advances. The idea was to snatch the white racist vote away from the Democratic Party, which had committed such unpardonable sins as enacting the Civil Rights and Voting Rights Acts and enforcing desegregation statues."

Herbert cites Ronald Reagan's first run for the presidency as an example. In the summer of 1980, Reagan chose the Neshoba County Fair in Philadelphia, Mississippi as the place to kick off his general election campaign. Three young civil rights workers (James Chaney, Andrew Goodman and Michael Schwerner) had been murdered there just 16 years earlier. It was, Herbert writes, "the perfect place to send an important symbolic message." The fair was "famous for its diatribes by segregationist politicians." (When the state legal system failed to prosecute anyone for the murders, eighteen men were prosecuted on federal conspiracy charges. Seven were jailed for up to six years. A hung jury let Edgar Ray Killen, a preacher and Klansman, walk free. The state finally prosecuted Killen in 2005 and he was convicted of manslaughter. But there were many in Mississippi who felt that he should have been left alone. They needn't have worried. Killen was in prison for about six weeks and then a judge ordered him released on bail pending an appeal.)

Reagan's running mate was George H. W. Bush. Herbert recalls that during his own run for president in 1988 Bush "thought it was a good idea to exploit racial fears with the notorious Willie Horton ads about a black prisoner who raped a white woman." He quotes Bush's campaign manager,

Lee Atwater, whose sleazy campaign tactics were at least as notorious as Karl Rove's are today. Atwater called the Horton case a "values issue, particularly in the South—and if we hammer at these over and over, we are going to win." He was right.

Enter Bush's son, George W, who, in Herbert's estimation, "has been as devoted as an acolyte to the Southern strategy.... Like so many other Republican politicians and presidential wannabes, George W. Bush was happy to appear at Bob Jones University in Greenville, S.C., at a time when the school was blatantly racially discriminatory."

This same ideological thread runs through the far right's dominant worldview: minorities—Hispanics, Asians, and especially blacks—are sucking up our tax dollars. Because of them Americans pay high taxes. It is a lie that is perpetuated like a myth. The federal government's direct contribution for food and housing to the poor is a miniscule percentage of our gross domestic product, and most of those receiving it are white. Americans do not pay high federal taxes. According to 1999 figures from the Organization of Economic Development and Cooperation, America ranks No. 28 out of 30 industrialized nations for total federal (or central government) tax burden. Tax revenue accounts for a relatively skimpy 26.02 percent of U.S. gross domestic product. Only Korea (24.3 percent) and Mexico (17.15 percent) had lower tax burdens.[76]

These figures are five years old. In light of the Bushies tax cuts for the rich, that percentage is undoubtedly lower now. Instead of paying our bills with tax revenue, America is borrowing the money and endangering our national security by making us a debtor nation to China.

I know it's a frightening picture. How do we fight them and reclaim the American dream of fairness and prosperity? I know we won't do it by lamenting the loss of the old southern Democratic Party. I say good riddance to their moldy, unjust values. I think we can do it by speaking the truth, knowing what the truth is, and framing issues from a progressive worldview. I believe there is a new progressive citizenry waiting to rise in the South and throughout the country, a citizenry waiting for the message, and waiting for the leadership to make it happen.

Eleven

Birth and Demise
of the Middle Class

———————◆•◆•◆———————

Teach a parrot the terms "supply and demand" and you've got an economist.

-Thomas Carlyle

It's the economy, stupid.

-Bill Clinton campaign slogan

Economics: The science that deals with the production, distribution, and consumption of wealth, and with the various related problems of labor, finance, taxation, etc.

-Webster's New World

L et's talk about economics and how the far right's screwing us to the wall. In the last chapter we recalled the birth of our nation, the industrial revolution, and capitalism. To get our arms around the fundamental differences between progressive and ultraconservative economic ideologies, we must understand the changing face of American capitalism: How America has gone from the Gilded Age of the robber barons in the 19th century to the New Gilded Age of the imperial CEOs in the 21st century.

> But while they prate of economic laws, men and women are starving. We must lay hold of the fact that economic laws are not made by nature. They are made by human beings.
>
> *-Franklin D. Roosevelt*

When Franklin Delano Roosevelt won the presidency in 1932, the laissez-faire economic policies of the United States and the "robber barons[77]" had led the world into the Great Depression. When accepting the Democratic nomination for president on July 2, 1932, Roosevelt promised "a "new deal" for the American people, and then followed through with a legislative agenda that created a slew of social-economic programs to give the government some control of the economy and provide for the welfare of the people. The very rich hated him and considered him a traitor to his class. In their worldview, he had created a welfare state, an unacceptable aberration of their idea of capitalism. They haven't forgotten or forgiven him, and there is not a doubt in my mind that the goal of the big business interests now ruling our country is to turn the clock back and undo the social progress he helped create in the 20th century.

> Economist Paul Krugman, when asked to define the economic policy of the Bush administration[78]: "There is no economic policy. That's really important to say. The general modus operandi of the Bushies is that they don't make policies to deal with problems. They use problems to justify things they wanted to do anyway. So there is no policy to deal with the lack of jobs. There really isn't even a policy to deal with terrorism. It's all about how can we spin what's happening out there to do what we want to do."

Here's another short, telling clip from Krugman's 2003 book, *The Great Unraveling: Losing Our Way In The New Century*: "It seems clear to me that one should regard America's right-wing movement—which now in effect controls the administration, both houses of Congress, much of the judiciary, and a good slice of the media—as a revolutionary power in [Henry] Kissinger's sense. That is, it is a movement whose leaders do not accept the legitimacy of our current political system.

"Am I overstating the case? In fact, there's ample evidence that key elements of the coalition that now runs the country believe that some long-established American political and social institutions should not, in principal, exist—and do not accept the rules that the rest of us have taken for granted.

"Consider, for example, the welfare state as we know it—New Deal programs like Social Security and unemployment insurance, Great Society programs like Medicare. If you read the literature emanating from the Heritage Foundation, which drives the Bush administration's economic ideology, you discover a very radical agenda: Heritage doesn't just want to scale back New Deal and Great Society programs, it regards the very existence of those programs as a violation of basic principals."

> Capitalism:
> ...Is a difficult, problematic term...characterized by...The accumulation
> of the means of production (materials, land, tools) as property into a few
> hands; this accumulated property is called "capital" and the property-
> owners of these means of production are called "capitalists." The means
> of production and labor is manipulated by the capitalist using *rational
> calculation* in order to realize a profit. So that capitalism as an economic
> activity is fundamentally teleological.
>
> *-Richard Hooker*

So let's take a short look at our economic history. What exactly is our heritage? Capitalism, in any sort of modern sense, is little more than 300-years old, even less in America. As we have seen, prior to the industrial revolution the nobility and the wealthy merchant class owned and controlled the limited means of production that existed. In agrarian and feudal societies barter was the major coin of the day; very few people had specie—gold, silver or whatever else passed for currency. That began to change first in Britain in the 1700s as early technology opened the door to greater and greater means of production, distribution and profits (the so-called first industrial revolution). From the 15th to the 18th century "mercantilism," a peculiar, early form of capitalism, prevailed in England. Although the mercantilist system was based on private property and markets, its fundamental focus was on the self-interest of the sovereign (the state), and not the individual.[79] As noted earlier, the constraints of Britain's mercantile system on the American colonies were one of the major causes of the Revolutionary War.

In the 1700s, when England's mercantile fleet of ships under sail was riding high, a British, Scottish-born philosopher and economist, Adam Smith, published *An Inquiry into the Nature and Causes of the Wealth of Nations* (1776). Coincidentally, it was published in the same year as the United States Declaration of Independence. Smith attacked the mercantile system: The central thesis of *The Wealth of Nations* is that capital is best employed for the production and distribution of wealth under conditions of government noninterference, or laissez-faire, and free trade. To explain this concept of government maintaining a laissez-faire attitude toward commercial endeavors, Smith proclaimed the principal of the "invisible hand": Every individual in pursuing his or her own good is led, as if by an invisible hand, to achieve the best for all. Therefore any interference with free competition by government is almost certain to be injurious.[80] In Smith's work, the term capitalism isn't used. Actually, the term may not have been introduced into the economic lexicon until Karl Marx's *Communist Manifesto* (1848), in which he used the term capitalism to attack its characteristics.

Interestingly, despite what the right-wingers would have you believe, the Constitution doesn't mention an economic system at all, nor should it; it's kind of apples and oranges. If one thinks only in economic terms divorced from all other aspects of life the fundamental purpose and meaning of human existence would boil down to productive labor and the distribution of products and services. The Constitution might have read "We the owners of capital and those that shall work and slave for us, etc. etc." Well, you get my drift. I believe the heart of the Constitution is the Bill of Rights—the rights of individuals, not corporations or vast international business empires whose invisible hands are more likely to pick your pocket than look after your best interest. A nation is more than just the buying and selling of goods and services.

When Adam Smith wrote his *Wealth of Nations*, he couldn't possibly have foreseen the industries and the means of distribution that would evolve in the 19th century, to say nothing of the 20th and 21st centuries. Smith was an Enlightenment philosopher; he envisioned individual freedoms—from the Crown—not a substitute system of financial overlords. I believe Smith would be aghast at what's happening in the United States in the 21st century. He was a humanist, not an ideologue.

The plain truth is that unmitigated capitalism is an abusive economic system that has proven not to work well in every country where it has been unleashed. It's like a Monopoly game wherein, lacking new technologies and expanding markets, the winners (corporations – global industrial empires) will own all the railroads, airlines and hotels and the game is over. Unlike a game, unless the government is an active participant in the economy, neither individuals nor groups of individuals (unions) are powerful enough to stand against capital. Marx saw capitalism as a class struggle between the bourgeoisie (capitalists who hold the reigns of production), and the proletariat (wage laborers who sell their time). Because he saw the working class as big-time losers in the mid-19th century, he thought the conflict would lead to a worldwide uprising of the people—a communist revolution—that would end capitalism and replace nation-states. As I indicated earlier, the link Marx made between capital and nation-states is particularly telling and contemporary in the United States.

The capital/labor conflicts would take the emerging industrial nations down different paths. By the early 20th century, England, France, Germany and Italy would turn toward socialism and state ownership of major industry. Russia would turn toward Communism with a capital C under Lenin and Stalin. Politically powerful labor parties would push the socialist movement in those countries, particularly in England. Labor unions in the United States never did form effective political parties, and consequently their effect on government hasn't been nearly as profound.[81] Regardless, the labor movement in the United States would spill a lot of blood and draw political attention with strikes and disruptions of service. In the 1880s there were almost 10,000 strikes and lockouts; close to 700,000 workers struck in 1886 alone.[82]

The notorious Chicago Haymarket Affair inspired many of those 1886 strikers. On May Day of that year union activists in Chicago called a one-day strike for an eight-hour workweek. Anarchists and other radicals joined in. Some thought the workers revolution was at hand. On May 3rd, police killed a striker outside the McCormick Reaper plant. A protest rally was called for Haymarket Square on May 4th. The rally was peaceful until, just as it was winding down, a bomb exploded and eight policemen were mortally wounded. Police cracked down on known radicals and labor leaders. Eight men were tried and convicted of conspiracy, even though the bomber was never identified and they could not be connected to the crime. Seven were condemned to death. Four were hanged. A fifth killed himself in jail before the state could hang him. The other three were later pardoned.

Fearful of the popular growth of socialism or a communist revolution in the 1930s, powerful wealthy industrialists in Italy, Spain and Germany supported the fascists. During that 1930s timeframe, there was also a big push toward fascism in the United States and Great Britain. Today, I can't help but feel, as baseball's Yogi Berra would say, "it's déjà vu all over again" in 21st century America. The difference is that today the rich ruling class fears nothing. It is motivated by opportunity and the lack of an effective opposition.

For 135 years, from independence until FDR's New Deal, the United States was a capitalist nation with a super big C. Perhaps this was best typified by President Calvin Coolidge (silent Cal) in a speech in Washington on January 17, 1925: "The chief business of the American people is business." During that 135-year period, America tripled in size both by acquisition and conquest. Plainly put, America was an aggressive imperialist power; and I believe that the invasion of Iraq and Bush's foreign policy indicate that our imperialistic nature lingers on. The link, the driving force now and then, is the heavy hand of capitalism—the quest for natural resources (oil), new markets, or living space (*Lebensraum*, as the Germans called it). [83]

So how did it work out? What happened before FDR? Those questions make me laugh because I think of Mel Brooks' 1981 movie, *History of the*

World: Part I. It's a really funny show based on the ludicrous premise of oversimplification. In attempting to frame some of the extremely serious issues in this book in a historical context, I often think of that movie; it gives me the *chutzpah* to continue writing.[84]

Wealth was held by the elite few and times were unbelievably hard for workers in America; the more adventurous followed the westward expansion, worked on laying railroad track, or joined the 1849 California gold rush[85]; few got rich but, cyclically, there was a lot of work and a lot of hard times. For southern slaves nothing changed until their emancipation in 1865, and then most simply continued to live in abject poverty as poorly paid wage laborers or sharecroppers. Coal and iron ore mining, and the production of steel were essential to the developing industries, but working conditions and wages for workers in the mines and steel mills were deplorable.

From the end of the 19th century until the Great Depression, America's doors were open to immigration. We needed workers and Americans always thought of immigrants as a source of cheap labor. Although the Irish and Italians led the rush, immigrants came from all of Europe and many from China. In the first 15 years of the 20th century alone, over 13 million people came to the United States, many passing through Ellis Island, the federal immigration center that opened in New York harbor in 1892.

In America's early factories, mills and mines, workers had no job security and no bargaining power; they worked for wages and under working conditions determined solely by the factory owners. Those factories often ran 24 hours a day, in two shifts of 12 hours, seven days a week. Many of the factories severely polluted their environments and their machinery maimed and killed workers. Food was scarce, many times only available at the company store, and health care nonexistent. Women and children were part of the workforce, and preferred because they cost much less than men. In the early years of the 19th century, children between the ages of seven and 12 years made up one-third of the workforce in U.S. factories. In addition, many adults held puritanical ideas regarding the evils of idleness among children and cooperated with employers to help them recruit young factory hands from indigent families.[86]

On the farms life was no better. There were many reasons, including, draught, soil exhaustion, a lack of legislative protection and, perhaps most important, overproduction.

The farther west the settlers went, the more dependent they became on the railroads to move their goods to market. At the same time, farmers paid high prices for manufactured goods as a result of the protective tariffs that Congress, backed by eastern industrial interests, had long supported. Over time, the Midwestern and western farmers fell ever more in deeply in debt to the banks that held their mortgages.

In the South, the fall of the Confederacy brought major changes in agricultural practices. The most significant of these was sharecropping, where tenant farmers "shared" up to half of their crop with the landowners in exchange for seed and essential supplies. An estimated 80 percent of the South's black farmers and 40 percent of its white ones lived under this debilitating system following the Civil War.

Most sharecroppers were locked in a cycle of debt, from which the only hope to escape was increased planting. This led to the overproduction of cotton and tobacco, and thus to declining prices and the further exhaustion of the soil.[87]

The wretched conditions of the period's working class were portrayed in novels by Charles Dickens, and in John Steinbeck's 1940 Pulitzer Prize-winning novel, *The Grapes of Wrath*.[88] The songs of Woody Guthrie are classically descriptive of the era. As PBS put it in *The American Experience*, "While the rich wore diamonds, many wore rags. In 1890, 11 million of the nation's 12 million families earned less than $1200 per year; of this group, the average annual income was $380, well below the poverty line. Rural Americans and new immigrants crowded into urban areas. Tenements spread across city landscapes, teeming with crime and filth. Americans had sewing machines, phonographs, skyscrapers, and even electric lights, yet most people labored in the shadow of poverty."

I think on a fundamental level Marx was wrong and Adam Smith was right. People need freedom and incentive to excel. But Smith was mistaken in holding that workers have an inherent power to bargain with capital. Without laws to level the playing field, and a government willing to enforce those laws, they do not. The power of the American people, while it lasts, is the freedom to vote.

The issue was bargaining power and one of the answers for the American worker was the labor union movement. The origin of labor unions actually goes back to the 12th century in Europe, when craft guilds were first formed to bargain with merchant guilds. In time, journeymen members of craft guilds organized their own associations to seek higher wages and working conditions. The earliest actual labor unions began to rise in Western Europe and the United States at the end of the 18th century. They were formed by skilled crafts workers in reaction to the rapid changes in the economic environment brought about by industrialization.

In the United States in the 1800s, the government, society on the whole and industry were extremely hostile to unions (as the Haymarket Affair makes clear). In Britain and on the Continent people were more socialistically inclined and more supportive of unions than in the United States. That remains the case today. Nevertheless, by the close of the Civil War big U.S. industries were emerging, and by 1900 numerous industries such as auto, steel, rubber, meatpacking and the railroads were making America an industrial powerhouse. The Trade Union Movement Historical Information website page puts it this way: "Between 1870 and 1934, unions in America were also trying to grow as well, but the captains of industry and the wealthy waged a bitter war against workers who tried to organize into a union. The creation of the U.S. trade union movement was the most violent in the world as a result of the wars waged against workers trying to organize into unions during this time."[89]

It was a capitalist's heyday. The sky was the limit, given the immense physical size of the country, natural resources of coal, iron ore, gold, and oil, sparsely populated regions, technological breakthroughs that opened up entire new giant industries, in transportation, communications, and on and on. But there was more than one fly in the ointment. Trusts and the robber barons controlled 90 percent of the nation's wealth; labor was growing more and more restive and vulnerable to any worldwide movement or ...ism that promised hope; the financial markets were insecure and manipulated, and there were continuous disruptive cycles of booms and busts, economic panics, recessions and depressions. Here are some of the notable dates of severe busts from Lexis Nexis: 1808, 1819, 1837, 1857, 1873, 1893, 1910, 1913, 1914, and then the granddaddy of them all, the crash of 1929.

Most thought the boom-bust cycles inevitable until along came John Maynard Keynes, who in the early 1930s wrote *The General Theory of Employment, Interest, and Money.* He advocated public works programs and deficits as a way to get the British economy out of the Depression.

By 1887 America was feeling the pain of a hundred years of government neglect and laissez-faire policies. Huge trusts were creating monopolies (and mega-millionaires) that made a joke of free enterprise, and union strikes were shutting down essential industries such as the railroads and steel. Those hands-off policies were backed by the judiciary, which time and again ruled against those who challenged the system. In this they were following the prevailing philosophy of the times. As John D. Rockefeller is reported to have said: "the growth of a large business is merely a survival of the fittest." This "Social Darwinism," as it was known, had many proponents who argued that any attempt to regulate business was tantamount to impeding the natural evolution of the species.

Hello Heritage Foundation, the Bush administration and Karl Rove! The whole ideology of the far right is Social Darwinism, eat or be eaten— that is their worldview, that is their compassionate conservatism, which, if they are given the chance, they will stick down our throats once again.

By the close of the 19th century sheer despair and social disruptions forced the first heavy interventions by government into the economy. It was the beginning of a populist reform movement in America. There was no choice. America was coming apart. Mind, the early interventions weren't to support labor; they were to control labor.

To control the trusts, Congress passed the Sherman Antitrust Act in 1890 to prohibit their formation, but Supreme Court rulings prevented federal authorities from using the act for years. Because of President Theodore Roosevelt's "trust busting" campaigns (1901-09) the Sherman Act was invoked with some success. Other legislation followed.

Big business turned the Sherman Antitrust Act against the unions as the judiciary upheld lawsuit after lawsuit claiming the unions to be in violation of the act. The Clayton Antitrust Act (1914) enacted under President Woodrow Wilson (1913-21) changed that. It excluded labor unions and agricultural cooperatives from the forbidden combinations in the restraint of trade, restricted the use of injunctions against labor, and legalized peaceful strikes, picketing, and boycotts. Under Wilson, the Federal Trade Commission was also set up.

Early labor law centered on railroads and was directed at setting up mechanisms to prevent strikes and disruption of service. The first labor law in the United States was the Arbitration Act of 1888, which authorized the creation of arbitration panels with the power to investigate the causes of labor disputes and to issue non-binding arbitration awards. The act was brought about by the Great Rail Strike of 1877, when workers across the country went out on strike in response to a 10-percent pay cut. Attempts to break the strike led to rioting and wide-scale destruction in several cities: Baltimore, Chicago, Pittsburgh, Buffalo and San Francisco. Federal troops were used to break the strike. In Baltimore, the state militia fired on strikers, killing 11 and wounding 40. The wage reductions remained in place, and the War Department created the National Guard to put down future disturbances.

The Arbitration Act was a complete failure. It did nothing to prevent or mitigate several serious labor incidents after it was enacted.

In 1892, riots erupted at Carnegie's steel works in Homestead, Pennsylvania. Carnegie's hired group of 300 Pinkerton detectives fired upon striking members of the Amalgamated Association of Iron, Steel and Tin Workers, killing 10 strikers. The National Guard was called in, non-union workers hired, and the strike broken. Unions were not allowed back in the plant until 1937. The battle at Carnegie's Homestead mill became the model for stamping out strikes: Hold firm and call in government troops for support.

Two years later, on May 11, 1894, workers of the Pullman Palace Car Company in Chicago struck to protest wage cuts and the firing of union representatives. In the wake of the 1893 world economic panic, Pullman had fired a third of its workers and cut the wages of those who remained by 30 percent. Their union, the American Railway Union, supported them and within days 260,000 rail workers complied and railroad traffic out of

Chicago came to a halt. President Grover Cleveland sided with Pullman, contending that the strike-related violence and boycotts interrupted mail service, and sent in troops to break the strike.

This was a breaking point. The labor movement lay in a shambles and wouldn't find new strength until the New Deal and FDR. But never again would American labor pose the same broad challenge to the claims of capital.

Congress attempted to correct the shortcomings of the Arbitration Act with the Erdman Act in 1898. The act also provided for voluntary arbitration, but made any award enforceable in federal court. The arbitration procedures were rarely used.

The Newlands Act, passed in 1913, was more effective, but rendered largely moot when the federal government nationalized the railroads on December 26, 1917 because of WWI. Immediately after exercising that authority, President Wilson's federal administrator of the railroad system issued orders protecting railroad workers' right to organize, while establishing a number of adjustment boards to settle employment disputes. Wilson's actions not only prevented a looming national strike but also set up the framework for broader railroad labor legislation (the Railroad Labor Act) after the railroads were returned to private ownership. President Wilson, a Democrat, had some other notable progressive legislative victories:[90]

- Underwood-Simmons Tariff Act (1913) – It was the first downward revision of the tariff since the Civil War and provided consumers with competitive pricing. To compensate for the lost revenue, a rider to the act created a small, graduated income tax.[91] The first income tax in America had been repealed in 1872. We'll examine taxation in America in the next chapter.

- Federal Reserve Act (1913) – The banking system was put under government supervision, loosening Wall Street's grip on the nation's purse strings. This act is considered Wilson's most significant accomplishment.

- Seaman Act (1915) – Considered the Magna Carta of American seaman, this act set standards for the treatment of merchant seamen.

- Keating-Owen Child Labor Act (1916) – The act limited the work hours of children, forbade the interstate sale of goods produced by child labor, and began a new program of federal regulation in industry.
- Adamson Act (1916) – This established an eight-hour workday for railroad employees and dramatically averted a potentially crippling railroad strike.

Woodrow Wilson was a visionary who did a lot for labor, framed in the tradition of keeping the peace and preventing strikes without providing direct welfare to workers. After the WWI Armistice in 1918, Wilson went to Paris to try to build an enduring peace. He later presented to the Senate the Versailles Treaty, containing the Covenant of the League of Nations, and asked, "Dare we reject it and break the heart of the world?" The Senate answered by voting it down. The United States would never be a member of the League of Nations, which was dissolved in 1946 and replaced with the United Nations.[92]

The American Federation of Labor (AFL), formed in 1886 with 140,000 members, continued to grow in the 20th century. The AFL had one million members in 1900, rising to four million by 1920. An additional million workers belonged to non-AFL affiliated unions.

During that time, the Communist Party gained complete control in Russia and was trying to expand its influence in the United States, particularly in the union movement. It was a terribly confusing time with the unions being branded as un-American and the government using sedition laws, arrests and expulsion to put the communists down. Part of the answer was for the government to further strengthen the country's labor laws to reinforce legitimate unions, rather than have them infiltrated by communist radicals with an international agenda. Following are the major pieces of legislation that evolved, and continue to regulate the labor movement in the United States today:

- The Railway Labor Act (1926) – This act, mentioned above, was the result of negotiations between the railroads and unions after Wilson returned the management of the railroads to private ownership following WWI. Simply put, the RLA specifies (1) the negotiation and mediation procedures that unions and employers must exhaust before they may change the status quo, and (2) the methods for resolving "minor" disputes over the interpretations or application of collective bargaining agreements. The RLA permits strikes over major disputes only after the union has exhausted the RLA's negotiating and mediation procedures, while barring almost all strikes over minor disputes. The newly emerging airlines were incorporated under the RLA in 1936.

- The Norris-La Guardia Anti-Injunction Act of 1932 restricts the employer's use of court orders to hamper union organizing drives and limit strikes. It also made yellow-dog contracts unenforceable in federal courts.[93]

- The National Labor Relations Act (NLRA) of 1935, also known as the Wagner Act, defines a set of unfair labor practices for employers. It requires bargaining with unions and non-interference with the workers' right to organize.

- The NLRA also established the National Labor Relations Board, an independent government agency that can investigate unfair labor practices and order the stop of such practices. The NLRB also runs certification elections in which workers decide if a particular union is to represent them in collective bargaining.

- The Labor-Management Relations Act of 1947, also known as the Taft-Hartley Act, curbed union power by permitting states to pass right-to-work laws. The legislation was vetoed by President Harry Truman but passed with the required two-thirds anyway. Because of Taft-Hartley, right-to-work legislation is being pressed in many state legislatures by the far right and remains a threat to unions. The Landrum-Griffin Act of 1959 set further union restrictions, barring secondary boycotts and limiting the right to picket.

- Presidential Executive Order 10988 (1962) – This Executive Order by President John F. Kennedy allowed employees of the federal government to organize and belong to labor unions.

In economic thinking, the fundamental purpose and meaning of human life is productive labor and distribution of products and services. So that there really is no such thing as economics unless you have the worldview that economic behavior can be separated out from other behaviors.

- Richard Hooker[94]

When FDR took office on March 4th, 1933 America was a deeply troubled nation. The stock market crash of 1929 was only a symptom of a dysfunctional economy that favored the rich and licensed the thieves. America had become a plutocracy—a nation ruled by the power of wealth. For the wealthy the Great Depression was an opportunity to expand their holdings; they were the only ones with money. For everyone else it was a fight for survival. Roosevelt had the courage to challenge the plutocracy. I think he was well aware that the country could not recover unless social values changed, and unless the distribution of wealth was brought into some kind of balance. I think Hooker's comments above are very apropos

Here are a few insightful quotes from FDR's First Inaugural Address; the first is quite famous:

"This is preeminently the time to speak the truth—the whole truth, frankly and boldly. Nor need we shrink from honestly facing conditions in our country today. This great nation will endure as it has endured, will prosper. So, first of all, let me assert my firm belief that the only thing we have to fear is fear itself – nameless, unreasoning, unjustified terror which paralyzes needed efforts to convert retreat into advance."

"In such a spirit on my part and yours, we face our common difficulties. They concern, thank God, only material things. Values have shrunk to fantastic levels; taxes have risen; our ability to pay has fallen; government of all kinds is faced by serious curtailment of income; the means of exchange are frozen in the currents of trade; the withered leaves of industrial enterprise lie on every side; farmers find no markets for their for their produce; the savings of many years, in thousands of families, are gone."

"Primarily, this is because the rulers of the exchange of mankind's goods have failed through their own stubbornness and their own incompetence, have admitted their failure and have abdicated. Practices of the unscrupulous money-changers stand indicted in the court of public opinion, rejected by the hearts and minds of men."

"True, they have tried, but their efforts have been cast in the pattern of an outworn tradition. Faced by the failure of credit, they have proposed only the lending of more money. Stripped of the lure of profit by which to induce our people to follow their false leadership, they have resorted to exhortations, pleading tearfully for restored confidence. They know only of a generation of self-seekers. They have no vision, and when there is no vision, the people perish."

FDR and his New Dealers drew heavily on the progressive ideas and programs of Teddy Roosevelt (FDR's fifth cousin, whom he admired) and Woodrow Wilson. It was to Roosevelt's advantage that along with his decisive presidential election the Democratic Party swept congressional elections across the nation.

The New Deal's accomplishments and failures are still hotly debated. As a history student, I've read volumes about the period. Born in 1937, I even lived during some of it. And as a union activist during my 37-year career as a commercial airline pilot I learned first hand about labor's struggle. In the 1960s, I was fired three or four times for my work as a representative in the Air Line Pilots Association, an AFL-CIO union. I never lost a day's pay but they were tough times. It's an interesting story that you can read about in my memoir, *A Good Stick: An Airline Captain Lives the History of 20th Century Commercial Aviation* (AuthorHouse, 2005).

Here's my take on FDR and the New Deal: Simply put, the New Deal changed America for the better. When Roosevelt speaks of a generation of self-seekers, his words resonate with me: "They have no vision, and when there is no vision, the people perish." Our Founders' vision of freedom had been hijacked by greed. I'm convinced that had it not been for men like Teddy Roosevelt, Woodrow Wilson and Franklin Delano Roosevelt,

America could easily have experienced a second bloody revolution. Starving people have little to lose. Unregulated capitalism does not work. The tyranny of great wealth is no different than the tyranny of the monarchs and emperors of the past.

What did the New Deal accomplish? First and foremost, it established the right of the federal government to regulate the economy. It leveled the playing field, which allowed labor effective collective bargaining, and for the first time used the country's wealth for public works programs specifically to employ people. It established Social Security, an insurance program to provide benefits to the elderly, handicapped, dependent children and the unemployed, paid for by employee and employer contributions. It is not and never was a welfare program. Social Security is a self-funded insurance program.

By abandoning the gold standard, the New Deal allowed more money to be put into circulation and devalued the holdings of the wealthy. To stabilize and bring honesty to the financial markets, it established the Federal Deposit Insurance Corporation (FDIC) and the Securities Exchange Commission (SEC).

It also created the National Recovery Act (NRA) to provide fair standards for labor unions and, when the Supreme Court found the NRA unconstitutional, followed with legislation that established the National Labor Relations Act (outlined above).

It set up the Tennessee Valley Authority (TVA), a public works program on an unprecedented scale, to curb flooding and generate electricity in the impoverished Tennessee Valley.

The Federal Emergency Relief Administration (FERA) provided bread lines and other aid to the unemployed. And the federal government employed people: the Civil Conservation Corp (CCC), Public Works Administration (PWA), and the Works Progress Administration (WPA).

But despite all those efforts unemployment remained high at the end of Roosevelt's first term. True to the accepted economic philosophies of the time, FDR had refused to abandon his efforts to balance the budget and accept deficit spending to spur an economic recovery. When unemployment rose again to 19 percent in 1938, Roosevelt implemented the only new idea he hadn't tried—the program put forward to him by that British "mathematician," John Maynard Keynes five years before. Roosevelt explained his decision in one of his famous fireside chats: "it was up to the government to create an economic upturn by making additions to the purchasing power of the nation."

Keynesian economic principals have saved industrialized nations from experiencing the drastic booms and busts ever since. It basically calls for the Federal Reserve (in the United States) to loosen the money supply by dropping interest rates and for the government to invest in social programs, even if that incurs temporary budget deficits.

Conversely, economists such as Milton Friedman, who advised Richard Nixon and Ronald Reagan, and David Stockman, who was Reagan's economic guru, are strong advocates for laissez-faire capitalism. This was brought to a pinnacle of lunacy with Reaganomics—his version of supply-side economics. The supply-siders maintained that tax breaks for the rich "trickle down" in the form of increased business and jobs. I say it's a con-job to give tax breaks to those who need them the least, and the only thing that trickles down doesn't smell too good. In running against Reagan for the Republican Party's presidential nomination for the 1980 election, George H.W. Bush called Reagan's supply-side policies "voodoo economics." On the other hand, his son, George W. Bush, has embraced voodoo economics hook, line and sinker, by giving massive tax cuts to the rich in the face of record-breaking deficits.

The New Deal and World War II would eventually take America out of the Great Depression and set the conditions for a short-lived middle class that was the envy of the world. It was a combination of federal control over the economic infrastructure, progressive taxation, strong unions, and a changed American worldview. No longer were workers perceived as a poverty-stricken class, immigrants and lawbreakers. The workers were returning GIs who had fought for their country and the law was on their side. And they wanted families, and needed homes, cars and appliances. Plus the GI Bill of Rights made getting homes easier, and even provided money for education and job training. America was investing in itself.

Economist and *New York Times* columnist Paul Krugman has written about the far right's failed economic policies, and at least two articles about the lost middle class. The first is titled "For Richer" and was published as an expanded magazine article on October 20, 2002. The second, titled "Losing Our Country" was published as an op-ed on June 10, 2005.[95] I think Krugman has it is right: Since the 1970s, all those sustaining forces that created the middle-class have lost their power. He writes, "Since 1980 in particular, U.S. government policies have consistently favored the wealthy at the expense of working families – and under the current administration, that favoritism has become extreme and relentless. From tax cuts that favor the rich to bankruptcy 'reform' that punishes the unlucky, almost every domestic policy seems intended to accelerate our march back to the robber baron era."

Krugman, speaking of his childhood on Long Island says, "…the America I grew up in—the America of the 1950's and 1960's—was a middle-class society, both in reality and in feel. The vast income and wealth inequalities of the Gilded Age had disappeared. Yes, of course, there was the poverty of the underclass—but the conventional wisdom of the time viewed that as a social rather than an economic problem. Yes, of course, some wealthy businessmen and heirs to large fortunes lived far better than the average American. But they weren't rich the way the robber barons who owned the mansions had been rich, and there weren't that many of them. The days when plutocrats were a force to be reckoned with in American society, economically or politically, seemed long past." Krugman was born in 1953.

I was born in 1937 and, although my family lived in Brooklyn, I spent my teenage years commuting to flight school at Deer Park Airport on Long Island. And as a young airline pilot I returned to Long Island to raise my family in Levittown, and then Long Beach. Krugman writes of an excursion to the North Shore to see the great Gilded Age mansions and I made the same excursion. Of course the robber barons were long gone but the mansions were still something to see. Being quite a bit older than Krugman, my middle-class memories go back further. I remember my parents listening to Roosevelt's fireside chats and witnessed their climb out of poverty.

The 1950s and 1960s were a time of great expectations and optimism— a time when those who worked hard, got an education or learned a trade could reasonably expect to earn a good living; a time when a family could enjoy a good lifestyle on the earnings of just one breadwinner. Most women were able to stay home and raise their families. When I think of the 1960s, I think of John Kennedy, Jackie and the dream of Camelot. Our leaders weren't telling us, as they are today, to be afraid. We were being told to look to the sky and reach for the stars. And we did, and eventually not only surpassed Russia in the space race but put men on the moon.

Some claim JFK originated supply-side economics because he launched legislation to drop the top income tax rate. What they usually overlook is that he dropped the rate from 91percent to 70 percent. It had been as high as 94 percent at the close of World War II. JFK also supported the unions. By his executive order, federal workers were for the first time allowed to join unions.

Even during the terrible, ill-advised war in Vietnam America was making social progress at home. While the war ultimately forced Lyndon Johnson not to run for a second term, he was a terrific civil rights president. His Great Society initiative and Medicare were monumental achievements. One cannot have economic justice without social justice; they are different sides of the same coin. Even though Johnson's guns and butter tax policy caused some inflation, it was modest, and the economy did well during his administration.

And then came Richard Nixon in 1969. He and Henry Kissinger would sign a peace treaty with North Vietnam in 1973, just in time for that year's presidential election, which Nixon won. And the world would see the last of our soldiers being evacuated by helicopter from the roof the American embassy in Saigon in 1975 as North Vietnam overran the south. It galls me to hear Nixon spoken of as a faulted but otherwise great president. He was a man who would do anything for political advantage, and America was better off when he was forced to resign.

Nixon's administration marked the beginning of the demise of the middle-class, mostly because of his politically motivated economic policies. To insure his reelection, he egged on the Federal Reserve chairman, Arthur Burns, to gun the money supply, cut the dollar loose from gold (devaluing it), and imposed phony wage and price controls in an effort to prevent the appearance of inflation before the election. The Arab oil embargo in 1973, along with Nixon's policies, escalated inflation and dropped America into a deep recession. They called it "stagflation." Between October 1973 and December 1974, the Dow Jones dropped 45 percent. I remember 1973 very well—you can't use coal to fuel airliners.

Gerald Ford mucked along serving out the remainder of Nixon's term after he resigned, but the economy, particularly for the middle class, never did rebound. When Jimmy Carter took office in 1977, double-digit inflation, unemployment, and a continuing deep recession—stagflation— were crippling the country. Unfortunately, by the time Carter figured it out it was too late; he became a one-term president. The economy and the Iran hostage situation cost him the 1980 election, providing a victory for Ronald Reagan. Economists now say Carter mistakenly concentrated on the recession, and switched gears to fight inflation only in his last year in office. Actually, the policies he set in place were working when Reagan took office.

That aside, I think Carter's biggest mistake was to follow bad advice and allow the passage of the airline deregulation in 1978. It has been a disaster for the airline industry and was the first of a deregulation trend that continues to turn America over to the whims of big business. And it was promoted by liberal thinkers such as Senator Edward Kennedy. The carrot was cheaper airline tickets; now we're beginning to understand the real cost to workers and society of non-government regulation.

I witnessed the fallout of airline deregulation first hand. The sharks moved in. Guys like Frank Lorenzo, Carl Icahn and Stephen Wolf leveraged airline buyouts with their own assets and then sold them out. Today few of the major airlines of the 1970s exist. Pan American, TWA, Eastern, Braniff and others are long gone. In 2005 the remaining major carriers of the 1970s are either in bankruptcy or on the verge; families have been destroyed and wages have plummeted in the airline industry.

Today's robber barons have become the lavishly paid CEOs of industry— nicely nestled in with boards of directors more interested in lining their own pockets than looking out for the stockholders. The compensation for CEOs skyrocketed. No longer are they simply managing companies. They are superstars of greed, betraying stockholders and workers alike. While the SEC looked the other way, billions of dollars were swindled at companies like Enron and Tyco as books were cooked with the complicity of major banking institutions under the watchful eye of accounting firms like Arthur Andersen. There's very little honor in corporate America today and, not surprisingly, there's very little worker loyalty.

Reagan continued the litany of the decline of the middle class. He gave tax breaks to the rich while running up giant deficits. Sound familiar? Some credit him as a genius for spending so much money on defense that the USSR was bankrupted out of existence trying to keep up. I think he was just feeding the military industrial complex, much as the Bush administration is doing now.

When Reagan broke the infamous air traffic controllers' (PATCO) strike in 1981, the labor movement was given a setback from which it has never really recovered. Reagan was ruthless. The air traffic controllers were locked out and never permitted to return to work and the labor clock was turned back.

Ultimately, a union's strength is determined by its ability to successfully go on strike to press its demands. The year before the PATCO strike in 1980 there were 187 work stoppages involving 1,000 workers of more. In 2003 only 14.

In 1960, the year I became a member of ALPA, 37 percent of American workers belonged to a labor union. Conversely, in 2004, 12.4 percent of the nation's wage and salary workers were members of a labor union. Of that number only about 8 percent were in the private sector.[96]

There are several reasons for the decline in union membership: The workers who built up the unions in the 1950s and 1960s (my generation) are now retired and out of the workforce, and young people today aren't interested. They don't know their heritage. There are far fewer manufacturing jobs. Those jobs have gone overseas to cheaper labor. And new-age technology companies such as Microsoft, Dell and Hewlett-Packard are non-union and many of their jobs are being outsourced to India and China.

Since 1973, the income gap between the very rich and the rest of us has continued to widen, so that the United States now has roughly the same distribution of income as in the 1920s, when a very small number of rich people controlled a large share of the nation's wealth. We became a middle-class society when the concentration of income at the top dropped sharply during the New Deal, and especially during World War II; this was the result (as mentioned earlier) of federal control over the economic infrastructure, progressive taxation, strong unions, and a changed American worldview. The economic historians Claudia Goldin and Robert Margo have dubbed the narrowing of income gaps during those years the Great Compression.

So it can validly be said that the middle class in America was merely a 30-year interregnum between the Gilded Ages of the robber barons of old and the 21st century imperial CEOs.

According to Krugman, the income of the average working family, adjusted for inflation, doubled between 1947 and 1973, but rose only 22 percent from 1973 to 2003. And much of that gain was the result of wives entering the labor force or longer working hours, not rising wages.

Since 1973, the average income of the top 1 percent of Americans has doubled, and is now equal to the share of the bottom 40 percent of the population.

In 1970 the top 0.01 percent of taxpayers had 0.7 percent of total income—that is, they earned only 70 times as much as the average. In 1998 the top 0.01 percent received 3 percent of all income. That meant that the 13,000 richest families in America had almost as much income as the 20 million poorest households. Those 13,000 families had incomes 300 times that of average families.[97] There are many reasons to believe the income disparity was higher in 2005 than it was in 1998.

So there you have it. You be the judge of your chances of making it big in the 21st century, because if you don't make big you're not going to make it at all, unless we get rid of the plutocracy now ruling America. It will have nothing to do with your intelligence, talent, skill or education. It's all about capital. And I don't think I'm being overly pessimistic. If you and you, dear readers, don't bring our politics back to life in America—with a passion worthy of the task—wealth is likely to progressively cement in new and less democratic regimes. Even if we continue to hold elections they will be meaningless, bought and paid for by the plutocracy. It will be a country in which only the well connected receive big rewards, and ordinary people have little chance of advancement, a country in which political involvement seems pointless, because in the end the interests of the elite are always served.

Part Three

The Issues

Twelve

America's Taxing Dilemmas

————————◆•◆•◆————————

Taxes, after all, are dues that we pay for the privileges of membership in an organized society.

— Franklin D. Roosevelt

I'm proud to pay taxes in the United States; the only thing is, I could be just as proud for half the money.

— Arthur Godfrey

The difference between death and taxes is death doesn't get worse every time Congress meets.

— Will Rogers

I like to pay taxes. With them I buy civilization.

— Oliver Wendell Holmes, Jr.

You guessed it. This chapter is about monetary policy and taxes. In just a few short lines FDR and Oliver Wendell Holmes described the fundamental importance of taxes in a civilized society. Arthur Godfrey and

Will Rogers, in their humorous way, expressed the natural conflict people feel about paying them. Yet, as we have learned, in the decade following independence our fledgling nation found it impossible to govern without the authority to levy taxes. Without revenue a government is powerless to function on behalf of its citizens. And that in a nutshell is the major threat the United States is facing today, not Al Qaeda or the Iraq war, but the fact that we are not raising enough tax revenue to pay our bills. Instead we are borrowing it, and one of our major public creditors has become communist China. Our major federal creditor is the Social Security Trust Fund, and it's going to have to start getting paid back by about 2017. To understand how the Bush administration and Congress are mismanaging our nation's purse strings we have to roll up our sleeves and analyze the data. Don't panic. You don't have to be an economist to get the big picture; you just need a strong stomach.

Grover Norquist[98] and his far-right pals, major instigators of the Bush's monetary policies, are far from economic geniuses. Quite the contrary, they are narrow-minded ideologues. To quote Norquist, "my goal is to cut government in half in twenty-five years to get it down to the size where we can drown it in the bathtub." Can you imagine? This "patriot" is talking about destroying our government! Their strategy is to "starve the beast," meaning, to starve the government of revenue it needs to function. It was the mantra of Reagan's administration and remains the common theme of the Republican majority ruling our country.[99] Their ideology of social Darwinism holds that at its core, government spending for the welfare of the public squanders the taxpayer's money. That private enterprise—not government—is the answer to all things. With that same perverse logic they have successfully legislated huge tax cuts for the very rich, and massive tax incentives and sweetheart deals for big business. Whether they actually believe what they preach or it's a greedy subterfuge is of little importance because the result is the same: America—you and I—are being taken to the cleaners and our nation is in peril.

But, you may ask, how can the far right be "starving the beast" when we're spending more money than ever before, $2.29 trillion in 2004? It is because most of the increased expenditures have been for Afghanistan and the Iraq war—which includes fielding an increasingly expensive mercenary army,[100] and for sweetheart deals for big business, such as Halliburton and their subsidiary Kellogg, Brown & Root. (Surely it is no coincidence that Dick Cheney was Halliburton's CEO before he became vice president.) The basic running costs of the conflicts are $6 billion a month; the Congressional Budget Office projected the defense budget for 2005 would be $493 billion. The revenue lost by Bush's tax cuts for the rich enacted between 2001 and 2003, on top of wartime military expenses, resulted in huge budget deficits. We are paying for those deficits by borrowing; we have increased the national debt by over $2 trillion dollars in four years—a breathtaking jump that has brought the total debt up to over $7.8 trillion.

The starving begins after 2005, when across the board "discretionary" program cuts will amount to $45 billion by 2009, then go downhill from there.[101]

Despite the protestations of Secretary of the Treasury John Snow and other administration spokespersons, the outlook for the economy at this writing in 2005 was deeply troubling. The recovery from the 2002 recession is at best anemic, favoring corporations and wealthy investors. We've lost three million manufacturing jobs and wages are falling behind the cost of inflation as jobs cascade overseas.

The Medicare Prescription Drug bill, which passed using phony numbers, kicked in on January 1, 2006. When the bill narrowly won passage in 2003, Congress voted on budget figures provided by the White House that projected a 10-year cost of $400 billion. Shortly after the bill was signed, that cost had risen to $534 billion. In February 2005, the projected cost was raised to a staggering $1.2 trillion, three times the amount that Congress had from the White House when it passed the bill.[102] The fiscal gap the law created over the next 75 years—not the financing gap for Medicare as a whole, just the additional gap created by the prescription drug legislation— will be $8.7 trillion. All for a stingy benefit that will leave many seniors with thousands of dollars worth of drug bills. Unbelievably, the legislation prohibits, I say again, *prohibits* the government from negotiating prices with the drug companies, thus negating the vast purchasing power of the program. It is a windfall for Bush's drug company buddies.

Congress passed and Bush subsequently signed into law two other massive pork barrel bills during the summer of 2005, an energy bill and a transportation bill. Mind, I strongly believe both pieces of legislation were necessary, and that investing in our infrastructure is money well spent. It is the pork and blatant giveaways to big business included in the bills that infuriate me. That is simply rotten economics and blatant political larceny.

The energy bill contains some positive measures but does nothing to reduce the sharply rising price of oil to American consumers (which is going to spike inflation and devalue the dollar) and fails miserably to reduce consumption. It gives $14.5 billion in tax breaks, and potentially more in loan guarantees and other subsidies to encourage oil and gas drilling, improve natural gas and electric transmission lines, build new nuclear power reactors and expand renewable energy sources. Out of that, several billion will go to Bush's oil company buddies—the same companies that have been enjoying the largest profits in the history of the world.

As this was written, the breaking news was that oil is selling at a record high of $67.10 a barrel [and was even higher in 2006]. By comparison, when OPEC turned off the oil spigot in 1974, the price soared to $11.65 a barrel (about $48 in 2005 dollars). Yet the Bush administration remains sanguine; after all, the oil companies are doing just fine.

Energy expert Gal Luft calls the energy bill "the sum of all lobbies."[103] What a shame. Energy independence should be our top national priority, much as John Kennedy made the space program a top priority during the Cold War. Without energy independence the economy of the United States will remain vulnerable and future oil wars (economic or military) inevitable.

The $286 billion transportation bill will fund all kinds of worthy projects, such as bridges, roads and bike paths over a five-year period (2004-2009). But it is also full of pork. Members of Congress have attached 6,350 special projects worth $24 billion, each one doling out something extra for the people in their own districts. This means 8 percent of the budget went to pork. Rep. Don Young, R-Alaska, the powerful chairman of the House Transportation and Infrastructure Committee, did particularly well—to the tune of nearly a billion dollars. His take includes $250 million for a bridge in Anchorage to be named Don Young's Way. And another $230 million for a bridge, almost as long as the Golden Gate on San

Francisco Bay, to connect the town of Ketchikan (pop. 14,000) to Gravina Island (pop. 50).

Vermont's haul was just below Alaska's, $331 million ($544 per capita); while New Hampshire, with twice the population of Vermont, got the least in the country, $69 million. Historically New Hampshire is always at the bottom of the barrel in federal grants. We're a big-time donor state. The reason is that most federal grants contain matching fund provisions. New Hampshire, with neither an income tax nor a general sales tax, spends among the least per capita in the nation ($1,477 in 2002), ranking number 45. Bush's home state of Texas, where he was governor, ranked number 49, spending $1,316 per capita. Texas does, however, have the distinction of leading the nation in executions, 346 since 1976. It's just a matter of priorities.

Congress also stuffed an extra $8.5 billion into the highway bill, bringing the real total to $295 billion, which some are calling highway robbery. They did it in the closing hours of legislative bargaining with the White House by claiming the additional money is merely a buffer that the states will return if not needed. You bet.

During his radio address on August 6, 2005, Bush made the following comments at the end of a litany of half-truths and distortions lauding his administration's economic accomplishments: "As Congress considers appropriations bills this fall, we will work with the House and the Senate to ensure that taxpayer dollars are spent wisely, or not at all…. We need to make the tax relief permanent, end the death tax forever, and make our tax code simpler, fairer and more pro-growth."

Translated, he thinks things are just super-peachy. There is no mention of the $2 trillion in national debt incurred on his watch, or the fact that our economy built on debt is unsustainable. Nor does he seem aware that if Congress does his bidding and makes the tax breaks permanent [they were extended in 2006] we will have a $4 trillion additional deficit by 2015, atop increased debt to the Social Security Trust Fund of $2.5 trillion—a total of $6.5 trillion.[104] America would essentially be credit-card bankrupt. We would owe a total national debt of $14.3 trillion. Interest payments would increase to over $700 billion a year, if we could find anybody to invest in us any longer. Which begs the question, what in the world will happen if these fiscal maniacs stay in power?

Some very smart people in America fear Norquist could have his way. If we don't encourage real economic growth, change our tax and trade policies, and once again invest in our future, the United States could well drown in a sea of red ink and drag the rest of the world down with it.

Among those who are crying wolf is Paul Krugman, a highly respected economist at Princeton University and columnist for the *New York Times*. (I have a great deal of respect for Krugman and have quoted him freely in this book.) In June 2005, as Krugman was passing through London, Liam Halligan, an economics correspondent at Channel 4 News UK, interviewed him.[105] Here are some extremely interesting excerpts of his report:

"Cornering Krugman during a flying visit to London, I raised the ongoing US-China trade talks. It is a hot topic: Congress is considering a bill to put stiff tariffs on –Chinese-made products if Beijing refuses to revalue its currency.

"'China has immense power in this trade row,' says Krugman. 'If it stops doing what it is doing, the Chinese government could easily trigger a global economic earthquake.'

"Sensing my surprise, Krugman lays out his argument. 'China exports lots of goods and foreign companies are investing heavily there, so it's running a huge trade surplus. But rather than keep all that money, Beijing is using it, overwhelmingly, to buy US government Treasury bills.

'America is very dependent on its housing market right now. Almost everything moving the economy forward relates, directly or indirectly, to our housing boom.' "That sounds familiar, but how does it link to China?

"Krugman then spells out the jaw-dropping extent of China's T-bill purchases: $200 billion in 2004 and possibly as much as $300 billion this year. Beijing, he says, is 'bankrolling America's huge budget deficit, now almost 5 percent of national income, to the tune of $1 billion per day.

'At some point,' he says, excited by the power of his logic, 'China could well decide to stop this. If so, the dollar falls sharply, US interest rates rise and our housing bubble bursts.'

"A pause. 'Quite simply,' he concludes, 'that would stop the American economy, the locomotive for the whole world, in its tracks. So, in this weird way, China is now the financial nexus keeping the global recovery going.'

"Krugman's analysis highlights the fact that the president has only limited ability to threaten China, given its 'key role' in propping up the dollar. 'There's no sign that anyone in government wants to face the unpleasant reality of our addiction to loans from abroad,' he says. 'If the US weren't so dependent on China buying T-bills, we would have become much more protectionist already.'"

Okay, let's roll up our sleeves and look at some of the data. Among the many indicators that economists use to judge the economic health of the nation, there are four key ones that are used widely in government press releases and so forth. These are Gross Domestic Product (GDP), national debt, US Government Budget Surpluses and Deficits, and Current-Account Balance (trade). The Consumer Price Index (CPI) is also widely used but is more of a measure of inflation. Here we'll discuss the first three, and save Current-Account Balance, trade and globalization for the next chapter.

The Congressional Budget Office defines **Gross Domestic Product** as the total market value of goods and services produced domestically during a given period of time. The components of GDP are consumption (both household and government), gross investment (both private and government), and net exports.[106]

The United States has a huge economy, the largest in the world. In 2004 the U.S. GDP was $11.7 trillion. In descending order the next six countries (in trillions) were: Japan $4.6, Germany $2.7, United Kingdom $2.1, France $2.0, Italy $1.7, and China $1.6.

In a presentation to the Alexandria, Virginia Rotary Club in January 2004 titled "Measuring the U.S. Economy," J. Steven Landefeld, director of the U.S. Bureau of Economic Analysis (BEA) spoke of the usefulness of GDP data. He proffered that the GDP provided an "Organized stream of volatile, partially incomplete – and sometimes overlapping and contradictory – data into a consistent and comprehensive picture of the economy." In other words, user beware. GDP is a very useful analytical tool if it is used in conjunction with other data—on its own it means little.

For instance David Chapman, director of the Millennium Billion Fund,[107] points out in his paper titled "Debt Illusion": "To the end of the second quarter 2003 US GDP rose $417 billion from $10,376.8 billion to $10,793.8 billion or 4% from the second quarter 2002. Debt, however, grew in the same period from $19,941.3 billion to $21,597 billion for a rise of $1,655.7 billion (8.3%). A ratio of 4:1 of Debt: GDP." The debt data Chapman is referring to isn't the National Debt but rather the Federal Reserve Flow of Funds Accounts of the United States. Flow of Funds represents debt from all sectors, government and private. It does not factor in unfunded liabilities such as Medicare, Social Security, Medicaid and pensions, making the data once again something of an illusion. Foreign debt is included in that data and is also reported in Current Account Balance—for the matching period, that was about -$500 billion.

Here's a tip. When the bean counters talk big numbers, they drop the zeros; thus the GDP used in the example above can be $10,783,800,000,000 or $10,793.8 billion or, if you don't want to count the small change $10.8 trillion (rounded out). Likewise our debt for the same period was $21.6 trillion.

GDP is not a measure of net worth—the type of information you have probably been asked to provide in applying for a bank loan. The bank, in judging your ability to repay the loan, judges your income, the value of your assets, and offsets that by your debt. GDP provides only one part of the balance sheet, the money spent on products, services or invested during a particular period of time; it's usually reported quarterly and collated annually. Consequently, to judge the financial condition of the nation, GDP must be weighted against money borrowed; the data from the Flow of Funds Accounts of the United States is one measure, the National Debt (government) is another.

Nor does GDP differentiate between money spent on education, health care or war—every dollar spent is counted. Inflation or, expressed another way, the value of the dollar, is another huge factor. For instance the GDP at the end of WW II was $223.1 billion. Corrected for inflation in chained year 2000 dollars it was $1,786.3 billion.

Population growth is also a factor in economic indicators. Between 1999 and 2005 the United States grew by over 24 million people or almost 9 percent. Which means that the economy would have to grow by that much just to stay even.

The national debt is your debt if you are a citizen of the United States. On July 26, 2005 we owed $7,87,946,479,699 or $26,540 each. A child born on that day came into the world owing not only the principal, which may never be paid down, but also inherited the obligation to pay the interest, about $150,000 over the child's lifetime at today's bargain-basement interest rates.[108] In 2004 the interest paid on the national debt was over $321.5 billion, making it the third largest budget item behind Health and Human Services (first) and Department of Defense (second). Social Security payments are off budget, paid from its own revenue source (payroll taxes called FICA). By comparison, NASA was budgeted at $15 billion, Education at $61 billion, and the Department of Transportation at $56 billion.

The definition of the national debt that I believe is most concise is by Morgan Stanley, one of the world's largest investment banks. Their definition: "The total value of all outstanding Treasury bills, notes, and bonds that the federal government owes investors is referred to as the national debt. Some of this debt is held by the government itself, in accounts such as the Social Security, Medicare, Unemployment Insurance, and Highway, Airport and Airway Trust Funds. The rest is held by individuals and institutional investors, both domestic and foreign, or by foreign governments."

It is important to understand that the national debt is not the same as the federal budget deficit, which is any federal spending that exceeds federal income in a fiscal year.

America is $7.8 trillion in debt and the debt is going up like an elevator. As you would expect, pundits could not help but put that kind of money into some sort of perspective. Here's one from *Business Week*: "One foot of dollar bills stacked up would be worth $1,800. If you stacked $7.8 trillion dollar bills on top of one another the pile would reach nearly 821,000 miles into space. That's 3.5 times the distance from the earth to the moon." (The moon is 239,000 miles above Earth.)

When the national debt was created in 1791, it stood at $75 million. In 1981, when President Reagan took office, it was $940,528 million. When Reagan campaigned for president, he focused on the national debt, claiming it was disastrously high. Compared to the productivity of the country, GDP, it was actually at its lowest level since 1932, and creeping lower. He fixed the problem. When he left office, it was $2,720,742 billion!

Here is a national debt graph that shows the time lines of our recent presidents and the national debt as a percentage of GDP.[109] This percentage is the proper and accepted way of adjusting the debt for inflation and for the country's growth. It is also used by the *Economic Report of the President*, and is the method of adjustment preferred by Alan Greenspan. This graph is from the Citizens for Tax Justice website.

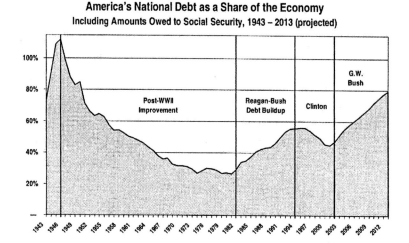

To bring the numbers down to size, let me relate it to my past family debt/income (my GDP) ratio. In 1961, as a young airline pilot with a wife and two children, I bought a modest two-bedroom home in Levittown, Long Island for $15,500 ($96,672 in 2005 dollars) on an annual income $8,000 ($49,895 in 2005 dollars). My monthly income was $667, mortgage payment about $80 (on a $14,000, 30 year mortgage @ 5.5 percent), so I could easily afford the house. My percentage of debt to annual GDP (my salary) was 175 percent. That's not bad for real property that will increase in value as the mortgage is paid down and inflation rises.

By comparison, in June 2005 The National Association of Realtors pegged the median price of a home at an all-time high of $219,000, just about the price that Levittown houses are selling for now. To buy that same house in 2005 with an income of $49,895 ($8,000 in 1961 dollars), using the same 10 percent down payment, my dept/GDP percentage would be about 400 percent, requiring a monthly payment of $1,136, which is not so good. In hot markets such as California, the median price of a home is $530,430—well out of reach of a median income family, which gives credence to the likelihood that the housing boom that is fueling our weak economic recovery may well be a bubble about to hiss out. Then, as Krugman pointed out, the housing boom is being supported by interest rates held at an artificially low level by the Chinese purchase of low interest T-bills.[110]

In 2004 the poverty threshold for a family of four was $19,484. These families are lucky to have a roof over their head. They are the families in the lowest 20 percent of income who are getting a whopping $71 tax break from Bush's tax cuts in 2005. The top 1 percent is getting a $38,141 break. The middle 20 percent got $684.[111] Sounds fair to the big shots.

Another popular website that tracks the national debt is the U.S. National Debt Clock.[112] They track the actual dollars owed, which makes an impressive measure but lacks the perspective of the GDP comparison. I'm including one because it too tells a tale.

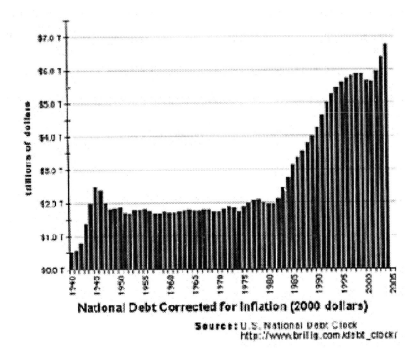

National Debt Corrected for Inflation (2000 dollars)

Source: U. S. National Debt Clock
http://www.brillig.com/debt_clock

In both graphs there is a wonderful symmetry that shows the narrowing income gap during what is called the Great Compression (1947-1973)— what I said earlier was that brief interregnum between the Gilded Age of the robber barons of old and the 21st century imperial CEOs, when for about 30 years it could validly be said that America had a middle class.[113] It was also when America was the envy of the world. As one can graphically see, during that period the national debt as a percentage of GDP shrunk from 110.3 percent (WWII debt) to 35.7 percent because of economic growth and inflation. But even in actual dollars the debt only increased modestly from $258.2 million to $469.8 million. The reason was that the top income tax rates were much higher, corporations paid more taxes, and we weren't creating zillionaires on the backs of working families. Naturally, the far right hated it.

When Reagan took office in 1981, the national debt, as a percentage of GDP, was the lowest it had been since the great depression in 1931 (32.5 percent). But, under Reagan and George Bush the elder (1981-1993), the national debt skyrocketed on both graphs. Under Clinton, the debt as a percentage of GDP first leveled and then went down. Under Bush the younger, it has resumed its steep climb and is higher now than it has been since the 1950s (65 percent of GDP).

The graph below tickles my funny bone because I've been called a tax-and-spend Democrat so many times. Guess who's spend and borrow. This California Democratic Party graph indicates not the total national debt but the increases per year in billions.

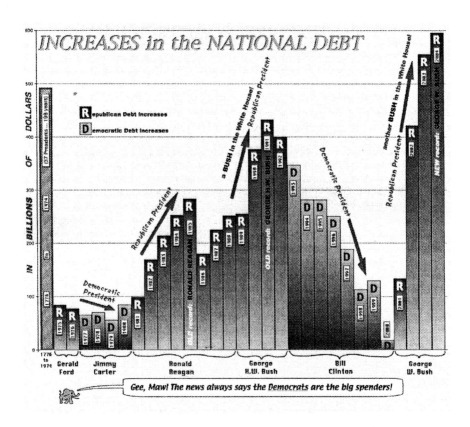

When Reagan railed about the national debt in his first presidential campaign, he had it wrong. It wasn't the debt that was the problem, it was inflation. Although in actual dollars the debt tripled during his presidency, in all fairness much of the increase was due to inflation and growth. As a percentage of GDP, the debt only increased from 32.5 percent to 53.1 percent. Still, for peacetime, this was unprecedented.

One of the reasons the federal portion of the national debt keeps increasing is because of the growth of the Social Security Trust Fund. Social Security is primarily a pay-as-you-go system, meaning that payments to current retirees and other beneficiaries come from current payment of payroll taxes (FICA) into the Social Security Trust Fund.[114] The Social Security Act specifies that trust fund surpluses can only be invested in securities backed by the full faith and credit of the federal government.[115]

Each business day, trust fund income that is not needed to pay expenditures on that day is invested in special-issue "certificates of indebtedness." These certificates mature on the next June 30. They are frequently redeemed prior to maturity to pay for Social Security benefits and other expenses. Whatever amounts have accumulated by June 30 are converted into special-issue bonds.[116]

In the latter part of the 1970s and early 1980s the fund began to experience deficits that hit a high of -$7.9 billion by 1982. In 1983, following the recommendations of the National Commission on Social Security Reform (chaired by Alan Greenspan), the Social Security tax (FICA) was increased so that it would be greater than necessary to pay for current expenditures, thus accumulating a reserve that could be drawn upon in anticipation of the retirement of the WW II baby boomers. At the end of 2004 that surplus stood at $1.7 trillion. The following graph from Social Security Online shows the growth of the fund.

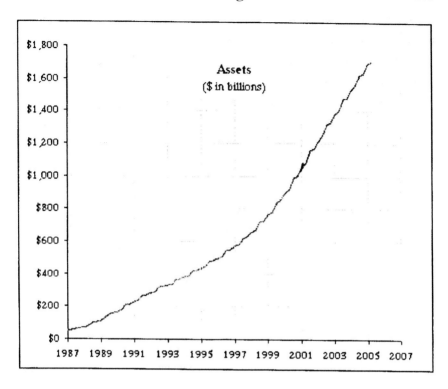

$1,800
$1,600
$1,400
$1,200
$1,000
$800
$600
$400
$200
$0

Assets
($ in billions)

1987 1989 1991 1993 1995 1997 1999 2001 2003 2005 2007

So, despite what Bush is telling us, Social Security is indeed solvent. It's as solid as the credit of the United States Government. In one of his foot-in-the-mouth speeches, Bush actually said he's looked at the Social Security Trust Fund and it's only paper in a file cabinet! I'm sure that was very reassuring to the public holders of our paper, foreign and domestic. We'll focus on Social Security in a coming chapter. As for the national debt; $1.7 trillion is now owed to Social Security Trust. The Congressional Budget Office projects that amount will increase to $2.8 trillion by 2010 and to $4.2 trillion by 2015. The Social Security Board of Trustees projects that by 2017 tax revenue will fall below expenditures and funds will begin to be withdrawn, and that without change the trust funds will be exhausted in 2041.[117]

What's confusing is that Social Security indebtedness is expressed as an off-budget surplus and offsets on-budget deficits. The trust fund has operated in the same manner since 1935. The only thing that changed is that in 1990 it was taken from being accounted for as part of general fund budget and is now accounted for as "off-budget." The reason for the change was ostensibly to show deficits more clearly and to take Social Security out of the fray of Congressional budget fights and machinations.[118]

So, no matter how you look at it, the national debt is real debt—both the federal and public portion. If we keep adding to the debt by continuing to run huge budget deficits, and with Bush goading Congress into making the 2001-2003 tax cuts permanent, the national debt will be $14.3 trillion by 2015. Without significant changes in fiscal policy, by 2009 and thereafter, the government is going to be spending more on interest on the debt than on all domestic discretionary programs put together—from education, to the environment, to law enforcement, to science, to transportation to veterans. By 2013 the annual interest on the debt will be over $700 billion. If this is permitted to occur, the very fabric of our society will begin to unravel, which could trigger a worldwide fiscal crisis.

The following graphs are from the Citizens for Tax Justice website, a paper titled "Bush's $10 Trillion Borrowing Binge" (September 11, 2003).

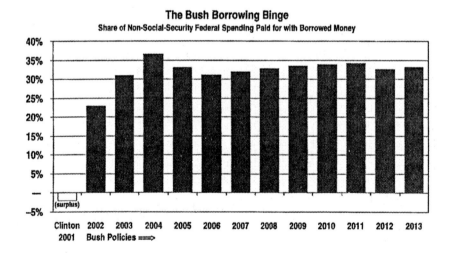

The Bush Borrowing Binge
Share of Non-Social-Security Federal Spending Paid for with Borrowed Money

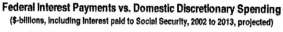

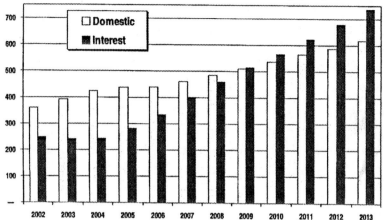

America is digging its own grave. Can we do anything? Sure, get rid of the gravediggers and stop digging.

The US Government budget surpluses and deficits provide data on our budget. Here's a brief definition of surpluses and deficits by LaborLawTalk.com: "Like other institutions, governments operate on a budget—or try to do so. When the expenditures of a government (its purchases of goods and services, plus its transfers (grants) to individuals and corporations) are greater than its tax revenues, it creates a deficit in the government budget. When tax revenues exceed government purchases and transfer payments, the government has a budget surplus (as in the late 1990s in the United States)."

So is Bush really responsible for this mess? Isn't it Congress that appropriates the money? The answer is both are responsible, but it is the president who sets the priorities, estimates the federal government's income and spending for the coming year and recommends funding levels for the federal government. It is the president's budget; he submits the budget to Congress by the first Monday in February every year.

While Bush and past presidents may claim that Congress pumps up their budgets and creates the deficits, historically it is simply not true. For instance, during President Reagan's term of office he proposed eight budgets with a total cost of $7,356 billion—Congress passed budgets that totaled $7,554 billion, an addition of $202 billion (2.75 percent), while the national debt increased $1,875 during his presidency (23.6 percent). Consequently, Reagan's budget *requests* accounted for almost all of the increase in the national debt during his tenure.

Reagan got what he asked for from Congress and so has Bush the younger. Both overestimated revenue assumptions based on a tax cut stimulus, and both paid for the tax cuts with debt. Congress' taste for pork is certainly a regrettable factor in American politics, but it is the president as chief executive officer who bears the primary responsibility for our budgets. The president has tremendous influence on the monetary policies of the United States. He has the power to veto a budget that congress sends back to him, and he appoints the secretary of the Treasury and the chairman of the Federal Reserve.

Okay. Why don't we pass legislation that requires the federal government to pass only balanced budgets? We did. In the face of ever-increasing budget deficits under Reagan in 1985, Congress enacted the Balanced Budget and Emergency Deficit Control Act. The act is better known as Gramm-Rudman-Hollings (GRH) after the Senate authors of the bill (Senators Phil Gramm of Texas, Warren Rudman of New Hampshire, and Ernest Hollings of South Carolina).[119]

GRH established "maximum deficit amounts." If the deficit exceeded these statutory limits, the president was required to issue a sequester order that would reduce all non-exempt spending by a uniform percentage. The law was an unworkable abortion that the Supreme Court struck down the following year, in 1986. Congress went back to the drawing board and revamped the law in 1987, the product some call GRH 2.

GRH 2 did absolutely nothing to stop the deficits, and by 1990 it was clear that the deficit was going to exceed the maximum debt limit. President Bush the elder and Congress addressed the issue by passing the Budget Enforcement Act (BEA) of 1990, which allowed the money to be spent. The act incorporated a pay-as-you-go rule (PAYGO) that required anyone proposing new tax cuts or entitlement expansions to come up with either a way of paying for them without enlarging the deficit or with 60 votes in the Senate to bypass the rule. The BEA was subsequently revised in 1993 and 1997 and expired at the end of fiscal 2002, PAYGO along with it.

In 2004 a watered down version of PAYGO was enacted that is scheduled to expire on September 30, 2008. It has no teeth, as long as tax cuts and entitlement increases are assumed in the budget resolution and no offsets are required.

Some credit the PAYGO for bringing the deficits under control during Clinton's administration. Perhaps it helped, but I think it was mostly a growing economy, encouraged by sound economic policies and leadership, that turned a $290 billion deficit into a $70 billion surplus the year Bill Clinton left office.

Ironclad fiscal rules don't work, although setting forth principles to guide fiscal policy can be very helpful. New Zealand has anchored the process for setting and changing fiscal targets in law. Its 1994 Fiscal Responsibility Act has been a model for a growing number of countries, including Australia, Britain, Brazil, and India.[120]

In the end, you can't legislate inflexible rules for a complex economy—there are too many variables. It takes political leadership and a willingness to put sound fiscal policies before political expedience or constituent/lobbyist pressure. Revenue flow and expenditures change with unforeseen circumstances and borrowing through special appropriations during a budget year, or budgeting a deficit, is sometimes the right thing to do. For instance, it is sound Keynesian policy to allow deficits to aid in the recovery of a deep recession, or to cover defense costs in time of war. However, it is lunacy to reduce taxes while you're doing it.

Let's look at the record of the federal budget since Bush took office and project it ten years into the future.

Center on Budget and Policy Priorities (CBPP), in an article presented by Richard Kogan and David Kamin (Revised October1, 2004), reported this: "Despite the economic recovery, the deficit has continued to rise. 2004 will be the fourth consecutive year of fiscal deterioration, following eight consecutive years of fiscal improvement...."

"The deficit is rising when it should be falling, indicating the emergence of a structural deficit: At this point in previous economic recoveries, deficits have almost invariably begun to shrink rather than to rise. The current economic recovery, however, is different; it has featured the largest deterioration in the government's fiscal position of any recovery since World War II. A substantial 'structural' deficit has developed that will persist as the economy grows, unless policies change."

The following chart is from the Congressional Budget Office's August 15, 2005 report.

CBO's Baseline Budget Outlook

(Billions of dollars)

	Actual 2004	2005	2006	2007	2008	2009	2010	2011	2012	2013	2014	2015	Total, 2006-2010	Total, 2006-2015
						In Billions of Dollars								
Total Revenues	1,880	2,142	2,280	2,396	2,526	2,675	2,817	3,075	3,312	3,481	3,660	3,848	12,695	30,071
Total Outlays	2,292	2,473	2,595	2,721	2,860	2,997	3,134	3,293	3,390	3,561	3,726	3,905	14,306	32,180
Total Deficit (-) or Surplus	**-412**	**-331**	**-314**	**-324**	**-335**	**-321**	**-317**	**-218**	**-78**	**-80**	**-66**	**-57**	**-1,612**	**-2,110**
On-budget	-567	-507	-503	-528	-554	-556	-564	-479	-347	-355	-344	-335	-2,706	-4,565
Off-budget[a]	155	176	189	203	219	234	248	261	269	275	278	279	1,094	2,456
Debt Held by the Public at the End of the Year	4,296	4,621	4,943	5,281	5,630	5,964	6,292	6,520	6,605	6,691	6,762	6,820	n.a.	n.a.
						As a Percentage of GDP								
Total Revenues	16.3	17.5	17.6	17.5	17.6	17.7	17.8	18.5	19.1	19.2	19.4	19.5	17.6	18.5
Total Outlays	19.8	20.2	20.0	19.9	19.9	19.8	19.8	19.9	19.6	19.7	19.7	19.8	19.9	19.8
Total Deficit	**-3.6**	**-2.7**	**-2.4**	**-2.4**	**-2.3**	**-2.1**	**-2.0**	**-1.3**	**-0.4**	**-0.4**	**-0.3**	**-0.3**	**-2.2**	**-1.3**
Debt Held by the Public at the End of the Year	37.2	37.7	38.1	38.7	39.2	39.5	39.7	39.3	38.1	37.0	35.8	34.6	n.a.	n.a.
Memorandum: Gross Domestic Product	11,554	12,271	12,967	13,655	14,372	15,106	15,836	16,578	17,331	18,105	18,903	19,729	71,937	162,582

Source: Congressional Budget Office.

Note: n.a. = not applicable.

a. Off-budget surpluses comprise surpluses in the Social Security trust funds as well as the net cash flow of the Postal Service.

This chart is based upon current law, and thus represents the effects of phasing out the tax cuts as scheduled. As you can see, the effect is dramatic; the Total Deficit (not counting money owed to the Social Security trust funds) is projected to fall to -$57 billion in 2015. As a percentage of GDP, the shrinking deficit clearly shows that the tax cuts represent very little economic growth and are mainly financed by debt.

The CBO also ran projections that took into account the president's proposed extension of expiring tax cuts, continuation of current Alternative Minimum Tax (AMT) relief, and a conservative estimate of future funding for the wars in Iraq and Afghanistan. The projected deficits never dip below $330 billion over the next 10 years and total $4.0 trillion over the 2006-2015 period. See Figure 2 below.

CBO Alternative Policies Increase Deficits
(Shows effect of phasing down of Iraq war and extending of tax cuts)

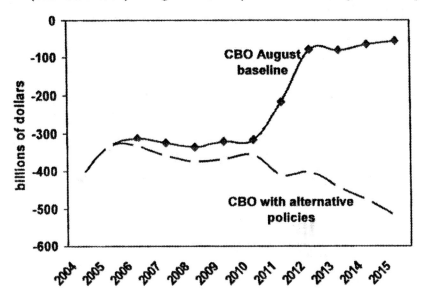

In its August 2005 report, the CBO concluded that the unanticipated increase in revenues in 2005 does not indicate a general improvement in the economic or budget outlook.[121] CBO's view of the economy is, if anything, slightly less sanguine than it was in January of that year. And unlike the administration, CBO has not significantly increased its projections of revenues in future years. When adjusted to account for the extension of the 2001 and 2003 tax cuts, continuation of AMT relief, and a more modest level of future funding for the wars in Iraq an Afghanistan, CBO budget projections show that deficits will remain quite high for the next 10 years. In short, CBO's report indicates that changes in the policies that have been pursued in recent years will be necessary to bring the deficits under control.[122]

The Brookings Institute, in a recent paper by Peter Orszag titled "The US Budget Deficit on an Unsustainable Path," reached similar conclusions: "Under reasonable projections, the budget deficit is likely to amount to about 3.5 percent of GDP in each year over the next decade." Brookings graph below.

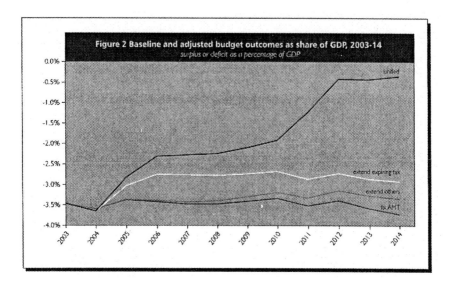

Figure 2 Baseline and adjusted budget outcomes as share of GDP, 2003-14
surplus or deficit as a percentage of GDP

Even open market/free trade champion Alan Greenspan, former two-decade chairman of the Federal Reserve, has admitted that he made a mistake in 2001, when he defended President Bush's controversial tax cuts. At a March 2005 Senate hearing, in response to questioning by Senator Hillary Clinton, Greenspan said, "We were confronted at the time with an almost universal expectation amongst experts that we were dealing with a very large surplus for which there seemed to be no end."

"I look back and I would say to you, if confronted with the same evidence we had back then, I would recommend exactly what I recommended then. Turns out we were all wrong."[123]

Again Greenspan before the Senate Budget Committee in April 2005:

Chairman Greenspan: "One of the real problems we had was allowing PAYGO to lapse in September 2002."

Senator (Jon) Corzine: "Do you think PAYGO rules should include both tax and spending decisions?"

Chairman Greenspan: "I do, Senator."

Chairman Greenspan: "Well, if PAYGO were in place all through this period you would not have the types of problems to which you're referring."

Chairman Greenspan: "The federal budget deficit is on an unsustainable path, in which large deficits result in rising interest rates and ever-growing interest payments that augment deficits in future years.... Unless this trend is reversed, at some point these deficits would cause the economy to stagnate or worse."[124]

Unfortunately, Mr. Greenspan's words of wisdom are a day late and a dollar short. It was he who supported the Bush administration's tax cuts for the rich in 2001, and it is he who shares the responsibility for creating the massive budget deficits we are facing today.

So it appears that the only ones who don't seem to know we are heading for a fiscal train wreck occupy the White House or sit on the right side of the aisle in Congress. (There are a few on the left side I'd like to see out of office as well.)

A sound budget, be it the family budget, a business budget or the budget of the United States is about priorities, honesty, and fiscal responsibility. It is the president's responsibility to present honest estimates of the government's income and expenditures when he presents his budget to Congress and the people. The Bush administration isn't being honest. They are cooking the books, way overstating expected revenues from the tax cuts, and way understating the true cost of the tax cuts and the cost of their sweetheart deals with big business.

In August 2005, the U.S. Census Bureau released its 2004 report on "Income, Poverty, and Health Insurance Coverage." Despite the fact that in 2004 the economy grew a strong 3.8 percent, the bureau reported that the median pretax income for households was $44,389, the lowest since 1997, after inflation. That's the longest stretch of income stagnation on record. Bureau graph below.

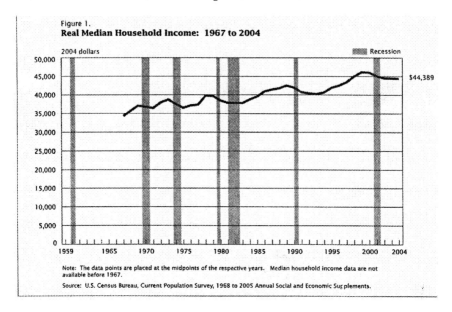

Figure 1.
Real Median Household Income: 1967 to 2004

Note: The data points are placed at the midpoints of the respective years. Median household income data are not available before 1967.

Source: U.S. Census Bureau, Current Population Survey, 1968 to 2005 Annual Social and Economic Supplements.

The economic recovery from the 2002 recession that the White House boasts about apparently is for only the very rich. Then there is that ugly problem of poverty, which keeps growing. In 2004, 1.1 million more people fell into poverty, bringing the number up to 37 million and rising—12.7 percent of the population. Census Bureau graph below.

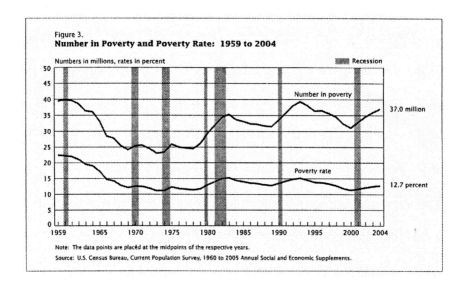

Figure 3.
Number in Poverty and Poverty Rate: 1959 to 2004

Note: The data points are placed at the midpoints of the respective years.

Source: U.S. Census Bureau, Current Population Survey, 1960 to 2005 Annual Social and Economic Supplements.

The bureau also reported that 800,000 additional workers found themselves without health insurance in 2004. It places the total number of uninsured at 45.8 million, but that's a statistical anomaly. Medicaid, along with Medicare and VA healthcare benefits are tallied as government health insurance programs, but Medicaid is not an insurance program; it is a welfare program that was enacted along with Medicare (an insurance program) whose funding is shared between the federal government and the states. The program is under tremendous financial stress and was likely to suffer budget cuts as congress prepared to find as much as $10 billion in savings to meet the stipulations required by budget reconciliation in 2005. If the 37.5 million on Medicaid (a 1.9 million increase from 2003) were factored in, the total uninsured would be a staggering 83.3 million people. Almost a third of America has no health insurance. We'll discuss the social safety net in a subsequent chapter.

The administration and the Congressional majority seem oblivious to the growing income inequality. Instead they are determined to make it worse by expanding the tax cuts and making them permanent, leaving the resulting debt to the rest of us. Let's look at some of their tax proposals.

The estate tax: Median income families and the impoverished will never pay a dime of what the Bushies call the "death tax." Under current law in 2005, estate tax is paid by only the wealthiest 1 percent of Americans. The estate tax exemption is $1.5 million ($3 million for a couple), with a top tax rate of 47 percent. In 2009, the exemption will be increased to $3.5 million ($7 million a couple) and the top tax rate will be reduced to 45 percent). In 2010, under present law, the estate tax is eliminated. Without change, after 2010 it would be reinstated as it was in 2002: $1 million ($2 million a couple) at 55 percent. Bush wants to eliminate the tax permanently.

All the rhetoric about saving the family farm and the assets of small family-owned businesses is absolute nonsense. Current estate tax law already includes sizable special tax breaks for family businesses and farms.

A CBO study found that very few family-owned businesses and farms would be affected under the $3.5 million exemption level set to take effect in 2009. And they say repealing the tax after 2010 could cost more than $70 billion a year in today's dollars, resulting in spending cuts or a larger federal deficit.

In other words, everyone else in America will pay dearly for a few hundred extremely wealthy families to get wealthier. Killing the tax has been the goal of some of the nation's largest family businesses, including Wal-Mart, Mars candies and Campbell's Soup. President Bush, Vice President Cheney and 11 other cabinet members will personally benefit up to $344 million if the estate tax is eliminated.[125] Yes indeed—the leaders of our government these days are very rich.

I know my wife and I would be thrilled to death to have the worry of leaving more than a $7 million inheritance to our children. How about you?

Plus, it is a myth to think of estate tax as double taxation—it's simply not true. Only a small portion of large estates is earned income, which has been taxed, but the unrealized capital appreciation of houses, farms, stocks, bonds, and real estate has never been taxed. Consequently, if they aren't taxed as an estate transfer it represents an untaxed windfall.

In addition, those who claim the government should not be taking half (45 percent) of a person's lifetime savings are making a false assertion. After exemptions and other deductions, the average tax paid is about 17 percent.[126]

As with many things inflation has been a factor in the estate tax, and for the Alternative Minimum Tax (AMT) as well, which we will discuss next. The answer is that the exemption for payment needed to go up. It was $1 million in 2002, a hardship for some far less than wealthy families. We should retain the estate tax as it will be under current law in 2009, with a $3.5 million exemption and a top rate of 45 percent. More than $500 billion in revenue loss could be averted over the subsequent decade (2014 – 2023) by retaining the estate tax at that level. To do so we should be considering other PAYGO revenue options.

Alternative Minimum Tax (AMT): Legislation was introduced on May 23, 2005 by the chairman and ranking minority member of the Senate Finance Committee, the Senate majority leader, and four other Finance Committee members to repeal the individual AMT. The bill does not include measures to offset the cost of repeal. If the legislation passes, it will add nearly $1.2 trillion to deficits and the national debt over the next decade, assuming the 2001 and 2003 tax cuts are made permanent.[127] The following graph is from a June 2005 report from the Center on Budget and Policy Priorities.

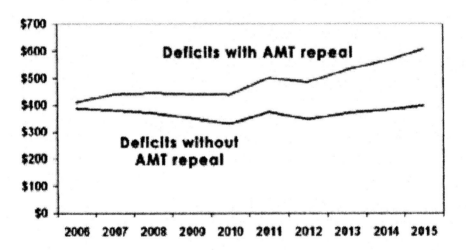

The AMT was enacted in 1969 to prevent a handful of super-rich Americans from taking advantage of tax laws to avoid paying taxes. Taxpayers who may be subject to AMT must calculate their tax liability under both the regular income tax and the AMT and pay the higher of the two amounts. The problem is that the AMT was never indexed for inflation, so that now it's hitting more and more middle and upper-middle class people.

Here's where it gets complicated with a hell of a lot of presidential and Congressional deceit involved. The president and Congress failed to rectify the looming problem with the AMT in crafting the $1.35 trillion tax cuts in 2001 because they wanted to maximize the size of the regular tax cuts. They literally built in a time bomb to get more tax cuts within the $1.35 trillion (the maximum allowed by the legislation) and they planned to come back in 2005 to get more AMT tax relief. What they did was provide AMT relief only through 2004 by increasing the exemption threshold, at a small cost of $14 billion—knowing that after 2004 the AMT revenue would mushroom and begin to restore a substantial portion of the 2001 tax—more than $292 billion.

So now these nut jobs are back at the trough, supported by many Democrats who are looking at the numbers and reelection. In 2005 only about 3.5 million taxpayers (fewer than 3 percent) will be affected by the AMT; by 2010 that number will grow to about 30 million, or 23 percent of all tax filers. By 2015 it will grow to over 40 million or a third of all taxpayers.

Interestingly, because of changes in the tax laws since the 1970s, the AMT no longer hits those with extremely high incomes. Because the top marginal rate under the regular income tax (which is 35 percent) significantly exceeds the highest tax rate under the AMT (which is 28 percent), CBO estimates that more than two-thirds of taxpayers with incomes greater than $500,000 will not be affected by the AMT. Their liability will be greater under the regular income tax.

The legislation introduced in May 2005 calls for repeal of the AMT, not reform. The CBO and the Joint Committee on Taxation estimate repeal would reduce federal revenues by $611 billion over the next ten years (2006-2015)—under current law, which means the tax cuts will sunset. If that revenue loss were not offset, the interest payments on the additional debt would total $179 billion over ten years, increasing the total cost of repeal to $790 billion.

With the extension of the president's 2001 and 2003 tax cuts, the additional revenue loss will be $343 billion over 10 years, bringing the total reduction in revenue resulting from AMT repeal to $954 billion. If the interest is added on to the debt, the cost of repeal climbs to $1.2 trillion over 10 years.

The best alternative is simply indexing the AMT for inflation from the income exclusion and other parameters that existed in 2004. That would greatly reduce the number of AMT taxpayers in 2010, by 82.5 percent overall. CBO estimates that if the AMT were indexed starting in 2007 revenues would be reduced by $385 billion in ten years, assuming the tax cuts are not extended. If they were extended, indexing would reduce revenues by about $630 billion over 10 years. Taking into account the increased interest payments, indexing would increase deficits by $758 billion over 10 years with the tax cuts extended—about $400 billion less than repeal would cost.

So America has serious budget choices to make. The Bush tax cuts have been extended when they should have been repealed. They are doing little or nothing to make the lives of the vast majority of people better, and the lost revenue is heaping huge amounts of debt upon us that darken our future. One way or the other it cannot go on, and we are in for a rough ride.

I think it is essential that the estate tax continue. We don't need vast inherited wealth in America; we need earned wealth. I don't want to live in a society that has only the very rich and the poor. I also feel the estate tax threshold should be higher than the $1.5 million that it is now and probably lower than it will be in 2009 at $3.5 million. And there should be an inflation index.

The AMT is particularly sensitive. It is a regressive flat tax that is no longer serving its purpose as inflation ensnares middle and upper middle-class families. Steve Forbes ran for president on a flat tax platform and enticed a lot of voters. Grover Norquist and his far-right pals consider the flat tax the crown jewel of tax reform. Don't buy it. America needs and should always have a progressive tax system—one in which those who have benefited from the collective wealth and energy of the nation pay their fair share.

Thirteen

A Nation in Hock

———◆•◆•———

On May 4, 2005 investor Warren Buffett gave a rare interview on CNN's "Lou Dobbs Tonight" show.[128] Buffett addressed a broad range of issues, including America's trade deficit. Here is some of the exchange.

Dobbs: You're investing—I think that's the correct way to put it—in currencies, not the dollar. The fact of the matter is, you have described what is happening in this context: tremendous deficits, rising debts as a result of budget deficits, trade deficit, those mounting debts that this country is taking on.

You are talking about something you refer to as a sharecropper society and economy. What does that mean to you, because to the rest of us, those are strong and powerful words for all of us but especially for those of us who are concerned about the middle class in this country, and who want this country to be all it is aspired to be.

Buffett: Well, if we keep doing what we're doing—and we have shown no signs of slowing down—the world will own a substantially greater percentage of this country or have our IOUs in the form of government bonds 10 years from now than now, and the cost of servicing the debt or the cost of paying dividends on the ownership will mean that we will send abroad a few percent of our GDP every year just to service the debts that arose from the over-consumption that has taken place currently. So, our sons will pay for the sins of their fathers, to a degree. Now, we'll always have a rich country. This is the best country in the world.

Sage words from Mr. Buffett. He had a couple of other gems worth sharing. In regard to a devalued dollar being a fix for the trade deficit, he said, "Well, I wrote an article 18 months ago in *Fortune* about import certificates. Just a change in the value of the dollar is probably not going to do much as we've seen in the last three years. I mean, the euro's gone from 85 cents to $1.29, and the dollar's fallen against many currencies, and the trade deficit keeps ballooning, so I think that we have to address it in some way that brings exports up and imports down and this import certificate idea would address that."[129]

In talking about the need to raise taxes, he said, "Yeah, The rich people are doing well in this country. I mean, we never had it so good."

"It's class warfare, my class is winning, but they shouldn't be."

He followed with comments about corporate America: "Well, right now corporate profits as a percentage of GDP in this country are right at the high. Corporate taxes as a percentage of total taxes raised are very close to the low historically. So, you know, corporate America is not suffering, I'll put it that way."

"I think that—you have seen companies be able to repatriate earnings with a very small tax that were taxed at very low rates abroad. Corporations are doing better in the total tax picture than the people I'm going to walk by on the street when I leave here."

The **current-account balance** measures the trade deficits or surpluses of a nation. The Bureau of Economic Analysis (BEA) defines it as: The net revenues that arise from a country's international sales and purchases of goods and services, plus net international transfers (public or private gifts or donations) and net factor income (primarily capital income from foreign property owned by residents of that country minus capital income from domestic property owned by nonresidents).

In other words, the balance of payments accounts is a record of all international transactions that are undertaken between residents of one country and residents of other countries during the same period of time.

The Balance on US Current Accounts is a record of all international transactions for both goods and services. Below is a chart and graph provided by the Global Policy Forum that shows the record from 1960. It is pretty sobering. When the data was charted, 2004's final numbers weren't available so the actual trade deficit was slightly different.

Balance on US Current Account: 1960-2004

Source: US Department of Commerce, Bureau of Economic Analysis

Balance on US Current Account: 1960-2004

Year	US$ Million	Year	US$ Million	Year	US$ Million
1960	2,824	1980	2,317	2000	-413,443
1961	3,822	1981	5,030	2001	-385,701
1962	3,387	1982	-5,536	2002	-473,944
1963	4,414	1983	-38,691	2003	-530,668
1964	6,823	1984	-94,344	2004*	-665,940
1965	5,431	1985	-118,155		
1966	3,031	1986	-147,177		
1967	2,583	1987	-160,655		
1968	611	1988	-121,153		
1969	399	1989	-99,486		
1970	2,331	1990	-78,968		
1971	-1,433	1991	3,747		
1972	-5,795	1992	-47,991		
1973	7,140	1993	-81,987		
1974	1,962	1994	-118,032		
1975	18,116	1995	-109,478		
1976	4,295	1996	-120,207		
1977	-14,335	1997	-135,979		
1978	-15,143	1998	-209,557		
1979	-285	1999	-296,822		

Source: US Department of Commerce, Bureau of Economic Analysis.

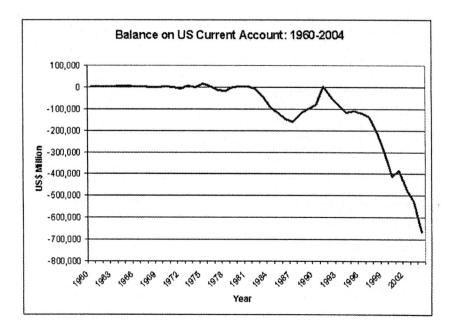

In 2004 the US imported $1,769 billion and exported $1,151 billion for a $618 billion deficit. As of June 2005 the deficit was $66 billion greater than 2004 for the same six-month period (Jan.-June). Due to the spiking price of imported oil alone it is highly probable that the 2005 trade deficit will be over $700 billion.

Amazing, but that's not the end of it; there would be the additional staggering costs of clean-up and rebuilding after Hurricane Katrina, which struck the Gulf Coast on August 29, 2005. Preliminary projections estimated the cost would be as much as $200 billion over the next few years ($62 billion was appropriated within weeks of the disaster).

Yet even that is just part of the equation. A large portion of the United States had been devastated (Louisiana and Mississippi were the hardest hit), shutting down production and putting a tremendous number of people out of work, which would cost the treasury untold numbers of tax dollars.

In agriculture alone Katrina damages were estimated to be over $2 billion, which would require billions in disaster relief programs, drive up the price of farm commodities and diminish our international trade position (grain is one of our chief exports).

Under existing tax law, the government had no alternative but to borrow money to cover the anticipated budget deficits. Some would come from the sale of bonds and T-bills to domestic buyers; a major amount would come from imported money (the sale of T-bills to foreign customers, thus increasing our trade deficit). We now owe the rest of the world over $3 trillion. Without a change in fiscal policy that number will grow to $10 trillion over the next 10 years. The interest on the debt will become our largest discretionary budget line item.

As discussed before, there is nothing wrong with incurring debt to deal with a crisis, and there is nothing wrong with using that revenue to invest in ourselves. That is what we should do. What's wrong is that the fiscal policies of those ruling our country have exacerbated the problem. Now we must heap needed debt on top of unneeded debt, wasted to give tax breaks to the top quintile of our nation's taxpayers.

The question that summer of 2005 was, when Congress reconvened in September 2005, would President Bush and the Republican leadership rethink their agenda of making the 2001-2003 tax-cuts permanent? Or further yet, given the magnitude of the growing budget deficit and aftermath of Katrina, would they do the responsible thing and immediately increase taxes? Not a chance.

Senator Judd Gregg (R-NH), powerful chairman of the Senate Budget Committee, had already announced that, despite the cost of Hurricane Katrina, the Republican leadership would continue to seek the permanent repeal of the estate tax. To cover the cost, they proposed cuts to social spending, including cutting Medicaid by $10 billion, reducing federal subsidies for student loans by $7 billion, and cuts to the food stamp program.

Democrats asked Gregg to delay the cuts in social spending, noting that the Katrina victims, many of whom were in or had been reduced to poverty, would need Medicaid for health care coverage, food stamps, student loans, and other assistance from the federal government. (Some of the heaviest cuts would be leveled upon the very area the storm ravaged.) Gregg rejected the call, telling Reuters that the cuts in social spending that would ostensibly hurt hurricane victims could actually benefit them. He gave as an example of his logic the cuts in Medicaid. The federal government and the states both administer the program to recipients. He reasoned that by cutting the federal allocation by $10 billion, the program would become easier to administer at the state level. This, he argued, would help the Katrina victims. That is the sort of "let them eat cake" logic that sparks revolutions.

President Bush showed how much he cared about workers in the South. On September 8, 2005 he issued an executive order allowing federal contractors rebuilding in the aftermath of Katrina to pay below the prevailing wage, thus exercising the "national emergency" provision of the 1931 Davis-Bacon Act, which requires federal contractors to pay at least the prevailing wages in the area where the work is conducted.

In terms of trade deficits, how times have changed. Balance of trade issues precipitated the American Revolution. Then, for a large part of our history, tariffs on imports were our chief source of tax revenue. Not so now. Due to open market agreements, our tariffs produce comparatively little revenue; in 2003 U.S. Customs collected $24 billion on imports of $1.5 trillion. Mind, I'm not suggesting that we close our borders with high tariffs. Most economists think that the Smoot-Hawley Act of 1930, which pretty much did close our borders with high tariffs, contributed to the length and depth of the Great Depression.

I am suggesting, as has Warren Buffett, that an element of fairness and reciprocity must be part of the deal—that there must be some limitations to totally open markets and free trade, and that those limitations can be far short of shutting markets down and still protect us. The United States participates in the General Agreement on Tariffs and Trade (GATT), the North American Trade Agreement (NAFTA), the recently enacted Central American Trade Agreement (CAFTA), and has at least 250 other trade agreements with various countries. Yet it would be difficult to say these agreements are working for us (although they are certainly working for multinational corporations) as we see jobs and our wealth flood overseas. Under NAFTA, what had once been a $1.7 billion trade surplus with Mexico, for example, was a $45 billion deficit as of early 2005. NAFTA has made a few Mexicans rich but, contrary to what most NAFTA boosters predicted, most Mexican workers are no better off. For some, pay and working conditions have worsened. The overall situation is not sustainable and somehow or the other the United States is going to have to do better or become a third-world country.

New tariffs would trigger retaliation from other nations and we would be back in a place where we don't want to be. So taking back some of the national sovereignty we gave over to multinational corporations under NAFTA and CAFTA may be a place to start. (As it stands, multinationals can demand huge compensatory payments from the federal government if local, state or federal laws, such as environmental restrictions, conflict with their profit expectations.) The trade agreements are a done deal, for now, but the United States could start reining in the corporations by outlawing offshore tax shelters and eliminating agricultural export subsidies, most of which benefit giant corporate farms.

Whatever the solutions, this country has to move away from the ongoing collusion with corporations (sharply intensified under the Bush administration) that is the hallmark of fascism.

Some say, among them many in the Bush administration, that the balance of payments is not a problem, that it reflects the willingness of the world to invest in the strength of the U.S. economy. To some extent that's true, but only to a point. When the U.S. balance of payments took a dip in the 1980s, it was characteristically different. Japan had developed highly competitive auto and electronics industries, and both Japan and the UK were investing in this country's physical assets such as hotels and real estate. They weren't bailing out our budget deficit by buying enormous amounts of T-bills as China is doing now.[130]

Incidentally, in 2004, according to the CIA's World Factbook, Japan had a $170 billion trade surplus, China a $30 billion surplus, and the UK had a deficit of $33 billion.

If we turn the clock back to the time of mercantilism, a trade surplus meant the nation acquired gold, and that enhanced the power of that nation to wage war. Of course now the most prized and necessary national commodity would probably be oil, but the link between wealth and the ability to wage war or to defend against an aggressor is still real. A nation flat on its back broke cannot defend itself.

My evil twin, the one who really likes Mel Brooks movies, can envision a scene he might play. The year might be 2012 or so, and the setting is the war room in communist China. A Chinese admiral is addressing a serious group of China's rulers and offering a solution to the troublesome problem of the U.S. Seventh Fleet patrolling the waters off Taiwan. He says, "Gentlemen, this has gone on long enough. America now owes us over $5 trillion and Americans are hooked on buying our stuff at Wal-Mart. Why don't we negotiate a deal for the fleet; we can easily afford to buy it, and how could Washington refuse?"

Silly, I know. But the truth is that capital does not have a nationality—it goes where profits can be made. If our government continues to give capital carte blanche authority over America's economic policies our nation is in peril. Nowhere is the disassociation between capital and state more apparent than with America's multinational corporations and the flood of outsourced American jobs.

Well-known writer-journalist Thomas Friedman has a book out that offers an extremely insightful prospective of globalization: *The World Is Flat, A Brief History Of The Twenty-First Century.*[131]

Friedman opens his book with a research visit to India. Here are a few lines from chapter one, "While I Was Sleeping."

No one ever gave me directions like this on a golf course before: "Aim at either Microsoft or IBM." I was standing on the first tee at the KGA Golf Club in downtown Bangalore, in southern India, when my playing partner pointed at two shiny glass-and-steel buildings off in the distance, just behind the first green. The Goldman Sacks building wasn't done yet; otherwise he could have pointed that out as well and made it a threesome. HP and Texas Instruments had their offices on the back nine, along the tenth hole. That wasn't all. The tee markers were from Epson, the printer company, and one of our caddies was wearing a hat from 3M. Outside, some of the traffic signs were also sponsored by Texas Instruments, and the Pizza Hut billboard on the way over showed a steaming pizza, under the headline "Gigabites of Taste!"

No, this definitely wasn't Kansas. It didn't even seem like India. Was this the New World, the Old World, or the Next World?

Friedman continued his research in China and Russia and reached the conclusion that the United States no longer has a competitive edge in world trade, that the playing field had been leveled—hence the title of his book. He postulates 10 forces that have flattened the world:

Flattener # 1 – The fall of the Berlin Wall on 11/9/89 "When the Walls Came Down and the Windows Went Up."

Flattener # 2 – The rise of the Internet. 8/9/95 "When Netscape Went Public."

Flattener # 3 - Work Flow Software "Let's Do Lunch: Have Your Application Talk to My Application."

Flattener # 4 – Open Sourcing "Self-Organizing Collaborative Communities."

Flattener # 5 – Outsourcing "Y2K"

Flattener # 6 – Offshoring "Running with Gazelles, Eating with the Lions."

Following is an African proverb that was translated into Mandarin and posted in an American auto parts factory in Beijing:

Every morning in Africa, a gazelle wakes up.
It knows it must run faster than the fastest lion or it will be killed.
Every morning a lion wakes up.
It knows it must outrun the slowest gazelle or it will starve to death.
It doesn't matter whether you are a lion or a gazelle.
When the sun comes up, you better start running.

Flattener # 7 – Supply-Chaining "Eating Sushi in Arkansas."

Flattener # 8 – Insourcing "What the Guys in Funny Brown shorts Are Really Doing."

Flattener # 9 – In-forming "Google, Yahoo! MSN Web Search"

Flattener # 10 – The Steroids "Digital, Mobil, Personal, and Virtual"

Friedman goes on to theorize that, although these flatteners have been around since the 1990s, they didn't have the internet/communications connectivity to truly have a global influence until the fall of the dot-coms. When the dot-coms were riding high, companies like WorldCom laid countless fiber-optic cables across the ocean floors, anticipating never ending growth in the dot-com businesses. Of course dot-com growth got stunted but the resulting cheap interconnectivity brought growth in other ways.

Multinational corporations are now able to link operations—in real time—all over the world. Outsourcing and offshoring are now no more complicated than building a facility across the road. The difference is that the price of labor is a whole lot cheaper in emerging countries now free to join a global economy.

The fall of the Soviet Union, the opening of communist China (China became a member of GATT in 2001), and India's open market policies have put a couple of billion very hungry people into the global labor force. But it will take generations before their purchasing power will make them major consumers of U.S. products and level the playing field for world trade.

In other words, they get the jobs; we get the bird.

India and China are also pumping tons of money into education. The locus of brainpower has shifted overseas. Their universities are new, are excellent, are focused on technology and business applications, and they are free. Only a small percentage of their huge populations qualify to attend—it's super competitive—but the numbers of students graduating now far outnumber graduates of our universities with similar high qualifications. Once out of school, Chinese and Indian graduates are more than willing to work for a tenth of the wages of U.S. workers; to them that represents giant upward mobility in a land where prices are low.

By comparison, the most recent international data, comparing students in the top 5 percent in terms of achievement, ranks the United States 23rd out of 29. It is pathetic.

One of the reasons we're getting left in the dust educationally is that the United States has yet to develop a coherent national education policy. "No Child Left Behind" is a political sop that has done little to ensure a uniform quality of education. The federal government has yet to put its money where its mouth is when it comes to education. If we are going to be able to compete in the world's markets, education must be a national priority, especially in science, math and engineering.

Instead, we have unfunded mandates that are crushing families with the highest property taxes in the world. Our universities are the most expensive in the world and, as we learned from Sen. Gregg, our Republican leaders were planning to cut the federal student loan program by at least $7 billion. It makes you proud to be an American.

There is another huge competitive disadvantage for American manufacturers—the cost of employee health insurance. All of the other countries that we are competing against have a national health-care system. We don't. Instead, we have made it a business cost that is no longer workable. Businesses are dropping employee insurance plans left and right—some choosing bankruptcy to get out from under their plans. Add to this company retirement plans that are underfunded and improperly regulated and you get some idea of the mess this country is really in. Once again Rome is burning while Nero fiddles.

I feel a certain empathy when Friedman speaks of the vast opportunities that have unfolded in recent years—opportunities that require relatively open markets and free trade to realize. It was uplifting to spend time in Germany as an international airline pilot in the late 1990s and to think of the hundreds of millions of people who had been given new freedoms. But that is still a work in progress. There is still a vast difference between the former Soviet block and Western Europe. I think the concept of the European Union is terrific, but it too is not without problems.

Let's be realistic. Russia is free from communism—great, now instead they have a capitalistic oligarchy with totalitarian tendencies. Communist China is now a member of GATT—great, but China is still a totalitarian nation with a huge population and a huge army.

The United States has been so badly led and so focused on the war in Iraq and terrorism that it seems we have forgotten what America stands for—and economic and social justice is part of that deal. Until we take back the moral high ground, the rest of the world isn't going to embrace us.

Our American way of life is in danger. We're not lions or gazelles, we are human beings with I think a higher calling than Social Darwinism.

And I must differ with Friedman: American workers do not have a level playing field. For them the world is not flat; it has been tilted uphill. We no longer have effective unions. The AFL-CIO has come apart at the seams with the Service Employees International Union (SEIU) and the Teamsters bolting the federation. Fewer than 12.5 percent of American workers belong to a union in any case. As this is written, the mechanics union for Northwest Airlines is on strike; the pilots, flight attendants and fellow workers are meekly crossing their picket lines. Not a peep from President Bush, although he had the power under the Railway Labor Act to end it and call for federal mediation. No way. The administration wanted the strike broken and labor rendered ineffective. That conforms to their ideology. (One result was that Northwest joined a long string of airlines seeking bankruptcy protection.)

So, friends, our Gross Domestic Product, Budget Deficit, the National Debt, the Trade Deficit, Globalization, Offshoring, Outsourcing, Downsizing and all the other capital letter issues come down to our values as a people. What do we want for our country? Our rulers will spin these numbers, and spin them and spin them. According to their propaganda, the tremendous cost of Katrina, a national disaster, will become a windfall, spiking our GDP; the national debt will be something for our grandchildren to worry about; Americans will just have work harder to lower the trade deficit; low wages and unemployment are only a problem for the lazy.

Until your turn comes.

Fourteen

The High Cost of Poor Government

———————◆•◆•◆———————

The Bush Paradox

With politics, the Bush administration has shown remarkable discipline… No recent president has got re-elected with controlling majorities in both houses of Congress, or been as successful in repositioning the national debate around his ideological view of the world.

With governing, it's been almost criminally incompetent…not since the hapless administration of Warren G. Harding has there been one as stunningly inept as this one.

The easy answer to the paradox is that Bush cares about winning elections and putting his ideological stamp on the nation, but doesn't give a hoot about governing the place. But that's no explanation because the two are so obviously connected. An administration can't impose a lasting stamp without being managed well, and a president's party can't keep winning elections if the public thinks it's composed of bumbling idiots.

Excerpts from "Bush Administration Paradox Explained," by Robert Reich[132]

I wasn't surprised that the Federal Emergency Management Agency bungled Hurricane Katrina in August 2005. Nor would I be shocked at the Bush administration using what was expected to be over $200 billion (of borrowed money) for rebuilding in the wake of Katrina to advance its conservative agenda and feather friendly corporate nests. It was an opportunity for the Bushies to proffer more tax cuts, privatize and deregulate as an emergency prerogative. They would continue to bungle and cast off responsibility because they didn't believe in government; they were running the country on the basis of political patronage and cronyism. We simply experienced the predictable result.

And sad performances would not be limited to FEMA. Look at the leadership of the Department of Homeland Security itself. What exactly was the department doing to protect us from terrorists?

The Environmental Protection Agency should have had a key role in Katrina's aftermath, yet the agency had lost most of its senior officials, who left in protest against the Bush administration's unwillingness to enforce environmental law and its attempts to rollback environmental gains.

At the Department of Housing and Urban Development, Bush had left seven top jobs vacant. Instead, he offered substandard wages and easing of affirmative action regulations. His answer to the impoverished victims Katrina left homeless along the Gulf Coast was a housing lottery that at best would only help a handful of the needy.

Then there is the Food and Drug Administration's cozy relationship with the drug companies, and Secretary John Snow at the Treasury Department.[133] Snow wasn't picked for his qualifications; he was picked for his political loyalty. The best and the most talented have left the treasury. A 22-year veteran economist told the *Washington Post* back in 2002 why he was leaving the department: "There is no policy…if there are no pipes, why do you need a plumber?"[134]

In a carefully worded statement on September 13, 2005, President Bush accepted responsibility for the Katrina fiasco "to the extent that the federal government didn't fully do its job right." What did he mean? He didn't acknowledge that the federal government has a responsibility to protect and assist cities and states against major disasters, such as hurricanes, floods, or international terrorism. Nor did he apologize for staffing FEMA with inexperienced political hacks. In his carefully choreographed address from New Orleans on September 15, 2005, standing before a Disney like backdrop, he spoke of distributing huge amounts of money but made no mention of how we were going to pay for it.

From the White House the next day, Bush again spoke of spending plans to rebuild, saying we'll do whatever it takes—and not raise taxes. We'll have to cut unnecessary spending, he intoned. The cuts, to the tune of $500 billion over 10 years, to come from social programs that those impoverished displaced people in the devastated areas need most. The Republicans were calling it "operation offset." It was their latest plan to annihilate America's social safety net.[135] The largest proposed cuts are targeted at Medicaid, "the health care safety net for low-income children, elderly, disabled, pregnant women and parents." The plan cuts $225 billion by converting the federal share of certain Medicaid payments into a block grant, and $8 billion more by increasing the federal Medicaid co-payments.[136]

By September 25th the FEMA-managed disaster relief fund had already allocated $15.8 billion of the $62.3 billion appropriated by Congress (to that date), of which $11.6 billion had been committed through contracts, direct aid to individuals or work performed by government agencies. More than 80 percent of the $1.5 billion in FEMA contracts were awarded without bidding or with limited competition.[137] The largest contract ($568 million) went to AshBritt, a Florida company with ties to Mississippi's Republican governor, Haley Barbour. Other contracts went to the Shaw Group and Kellogg, Brown & Root, a subsidiary of Halliburton. Lobbyist Joe Allbaugh, Bush's former campaign manager and a former leader of FEMA, had represented both companies. It seems it pays well to have friends in Washington.

Here is an astute overseas observation in the aftermath of Hurricane Katrina by Janadas Devan, a *Straits Times* (Singapore) columnist, as he tried to explain to his Asian readers how the United States is changing.[138] "Today's conservatives," he wrote, "differ in one crucial aspect from yesterday's conservatives: the latter believed in small government, but believed, too, that a country ought to pay for all the government that it needed.

"The former believe in no government, and therefore conclude that there is no need for a country to pay for even the government that is does have… [But] it is not only government that doesn't show up either, government is starved of resources and leached of all its meaning. Community doesn't show up either, sacrifice doesn't show up, pulling together doesn't show up, 'we're all in this together' doesn't show up."

Again, welcome to America in 2005.

On September 14, 2005, the day before Bush gave his speech in New Orleans, both Delta Airlines and Northwest Airlines, two of the nation's largest carriers, filed for bankruptcy. They joined United Airlines and US Airways (already operating in bankruptcy), putting almost half of U.S. airline capacity in Chapter 11. Incredibly, Bush didn't mention the bankruptcies in his New Orleans speech or the following day from the White House, nor had his administration uttered a single word about this national disgrace. Yet, despite their silence, it is a monumentally serious matter that endangers one of our nation's major transportation systems, and directly affects almost 200,000 American workers, many more indirectly. It is again a failure in leadership that is being swept under the rug. Our federal government accepts responsibility for none of it.

It would be easy to attribute the airlines' financial woes to 9/11/2001, the spiking cost of jet fuel or even to Katrina. The Air Transport Association estimates that from 2001 through 2004, the industry posted net losses of $32.3 billion; losses of $10 billion are expected in 2005. That is an easy explanation, but it misses the whole truth by a generation.

The airline industry collapse was the direct result of the financial chaos brought about by deregulation. The national mania to deregulate began with the Airline Deregulation Act of 1978; it led in varying degrees to deregulation of banking, trucking, railroads, buses, telephones, cable TV, stock exchange brokerage, and now electricity.

I believe the reason President Jimmy Carter and Senator Ted Kennedy (both of whom I hold in high esteem—but not on this) bought into airline deregulation in 1978 was the lure of cheaper airfares everyone thought would result from open market competition. It is the common thread throughout the deregulation/government privatization argument. Back then the airlines were re-equipping with expensive jet aircraft, the price of jet fuel had escalated sharply, and inflation was rampant. The Civil Aeronautics Board (CAB) awarded all airline routes and set prices. The board (or it's predecessor, the CAA) had regulated the industry since the 1930s, and many felt it had turned into a "good ole boys club" favoring the established airlines and stifling competition. To a large extent that was true; the CAB needed to be reformed. What happened, though, was an immoderate turn to the extreme opposite.

It started in 1975 with Senator Kennedy's congressional subcommittee hearings in regard to federal oversight of the airline industry. Alfred Kahn, a professor emeritus of political economy at Cornell University and a leading figure on the issue at the time, joined by other open-marketers, pushed hard for deregulation. (Kahn served briefly as chairman of the CAB in 1977.) The hearings ultimately resulted in legislation and the Airline Deregulation Act.

Sure we got cheaper fares and a gaggle of no-frills, cut-rate airlines— for a while—but it was at the expense of a stable public transportation industry. Since 1978, one hundred airlines have gone bankrupt. The vast majority of them were liquidated. Airlines such as TWA, Pan American, Eastern, Braniff, People's Express, and a host of others simply went down the drain, taking many working families along with them. And the destruction goes on today. Was it worth it? I don't think so. America needs a better-regulated airline industry, not an unregulated industry. It simply doesn't work.

I was an airline pilot from 1959 until 1997 and I witnessed the carnage of broken families and shattered careers.[139] For a time in the 1990s airline mergers and the vastly increased productivity of wide-body jet aircraft offered a glimmer of hope and profitability. I personally benefited from that short period of time by flying wide-body aircraft overseas. It didn't last long, however, before low cost airlines paying cheap wages flooded the market with seats. Many of the seats were on brand new (consequently low maintanence) aircraft, supplied by the aircraft industry—many from Air Bus Industries, a European, government-supported manufacturer.

It is of interest to note that during the industry's formative years aircraft manufacturers were joined at the hip with the airlines by stock holding companies. It was antitrust laws that forced the manufacturers to divest of airline ownership. Now apparently the manufacturers have found a way around it by deals (leases and sales) that allow them to suck the money out of the airlines while accepting none of the responsibilities of ownership. When an airline fails, the manufacturer, as a secured creditor, simply takes the aircraft back and leases or sells it again. Needless to say there are all sorts of tax incentives to match the process.

Today's airline fares are a crapshoot; rarely are any two seats sold for the same price on the same flight. Sure you can get cheap fares if you're able to plan months ahead, and travel during high tide or various unknown phases of the moon. If you need to go somewhere tomorrow, the price is astronomical—corrected for inflation, the highest in history. Meals are a thing of the past; service stinks; seats are unbearably cramped and passengers are herded around airline terminals like sheep. It's no longer much fun to travel by air.

A lack of sound public policy, which is the responsibility of government, is killing the airline industry. For instance, there wasn't an airline pilot in the world who didn't realize that an incident similar to 9/11 could occur. As an international captain, I received frequent FBI briefings as to the threat level—everyone knew. Unfortunately, in the years before 9/11 our Republican friends in Congress were busy distracting government with the impeachment of President Clinton; nobody was paying attention. Nor did anyone in the industry have the courage to spotlight the deficiencies of domestic airline security. The fix would cost the airlines money and inconvenience passengers. As it worked out, the cost of neglect was far higher.

The financial ramifications of 9/11 on the airlines required real government intervention—not the unaffordable, inadequate government loans that the Bushies came up with. The airlines needed a true emergency response and they got the FEMA treatment.

The price of crude oil, and consequently of jet fuel, may fluctuate but it is not going to go down to earlier levels. Yet the United States flatly refuses to recognize that major industries, including the airlines, are in danger. If we hope to have a functional airline industry we need price controls and must stop overcapacity. The only other (socially regressive) solution is to stop the pretense of antitrust and allow megaindustries to emerge with no competition. That is essentially what's happening now in other industries with globalization—international megacorporations feeding off of cheap labor. Let's not kid ourselves; it is the ultimate end game of a laissez-faire, unregulated economy.

The other driving forces in airline bankruptcies are underfunded defined pension plans and the escalating cost of employee health insurance. Under our present bankruptcy laws, companies are allowed to default on those plans when reorganizing under Chapter 11. The liability is then turned over to a federal agency called the Pension Benefit Guaranty Corp (PBGC).[140] In 2005, the fund already faced a $23 billion dollar gap in what it takes in through corporate premiums and what it has promised to pay retirees. If Delta and Northwest default on their pension plans, as have US Airways and United Airlines under Chapter 11, the gap could widen by as much as $12 billion.

The head of the Congressional Budget Office told Congress in June 2005 that the fund would need a fivefold increase of premiums companies pay into the fund to meet its projected $71 billion deficit over the next decade. While the PBGC receives no direct public tax money, the guarantor is the U.S. Treasury.[141] The relationship is much like that of the Federal Deposit Insurance Corporation (FDIC). And the need for a federal bailout in the future is almost a certainty.

The first round of corporate dumping of pension plans was with the collapse of the steel industry in the mid-1970s. Between 1975 and 2002 the PBGC has paid $9.4 billion in claims to retired steel workers.

Although covered by the PBGC, higher wage, professional employees get hammered. The fund will pay only up to $45,614 if you retire at 65. Pilots are required by federal air regulations to retire at 60, thus lowering the maximum coverage considerably. I have former colleagues at US Airways, retired after many years of service, who have seen their benefit cut by a third or more by the PBGC. I was lucky. I was able to take a lump sum payout when I retired in 1997 (after 37 years of service). Consequently, I had no connection with the airline's pension plan when it went bankrupt.

US Airways was also allowed in bankruptcy to cancel life insurance coverage, which was part of our retirement package, and health insurance (Medicare supplemental). Those still working have seen their health insurance plans emasculated by higher employee premiums and fewer benefits.

Health insurance costs have steadily outpaced inflation and wages, and for industries with a large number of employees, such as the airlines and auto manufacturers, the additional cost has become a major burden. In 2005, the average premium for a family hit $10,880, with employers paying an average 74 percent of that cost and the workers paying the rest.

Many in the financial world fear that auto manufacturers will be next in corporate bankruptcies following the airlines. Whatever it takes to get out from under their pension and health plans. On the world market, American manufacturers are competing with industrial nations that have national health plans and that is a giant competitive advantage.

In June 2005, General Motors Corporation, which employs about 150,000 workers, announced it planned to cut 25,000 jobs and close an unspecified number of plants in the United States over the next three-and-a-half years. At GM the average cost of providing health care and pension benefits is around $1,360 a car. Both GM and Ford were locked in difficult cost cutting negotiations with the United Auto Workers over reducing retirement and health care costs.

Is anyone in Washington paying attention? I think not.

Deregulated industries all share similar characteristics: labor is devalued and wages stagnate or go down; prices go down for a while (setting the hook) then escalate as big players stifle or eliminate competition; many times customers and stockholders are exposed to fraud, and invariably services deteriorate.

Much to my chagrin, President Jimmy Carter, a Democrat, turned out to be a deregulation dynamo. Besides the Airline Deregulation Act of 1978, he supported and signed into law legislation that greatly loosened controls on banking, trucking, and the railroads. Mind, all those were in trouble and in need of regulatory modernization to match the times. But Carter, an extremely ethical, honest Washington outsider from Georgia, got taken to the cleaners by special interests.

Banking. On March 31, 1980, President Carter signed into law the Institutions Deregulation and Monetary Control Act of 1980. The Monetary Control Act has nine Titles, which collectively took the lid off banking in the United States. It changed reporting requirements to the Federal Reserve Board, reserve requirements, eliminated interest rate ceilings, permitted banks of all sorts to market checking accounts, eliminated state usury ceilings, and loosened up foreign investment in U.S. institutions.

Prior to the act, the Savings & Loans (also called thrifts) served as the major vehicle for home mortgages, with deposits secured by the FDIC. The S&Ls collected deposits, paid interest and loaned the money out in 20 to 30 year mortgages to finance homes. Because the interest paid was lower than the interest charged, the S&Ls made money. Commercial banks, on the other hand, were restricted by the Federal Reserve Board to pay 3 percent or less on deposits. The S&Ls were not restricted and paid 1-and-a-half to 2 percent more to attract funds, and charged 2-and-a-half to 3 percent more on mortgages, which generated a comfortable profit.

After 1980 it was a whole new ball game. The S&Ls, suffering from holding long-term, low-interest mortgages, were now in competition with commercial banks for deposits. At the same time, the Monetary Control Act eliminated state usury interest rate ceiling on mortgages, and permitted the S&Ls to grow and branch out from just serving local communities. Federal deposit insurance was also increased to $100,000, doubling the exposure of bank failures for the FDIC. Between 1982 and 1985, under the Reagan administration, the S&Ls tripled in size and mortgage interest rates went through the roof, topping 18 percent.

It was wild, and unsustainable and spawned wheeling and dealing of massive proportions. Figures such as Charles Keating were caught feeding campaign contributions of $1.3 million (collectively) to the famous "Keating Five" U.S. senators. Keating went to jail. The senators offered up a mea culpa and carried on in the fine tradition of legislative excellence. (Arizonan John McCain was the only Republican involved. But he was absolved of any involvement in the influence peddling scheme, as was John Glenn of Ohio. The other senators named but not absolved were Dennis DeConcini, D-AZ, Alan Cranston, D-CA and Donald Riegle, D-MI.)

Another factor that buried the S&Ls was the huge change in the income tax law Congress passed in 1986. Before the tax law change, taxable income from any source could be offset by any business loss, including investment real estate. The new IRS code specified that only at-risk income for the investment could be written off—not income from other sources, such as salary. As a result, condos, secondary homes, and real estate speculation crumbled.

Reagan did his part to assure a financial meltdown by reducing the Bank Board's regulatory and supervisory staff. A starting examiner was paid only $14,000 a year and the average experience on the job was two years. It seems that Bush the younger and Reagan had much in common when it comes to not taking governing seriously.

By the time Reagan left and Bush the elder entered office, Bush faced a disaster as hundreds of S&Ls became insolvent. One of his first acts was to propose a $126 billion bailout to cover insured depositors. It would ultimately cost American taxpayers over $90 billion after seized assets were liquidated (about $140 billion in 2005 dollars).

There were other costs that cannot be calculated: lost jobs and careers, the unproductive loss of capital and the diversion of savings into excess overbuilding of office space, inflated prices paid for real estate, and loans on wastelands. America had been successfully swindled.

More than 500 S&Ls failed in the fiasco.

One has to wonder how exposed America is today to another banking crisis driven by low interest mortgage loans on over-inflated real estate prices. We've spoken about the Chinese holding down U.S. interest rates, but there are other modern banking practices at play also.

Because of the housing boom, lenders were competing by offering all kinds of risky loans with low payments to desperate homebuyers. There are interest-only, option-payment, 40-year fixed, piggyback loan, low-doc loan; all are have the same goal: to help you afford an expensive home by letting you put off paying down your mortgage.[142]

There is considerable risk to these weird mortgages. If you are a buyer, the risk is that you won't be able to afford the loan payments in a few years. But even for the 75 percent of borrowers with fixed-rate loans, or the lucky 35 percent of homeowners with no mortgages, this bizarre loan lunacy poses a risk to your home's value. That's because the rash of nontraditional loans has encouraged real estate speculation and has driven up prices. This will intensify the crash if prices soften and homes are worth less than their mortgages.

Sales of existing homes were at record levels, reaching an annual rate of 7.35 million in June 2005.

Are portions of the banking industry exposed to failure? If interest rates rise and property values fall, who's left holding the bag when homeowners default on their loans? Is the Federal Reserve concerned? Is anyone in the Bush administration concerned? You know the answer to that.

There are a few other aspects of bank deregulation one should think about when judging its success or shortcomings:

Banks no longer employ large numbers of workers; they've been dramatically cut due to technology and ATMs. Great. But don't plan on a career in banking. In some areas bank tellers are as scarce as hens' teeth. You have to deal with electronic machines, which is not quite the same thing as dealing with a live human being.

Forget about savings accounts. Banks no longer pay reasonable interest on deposits so there is little reason not to keep your money under the mattress. Yet our financial wizards whine that people aren't saving. Aside from the fact that Americans living on frozen wages have little money to save, why would they use a bank, which pays practically nothing compared to the cost of inflation?

Credit card interest rates and bank fees are so outrageously high they border on usury. Of course usury isn't prohibited any longer as far as banks are concerned. A bill paid one day late incurs outrageous fees, usually $35 or more, no matter what the balance on the account. Although banks cry over credit card defaults, they must be doing well with them; they mail them indiscriminately and frequently to just about anyone, regardless of their credit history.

As for me, I'm concerned about our banks and financial institutions. I'm beginning to feel that there is nobody in charge, not the Treasury Department, and not the Federal Reserve. It's pretty depressing. Whoops, that's perhaps the wrong word to use.

Here are a few tidbits about other deregulated public service industries. As we learned earlier in the book, by the 1880s the "robber barons" had a stranglehold on interstate commerce through ownership of the nation's railroads. To establish control, the federal government created the Interstate Commerce Commission (ICC) in 1887, which was signed into law by President Grover Cleveland. The ICC regulated the railroads, and trucking (when trucks came into being), and even interstate telephone service between 1910 and 1934. In 1934 this authority was transferred to the Federal Communications Commission.

By the late 1960s the ICC was under criticism for strangling both the railroad and trucking industries, which led to a string of congressional actions in the 1970s and 1980s to reduce its powers. By 1995, with most of the ICC's powers already eliminated, the agency was abolished, transferring what powers remained to the Surface Transportation Board.

Railroads. The National Passenger Corporation (known as Amtrak) provides America's limited intercity passenger rail service to about 500 stations.[143] Although Amtrak was established by the federal government as a private, for-profit company, it has needed and received federal subsidies every year since it began providing service in 1971. In 2003 Amtrak received over $1 billion.[144] Amtrak's authorization expired in 2002 but the company limps along, year to year, kept afloat by additional congressional appropriations.

Prior to the formation of Amtrak, railroads provided both passenger and freight service. As air service captured the long distance market and the interstate road system provided an easy alternative to short and medium distance markets in the 1960s, the railroads began hemorrhaging money. The creation of Amtrak was essentially a federal bailout for the railroads, relieving them of an unprofitable segment of their business.

Local commuter rail service (some provided by Amtrak) is active in some places, such as the New York City area, but on the whole Americans go to work by car, cars that guzzle precious gasoline.

On the other hand, according to the Association of American Railroads, U.S. freight railroads are the world's busiest, moving more freight than any rail system in any other country. In fact, U.S. railroads move more than four times as much freight than all of Western Europe's freight railroads combined. (A significant portion of that tonnage is in coal, used to fire electric power plants.)

I think if the government doesn't simply let Amtrak go belly up as part of "operation-offset," the railroad will be forced to eliminate long distance service altogether and concentrate on the Northeast corridor and some other high-density commuter routes.

One way or the other, our nation is in trouble; we have equated deregulation with lack of governance. That is wrong and it is not working. Amtrak, our national passenger railroad, is broke, our airlines are bankrupt, and the family car is running on empty. Hello...

Trucking. America moves a lot of stuff by truck, unburdened by many interstate trucking regulations or expensive union contracts. Prior to deregulation, long-haul truck driving was a respected, well paying job. Now it's a fight against long hours, poor rest and low wages. Truck drivers used to be the pros of the road; some still are, but many are involved in way too many accidents. Our interstate highways are often lined with trucks rushing goods to markets that no longer carry inventories; it's the modern rapid distribution system. But who's really paying for it? What's going to happen when the cost of fuel drives the CPI through the roof? How many independent truck drivers will be forced out of business? Maybe America has to ship less and value truck drivers (and airline pilots) more.

Telephones. I bet no more than a handful of people can interpret today's phone bill or truly know anymore who provides all of the aspects of their telephone service. There is tremendous overlap. It seems everybody is capable of providing the same services—local, long distance, Internet access, wireless…. The list goes on and on. But don't try to get someone to come into your house to install or fix your phone; nobody does that any longer. On the plus side, there is no question that long distance phone rates are far lower than they were before the breakup of AT&T in the mid-1980s. As far as wireless service and high speed Internet access go, most Americans in rural areas would be better off in Japan, China or Finland.

Broadcast and Cable TV. There used to be just a few national broadcast networks, such as CBS, NBC and ABC, and lots of local, independently owned stations. Now the broadcast networks, cable TV, radio, movie production, and just about anything communicative is in the hands of four giant corporations: AOL Time Warner, Viacom, Walt Disney, and News corp. It is a dangerous concentration of power that all Americans should be extremely concerned about. Those giants control our news and influence our values.

The independence of public broadcasting is in danger too. The Corporation for Public Broadcasting (CPB) is a congressional chartered agency that passes federal money to hundreds of public TV and radio stations. National Public Radio (NPR) and the Public Broadcasting Service (PBS) depend on the federal support of those stations for about 15 percent of their revenue. House Republicans proposed on September 20, 2005, as part of Operation Offset to eliminate federal funding for CPB. The GOP said that zeroing out CPB would save $400 million in 2006 and $5.5 billion over the next 10 years.

In June 2005, CPB appointed Patricia Harrison, a former co-chairwomen of the Republican National Committee, as its next president and chief executive. It was an obvious Republican attempt to deal with what conservatives call a left-wing bias in the nation's public television and radio stations. Kenneth Tomlinson, chairman of the board of CPB, has revealed that he paid $14,170 in taxpayer funds to a researcher from a conservative organization who monitors the "Now" program with Bill Moyers for "political objectivity." The CPB board reportedly did not know about the payment.

At this point it wouldn't take much of an imagination to envision future generations of Americans huddled around illegal short-wave radios, trying to get the news from parts of the remaining free world—the part where elected governments still rule and not megacorporations.

The New York Times
October 1, 2005

WASHINGTON, Sept. 30 – Federal auditors said on Friday that the Bush administration violated the law by buying favorable news coverage of President Bush's education policies, by making payments to the conservative commentator Armstrong Williams and by hiring a public relations company to analysis media perceptions of the Republican Party.

In a blistering report, the investigators, from the Government Accountability Office, said the administration had disseminated "covert propaganda" in the <u>United States</u>, in violation of a statutory ban...

Electricity. Prior to 1996, the generation, distribution and sale of electricity was virtually a monopoly. Some communities and electric cooperatives purchased some or all of the electricity but used their own power lines, which they maintained, and sold the electricity to each customer. By the 1990s the cost of electricity was zooming and some looked to the deregulation of the airlines, banking and telecommunications as example to follow. (The continuation of deregulation mania.) The idea was to purchase power from "competing" generating plants over the interlocking electric power line grid.

In 1996, California launched electric deregulation by allowing power utilities to compete for customers within and across its borders. By 2000,

23 states and the District of Columbia had rushed down the path of electricity deregulation. My home state of New Hampshire was one of them; earlier in the book, I noted that I played a very minor role in encouraging that to occur.

It has worked reasonably well in New Hampshire, but nationwide residential consumers have found little reason to switch to new power providers, and promises of lower prices and a reliable electricity infrastructure have failed to materialize. The California energy crisis of 2000-2001, the financial scandals of energy giant Enron, and the massive Northeastern blackout in August 2003 have convinced many policymakers, consumers and even some power companies that electric generation competition isn't the answer.

Deregulation spurred massive rate hikes when Houston-based Enron, an energy trading company, manipulated California's energy market.[145] The power grid is sensitive to distribution overloads, and dependant on the purchase of "spot" generation. Huge coal fired and nuclear generators feed the normal running pool of power but depend upon smaller oil-fired generators to handle peak overloads—thus the system was easily manipulated. The scoundrels at Enron manufactured the need, then charged top dollar to fill it. Essentially deregulation enabled Enron to defraud its customers, stockholders, and employees.

That said, America's need for reliable electric power continues to grow and our system is extremely tenuous. In my judgment, the energy bill of 2005 comes up far short of cutting the mustard.

Special Interest Laws & Regulations – the rottenest legislation money can buy.

The 2005 bankruptcy reform bill (the Orwellian-sounding "Bankruptcy Abuse Prevention and Consumer Protection Act of 2005,"), which became effective October 17, 2005, made it much harder for families in distress to write off their debts and make a fresh start. Instead, many debtors will find themselves on an endless treadmill of payments.

Under the old law, individuals usually filed for bankruptcy under Chapter 7 or Chapter 13. In a Chapter 7 bankruptcy, your assets (minus those exempted by your state[146]) are liquidated and given to creditors, and many of your remaining debts are cancelled, giving you a "fresh start."

In 2004, over 1.1 million people filed for Chapter 7, the vast majority the result of severe misfortune—not a deliberate attempt to circumvent debt. Studies have found that half of bankruptcies were the result of medical emergencies, the rest overwhelmingly the result of either job loss or divorce.

Prior to the new law, it was up to the court to determine if you qualified for Chapter 7 bankruptcy. Now the court has very little discretion. Your income is subject to a two-part means test. First, to a formula that exempts certain expenses (such as rent and food) to determine if you can afford to pay 25 percent of your "non-priority unsecured debt," such as your credit card bills. Second, your income is compared to your state's median income. You are not allowed to file for Chapter 7 if your income is above the state's median and you can afford to pay 25 percent of your unsecured debt. Instead you may be allowed to file for Chapter 13.

Under the new rules for Chapter 13, the court must apply living standards derived by the IRS to determine what is reasonable to pay for rent, food and other expenses to compute how much of your debts you have to pay.

Thanks to our far-right friends, and some Democrats fond of large campaign contributions, the only "fresh starts" are now for the very rich, who retain many mechanisms that allow bankruptcy to be used as a financial tool.[147] The rest of America is now being forced into what Paul Krugman has called a "Debt-Peonage Society."[148] Are debtor prisons far behind? (Prisons are now a growth industry in America.)

This terrible law now welcomes home our returning troops from Iraq, a large number of whom will have lost their jobs and careers because they were pressed into extended service, and greets the tens of thousands of people who lost their homes and everything in Hurricane Katrina. No fresh start for them if needed.

Bank, credit card companies and retailers had pushed hard for this legislation since 1997. You would think they were hurting. Not quite. In 2004, the credit card industry took in $30 billion in profits. All that high interest, nonexistent repayment schedules, and ridiculously high fees pay off pretty well. Oh, and if those defaults really hurt them, it is unlikely that they would be sending out tons of credit cards to everyone with a mailing address, regardless of their credit rating. Defaults are just part of the cost of doing business.

The new law is a nice gift to the credit card industry, though; it stands to receive $1 billion or more from repayment plans due to the expected increase in Chapter 13 filings.

The change is also a trip-wire for lawyers. Under the new law, if information about a client's case is found to be inaccurate, the bankruptcy attorney may be subject to various fees and fines.

Following is a brief note to me about the law from a good friend and leading New Hampshire bankruptcy attorney, whom I asked for an opinion. He'll remain unnamed out of respect for his legal practice.

Jerry,

It took 8 years to get this law passed. It in effect puts a lot of lawyers out of business, because the lawyer has to certify to the accuracy of all of the debtors financial affairs.

The malpractice insurance premiums are being increased and in some situations the insurance company is refusing to insure any lawyer doing bankruptcy.

There's a lot more...it will take more than 8 years and a new administration to correct this.

Well again we shouldn't be surprised. It is no secret that the far right feeds off the banking and insurance industry and has little use for lawyers or other professionals.

Class-action lawsuit bill. On February 18, 2005, President Bush signed into law a class-action bill that sharply limits the ability of people to file class-action lawsuits against companies.[149]

The measure has been attacked by civil rights organizations, labor groups, consumer organizations and many state prosecutors and environmental groups, who say it would sharply curtail important cases and provide new protections for unscrupulous companies. Many federal and state judges and state lawmakers have also criticized the bill, saying it will strip states of an important role in judging such contests and could add a considerable number of cases to badly burdened federal dockets.[150]

Mr. Bush, on the other hand, had this to say:

"Our country depends on a fair legal system that protects people who have been harmed without encouraging junk lawsuits that undermine confidence in our courts while hurting our economy, costing jobs and threatening small businesses.

"The class-action bill is a strong step forward in our efforts to reform the litigation system and keep America the best place in the world to do business."

"This bill is one of the most unfair, anti-consumer proposals to come before the Senate in years," said Sen. Harry Reid of Nevada, the minority leader. "It slams the courthouse doors on a wide range of injured plaintiffs. It turns federalism upside down by preventing state courts from hearing state law claims. And it limits corporate accountability at a time of rampant corporate scandals."

Well, for all that I'm sure Bush had no pangs of conscience signing the bill into law. It is a giveaway to large manufactures and the insurance industry—small businesses have never been involved with class-action lawsuits. But automakers, drug companies, and environmental polluters have now been given a pass.

The far right doesn't want justice for all; it wants justice for the select few.

Medical Malpractice Tort Reform will be the next shoe to fall if Bush has his way. Prompted by the insurance industry, the far right claims that the high cost of medical malpractice insurance is the result "junk lawsuits" and "jackpot justice" (high jury awards). And once again it is not true.

Studies by both the federal government and insurance organizations show an average annual rate increase over the last decade (1990-2000) of about 3 percent, adjusted for inflation. Rates skyrocketed in 2002 when the stock market turned sour. Insurance companies make money by investing premiums, not off the premiums themselves. They simply began doubling and tripling the insurance rates for doctors to cover their investment losses. Other types of insurances went up as well.

What we really need to reform is the insurance industry. I think we will be getting a wakeup call when the price of homeowner's insurance skyrockets in the wake of Katrina. Guess who will be paying to replace those expensive homes at the water's edge. We all will.

Republicans have proposed federal legislation that would dismantle state judicial authority and preempt all existing state laws governing medical malpractice lawsuits with the following:[151]

- Caps on non-economic (pain and suffering) damages at $250,000;
- A 3-year statute of limitations to initiate lawsuits, or one year from discovery; statute of limitations for children until age 8;
- Limits on attorneys fees whether in settlement or judgment;
- Collateral source benefits may be introduced into evidence in court;
- Periodic payments are ordered for future damages exceeding $50,000;
- Standard guidelines for awarding punitive damages (clear and convincing evidence);
- Prohibitions on instructing a jury about any limitations to damage awards;
- Punitive damages may not be awarded against the manufacturer or distributor of a medical product approved by the Food and Drug Administration;
- A specific statement that the provisions would preempt all state laws not in conformance with the standards presented.

The proposed legislation is unbelievable. It infringes on the prerogatives of state legislatures, sets the value of human life at a paltry $250,000— except for income loss for the wealthy. If passed it will be nothing more than a windfall for the insurance industry.

In 2004, claims against doctors and other medical professionals actually dropped 8.9 percent, to $4.6 billion. All the data shows that jury awards are not out of control; in fact in conservative states such as New Hampshire large awards almost never occur. In the larger scheme of things, $4.6 billion represents just a fraction of 1 percent of the total annual amount America spends on health care. If there were no malpractice lawsuits whatsoever, it would not affect the skyrocketing cost of your family's health insurance at all.

The real question is why are there so many legitimate medical malpractice lawsuits in the first place? Amazingly, at least 100,000 people die in hospitals every year (not counting those outside of hospitals) due to medical malpractice. That's more than die from highway accidents, breast cancer or AIDS.[152] Many more survive medical malpractice but suffer needlessly. Our government should be concerned enough to make it a national priority to find out why and correct it. I think we would find a large contributing factor is that the health-care system is under tremendous financial stress, while segments of it are milking the system for all it's worth.

As a former airline pilot and check airman, I know the importance of open, above board peer review. If the airline industry had accident fatalities equivalent to the medical profession there would be a large airliner crash every day!

Unfortunately, professional peer review seems to be lacking in medicine. I know from a dear friend, who was a doctor unjustly accused, that the system is relying heavily on secretive "whistleblowers." These are unknown accusers protected by the law, their anonymity guaranteed so as to preclude legal recourse by those they accuse. That is wrong. Doctors shouldn't have to endure faceless accusers with perhaps personal motives. That is nothing more than a witch-hunt. It is unfair, it ruins reputations, and the evidence shows it doesn't work. [153]

According to National Practitioners Data Bank, between 1990 and 2004 just 5.5 percent of doctors were responsible for 57.3 percent of all malpractice payouts. Each of these doctors has made at least two payouts. The sum total of payouts for that period was over $27 billion. I think the medical profession has good reason to get its act together.

Reuters (London) reported on March 25, 2002 that Western Europe, Not the US, Ranks as the World's Healthiest Region.

A survey of people in 175 countries ranked nine Western European countries in its top 10, with Belgium heading the list followed by Iceland, the Netherlands, France, Switzerland, Austria, Sweden, Italy and Norway.[154] The United States ranked 17th just behind Israel.

On the other hand the United States spent 13.1 percent of its GDP (2002), or $4,180 per capita on health, compared to Belgium's $2,172; a total of about $1.5 trillion in the sample year.

Sooner or later America is going to have to choose between caring for its people with an inclusive national health plan and continuing to feed special interests. Our lives are on the line.

Federal Minimum Wage. The federal minimum hourly wage in the United States has been $5.15 since 1997. Corrected for inflation, that means a minimum wage worker in 2005 has had a cut in pay of about a dollar an hour since 1997, a decrease of about $2,000 a year in purchasing power.

Members of Congress (House and Senate), on the other hand, have seen their annual pay increase from $136,623 in 1997 to $162,100, an increase of $25,427; they've kept up with inflation very well.

A member of Congress earns over 15 times that of a full-time minimum wage worker. In March 2005, the Senate voted down a proposal by Sen. Kennedy to boast the minimum wage, in steps, to $7.25 an hour—a $2.10 increase. The vote was 49-46. Yet the Republican majority continues to vote for every tax break under the sun for the very rich.

In 2003, 2.7 percent of America's hourly workers over 16 years of age earned $5.15 or less.[155] That was over two million workers! It is a national disgrace that makes America unique in having a large underclass of people working full-time jobs and living in poverty.

Although many states have legislated higher hourly minimum wages, my home state of New Hampshire isn't one of them. Our far-right legislature voted it down yet again in 2005, claiming it would be too big a burden for employers and result in minimum wage workers being laid off. What a joke, in a state where the median family income is one of the highest because of our ratio of the extremely wealthy.

There are many, many more terrible, unfair special interest laws on the books, and it looks like more are in the making, but that's all I can stomach for now.

Fifteen

Owning Our Own Poverty

———•◆•———

White House Fact Sheet – America's Ownership Society: Expanding Opportunities[156]

"…if you own something, you have a vital stake in the future of our country. The more ownership there is in America, the more vitality there is in America, and the more people have a vital stake in the future of this country."

- President George W. Bush, June 17, 2004

Building a Real "Ownership Society"[157]

President Bush has proposed several initiatives to create an "ownership society." The premise that we want to be a nation of owners is attractive and deeply rooted in the American psyche. Ordinary people want the financial security, opportunity, and liberty that come with owning assets. A home owner has more security, and hence more liberty, than a renter. A person with a pension or a savings account can look forward more confidently to retirement than one who must keep working out of financial necessity. An individual who "owns" skills and educational qualifications is better bolstered against economic change and more able to get ahead financially than one who is unskilled….

> The new push for an ownership society, ironically, comes at a time when
> government social investments and protective regulations are being reduced
> and when a variety of risks (such as health insurance and pensions) are being
> shifted from large institutions (employers and government) onto individuals. In
> this context, the wrong sort of ownership society may actually make Americans
> less secure and less independent...

You've got to hand it to them; the far-right spin machine is excellent. Of course people want to own their own assets. America has a long tradition of ownership going back to the westward expansion of our country and the land-tenure laws crafted by Thomas Jefferson. The laws opened the new lands to freeholders rather than allowing us to grow as a nation of huge landholders or feudal "lords," as was the case in England and throughout Europe. That policy continued in the 19th century under President Lincoln with the Homestead acts and land-grant college legislation and, after Lincoln's death, with the abortive efforts of the Freedmen's Bureau to give emancipated slaves their "40 acres and a mule."

When Bush declared, as he did in his acceptance speech at the Republican National Convention that, "ownership brings security, dignity, and independence," few Americans would disagree. Characteristically for Bush, however, his push for an ownership society came as his administration was slashing government social programs and protective regulations, when a number of risks (such as health insurance and pensions) were being shifted away from employers and government onto the backs of individuals. He offered the wrong sort of ownership society that threatened to turn the clock back to when Americans overall were far less secure, and when only the wealthy enjoyed the luxury of any degree of financial security.

As we have seen, it took the Great Depression, and FDR to bring bipartisan political support for his "New Deal," to find a way for the vast majority of middle-class and working-poor families to cope with the multiple risks of our market economy. Many of those risks were at the time beyond an individual's control, risks such as illness, unemployment, destitution in old age, hazards from defective products, polluted natural resources, industrial accidents, corporate and financial frauds and other personal disasters.[158] What developed was a "social safety net" to help mitigate the risks of a capitalistic, market economy. Of course it took a worldwide financial calamity and our country flat on its butt to make that happen.

The creation of a social safety net represented a huge change in the relationship between our government and its people. For much of its history, the United States was similar to most of the countries in Europe. We had a small, wealthy class of aristocrats and merchants, and the rest of society scraped to get by. For the vast majority of our citizens, the risks of life—jobs, income, education, health care, personal security—were "privatized" rather than shared. If one experienced tough luck, too bad—there was no social safety net, nor was it considered the proper role of government to provide one. This is the glorified era the far right wishes to take us back to.

FDR's administration was followed by a succession of others, both Democratic and Republican, that worked to expand protections and opportunities for everyday people—and, as we have seen, America prospered.

It was the shifting of risk from the individual to risk mitigated by society that molded the American middle class, which became the envy of the world. It created a unique balance that permitted the dynamism of a market system while protecting individuals against catastrophic risks beyond their control. It took government to do it. Big business would not, and individuals could not, bring balance to the system. The tools used were taxation, social investment, and regulation—all the things the far right despises. Many of the wealthy considered Roosevelt a traitor to his class, if not the devil incarnate.

Then along came Ronald Reagan (1981-1989) and the far right began its assault in earnest on the institutions and safeguards that created the middle class. Reagan, actor turned politico, was their willing champion. And it has been downhill ever since (with something of a pause under President Clinton). The far right's spin doctors cleverly turned our myths and prejudices against us, beating us to death with a aggrandized macho image of America's strong-willed, hard-working, self-made men. A delusion that they preach made America great. Inversely, they use that delusion to portray the poor as weak, a willful drain on society that picks the pockets of real men.

Subliminally, many Americans are also swayed by ingrained racial prejudices that equate poverty with the color of skin, when in truth (although a higher percentage of people of color are poor because of limited economic opportunities) vastly more whites live in poverty.[159]

This concocted worldview is a boldfaced lie. What made our nation great were public policies and ruling governments that enabled individuals to live with a degree of security and dignity, policies that need to be expanded, not dismantled, to stop America's economic decline into a second-rate debtor nation.

Americans have been brainwashed into equating risk taking with potency and manliness—after all, nobody wants to be a wimp or a girly-man. Oh yes, glorifying risk is a masculine thing; most women don't seem to feel the need to have brass balls (although a few do).

In talking about my personal identification with a more feminine than masculine prospective of "risk," my wife Sue said I "relate easily with women because they live their lives with people who are dependant on them 24-hours a day; they relate because you experienced a compressed version of that as an airline captain. Women are multi-leveled from childhood." Hmm. I think we need more women in politics.

Just imagine: We now have a strutting president who said of the war in Iraq "bring it on," and a foreign policy that has been usurped by the vice president and secretary of defense, the fearless war hawks of the "Cheney-Rumsfeld cabal."

Consider these comments by Lawrence Wilkerson, a retired Army colonel who served as chief of staff to Secretary of State Colin Powell, in a mid-October 2005 talk before the New America Foundation, an independent public policy institute.

> We have courted disaster in Iraq, in North Korea, in Iran. Generally, with regard to domestic crises like Katrina, Rita … we haven't done very well on anything like that in a long time. And if something comes along that is truly serious, something like a nuclear weapon going off in a major American city, or something like a major pandemic, you are going to see

the ineptitude of this government in a way that will take you back to the Declaration of Independence.

The case that I saw for four-plus years was a case that I have never seen in my studies of aberrations, bastardizations, perturbations, changes to the national security decision-making process. What I saw was a cabal between the vice president of the United States, Richard Cheney, and the secretary of defense, Donald Rumsfeld, on critical issues that made decisions that the bureaucracy did not know were being made.

When the time came to implement the decisions, they were presented in such a disjointed, incredible way that the bureaucracy often didn't know what it was doing as it moved to carry them out.

Where was the president? According to Wilkerson, "You've got this collegiality there between the secretary of defense and the vice president, and you've got a president who is not versed in international relations and not too much interested in them either."[160]

In other words, thanks to Cheney and Rumsfeld, and President Bush, who empowered them, the United States is mired down in a dead-end strategy in Iraq, and our foreign policy is a disaster. In five years they helped turn a handsome federal budget surplus into the largest deficits in the history of our country. They admit to no errors in judgment; that would be unmasculine. How many more will have to die and suffer because our leaders are afraid of not being "real men?" Are they the caliber of people we want to lead us? I think not.

The Bush administration has an economic plan, though—and it's not the New Deal. On the table to be slashed by "Operation-Offset" in 2005 was our social safety net: Social Security, Medicare, Medicaid, Temporary Aid to Needy Families (TANF), food stamps, and a host of other government social programs that invest in our future. All while making permanent massive tax breaks for the very rich.

At the same time that they were trying to privatize risk, there was a continuing thrust to "privatize" government services, such as the United States Postal Service, the Weather Bureau, public education, air traffic control, major elements of the military, and prisons – to name a few. (These we'll discuss in the next chapter.)

Oh yes, the Bushies and the Norquists have a vision for America, and it is important that you and I and anyone else who loves our country understand the scope of what these incompetents are trying to do and prevent it before it is too late.

Health care

The United States is the only industrial nation in the world that does not have an all-inclusive national health-care system. Since WWII, health insurance has been largely a fringe benefit of high-quality employment. The problem is that for the last two decades good jobs with benefits have evaporated, and along with the loss of those jobs, fewer and fewer families have health insurance. Additionally, the benefits that remain are requiring larger and larger employee-paid contributions and shifting out-of-pocket costs to the workers. The combination of high deductibles and other restrictions, such as services and drugs covered, and limited choices of doctors and hospitals are making health-care insurance increasingly unreliable.

National Health Care Spending

- In 2003, health care spending in the United States reached $1.7 trillion, and was projected to reach $1.8 trillion in 2004.
- Health care spending is 4.3 times the amount spent on national defense.
- In 2003, the United States spent 15.3 percent of its Gross Domestic Product (GDP) on health care. It is projected that the percentage will reach 18.7 percent in 10 years.
- Although nearly 45 million Americans are uninsured, the United States spends more on health care than other industrialized nations, and those countries provide quality health insurance to all their citizens.

- Health care spending accounted for 10.9 percent of GDP in Switzerland, 10.7 percent in Germany, 9.7 percent in Canada and 9.5 in France, according to the Organization for Economic Cooperation and Development.
- Total out-of-pocket spending on health care rose $13.7 billion, to $230 billion in 2003.

The Nation Coalition on Health Care[161]

In 2004, about 175 million Americans (59.8 percent) were covered by private- employment based health-care insurance.[162] Employer health-care insurance premiums increased by 11.2 percent, nearly four times the rate of inflation. The annual premium for an employer health-care plan covering a family of four averaged nearly $10,000. That was expected to surge to $14,545 in 2006.

The Census Bureau further reported that in 2004, 45.8 million people (15.7 percent) had no health-care insurance at all. By 2006 that number was expected to exceed 51 million.

Medicaid covered 37.5 million people (12.9 percent) in 2005. Medicaid (Social Security Act Amendment 1965) is a federal/state entitlement program that pays for medical assistance for certain individuals and families with low incomes and resources. It is a means-tested "welfare" program jointly funded by the federal and state governments.[163]

Medicaid also pays 68 percent of the cost of nursing home care in the United States.[164] It again is a means-tested program that requires long-term residents to essentially be indigent and surrender all assets to the state. Nursing home care accounts for about a third of the cost of the Medicaid program. (All of this was before the cuts Congress was proposing in 2005.)

In 2004, the Department of Health and Human Services (HHS) budget for Medicaid was over $176 billion with the states' matching funds for a total of about $352 billion. In 2006, the total amount is expected to increase to $384 billion.

If one includes those on Medicaid, about one-third of our population (more than 83 million people) does not have health care insurance.

Medicare (Social Security Act Amendment 1965) covered 40 million people (13.7 percent). Medicare is the national health care insurance for people age 65 or older; some people under age 65 with disabilities, and people with End-Stage Renal Disease (ESRD), which is permanent kidney failure requiring dialysis or a kidney transplant. In 2004, the Hospital Insurance (HI) Trust Fund – Part A of Medicare - paid out $170.6 billion for inpatient hospital and related care.

Medicare Supplementary Medical Insurance (SMI) – Part B – paid out $138.3 billion, for a total Medicare expenditure of $308.9 billion. In 2006, after the Medicare Prescription Drug plan – Part D kicked in, the total amount was expected to increase to $438 billion.

Military benefits (VA, CHAMPUS, and subsets) covered another 10 million people (3.7 percent). The Veterans Administration's budget authority for 2004 was about $28 billion.

The skyrocketing cost of this ridiculous national hodge-podge health-care system is a crisis, a crisis more imminent and of larger proportion than the projected exhaustion of the Social Security Old Age and Survivors Insurance (OASI) Trust Fund in 2041.

Because of complexity and waste, the United States spends more than any other nation—nearly $300 billion and rising—just to administer its health-care system.

Medicare (Part A) is paid for by the payroll tax (FICA and SECA), with money that flows through the Social Security Medicare Hospital Insurance (HI) Trust Fund. The HI tax rate is 1.45 percent of all earnings, payable by both employees and employers for a total of 2.90 percent. The HI Trust Fund reserves are expected to be exhausted by 2020.

The optional Medicare (Part B), Medicare Supplemental Insurance (SMI), does not have a trust fund. It is a pay-as-you-go system funded by beneficiary premiums and general fund revenue. In 2004, the premiums paid less than a third of SMI; the general fund paid $100.9 billion.

The optional Medicare (Part D)[165], the prescription drug benefit that began in January 2006, is a subset of SMI and funded the same way—beneficiary premiums and general fund revenue. It was projected that the program will require $1.1 trillion from the general fund over the first 10 years.

In 2006 the basic Medicare premium for (optional) Part B shot up 13 percent to $88.50 a month. That cost was added to by as much as $32 a month or more for the new (optional) prescription drug benefit – Part D. The combined premium for doctors' services, outpatient hospital-care and prescription drugs comes out slightly higher than $120 a month. Quite a chunk, when compared to the average monthly Social Security benefit in 2005 of $955.

Bush's solution, Operation-Offset: Make the tax cuts for the rich permanent, cut Medicaid—the welfare program that our most needy (seniors, women and children) rely on most; shift from employer based health-care insurance to individual health-care insurance policies with very high deductibles; and of course protect the administration's sweetheart deals with the insurance and drug companies.

The administration was touting the Health Savings Accounts,[166] which allow limited tax-free contributions for only those enrolled in a very high deductible health-care insurance plan. These guys just don't get it. People struggling to live day-to-day don't have money to put aside for Health Savings Accounts.

As this is written, House Republican leaders have pledged to increase the targeted entitlement cuts in 2006, from $35 billion to $50 billion, impose across-the-board spending cuts and rescind spending already approved—all to offset the cost of hurricane relief.[167]

In October 2005, the White House killed a $8.7 billion proposal by U.S. Senate Committee Finance Chair Chuck Grassley (R-Iowa) and ranking committee member Sen. Max Baucus (D-Mont.) that would have allowed the federal government to pay 100 percent of Medicaid costs for Katrina survivors through the end of 2006, and to expand Medicaid eligibility from traditional categories—such as women and children—to include poor, childless adults.

America can only stop this madness if we join other advanced countries and treat access to health care as a right rather than a privilege. Then we must establish an insurance pool that includes everyone and requires everyone to participate, one that is underwritten, or guaranteed, by the federal government. Only then can we spend our collective money wisely and get fair value for our dollar, rather than being taken to the cleaners by the HMOs, insurance, and drug industries.

Reform must also be systemic and systemwide. Our present health-care system is elaborately interconnected. A piecemeal approach to reform won't work, because it will result in gains for some offset by losses for others. For example, our Social Security Trust Fund Trustees tell us that Medicare can be "fixed" by either increasing the payroll tax (premiums), reducing benefits, or a combination of both. But that merely privatizes the burden or shifts it onto secondary insurance and would do nothing to make our total health-care system more efficient and affordable.[168] In the meantime, HHS has already launched a program of Section 1115 "waivers" targeting Medicaid eligibility and reducing already meager benefits. This doesn't fix the system, either. It eliminates access to health care for our most needy and shifts the costs to our nation's emergency rooms and ultimately to the rest of the system, including private payers and Medicare.[169]

And it isn't only the cost; it is the quality of health care that needs desperately to be improved. As the National Coalition on Health Care puts it, the United States has "An Epidemic of Sub-Standard Care."

"The American health care system provides excellent care to many of its patients much of the time, but, on the evidence, not to enough of its patients enough of the time." As a series of landmark reports from the Institute of Medicine has documented, there is a "quality chasm"— a wide gulf between the care that patients should receive and the care that is actually delivered. As I noted earlier, there were 100,000 medical malpractice deaths in U.S. hospitals in 2004.

Is reforming America's health-care system politically possible? The first step needed would be a vigorous bipartisan national debate; the next is prompt action. I don't think there's a chance in hell that the Bush administration will move in that direction. Nor, unfortunately, do I believe will the Democrats. Health-care reform was the first thing on Bill Clinton's agenda when he took office in 1993—and he and Hilary got fried. Over a decade later, to mention a national health-care system is synonymous with "socialized medicine," and political suicide.

As much as I'd like to be optimistic about the chances of health-care reform, I think that so long as those in power are able to shift the risk and pass the cost down to future generations, nothing will change.

Social Security

There's little question that the 70-year-old Social Security Act (1935) has been the most successful social program in American history.

Today, Social Security lifts 13 million seniors above poverty. Half a century ago over a third of seniors lived in poverty—today, while still too many, it is less than 10 percent (3.5 million).[170]

Yet only half the beneficiaries of Social Security receive benefits solely because they are retired. The rest are adults with disabilities and their dependents, widows and widowers, and children whose parents have died.

According to the National Academy of Social Insurance, over five million children under age 18 receive part of their family income from Social Security; in contrast, only around four million children receive Temporary Aid to Needy Families (TANF). The Center on Budget and Policy Priorities found that a million more children would be in poverty if not for Social Security.[171] The U.S. Census Bureau reports that in 2004 slightly over 13 million children under age 18 lived in poverty.

Social Security is much more than a normal retirement program and provides benefits that a "private" pension plan could never afford to provide. Social Security is a mandatory social "insurance" program that is supported by a dedicated tax, just like highways and airways are supported by a dedicated tax on gasoline and airfares. The American worker and employers pay into a system that defuses "risk." It is as simple as that. It is a part of the social safety net and was never meant to preclude employment-based or private pension plans.

On February 2, 2005, in his State of the Union address, President Bush told the American people that Social Security is "headed for bankruptcy," and outlined in general terms a proposal based on partial "privatization" that would allow workers under 55 years old to have the option of setting aside four percentage points of the their payroll taxes in individual accounts (at the present time an employee is taxed 6.20 percent, on wages up to $90,000, which is matched by the employer).[172] He went on to say that privatization was "revenue neutral" and would not affect projected shortfalls in Social Security tax receipts. He never suggested specific benefit cuts, saying, "All ideas are on the table," and that he was opposed to increasing payroll taxes. He alluded to options linked to former Democratic officeholders who would reduce benefits for those with higher incomes (indexing).

Bush has been pushing the same line since Karl Rove, Grover Norquist and other far rightists helped him frame his gubernatorial campaign in Texas. Norquist, the Heritage Foundation and the Cato Institute want to privatize Social Security as the first step toward killing it. Ideologically, they view the program as a redistribution of wealth—the antithesis of the unrestricted, capitalistic, open market society they wish to take us back to. Yet with Bush as standard-bearer, the Republicans are on a crusade to redistribute wealth from the bottom up. That doesn't bother them a bit.

And again Bush and his cronies are lying to the American people.

As discussed in Chapter 12, Social Security is far from facing bankruptcy. In fact, after paying all beneficiaries fully from payroll taxes, the Old Age and Survivors Insurance (OASI) Trust Fund will continue to grow to $4.2 trillion by 2015. It is true that by 2017 tax revenue will fall below expenditures and funds will have to be withdrawn, and that without change the trust fund will be exhausted by 2041.[173] But even if that were to occur the system would not be "bankrupt." Social Security revenue would continue to cover 81 percent of the promised benefits. Still, there is a long-term financing problem, but it's a problem of modest size.

A recent report by the Congressional Budget Office finds that the trust fund could be extended into the 22nd century with no change in benefits with additional revenues equal to only 0.54 percent of GDP. In reference to the CBO report, columnist Paul Krugman notes, "That's less than 3 percent of federal spending – less than we're currently spending in Iraq. And it's only about one-quarter of the revenue lost each year because of President Bush's tax cuts – roughly equal to the fraction of those cuts that goes to people with incomes over $500,000 a year."

Mr. Bush is inventing a short term Social Security crisis that can only exist if the federal government defaults on the Treasury's obligations to the trust funds. While default is an incredible scenario, Bush has after all said that trust funds were meaningless, "just pieces of paper in a drawer."

Bush and the far right know that the only way they can privatize and ultimately kill Social Security is by creating a crisis and then convincing young workers that they can get something for nothing—the basis of all cons.

Given the modest amount of money involved, any number of packages would secure the retirement program with no major change for generations to come. The easiest, proposed by Warren Buffett, and the one that I support, is to simply remove or greatly increase the $90,000 wage cap on the OASDI portion of the payroll tax. But there are other schemes that would work as well without reducing benefits.

Reducing benefits would be a mistake; for many low-income households, Social Security benefits already do not provide even a poverty level income. Another major objection to reducing the benefit for middle to high-income families is that it would turn Social Security into a welfare program, and that would ultimately consign it to the scrap heap.

What aren't so easily fixed as the retirement piece of Social Security are Medicare and Medicaid. But, as indicated earlier, neither program can be made right independently; the United States must reform its entire health care system.

Holistically, retirement income is often compared to a three-legged stool. Two legs of the stool are employer-based retirement plans and individual savings. Social Security is the third.

Employer-based plans fall into two broad categories:

- Defined benefit plans, which provide a specific benefit on an employee's earnings record. The employer generally holds contributions in a single, companywide account—these are the type plans that are getting dumped onto the Pension Benefit Guarantee Corporation (PBGC) by companies in bankruptcy (steel, airline – auto next?), leaving workers and taxpayers largely holding the bag.
- Defined contribution plans such as 401(K) and 403(B) plans, in which the size of the benefit depends on the amount of contributions made to an individual's account and the rate of return on the funds invested.

Contributions are generally held in an individual, tax-advantaged account in the employee's name—these monies are the employee's and cannot be touched in a company bankruptcy.

Individual Savings Accounts:

- Traditional Individual Retirement Accounts (IRAs), or private retirement accounts that offer "front-loaded" tax benefits (contributions are tax-deductible, and withdrawals are taxed as ordinary income).
- Roth IRAs, or private retirement accounts that offer "back-loaded" tax benefits (contributions are not tax-deductible, and withdrawals are tax free).
- Simplified Employer Pension (SEP) plans, or IRA-like accounts into which employers make direct deposits.
- Keogh plans, tax-deferred retirement savings plan for people who are self-employed.

When one examines the retirement possibilities of very-low-income workers the outlook is dismal. Social Security benefits alone will not provide even a poverty-level income, and there are many obstacles blocking low-income families from accumulating retirement savings (like those indicated above) to supplement their Social Security benefits. This is largely because lower tier workers are more likely to lose a job or not have health insurance and require public assistance. Once in the system, such families are rarely able to accumulate even a modest amount of retirement savings.

Means-tested benefits programs, such as Medicaid, Temporary Assistance for Needy Families (TANF), federal and state housing assistance, and the federal food stamp program, require that individuals not have countable assets set by the particular program. That asset limit is usually $2,000 or in rare instances $3,000, and has been for over thirty-years, with no adjustment for inflation. In addition, retirement savings programs (401Ks, 403ks and IRAs) are treated inconsistently from program to program and state to state.

In other words, in the United States to receive help from the social safety net families and individuals have to be flat broke, and from that position it's very hard to recover and grow old with any degree of economic security.

At the same time the federal and state governments prohibit even a modicum of savings for those who receive aid, they provide about $150 billion a year in tax benefits to those not down on their luck to encourage retirement savings, primarily through employer-based retirement plans and IRAs.[174]

In analyzing the problem, the Center on Budget and Policy Priorities (CBPP) suggests the following:

- Congress could amend the tax code so that retirement accounts that receive preferential tax treatment (such as 401(K) plans and IRAs) are disregarded for purposes of eligibility and benefit determinations in federal means-tested programs.
- For many programs, states can eliminate the asset test and consider only income when determining eligibility, raise the asset limit, or not count retirement savings accounts toward the asset limit.

I think the changes CBPP recommends would be sound public policy. In the long run, society would come out ahead if people could achieve financial independence—nobody wants to be on welfare. As the income gap widens in the United States and high-quality jobs vanish, Social Security and our social safety net have become increasingly important. Many people are only a job loss or a family illness away from needing some sort of temporary public support, yet in the United States, because of niggardly means-tested welfare programs, getting that help can mean a life sentence of poverty imposed by the federal and state governments.

Through October 8, 2005 more than 1.47million Americans filed bankruptcy petitions – most due to medical bills or job loss. The number of filings was up 19.4 percent from the same period in 2004. In a rush to beat the October 17th deadline before the new 2005 bankruptcy law went into effect, over a hundred thousand petitions were filed in the second week of October alone. As I said earlier, under the new law, means testing prevents many lower and middle-income people from filing under Chapter 7 (no fresh start). Instead they are forced to file under Chapter 13 and obligated to long repayment plans that will lock many families into poverty for years.

Eliminating the Chapter 7 option for every-day-people was the Bush administration's early Christmas present to the credit card industry. The new law, however, retained all of the bankruptcy asset shelters available to the wealthy. Corporations remain totally free to dump their defined benefit retirement plans and health insurance plans for retired and current workers under Chapter 11. Yet none of this was of interest to our leaders in Congress.

Poverty

The United States has the highest overall poverty rate among the world's wealthiest countries. We rank number one on the list of shame, with 17 percent of our population below the poverty line, defined by the Organization for Economic Cooperation and Development (OECD) as less than 50 percent of median income. Several Scandinavian countries had the lowest rate: Finland (5.4 percent), Norway (6.4 percent), and Sweden (6.5 percent). These were followed by Germany (7.5 percent), France (8.0 percent), Netherlands (8.1 percent), Denmark (9.2 percent), and Canada (12.8 percent).[175]

The United States also has the highest child poverty rate (21.9 percent), and the second-highest elderly poverty rate (24.7 percent).

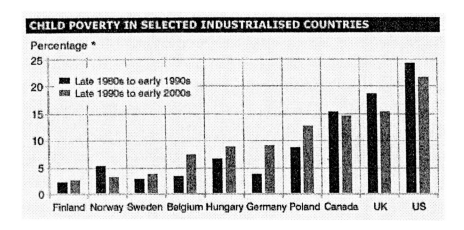

CHILD POVERTY IN SELECTED INDUSTRIALISED COUNTRIES

Percentage *

Late 1980s to early 1990s
Late 1990s to early 2000s

Finland Norway Sweden Belgium Hungary Germany Poland Canada UK US

*Percentage of children living in families whose income is less than 50 percent of the median adjusted disposable income of all persons. Source: UNICEF

Following the Office of Management and Budget's (OMB) Statistical Policy Directive 14, the U.S. Census Bureau uses a set of money income thresholds that vary by family size and composition to determine who is in poverty. The resulting weighted poverty level is considerable less than 50 percent of median household income. By that measure the US Census Bureau reports:

- The official poverty rate in 2004 was 12.7 percent, up from 12.5 percent in 2003.

- In 2004, 37.0 million people were in poverty, up 1.1 million from 2003.

- Poverty rates remained unchanged for Blacks (24.7 percent) and Hispanics (21.9 percent), rose for non-Hispanic Whites (8.6 percent in 2004, up from 8.2 percent in 2003), and decreased for Asians (9.8 percent in 2004, down from 11.8 percent in 2003).

- The poverty rate in 2004 (12.7 percent) was 9.7 percentage points lower than in 1959, the first year for which poverty estimates are available (Figure 3). From the most recent low in 2000, both the number and rate have risen for four consecutive years, from 31.6 million and 11.3 percent in 2000 to 37.0 million and 12.7 percent in 2004, respectively.

- For children under 18 years old, both the 2004 poverty rate (17.8 percent) and the number in poverty (13.0 million) remained unchanged from 2003. The poverty rate for children under 18 remained higher than that of 18-to-64-year olds (11.3 percent) and that of people aged 65 and over (9.8 percent).

- Both the poverty rate and number in poverty increased for people 18 to 64 years old (11.3 percent and 20.5 million in 2004, up from 10.8 percent and 19.4 million in 2003).

- The poverty rate decreased for seniors aged 65 and older, 9.8 percent in 2004, down from 10.2 percent in 2003, while the number in poverty in 2004 (3.5 million) was unchanged.

- The number of families in poverty increased to 7.9 million in 2004, up from 7.6 million in 2003, while the poverty rate remained unchanged at 10.2 percent in 2004.

The poverty rate and the number in poverty showed no change between 2003 and 2004 for the different types of families: In 2004, married-couple families (5.5 percent and 3.2 million), female-householder, no-husband present families (28.4 percent and 4.0 million), and male-householder, no-wife-present families (13.5 percent and 658,000).

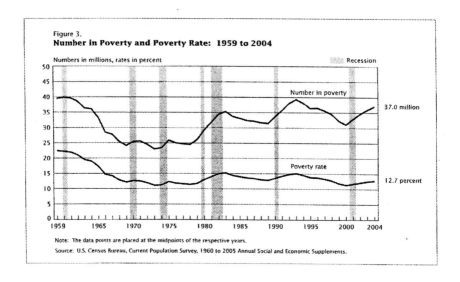

Figure 3.
Number in Poverty and Poverty Rate: 1959 to 2004

Note: The data points are placed at the midpoints of the respective years.
Source: U.S. Census Bureau, Current Population Survey, 1960 to 2005 Annual Social and Economic Supplements.

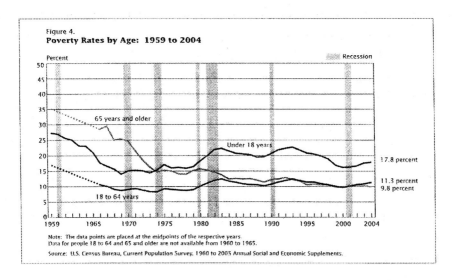

Figure 4.
Poverty Rates by Age: 1959 to 2004

Weighted Average Poverty Threshold in 2004, by Size of Family
(Dollars)

One person	9,645
Two people	12,334
Three people	15,067
Four people	19,307
Five people	22,831
Six people	25,788
Seven people	29,236
Eight people	32,641
Nine people	39,048

Median Pretax Household Income
$44,389

Let's get back to the question of "risk" in the United States. What is the risk of falling into poverty? It is not 12.7 percent as the Census Bureau computes it. That is the overall risk. An individual's risk depends upon what cohort of the population you fall in. If you are a female-householder with no husband, the risk is 28.4 percent; if you are black it is 24.7 percent, Hispanic 21.9 percent, or a child 17.8 percent. These are amazing numbers.

There is plenty of data showing that adolescent, non-marital childbearing results in a very high risk of poverty for mother and child or children, and that for every year pregnancy is delayed into maturity that risk goes down. Others that are more likely to live in poverty are people of color, people with disabilities, and children. Added to that there are the risks related to employment and barriers to employment. These include, but are not limited to, education, the availability of jobs, job protection, and livable wages.

Clearly, when it comes to economic well being, far too many people in the United States are not doing well, while the top percentile of people are accumulating more wealth and doing better than ever before. A growing majority of what used to be our middle class is barely afloat, lucky to tread water. And 37 million people in the wealthiest nation on Earth live in poverty.

The federal budget can be divided roughly into three parts: (1) interest on the debt, (2) defense and international affairs, and (3) domestic programs. As we have seen, the country's domestic programs form our "social safety net—mainly Social Security, Medicare, and Medicaid, and what are called other domestic budgetary outlays. We covered the first three earlier in the chapter. The last category consists of programs for children, welfare, education, the environment, community development, housing, energy, transportation, and justice—the very programs that safeguard working-families' lives the most and that the majority of Americans depend upon. Yet despite the fact that the poverty rate has steadily increased over Bush's entire time in office, and despite the fact that the United States tops the list of the wealthy nations poverty list of shame, it is the domestic programs that are under the Bush administration's axe.

Welfare, which has long been an easy target, really has two meanings. In one sense, it refers to all government programs providing benefits to impoverished Americans. The major programs are Medicaid, food stamps, Supplemental Security Income (SSI) and HUD housing programs.

When the far-right politicians and the unknowing speak of welfare, they are usually referring to what was Aid To Families with Dependent Children (AFDC) and is now Temporary Assistance to Needy families (TANF). TANF is primarily provided to single parents and has always been a small part of the overall welfare scheme. (See pie chart below.) To qualify for these programs, applicants must meet income and resource limitations that are actually well below the poverty line. The HUD and food stamp programs are federally funded; the others involve federal and state funds.[176]

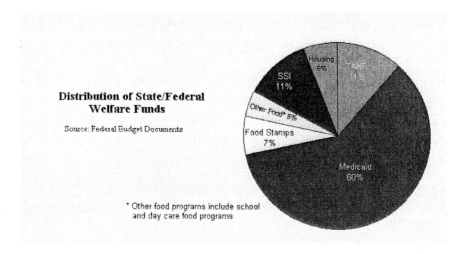

Distribution of State/Federal Welfare Funds

Source: Federal Budget Documents

* Other food programs include school and day care food programs

The truth is that welfare, or aid for the poor, has always been extremely parsimonious in the United States. Going back to colonial days local communities didn't hand out money, they warehoused the poor in "poor houses," or "work houses," and charity was a matter for the church. In the face of the Depression, with limited public and private resources exhausted, parts of the Social Security Act gave relief to the unemployed and the poor. Prior to the Social Security Act a federal welfare system didn't exist, and those states and cities that had programs were few and far between and extremely limited.[177]

The Social Security Act of 1935 not only provided benefits for retired workers but also for workers with disabilities, dependents, and children whose parents had died. These are SSDI benefits under Title II, and are entitlements paid for with FICA taxes. They are not welfare.

The Act further provided grants to the states (Title I) for Old Age Assistance for the Aged (OAA), and (Title IV) Aid to Dependent Children (ADC). Both of these were means-tested entitlements funneled through the state to individuals, with shared federal/state government funding.

These were federally entitled welfare programs. OAA still exists; ADC does not.

ADC made no provision for assisting a parent or other relative in the household, although it did specify that the child must live with a parent or other close relative to be eligible for federal aid. It was not until 1950 that the federal government began to share in the maintenance costs of a caretaker relative.

Congress later *allowed* states to claim federal reimbursement for assisting other persons under the renamed Aid to Families with Dependant Children (AFDC), but it wasn't until 1984 that all states were *required* to provide benefits for a second incapacitated or unemployed parent. Effective in 1990, in some states benefits to a second qualified parent were limited to six months yearly.

Section 1115 of the Social Security Act, established in 1962, allowed the waiver of specific parts of AFDC law (namely, provisions setting forth requirements for state plans) in order to enable a state to carry out projects that the secretary of HEW (Health, Education and Welfare, now Health and Human Services) judged likely to promote the objectives of AFDC.[178] Presidents Reagan, Bush, and Clinton all promoted waivers for state experimentation. The Clinton administration approved waivers from more than 40 states, many of them for statewide reforms, before the passage of the law repealing AFDC on August 22, 1996.

AFDC was a miserly program that paid niggardly cash benefits, but it was an entitlement from the federal government given to the people. What followed in 1996 was the ultimate Section 1115 waiver; Temporary Aid to Needy Families is an entitlement to the states to use the funds as they see fit.

The only Social Security cash welfare benefit that remains is (Title XVI) Supplemental Security Income (SSI), which was enacted in 1972. SSI only provides benefits to the disabled who lack the insured work record required for SSDI. SSI is a means-and-resource-tested welfare program. In 2005 the maximum SSI benefit was $579 for an individual, $869 for a couple, and $30 if an individual is institutionalized.

President Lyndon B. Johnson's War on Poverty and Great Society programs in the 1960s picked up where the New Deal left off—and the far right hated him with much the same enthusiasm as it hated FDR.[179] Under his leadership, in 1965 Social Security was expanded to include Medicare (an insurance program), and Medicaid (an entitled welfare program). In that same year the Department of Housing and Urban Development (HUD) was established by the Housing and Urban Development Act.

Medicaid, HUD, work training, and an expanded food stamp program provided needed additional relief for middle-class and poor families, and for those receiving AFDC benefits. But by the Reagan era the spin-doctors were out in force and had their guns turned on "welfare." According to them, hordes of lazy people were receiving benefits indefinitely and refusing to work. And it was never true. Most received benefits for a short period of time. Why would they purposefully stay on welfare? The cash benefit never exceeded a third of the poverty level income, and combined with food stamps rarely brought recipients above half the poverty level.

Was there welfare fraud? Of course, as would be expected some people filed phony claims or hid income or assets, particularly in pre-computer days. But the largest frauds probably were in the collusion between realtors, landlords and those responsible for providing housing for those on welfare. In the 1960s I saw this collusion working in Long Beach, New York. Welfare landlords were advanced money that they then would use to buy old, rundown buildings. Then, with no money of their own at risk, rent them to welfare tenants for exorbitant amounts. As I recall, a few gentlemen did some hard time over welfare housing in Long Beach.

Some called it welfare dumping and I believe in varied forms it still goes on legally throughout the country. For example, Berlin, New Hampshire has welfare recipients imported from all over the state and beyond to occupy decrepit rental units that would otherwise go unrented. In Berlin, those being placed have very few job opportunities and put stress on the community's limited public resources. Is Berlin an example of good public policy? I don't think so.

In any case, the myth of welfare recipients rampantly defrauding the taxpayers and living in luxury gained momentum, rising to a political crescendo to reform welfare during President Clinton's first term of office.

After a series of threatened vetoes, a deal was struck between Congress and the White House, and Clinton signed the Republican-sponsored Personal Responsibility and Work Opportunity Reconciliation Act (PRWORA) into law in 1996. The law had a five-year funding authorization that has been extended from year to year since.

As noted earlier, the welfare program is called Temporary Aid to Needy Families (TANF). To further confuse the issue, states call their programs under TANF different names as well. After weeks of research, I found that very few of the good folks at the New Hampshire Department of Health and Human Services understand the intricacies of the interrelated programs under TANF; it is extremely complicated. So if you were planning to sign up it would be a good idea to get your Harvard Law School degree first. I hope you'll never have to, but all Americans should understand how our welfare system works and feel compassion for those who are forced to use it.

TANF: the Bottom Line

- Able-bodied adults between the ages of 18 to 65 without a dependant child are ineligible for TANF. Cities and towns are usually required by state law to provide some aid. The *Washington Profile* reports that about 3.5 million U.S. residents (about 1 percent of the population), including 1.35 million children, have been homeless for a significant period of time. Over 37,000 homeless individuals (including 16,000 children) stay in shelters in New York every night. This information was gathered by the Urban Institute, but actual numbers might be higher.[180]

- Another study, which surveyed 777 homeless parents (mainly mothers) living in 10 U.S. cities showed that 22 percent of the respondents left their homes because of domestic abuse.

- Current TANF benefits and food stamps combined are below the poverty level in every state; in fact, the current average maximum

TANF benefit in the United States for a single mother of two children is less than 40 percent of the poverty level.[181]

Thus, contrary to popular belief, welfare in the United States does not provide relief from poverty but merely allows some recipients, for a limited period of time (24 to 60 months, depending upon the state), to join the ranks of the working poor. In New Hampshire, all able-bodied adults receiving TANF, ages 16 to 60, are expected to work, attend school, or undergo job training. The state promises to help them find work. This approach has generated some widely bruited successes nationwide, but usually, when their TANF time limit runs out, recipients are at best left with low-paying service jobs that do not meet their needs. Others simply disappear into the dark depths beneath the social safety net.

It is with a macabre sense of humor that I note the 2005 Executive Summary of the Department of Health and Human Services' annual report to Congress (required by the Welfare Indicators Act of 1994). They reported: "Trends in dependency are similar to the more well-known changes in TANF and food stamp caseloads. For example, the percentage of individuals who received AFDC/TANF cash assistance fell from 4.6 percent to 1.9 percent between 1996 and 2003. Food stamp recipiency rates fell from 9.5 percent in 1996 to 6.1 percent in 2000 and 2001. Since then, the food stamp recipiency rate has increased to 7.3 percent in 2003."[182]

Congratulations HHS! Let's hear it for the Republicans! In 2004 only 1.9 percent (5.5 million) of the 12.7 percent (37 million) Americans in poverty received any cash from their government. And a whole bunch of others went hungry because of cuts in the food stamp program.

Wow! Cutting welfare must be a budgetary necessity. Baloney. Following is a pie chart of the president's budget for HHS for 2006: [Source Federal Budget document]

Composition of the Budget

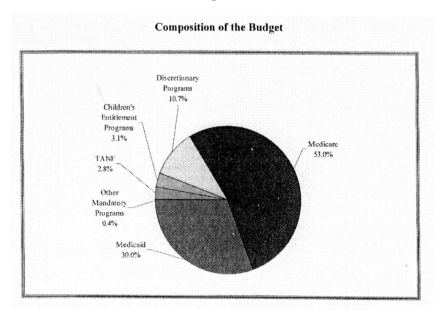

TANF represents merely 2.8 percent of HHS' budget, $18,164 billion, or about $3,302 per TANF recipient (average). The biggest slice of the pie is Medicare ($340,412 billion), which is mostly funded by the Social Security HI Trust Fund, SMI premiums, and about $100 billion from the General Fund. Of course the General Fund contribution increased dramatically with the advent of the prescription drug program.

The largest welfare program is Medicaid ($192,718 billion).

As with our health-care system, our welfare system is a hodge-podge of programs that are inadequate, inefficient, and failing to keep up with the needs of the 21st century.

Is there anything we can do? Sure. First we must require U.S. corporations and the rich to pay their fair share of the tax burden. As it is now, risk in America is increasingly falling upon individuals without the resources to cope with it. We must focus on education, affordable housing, job creation and fair wages—all factors that would prevent people from falling into poverty. Most of all, we must recognize the urgency of change or face the consequences of an economic meltdown. Don't forget, in 1928 no one foretold the Great Depression.

I certainly hope that America will never have to endure another Depression. Optimistically, I don't think we will, because times have changed. I do think, however, that the economy of the United States is being terribly misguided, and that until we get back on course our social safety net is more important than ever, and in 2005 it was far from up to the task.

Sixteen

Retooling for a Global Economy

—•—◆—•—

♫ Hello Brother (Lyrics)

A man wants to work…for his pay

A man wants a place…in the sun

A man wants a gal proud to say

That she'll become his lovin' wife

He wants a chance to give his kids a better life

Well hello ah…hello brother

You can travel all around the world and back

You can fly or sail or ride a railroad track

But no matter where you go you're gonna find

That people have the same things on their minds

A man wants to work…for his pay

A man wants a place…in the sun

A man wants a gal proud to say

That she'll become his lovin' wife

He wants a chance to give his kids a better life
Well hello brother, hello

He wants a chance to give his kids a better life, yes
Well hello, hello, brother hello
I said hello, hello, brother hello

Louis Armstrong

It was a Depression song. When Satchmo sang, "A man wants to work…" everyone knew in his or her heart what he meant. What does George W. Bush mean when he boasts about America's "entrepreneurial spirit?" I'm one American who is sick to death of hearing him prattle about the virtues of being an entrepreneur. The words come from a rich man's son who has never really had to work and could not even run a successful business. During the Depression there were plenty of entrepreneurs; they were selling apples on street corners. The problem was there were no jobs, and people didn't have the money to feed themselves or pay the rent. Now as then, what most men and women want and need is a job—a job that pays a decent wage, offers benefits, and has a modicum of security so that they can raise a family. That's the American dream, and that is where the Bush administration has failed miserably.

From December 2000, the month before Bush took office, through March 2005, the official U.S. unemployment rate climbed from 3.9 percent to 5.2 percent—representing 7.7 million unemployed workers. And that doesn't even begin to tell the tale. To get a fuller picture you have to look at other data presented by the U.S. Bureau of Labor Statistics (BLS), not just the unemployment rate.[183] The unemployment rate is simply the ratio of unemployed to the civilian labor force expressed as a percentage [i.e., 100 times (unemployed/labor force)]. It is significant that only those who have said they looked for work in the preceding four weeks are reported as unemployed.

The 7.7 million officially unemployed represents only about 57 percent of all U.S. workers—approximately 13.6 million, according to the BLS—who are either unemployed, underemployed in part-time jobs out of economic necessity, or who have become so discouraged that they have given up looking for work. The following graph is from the AFL-CIO website.

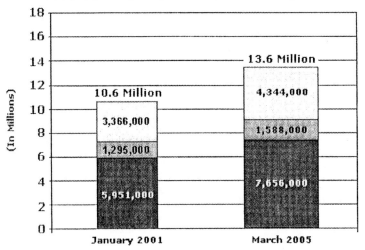

The Bush Record Since January 2001
The number of unemployed and underemployed persons has jumped by 28 percent since January 2001.

Black – Officially unemployed

Gray – Marginally attached (unemployed White – Part Time for economic reasons

Satchmo had it straight, "♫...no matter where you go you're gonna find...That people have the same things on their minds...♪" People do have shared dreams but unfortunately governments can and often do have different national goals. Many in the world—rightly or wrongly—blame the United States for pushing the current economic model of globalization, free trade, open markets, privatization and fiscal austerity that they believe has resulted in increased social inequality. They see the United States and the World Trade Organization (WTO) in the same light, as a superpower and an organization whose prime mission is to pry open markets for the benefit of transnational corporations at the expense of national and local economies—workers, farmers, indigenous peoples, women and other social groups, health and safety, the environment; and animal welfare.[184]

Meetings of the WTO and other economic summits, such as the fourth Summit of the Americas held at Mar del Plata, Argentina in early November 2005, consequently have drawn massive demonstrations targeting the United States.[185]

At the first Summit of the Americas in 1994 Bill Clinton proposed a hemispheric free trade agreement that would stretch from Alaska to Tierra del Fuego, to be called the Free Trade Area of the Americas (FTAA). Bush and his entourage came to the fourth summit hoping to revitalize FTAA, which was supposed to be completed by 2005. It didn't happen.

Just a few blocks from the summit, Hugo Chávez, Venezuela's colorful leader, rallied a soccer stadium filled with at least 25,000 people against the United States. (The United States imports about 1.299 million barrels of oil a day from Venezuela. (Chávez is a socialist; Bush is capitalist with a big C.)

"Every one of us has brought a shovel, because Mar del Plata is going to be the tomb of FTAA," Chávez said. "FTAA is dead, and we, the people of the Americas, are the ones who buried it."

While I don't agree with the demonization of the WTO, leaders like Chávez deserve to be heard, and the problems associated with the United States' current trade policies need to be addressed. As far as the FTAA is concerned, I think Chávez had it right. According to *The New York Times*, "the feeling among many Latin Americans" is that the United States came "with little to offer other than the usual nostrums about free trade, open markets, privatization, and fiscal austerity, the same recipe that has vastly increased social inequality throughout Latin America during the past decade."

To better understanding globalization, free trade, and the affect on jobs, it's useful to establish a recent time line of United States' trade agreements:

- The General Agreement on Tariffs and Trade (GATT) was a result of the Bretton Woods Agreement (1947). The GATT is very similar to a treaty; it is classed as a Congressional-executive agreement.[186] It is based on the *"unconditional most favored nation principle."* This means that the conditions applied to the most favored trading nation apply to all trading nations. (The one with the least restrictions.) In 1998 Most Favored Status was changed to Normal Trade Relations.

- Signatories of GATT meet periodically to negotiate new trade agreements. The Uruguay Round, which ended in 1994, rolled GATT into the World Trade Organization (WTO). The Uruguay Round also put into place comprehensive international rules about which policy objectives so-called independent countries are permitted to pursue and which means a country might use to obtain WTO-legal objectives. It established the World Trade Organization (WTO) as a powerful new global commerce agency, which transformed GATT into an enforceable global commerce code.

- On January 1, 1994, the North American Free Trade Agreement (NAFTA) was implemented. (The same year Clinton proposed FTAA.) It is an agreement between the United States, Canada, and Mexico. Both NAFTA and the WTO had bipartisan support, and that of many of the world's largest corporations. Remarkably, however, many of NAFTA's most outspoken boosters in Congress and among economists never read the 900 hundred-page-document.

- The Central American Free Trade Agreement (CAFTA) is an agreement between the United States, five Central American nations (Guatemala, El Salvador, Honduras, Costa Rica and Nicaragua), and the Dominican Republic. It was signed May 28, 2004, and on July 27, 2005, was approved in the middle of the night by an extremely narrow (217-215) majority in the U.S. House of Representatives.

As of 2005, there were 148 members of the WTO, including Communist China, which became a member in 2001. Russia has held talks on WTO accession with 54 countries, of which 36 have signed bilateral agreements, and still needs to complete negotiations with 13 more countries, including the United States, Canada, Brazil, and Australia. Russia hoped to conclude negotiations for accession to the WTO by the end of the 2005.[187]

After a decade of the WTO and NAFTA, how is it working out? The answer is mixed at best. America's largest multinational corporations are awash in profits, and America's workers (joining the European Union and Japan) are on the ropes. Between 2001 and 2004 over 2.9 million manufacturing jobs have been lost in the United States. In fact, manufacturing is at its lowest level in 45 years, according to the BLS. As a share of total jobs, manufacturing has declined since its peak of 40 percent just after World War II to 27 percent in 1981 and now stands at about 12 percent. Of these, the Progressive Policy Institute (PPI) has estimated that around 840,000 manufacturing jobs have been lost since the beginning of 2001 due to increased imports and decreased exports—jobs that have been shipped overseas to cheap labor. (BLS graph below)

While it's true that increased productivity because of technology accounts for most of the decline in manufacturing jobs, it is equally true that it's darned hard to find something made in America, certainly not at Wal-Mart, which imports over 60 percent of its goods from China.

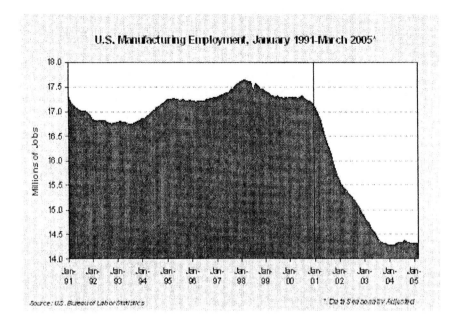

U.S. Manufacturing Employment, January 1991-March 2005[*]

Source: U.S. Bureau of Labor Statistics　　　*[*] Data Seasonally Adjusted*

How many and what other kinds of jobs (aside from manufacturing) are at risk to offshoring? (See Chapter 13—Friedman, *The World is Flat*.) PPI estimates that the new digital economy is enabling as many as 12 million information-based jobs—once considered relatively immobile—to locate virtually anywhere across the globe. Forrester Research estimates that American companies will move 3.4 million jobs offshore by 2015.

Testifying to a Congressional Hearing in September 2005, Robert Baugh, AFL-CIO Industrial Union Council executive director, offered this analysis:

> Our unions and their members have grave concerns about the future of manufacturing and the economy. There is something fundamentally flawed with the business practices of our nation's largest corporations.
>
> Over the past decade a dominant business model, supported by government trade and tax policy, has emerged in the American economy that promotes the outsourcing/offshoring of American manufacturing. The loss of our manufacturing capacity – the intellectual and technical

capability to make things – is a profound threat to the nation's economy and our national security...

The trade picture (chart below) tells the other side of the employment story. It is a disaster. The 2004 $666 billion goods trade deficit is headed toward $700 billion – more than 6 percent of the GDP...

Over the past five years our so-called free trade policy with the Chinese government has resulted in the largest bilateral trade deficits between any two countries in the history of the world (second chart below)...

Our union members and the communities they live in know that manufacturing means good jobs and healthy communities. They know that our nation's economic and national security are dependent upon a strong manufacturing base.

There is a simple truth that the working families of this nation understand...if we don't make things we have nothing to trade and if we have nothing to trade can never solve the trade deficit.

They also understand that the loss of skilled workers, R&D, engineering, design, etc. means the next best idea, the next innovation, the next generation of products, the next investment will be made somewhere else, not here.

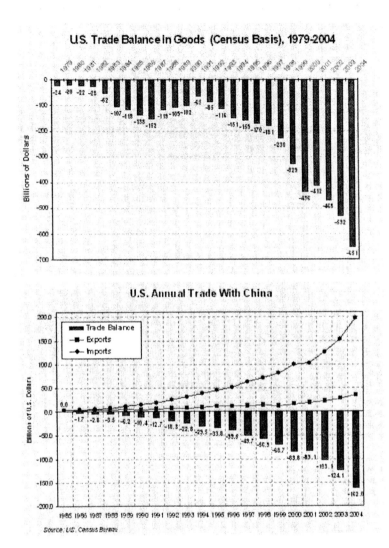

U.S. Trade Balance in Goods (Census Basis), 1979-2004

U.S. Annual Trade With China

Source: U.S. Census Bureau

In the 1990s the concerns of globalization on U.S. jobs were a hot issue when Congress was faced with the two most transforming trade agreements of the 20th century, NAFTA and the Uruguay Round of the General Agreement on Tariffs and Trade (GATT), which established the WTO.

Democratic President Bill Clinton, along with the Republican majority and conservative Democrats in Congress, worked hard to push the trade agreements into law. Opposed were pro-labor Democrats and a few Republicans, such as Strom Thurman and Jesse Helms—who correctly predicted the destruction of the textile industries in their home states. The unlikely bedfellows of Ross Perot, Ralph Nader and Pat Buchanan, who were running against Clinton for the presidency, were among the outspoken opposition.

While the proponents claimed free trade and globalization would create hundreds of thousands of new jobs because of export markets, the opponents called the trade agreements a surrender of national sovereignty and predicted the "great sucking sound" of jobs leaving the country.[188]

Then the debate was over the balance of manufacturing jobs; on that basis, a decade later the evidence clearly shows the United States has been a loser. But no one foresaw the ramifications that cheap interconnectivity would have on outsourcing. Nor did anyone foresee the growth of Wal-Mart, or the trade imbalance that has spiraled out of control in the 21st century (over $2 trillion 2000-2004).

I am among those who think we need to seriously regroup. The United States is digging a hole for itself and the first thing we need to do is stop digging.

The overall jobs outlook is deeply disturbing. It is not only the growing number of unemployed; it is the quality of the jobs.

The following is from an analysis by the Center on Budget and Policy Priorities titled "The Lukewarm 2004 Labor Market: Despite Signs of Improvement, Wages Fell, Job Growth Lagged, and Unemployment Spells Remained Long," revised February 17, 2005:

Among nearly all groups of workers, wages fell, relative to inflation.

Inflation-adjusted wages grew throughout the recession of 2001 and the jobless recovery that followed. However, by 2003, the persistently weak job market began to take its toll on wage growth, and last year the hourly wages of most workers either remained flat or dropped relative to inflation. (Throughout this analysis, all wage changes are expressed after making an adjustment for inflation.)

This period also represented a return to growing wage inequality, as wages grew faster among workers at the top of the wage spectrum than among other workers. For example, among men, the hourly earnings of the worker right in the middle of the wage spectrum was essentially the same in 2004 as in 2000 (down 0.2 percent), while hourly earnings rose 7.7 percent for the worker at the 95th percentile (five percent of workers have wages higher than this worker, 95 percent have wages lower than this worker).

Further, from 2003 to 2004, the *only* education group that experienced gains was the group where workers had been to graduate school. All other groups—workers with less than a high school education, with a high school education, with some college, or with a college degree—experienced either flat or falling wages.

Table 3: Annual Changes in Real Hourly Wages by Education and Gender, 2000-04					
All	*Less than High School*	*High School*	*Some College*	*College*	*Advanced Degree*
2000-03	1.2%	1.1%	0.7%	0.7%	0.7%
2003-04	-0.8%	-0.5%	-0.3%	-1.0%	1.1%
Men					
2000-03	1.0%	0.5%	0.2%	0.8%	0.8%
2003-04	-0.7%	-0.3%	0.0%	-1.1%	2.0%
Women					
2000-03	1.4%	1.8%	1.3%	0.9%	0.9%
2003-04	-1.4%	-1.1%	-0.9%	-1.1%	0.1%

Source: EPI analysis of CPS data.

Note: All 2000-03 changes are statistically significant at the 0.05 level, except male, some college. For 2003-04, these changes are significant: College, all; HS, Some College, and College, female, (the latter two at the 0.1 level), and male,

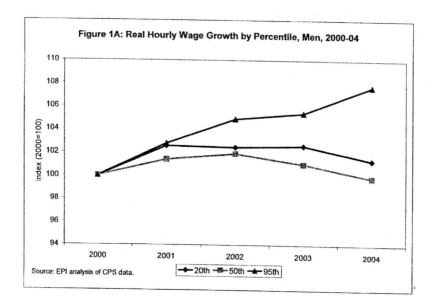

Figure 1A: Real Hourly Wage Growth by Percentile, Men, 2000-04

Source: EPI analysis of CPS data.

Note: After this report was published, monthly reports by the BLS continued to show a decline of over 2.3 percent, after inflation. By that measure, average pay for an hour's work has less purchasing power than it had four years ago—since the Republicans have ruled. And even that doesn't reflect the airline and automotive wage concessions given by workers late in 2005.

Another factor in judging the success or failure of our trade and tax policies is the growing disparity between the very wealthy and working class families. (See Chapter 11 – "…the middle class was merely a brief interregnum between the Gilded Ages of the robber barons of old and the 21st century imperial CEOs.") The data used in Chapter 11 was from a 1998 report by economic historians Claudia Goldin and Robert Margo. The following update is from an October 17, 2005 report by the Center on Budget and Policy Priorities titled "New IRS Data Show Income Inequality is Again On the Rise":

New figures from the Internal Revenue Service show that income disparities grew substantially from 2002 to 2003. After adjusting for inflation, the after-tax income of the one percent of households with the highest incomes shot up in 2003 by an average of nearly $49,000 per household while the after-tax incomes of the bottom 75 percent of households fell on average. The term "household" here refers to tax filers with positive amounts of adjusted gross income.

The IRS data are especially important because they provide the first full snapshot of trends since 2002 at the top of the income spectrum; Census data through 2004 fail to capture this information because they omit a substantial share of the income at the top of the income spectrum (such as all capital gains income and all earnings above $999,999 per year). The less complete Census data as well as other information do suggest, however, that income disparities have widened further since 2003 and that it has been an uneven recovery.

Income disparities are again widening in the United States even though they were already at near-record levels. Data from the Congressional Budget Office that go through 2002 show that income inequality that year was wider than in all but six years (1988 and 1997-2001) since the middle of the 1930s.

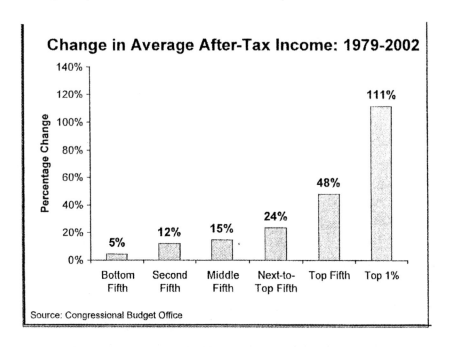

Change in Average After-Tax Income: 1979-2002

Source: Congressional Budget Office

Average After-Tax Income by Income Group (in 2002 dollars)				
Income Category	1979	2002	Percent Change 1979-2002	Dollar Change 1979-2002
Lowest fifth	$13,200	$13,800	4.5%	$600
Second fifth	$26,700	29,900	12.0%	$3,200
Middle fifth	$38,000	$43,700	15.0%	$5,700
Fourth fifth	$49,800	$61,700	23.9%	$11,900
Top fifth	$87,700	$130,000	48.2%	$42,300
Top 1 Percent	$298,900	$631,700	111.3%	$332,800

Source: Congressional Budget Office, *Effective Federal Tax Rates: 1979-2002*, March 2005.

There is no question that the current international trade policies of the United States are unsustainable and a contributing factor to a growing jobs crisis. But there is a tremendous division of opinion of what to do about it.

There are those, some in the Democratic Party, who are advocating getting out of the WTO, NAFTA, CAFTA, and returning to only bilateral agreements with other nations that are clearly in the best interest of American workers and our country.[189] They say our present trade policies have benefited business and the wealthy, not the American worker, and have widened the gap between rich and poor. They further believe that current trade practices have been harmful to the environment, to international labor standards, and to poor countries; and are unhappy because they believe that while U.S. trade practices are fair, most other countries' are not.

I agree to some extent but don't think getting out of the WTO or other "free trade" agreements is the answer. Nor do I think U.S. trade practices are all that fair, particularly to poor countries. To a large extent I believe, as expressed in these pages, that it is a failure of our domestic priorities that is lowering the average Americans standard of living, which is being exacerbated by our trade policies. Of course we must bring exports up and imports down, but that has to be done without closing the door on international trade. One idea, proposed by Warren Buffett, is the use of import certificates (see Chapter 13).

Going back a decade, the proponents of the WTO and NAFTA were swept up in an ideological dream—the Cold War was over, the Berlin Wall was down, and the vision of open markets was irresistible. I shared that dream. As an international airline pilot, I thought the world was on the cusp of a great new dawn, that modern air travel would bring people together and international trade would not only improve the quality of life for a large portion of the world's population, but also diminish the possibilities of war. I think that's still true—but the way we are going about it isn't working at all well.

For starters, there is no such thing as "free trade," anymore than there is the proverbial free lunch. Nation-states and transnational businesses will *always* seek trade advantages and new markets, without surrendering their own. (Chapter 11, reflections on capitalism)

Nations, for instance, can manipulate their currency to keep the cost of exports low and that of imports high (as China has done). By not investing in its people, the standard of living and the cost of labor can be kept low, and other national goals pursued. And then the environment can be raped for short-term gains; we do a pretty good job of that, as does India, China, and Mexico, to name a few (more in the next chapter). If U.S. negotiators were doing their job, these practices would not be tolerated by our trade agreements. But they're not doing their job and that has given the United States a black eye and put us at a competitive disadvantage.

I think the idealism that ushered in the WTO has to give way to more pragmatic solutions that protect our national interest while encouraging open world markets. It is a very delicate balancing act, wherein intention means all.

U.S. policies are skewed toward big business, not workers, neither here nor abroad. In many ways we are back to the days of the robber barons; only now they are the CEOs of multinational corporations. I think these guys have to be reined in and reminded that America is still the world's largest economy and the world's largest market. If America's multinational corporations want the use of our military umbrella, and want access to our domestic markets, moving units of their businesses offshore should not permit them to shelter profits from taxation and bypass their responsibility to the American people. *But that's what our government is allowing now, and it is wrong.*

That is one reason I am leery of "fast track" authority, which Congress has authorized for Bush until April 2007. With fast track, the current "Doha Round" of WTO negotiations could turn into a disaster.[190] For instance, Bush's authority does not force him to include protection for the environment and workers' rights in our trade agreements, lacks adequate procedures for consultation with Congress and the public, and limits debate about trade policy.

I don't like the idea of Grover Norquist and far-right think tanks influencing policies for our trade negotiations. Ultimately, what it comes down to is trust in our government, and the Bush administration does not have my trust, not in domestic policies, and not in foreign policies, including international trade agreements.

On the face of it, our national sovereignty isn't endangered by the WTO anymore than it is by the United Nations. The WTO is an organization of governments. (The private sector, non-government organizations, corporations and other lobbying groups do not participate in WTO activities, except in special events such as seminars and symposiums.)

The WTO does not tell governments what to do. WTO's rules—the trade agreements—are the result of negotiations between the member governments. The current set were the outcome of the 1986-94 Uruguay Round negotiations, which include a major revision of the original General Agreement on Tariffs and Trade.

GATT is now the WTO's principal rulebook for trade in goods. The Uruguay Round also created new rules for dealing with trade in services, relevant aspects of intellectual property, dispute settlement, and trade policy reviews.[191]

In short, within the WTO framework nations negotiate trade agreements—the WTO settles disputes. The United States has the right to say no to proposed trade agreements by WTO members or to renegotiate them.

In regard to disputes, this is from the WTO website:

> The only occasion when a WTO body can have a direct impact on a government's policies is when a dispute is brought to the WTO and if that leads to a ruling by the Dispute Settlement Body (which consists of all members). Normally the Dispute Settlement Body makes a ruling by adopting the findings of a panel of experts or an appeal report.
>
> Even then, the scope of the ruling is narrow: it is simply a judgment or interpretation of whether a government has broken one of the WTO's

agreements—agreements that the infringing government had itself accepted. If a government has broken a commitment it has to conform.

The WTO cannot enforce its decrees. It can only grant complainants permission to retaliate by imposing their own tariffs on products imported from the unrepentant country. According to Steve Seidenberg in the National Law Journal, defiance of the WTO is a growing trend. A recent study indicates that one in seven judgments rendered by the WTO's dispute mechanisms have been ignored.[192]

In all other respects, the WTO does not dictate to governments to adopt or drop certain policies.

Has the WTO has evolved into a kangaroo court weighted against the United States? I don't think it has; rather, I think some of our trade agreements need to be renegotiated, including steel, and textiles. Poorer agricultural countries are being priced out of world markets by the huge subsidies given to EU and U.S. farmers. On the other hand, imported steel and textiles have just about killed U.S. domestic production of those commodities. Those industries and their unions have advocated getting out of the WTO.

On balance, I think if the United States were to withdraw from the WTO it would be at its own peril. As it is, in the last 10 years the GATT agreements have been supplanted by a patchwork of bilateral and regional treaties, such as NAFTA and CAFTA—albeit subject to WTO rules.

It must be said, however, that treaties such as NAFTA and CAFTA have indeed undermined our national sovereignty, in that they have elevated multinational corporations to the virtual status of sovereign nations with the power to challenge and potentially override federal, state and local laws and regulations. Under NAFTA's Chapter 11, corporations can demand that a legal restriction (an environmental regulation, for example) be eliminated or that the federal government compensate the corporation for lost profits.

A case in point is a Canadian corporation's (Methanex) demand for compensation because of a California ban on MTBE, a gasoline additive for which it produces a component. NAFTA rules give the state no legal standing, so the federal government has to defend the state regulation. As of early 2005, U.S. taxpayers had already shelled out $3 million to ward off the corporate demand.

By that same time period, 42 corporations had sued the governments of the United States, Canada and Mexico for a total of more than $28 billion. UPS, for example, claimed that it was an illegal public subsidy under NAFTA rules for the Canadian postal service to deliver parcels.

CAFTA enhances that corporate power. Under NAFTA, U.S. corporations could not sue federal state or local governments in this country. CAFTA allows them to do exactly that through their foreign subsidiaries, if the subsidiary does an active business abroad and is not just a foreign post office box. And that is only one example. (See the Global Trade Watch website: www.tradewatch.org)

Lest we forget, many wars have been fought over international trade. When the GATT was established after WW II, in 1947, the goal was to encourage trade, and to prevent trade wars that have a way of turning into military conflicts. This remains an important consideration. If the WTO is broken, we should help fix it, and be a true world superpower by providing the leadership to do so.

One thing is for sure. The billions of workers from the former Soviet Union, China and India who joined the world labor market with the end of the Cold War and the advent of dot.com high-speed connectivity, have raised the competitive bar for American workers. And cope and compete we must; economic isolation is not an option

The question is, how?

On the plus side, *if* the new competing countries use their newfound wealth to increase the standard of living of their people, their purchasing power would go up, and they too would become consumers for our exports; a balance would develop *if* open markets were fairly constructed. But that could take years, if not decades, of conscientious governance, and that is not what's happening now. In the meantime, the bottom line is jobs lost are jobs gone and most are not going to come back. The paradigm for America's workers has changed and our government has serious choices to make. Either we accept a diminished, uncompetitive workforce or keep up with the times.

As I see it, these are the choices. We can continue what we're doing now and allow the further polarization of wealth with multinational corporations coining money, tax breaks for the rich, and a growing military budget; or we can change course, invest in ourselves, as FDR did with the New Deal, invest in retraining workers and providing the best education in the world to our children, and perhaps most of all insist that even America's most menial jobs have value and provide a living wage.

When it comes to economic policy, the simple truth is the Bush administration doesn't have one. "...They don't make policies to deal with problems. They use problems to justify things they wanted to do anyway. So there is no policy to deal with the lack of jobs..." (See Chapter 11 – Paul Krugman)

For the poor and needy, the Republicans in Congress have a Marie Antoinette mindset: "If people have no bread, let them eat cake." This attitude was never more evident then when in the closing hours of Congress, before a two-week vacation for the Thanksgiving recess of 2005, Republicans congratulated themselves on passing legislation to reduce deficits by $50 billion over five years.

The measure would limit spending for the first time in a decade on Medicaid, food stamps, student loans and other benefits that normally rise with inflation and eligibility. The bill was passed in a post-midnight vote (217-215), with all the Democrats voting in opposition, along with 14 GOP rebels. Democratic leader, Rep. Nancy Pelosi, said of the bill, "The Republicans are taking food out of the mouths of children to give tax cuts to America's wealthiest. This is not a statement of America's values."

Oh, and before these people went on vacation, they refused to reconsider an automatic pay raise for themselves of $3,100 to go into effect in January 2006. They got a raise of $4,000 in 2005, for a total of $28,000 since 1997. For low-income workers, on the other hand, the minimum wage was last increased in 1997 and stands at $5.15 an hour. Congress voted yet again not to increase it earlier in 2005.

So I have no illusions; the things that we can do to pull ourselves out of the rut we're in are not going to happen unless there is a change in the balance of power in Washington. The best we can hope for is that an informed citizenry will make that happen.

As I recounted earlier, when FDR faced the Great Depression, the unemployment rate was 19 percent. Although he moved quickly to establish programs to create jobs, there was little federal money to invest in them. Following the precedent of his times, he balanced federal budgets during his first term of office. It wasn't until his second term that finally, in desperation, he listened to the advice of John Maynard Keynes and loosened up the money supply by dropping interest rates and allowing temporary budget deficits. It worked.

The economic problems we are facing in the 21st century are not yet as crippling as those of the 1930s, but if we don't act soon our jobless situation and income inequality are going to get worse. The jobless recovery, exacerbated by globalization, budget and trade deficits could easily turn into the next recession, spread throughout the world, and slip out of control.

It is an interesting dichotomy that in 2005, the United States and much of the world were facing stagnant employment rates (and wages), and inflation—a replay of the "Stagflation" of the 1970s.[193] From June 2004 through 2005 the Federal Reserve had raised overnight interest rates on loans between banks 12 times, from 1 percent to 4 percent to combat inflation—inflation, albeit largely fueled by a rise in the price of oil and the housing boom. Yet how much should the Fed increase interest rates with the poor job market that exists? I think a large part of the problem is that Alan Greenspan has been in league with the Bush administration by underplaying the seriousness of America's jobs crisis. I hope that Ben S. Bernanke, the new chairman of the Federal Reserve, will not.

How did we get this screwed up? Easy, because of Reagan's supply-side economics that the Bush administration has brought to a new pinnacle of lunacy, combined with a war being fought on borrowed money. The tax cuts for the rich don't work; they didn't work for Reagan and they are not working now. Certainly not while we are fielding a large military force in Iraq that is costing a billion dollars a week. While it is true that rescinding or at least allowing many of the tax cuts for the rich to twilight on schedule will go a long way toward closing the deficit, I am among those who would allow short-term deficits to continue and pump money into job creation and retraining and education. After all, short-term deficits are what allowed the New Deal to work.

Consequently, I hope Bernanke and the Fed give job creation priority over draconian price stabilization. Sure, we needed to increase the interest rates to cool the housing boom, as the Fed has done, and we may need to raise them more. But the flip side can be positive too. Higher Fed interest rates will force the Treasury to pay a higher yield on T-Bills, which will encourage the large amount of foreign investment in the U.S. economy to continue.

While the sale of T-Bills would add to the national debt and keep the Balance of Currant Accounts deficit high for a while; the import of investment money—if not used to fuel an overheated housing market and compensate for tax cuts—would be extremely desirable, and help offset the huge trade imbalance of goods. This only makes sense if the foreign investment is used to help fund long-term solutions to strengthen the middle class against the impact of technology and globalization.

It is rather a unique opportunity to use the vast economy of the United States to our advantage, an opportunity FDR never had. In the 1930s, there were few foreign investors or countries capable or willing to invest in our economy. I think if John Maynard Keynes were still around, he would approve of temporary budget deficits used for such purposes. Here is one of his apropos quotes:

Capitalism is the astounding belief that the most wickedest of men will do the most wickedest of things for the greatest good of everyone.

As this is written, Bernanke is still a question mark. Is he a hawk or a dove on fighting inflation? His writings and his record at the Fed suggest he will be in line with the Fed consensus to maintain price stability. On the other hand, his writings seem to emphasize the need for flexibility and "constrained discretion."

At a Senate confirmation hearing on November 15, 2005, Bernanke told lawmakers that it was a "false dichotomy" to assume that low inflation was at odds with rising wages and greater income equality. He further said, "Middle-income living standards, and poverty for that matter, are best addressed through employment growth. By maintaining low inflation and low expectations of inflation, you can create new employment."

And in describing his approach, he sharply distanced it from those of some central banks that focus almost exclusively on an inflation target and not at all on promoting growth. "I don't agree with that," Bernanke declared flatly.

In sharp contrast to Greenspan, Bernanke immediately made it clear that he did not want to comment on fiscal policy. While Greenspan supported Bush's tax cuts in 2001, a move that many lawmakers said set the stage for the huge deficits that followed, Bernanke said he would not comment on any tax or budget proposals.[194]

Though I like what Bernanke said at his confirmation hearings, it is disconcerting that he was Bush's chief economic adviser (for a few scant months) prior to his nomination. We'll have to wait and see how independent the new Fed chairman is once free of the White House.

Bernanke's awareness of the link between the rising poverty level and the shrinking middle class is particularly encouraging, but the question is what to do about it.

In order to provide the American worker with economic security, and make our nation more competitive in international trade, *we must first recognize that our semi-privatized social safety net and welfare state system is no longer viable.*

The economic model of the 1960s was built on the premise that American workers at big companies—usually under union contracts—could depend on those companies to guarantee job security, health care and a dignified retirement. That was the deal.

As new technologies continue to change industries, so go the big corporations. A good example of that is the U.S. steel industry—employment there fell 60 percent between 1968 and 2000. Add into this equation government deregulation and globalization, and America's workers have found their economic security as fragile as the future of the companies they work for. To put it simply, many of America's corporate giants are no longer able to hold up their end of the deal, because they themselves are in peril. Witness the steel, airline and automotive industries. Broken promises, shattered lives.

As Paul Krugman put it in his November 28, 2005 New *York Times* column, "Such deals were, in a real sense, the basis of America's postwar social order. We like to think of ourselves as rugged individualists, not like those coddled Europeans with their oversized welfare states. But as Jacob Hacker of Yale points out in his book *The Divided Welfare State*, if you add in corporate spending on health care and pensions—spending that is both regulated by the government and subsidized by tax breaks—we actually have a welfare state that's about as large relative to our economy as those of other advanced countries.

"What went wrong? An important part of the answer is that America's semi-privatized welfare state worked in the first place only because we had a stable corporate order. And that stability—along with any semblance of economic security for many workers—is now gone."

It is essential that economic security for American families be restored, and that our social safety net be brought up to the standards of other leading industrialized nations. American businesses cannot be competitive if they have to carry the burden of a privatized welfare state. In this regard, here is a short wish list of goals:

- Establish a national health care insurance system that is all-inclusive and not employment based. Such a system would replace Medicare (A, B and D), and Medicaid (including long-term nursing home care). Fixing our nation's dysfunctional health-care system would go a long way toward making American industry more competitive and a giant step in fighting poverty.

- Remedy the projected long-term fiscal shortfall of the Social Security Old Age and Survivors (OASDI) Trust Fund, without reducing benefits or privatization.

- Pass legislation that protects company defined benefit plans and assures full payment of benefits to workers and retirees backed by the federal government.

- Reinforce our direct aid welfare programs, including Temporary Aid to Needy Families (TANF), Supplemental Security Income (SSI), food stamps and Department of Agriculture food pantries, and Housing and Urban Development supplemental housing. Collectively, these programs should bring families up to the poverty line—not keep families living in poverty.

Will the far right ever do these things? Not a prayer: They're busy chopping our social programs. Nonetheless, it would be prudent for our nation's leaders, Democrat or Republican, to keep in mind that if the gap between the rich and the poor widens, our country will become increasingly politically unstable. This has been so throughout history, was so in the 1930s and is so today.

A recent example is the weeks of rioting in France during the autumn of 2005. Reminiscent of the Black violence in several American cities in the 1960s, the French youths rioting, mostly Muslim, were doing so because they have been socially and economically excluded. (The unemployment rate in France in April 2005 was 10.2 percent; in the Muslim ghettos it was about 40 percent.) As Olivier Roy, a professor at the School for Advanced Studies in Social Sciences, put it, "Americans, for their part, should take little pleasure in France's agony—the struggle to integrate an angry underclass is one shared across the Western world."

Another example is Germany. In a strange election in November 2005, the conservative Christian Democratic Party was able to put together a "grand coalition" with the more liberal Social Democrats, which resulted in the ouster of Chancellor Gerhard Schröder, who had dominated German politics for years. The political shakeup was the result of Germany's stagnating economy and a postwar unemployment rate high of 12 percent.

The comparative unemployment numbers of France, Germany, and the United States is deceiving. Both of those countries have a much more expansive social safety net than we do, strong unions, contract agreements, and laws that encourage full-time employment at a livable wage. (Albeit, since the 1970s both France and Germany have reduced the workweek to 35 hours, and limited the use of overtime in exchange for more leisure time, and job creation.)[195] Consequently, the level of pain created by their unemployment rate of 10 to 12 percent is actually similar to what ours would be if we factored in underemployed and discouraged workers; for Blacks and Hispanics it would be higher yet.

Does anyone doubt that an angry underclass is rising in America? I sure don't.

Jobs

Whether it is jobs going offshore or jobs lost to technology, we desperately need a national strategy to deal with it—a strategy that will create jobs, keep the jobs we have and train, retrain, and educate our workforce to fill them. It is a dynamic process in which the United States has been lagging way behind for decades.

Businesses that employ workers are created by the need of a product or a service. That product could be a farm product or a jet airliner; the service could be provided by a medical professional, plumber or the Internet. The list is endless and actually tracked to a large extent by the Bureau of Labor Statistics (BLS); there are hundreds of job classifications. But what do you do if the product you produce or the service you perform isn't needed anymore?

For example, Swiss watches were the best in the world. Yet electronic watches that cost a fraction of the price and kept better time replaced them virtually overnight. Another example would be carburetors. Once they were a vital component of all the internal combustion engines that powered our automobiles and trucks—then, zoom, they were replaced with fuel injection systems. The paradigm shift forced those businesses and workers to either change, close shop, retrain or leave the workforce.

Those two examples were the result of the rapidly changing world of mechanization and technology; in the 21st century, outsourcing and globalization are multiplying the problem. Large businesses protect themselves with diversity and research and development. As an example, the General Electric Corporation has something like 137 diverse businesses located both here and abroad. If one of those businesses or locations goes sour, they close it and use the resources elsewhere.

On the other hand, the United States has never developed a strategy for displaced workers, when plants close or their job skills are no longer needed. These workers find that losing a good job can mean a tremendous loss of earnings and benefits. This has been a growing problem since the 1980s. Age discrimination, although ostensibly illegal, contributes to the problem; few employers want to invest in expensive on-the-job training for a 50 or 60-year-old.

America has to create a new social contract for workers. We need an economic model that offers affordable retraining, and laws that prevent corporations from treating workers simply as an expendable cost of doing business. When plants are closed or businesses move offshore, there should be more than just a wink and nod to relocating workers or retraining them—there should be an economic commitment.

Then we must hold our government accountable for upholding that social contract and expect our political leaders to do everything possible to keep the good jobs that exist. Of those good jobs, civil service (federal, state, and local) has been a bedrock employer of the middle class since the days of FDR.[196] Those jobs have offered pay rates slightly lower than the private sector, traded for job security and benefits. During good times or bad, those jobs have had an important stabilizing influence on our economy for over 70 years.

In October 2005, the BLS reported total government employment at about 22 million. Compared to other sectors, (farming, 8 million; manufacturing, 14 million; construction, 7 million; retail trade, 15 million; professional and business services, 17 million; education and health services, 17 million; leisure and hospitality, 13 million [All numbers are rounded]) *the government is by far our largest employer.*

The military has also historically been a refuge when jobs are scarce. The Armed Forces have about 1.4 million active-duty personnel.[197] Not surprisingly, most of our "all-volunteer" army is drawn from financially stressed young men and women in jobless rural areas.

To entice enlistments the military is offering signing bonuses up to $30,000 for jobs in high demand, and up to a $150,000 cash bonus for reenlisting if you are in Special Forces. And all recruits are eligible for up to $50,000 to offset the costs of higher education and up to $65,000 to pay back college loans. Not to mention generous housing, childcare, and health benefits.

Not a bad deal, if you can avoid getting blown up or shot in Iraq or Afghanistan, but not good enough to entice America's rich kids. The truth is if America's job situation improves and the war in Iraq continues the military is going to have an even harder time meeting its enlistment quotas.

I have always felt that, when it comes jobs, every person creates a new job when born. In the pre-mechanized agrarian world this was self-evident. A farmer needed sons to help work the fields. Women didn't outlive men (because of the high mortality rate of childbirth) as they do now, and people overall died at a much younger age. In essence, the dynamic was reversed; there were more jobs than people to fill them. As we discussed in the worldview section, the industrial revolution changed all that and, unfortunately, we are still struggling to come up with an economic model that works.

A large part of the problem is the American model of capitalism. At the core of our ideology is the sale of goods or services to make a profit. As discussed earlier, the United States has developed industries and huge businesses that, although facing difficult times, have done that very well. What we haven't done well at all is learn how to invest in ourselves as a society. FDR created works projects like the Tennessee Valley Authority electric power system, the WPA, and other public works projects that both invested in our infrastructure and created jobs. These were carefully managed by government agencies.

In contrast, the federal government of late dispenses pork—bridges that go nowhere and tax breaks to a petroleum industry that is awash in windfall profits.

Yet America's infrastructure is seriously in need of investment—investment that, if managed properly by competent government agencies, would reinforce the middle class and create good paying jobs.

In 2005, the American Society of Civil Engineers (ASCE) issued a report card for America's infrastructure. The report card assessed 15 infrastructure categories individually, and collectively gave the system a "D." The assessed categories included aviation, bridges, dams, drinking water, energy (national power grid), hazardous waste, navigable waterways, public parks and recreation, rail, roads, schools, security, solid waste, transit and wastewater. [Both roads and transit have worsened since the last report card. Roads went from a D+ to a D and transit from a C- to D-.]

ASCE estimates that $1.6 trillion over five years will be needed to remedy "current and looming problems." According to ASCE, that level does not include estimates for infrastructure security needs. Note: The report card was issued early in 2005 before the devastation of Hurricane Katrina and other hurricanes that wrecked havoc in the South. The early estimate of rebuilding after Katrina was $200 billion, but by late 2005 only a portion of that had been allocated since President Bush made his empty promises months before.

Then it is amazing that, given the importance of civil service jobs, the mental midgets ruling our country are committed to "privatizing" government to save money.

Here again, their program is a lie. It is a proven fact that government services turned over to private companies have invariably cost the taxpayers more while providing degraded services. The workers wind up earning less, with fewer benefits and less job security, while the private companies reap large profits. It has become the American economic model—shrink government and grow the corporate empires.

Privatization

At risk for privatization are Social Security, Medicare, education, U.S. Postal Service, U.S. Weather Bureau, air traffic control, and prisons.[198]

Social Security: At the end of 2005, Bush's attempt to privatize Social Security for the moment seemed to have fallen by the wayside under a crush of ethics problems and Iraq war news. But for so long as the Republican far right is in power, rest assured it will continue to try to get its foot in the door.

Medicare: As Paul Krugman pointed out in a column on November 18, 2005, "The Medicare drug benefit is an example of gratuitous privatization on a grand scale."[199]

Here's some background: In many areas of the country elders on Medicare have long been offered a choice between standard Medicare, in which the government pays the medical bills directly, and plans in which the government pays a middleman, like an H.M.O., to deliver health care. The theory was that the private sector would find innovative ways to lower costs while providing better services.

It never happened. Studies have found that the managed-care plans have higher administrative costs than the government, and end up costing Medicare more, not less.

But despite the facts, privatization has become a goal in itself. Medicare D (drug coverage) went further than merely offering a choice of subsidized private plans; it made them mandatory. To receive the drug benefit, one must sign up with a plan offered by a private company. The result is tremendously confusing because the competing private plans are different in ways hard to assess. In the end, America will be spending a ton of money and getting little for it. The private insurers and drug companies however are guaranteed by the federal government to do very well.

Education: The thrust to privatize education is centered on the diversion of government money from public schools to religious schools, vouchers, and charter schools. At the state university level it comes from the dwindling state funding of university budgets.

Private schools have always been an uncontested alternative to public schools in America. The conflict arises with the use of public money for tuition. If a family wishes to send its child to a private school, should the community and state be required to offset the cost? This is a particularly thorny question if it is a means of circumventing the Constitutional prohibitions against subsidizing religious practice and instruction (85 percent of private schools are religious).

What has evolved in recent years, politically pushed by the religious far right under the guise of school choice, is the use of tuition vouchers. It is a way of diverting tax dollars away from public schools. In the words of Grover Norquist, "We win just by debating school choice, because the alternative is to discuss the need to spend more money....." Obviously, this is obfuscation to avoid the issue; we need to invest more money in our public schools.

In June 2002 the U.S. Supreme Court reversed an appeals court decision 5-4, ruling that a pilot voucher program in Cleveland, Ohio did not infringe upon the constitutional separation of church and state. The reasoning was that although most of the vouchers went to religious schools, secular schools were also available.

After learning of the ruling, Sen. Edward Kennedy, D-Mass, then chairman of the Senate Health, Education, Labor and Pensions Committee, released a statement slamming the voucher program. "Private school vouchers may pass constitutional muster, but they fail the test when it comes to improving our nation's public schools. It's flat wrong to take scarce taxpayers dollars away from public schools and divert them to private schools," Kennedy said. "Despite the Court's ruling, vouchers are still bad policy for public schools, and Congress must not abandon its opposition to them."

I agree wholeheartedly with Sen. Kennedy. While superficially school vouchers might seem a way to increase options for poor parents to educate their children, it comes at a heavy price. These programs subvert the principle of separation of church and state, divert funds from public schools, hold students to different standards, and fundamentally threaten our system of public education.

Charter schools are publicly funded elementary or secondary schools that are privately owned businesses. Quite a mouthful isn't it? They sprang up in the 1990s, basically on the premise that free from some of the rules, regulations, and statutes that apply to other public schools they could be held accountable for results, which are spelled out in each charter school's charter. (It's another twist on the deregulation that was discussed in Chapter 14.)

By 2004, nearly 3,000 of them had been launched since state legislatures began passing charter legislation in the 1990s. They now exist in 37 states plus the District of Columbia and Puerto Rico, enrolling approximately 750,000 students. However, more than one-third of those schools had been in operation for three years or less, while more than 400 other charter schools had gone out of business between 1991 and 2004.[200] (In 2005, New Hampshire had seven small charter schools with a total enrollment of under 200 students.) As a candidate for the New Hampshire Senate I did not support them.

Proponents claim that chartering is a radical educational innovation that is moving states beyond reforming existing schools to creating something entirely new. Opponents say that educational and financial accountability is proving to be elusive.

In a study that tracked North Carolina students for several years, professors Robert Bifulco and Helen Ladd found that students in charter schools actually made considerably smaller achievement gains than they would have in traditional public schools.

I think that while experimentation in educational methods is important, America needs greater accountability, not less. We'll discuss the need for national educational goals later in the chapter.

As reported in the *New York Times* on October 16, 2005, "Taxpayer support for public universities, measured per student, has plunged more precipitously since 2001 than at any time in two decades, and several university presidents are calling the decline a de facto privatization of the institutions that played a crucial role in the creation of the American middle class."[201]

The share of all public universities' revenue derived from state and local taxes declined to 64 percent in 2004 from 74 percent in 1991. But it varies greatly from state to state. About 25 percent of the University of Illinois' budget comes from the state; Michigan about 18 percent; and Virginia 8 percent; 22.7 percent of the University of New Hampshire budget will come from the state in 2006.

"At those levels, we have to ask what it means to be a public institution," said Katharine C. Lyall, an economist and president emeritus of the University of Wisconsin. "America is rapidly privatizing its public colleges and universities, whose mission used to be to serve the public good. But if private donors and corporations are providing much of a university's budget, then they will set the agenda, perhaps in ways the public likes and perhaps not. Public control is slipping away."

United States Postal Service: The former name of the United States Postal Service (USPS) was the Post Office Department, a cabinet department headed by the United States Postmaster General. President George Washington established the department in 1792.

It was changed from a cabinet department to a government owned corporation by the Postal Service Reorganization Act that took effect on July 1, 1971. During the 1960s, the Post Office Department was under fire because it was said to be "not capable of meeting the demands of our growing economy and our expanding population."[202] It was also said that political patronage reigned supreme, with 33,000 postmaster jobs and some 30,000 rural carrier positions filled by political arrangement.

The Postal Reorganization Act didn't come without a struggle however.[203] On St. Patrick's Day, 1970 Letter Carriers Branch 36, which covered Manhattan and the Bronx, took a strike vote, and walked out. By March 21, one-third of the postal workforce was on strike, the first major strike by federal workers since the founding of the United States. On March 23, President Nixon declared a national emergency, and announced that he would send the National Guard into New York City to move the mail. Within two days, the strike was over.[204]

Reorganized, USPS has worked out extremely well. The Postal Service is basically self-supportive. Prices have been relatively stable—in real dollars, the 37-cent stamp costs little more than the 8-cent stamp cost in 1968. The Postal Service budget still runs slightly in the red; in 2004 it was a $4 billion off-budget outlay (it stands as an off-budget line item along with Social Security).

In August 2004 the Postal Service employed over 781,000 postal clerks and letter carriers who earned more than $52,000 a year, including benefits. The median pretax household income in America reported by the Census Bureau was $44,389, so these are good jobs—jobs that are targeted by the Heritage Foundation, the CATO Institute, and the far right for "privatization."

One of the reasons given is that e-mail is cutting down on so-called snail mail, which is true; mail volume growth, which had averaged 4.5 percent in the 1980s and half that in the 1990s is now nearly zero. But it is also true that the Postal Service is essential to the American economy, and not just for the 781,000 postal jobs. The U.S. mailing industry employs nine million workers and constitutes about eight percent of the nation's gross domestic product. If the USPS fails, can companies such as UPS and FedEx do the job? It is worth considering that one week's USPS volume equals one year's UPS volume; two days' Postal Service volume equals one year's FedEx volume.[205]

The Postal Service does have serious problems as we go deeper into the 21st century, but the solution most certainly isn't privatization. The service is chartered as a government owned corporation, so the answer is our federal government has to do its job and manage it.

It is like everything else our far-right rulers are doing. Not knowing how to govern, they feather the nest of the very rich and hope they will do it for them before it's noticed that they are incompetent.

National Weather Service: Unbelievably, in April 2005 Sen. Rick Santorum, an archconservative Republican from Pennsylvania, introduced the National Weather Service Duties Act of 2005 (S. 786). The legislation would have limited the information that the National Weather service can provide to the public, in what Republican aides describe as an effort to make sure that private weather companies—particularly those in Santorum's home state—can compete in the marketplace and retain jobs.

What Santorum's aides failed to say was that employees of AccuWeather, one of the companies arguing for the legislation, have contributed at least $5,500 to Santorum since 1999, according to Federal Election Commission reports.

It was terrible "privatization" legislation that would change the important role of the National Weather Service to provide free information for the public as well as to airplane pilots and farmers, who are among some six million people who each day access weather service data on the Web pages of the National Oceanic and Atmospheric Administration, or NOAA. As an airline pilot, I was one of those people for many years; the service and information is the best in the world.

Fortunately, Santorum's bill had no co-sponsors and didn't go anywhere.

Almost four in 10 atmospheric scientists, commonly called meteorologists, work for the federal government; the rest work for the media as weathermen (and women) or for private weather companies, such as AccuWeather. In 2002, atmospheric scientists held about 7,700 jobs, with the federal government accounting for about 2,900.

In 2003, the average salary for a meteorologist employed by the federal government was about $74,528. Good jobs held by dedicated, talented people.

Air Traffic Control: Air traffic control (ATC) in the United States is primarily the responsibility of the Federal Aviation Administration. The military has its own system that is coordinated into the national/international ATC systems. Air traffic controllers held about 26,000 jobs in 2002. Of these, the FAA, which is part of the federal government, employed the vast majority.

The median annual salary of air traffic controllers in 2002 was $91,600, with an excellent benefit package. While it is expected that the need for controllers will increase with the demand of air travel, this will be moderated both by technology, and the FAA's use of "private" nongovernmental facilities—mostly local control towers with lower density traffic.

There were actually 2,000 fewer air traffic controllers employed by the FAA in 2005 than there were in 2003. And the trend to privatize ATC was likely to continue under the policies of the Bush administration.

Prior to landing my first airline job as a pilot, I took a job as an air traffic controller in 1959, and went through the six-week training course at the FAA Academy in Oklahoma City. It was a great experience and proved to be a big help throughout my 37-year airline career. Let me tell you, you can get just as dead in a collision at a low-density airport as at JFK, and you want highly trained and dedicated professionals at both.

Some things are just too important to the public safety to be privatized, and here again it has become our government's policy to give away good and stable jobs.

Prisons: At this point I have to tell you that while I have a lot of experience with the National Weather Service and the air traffic control system, I've never set foot in an operational prison. The closest I've come was to tour Alcatraz in San Francisco Bay long after the facility had been closed.

But I did become familiar with the prison privatization issue when I ran for the New Hampshire Senate. Then Republican Governor Craig Benson (he later lost to Democrat John Lynch) was hot to trot to ship New Hampshire prisoners off to some commercial gulag in the South. As part of my platform, I opposed Benson's plan on ethical grounds. It is just wrong to send prisoners far away from their families and support systems, and certainly would increase recidivism. It is no different than the French sending prisoners off to Devils Island in the Caribbean.

To put the problem in perspective, here's some data from a U.S. Department of Justice study issued in February 2001, titled "Emerging Issues on Privatized Prisons:"

- It is estimated that worldwide there are 184 privately operated correctional facilities, which hold 132,346 inmates.

- Within the United States, a total of 158 private correctional facilities are operating in 30 states, Puerto Rico, and the District of Columbia. Texas has the most facilities (43), followed by California (24), Florida (10), and Colorado (9). Most private correctional facilities tend to be concentrated in the southern and western United States.

- Another 26 private facilities operate in three other countries, with Australia (12) and the United Kingdom (10) topping the list.

- Total revenue allocated to private prisons and jails is estimated at $1 billion.

What is startling is that as of 2003, the total number of people held behind bars in the United States, including federal and state prisons and local jails, now exceeds 2.2 million. This is far more than China (1.4 million) or Russia (920,000). During the 1990s, aggregate state spending on corrections ballooned from $17.2 billion to almost $23 billion.[206] So one could say prisons have turned into a growth industry in America.

Although only a small percentage of U.S. prisoners are held in private facilities (less than 7 percent), the anticipated cost savings of 20 percent has never materialized; the average has been 1 percent, and most of that was achieved through lower labor costs.

There are other issues concerning "private" prisons that concern the Bush administration's treatment of political prisoners that we'll discuss in a coming chapter.

In wrapping up this short look at the ramifications of privatization, I'd like to recommend a new book, *The Fox In The Henhouse: How Privatization Threatens Democracy,* by Si Kahn and Elizabeth Minnich. The authors expose the damage privatization has done in several areas of society, including schools, prisons and the military. They argue that instead of privatization serving the public good, it rewards powerful corporations intent on replacing the government with a "private profit culture" in which there is limited public accountability.

A review of his book quoted Si Kahn: "In *The Fox in the Henhouse,* we're making an argument that we think is somewhat different. Don't think about privatization in terms of the usual arguments that the government gives or that are given by the corporations, which say, 'Oh. This is about saving money for the taxpayer, this is about efficiency.' What we're doing is the largest transfer of public wealth to private pockets in the history of this country. We're seeing this in Iraq, where the goal of this administration is to see how much of the money that should be going to all sorts of other issues and other causes can be put into private pockets. Think Halliburton. Think Lockheed Martin. This is what is going on, and it is the undermining of public space, of the public good, of public welfare, is a deliberate strategy to undermine the ground that belongs to all of us: the common wealth, the commons, those things that create public good, that create a humane society."

Education and Retraining

To remain competitive in the 21ˢᵗ century, the United States is going to have to make a full national commitment to having the most educated citizenry in the world.

Much like with our ranking in health care, Americans have been brainwashed into thinking that our educational system is the best in the world, and that is no longer true. Studies show we are losing ground in education, as peers around the world pass us by in student achievement and school graduations.

A report released by the Paris-based Organization for Cooperation and Development in September 2005, showed that among adults age 25 to 34, the United States is ninth among industrial nations in the percentage of its population that has at least a high school degree. In the same age group, the United States ranks seventh, with Belgium, in the percentage of people who hold a college degree. Barry McGaw, the organization's director of education said, "By both measures, the United States was first in the world as recently as 20 years ago."

The Program for International Assessment, a data gathering part of the organization that compiles reports on the reading and math skills of 15-year-olds, found that the United States ranked 24ᵗʰ out of 29 nations surveyed in math literacy. The same result for the United States (24ᵗʰ out of 29) was found when applying math skills to real-life tasks.

The top performers included Finland, Korea, the Netherlands, Japan, Canada and Belgium.

Given what the United States spends on education, its relatively low student achievement through high school shows its school system is "clearly inefficient," McGaw said.

At all levels of education, the United States spends $11,152 per student. That's the second highest behind the $11,334 spent by Switzerland.[207]

The Organization for Cooperation and Development (a 30-nation organization) develops the yearly rankings as a way for countries to evaluate their education systems and determine whether to change their policies.

When it comes to a national education policy, the truth is the United States doesn't have one (as we don't have a coherent economic policy).

Consequently, we are a nation of extremes, with the quality of education dependent upon the wealth of the community a child lives in and the financial resources of parents. These disparities are widening with America's income gap.

I grappled with understanding education funding as a state Senate candidate. In New Hampshire, as in most states, the lion's share of local property taxes goes to education, which makes "local control" a core issue in American politics—the logic being that "control" should rest with those who pay the bills. In times past, when schools educated the citizenry for local needs, that was workable. But as the nation's need for skilled and highly educated workers increased, who was to set the standard for public schools: the local school boards with an eye to their tax dollars and parochial issues, or the state and federal governments with a broader economic and constitutional responsibility?

For instance, should a school district allow school prayer, sex education, or the teaching of evolution as opposed to "Intelligent Design," a repackaging of biblical creationism.

The problem has never been resolved because it is a political hot potato. Property rich communities want the ability to spend the money on schools to give their kids a good education and the poor school districts throughout the nation are falling farther and farther behind their rich counterparts. Because they have the power to legislate, the state and federal governments mandate certain standards, but they haven't fully funded the mandates.

Poor school districts in state after state have sought relief in the courts. The result of those litigations vary from state to state, but on the whole the courts have ruled that the state has an obligation to financially support an adequate K-12 education for all of its citizens—none has really defined what an adequate education is, however.

So, one way or the other, states have had to financially support local school districts. The breakdown of school funding is inconsistent from state to state, with local property taxes paying anywhere from 50 to 80 percent of school expenditures, and federal and state tax dollars picking up the tab for the rest.

In New Hampshire, which is one of only a few states without either an income tax or a broad-based sales tax, the state merely redistributes property tax from the wealthy school districts to the poor. The issue has been contentious for more than a decade and is once again before the court as this is written.

All the data indicates that students in wealthy school districts rank better in testing and are more likely to graduate from high school and successfully complete a college education. In 2004, only 70 percent of American students entering high school graduated. That statistic is even worse for minorities, with only 50 percent of Blacks and 53 percent of Hispanics earning a high school diploma.

Two Washington think tanks, the Center for American Progress and the Institute for America's Future say an urgent new commitment to public education, much stronger than the No Child Left Behind law, must be made if America's downhill slide in education is to be reversed.[208] The two groups established the National Task Force on Public Education. The report titled "Getting Smarter, Becoming Fairer" from which this information was drawn was released in August 2005. It is an excellent, comprehensive plan for the future of education in America (104 pages), which can be accessed on line at: http://www.americanprogress.org/site/pp.asp?c=biJRJ8O VF&b=994995

The task force found that much of the nation's public education system is a shambles. And kids that need the most help—poor children from inner cities and rural areas—often attend the worst schools: "Young low-income and minority children are more likely to start school without having gained important school readiness skills, such as recognizing letters and counting.... By the fourth grade, low-income students read about three grade levels behind non-poor students. Across the nation, only 15 percent of low-income fourth graders achieved proficiency in reading in 2003, compared to 41 percent of non-poor students."

Not only is the picture horribly bleak for low-income and minority kids, but we find that only 41 percent of non-poor fourth graders can read proficiently.

The report restates the point made by Bill Gates and Thomas Friedman earlier in this book, a point that by now should be clear to most thoughtful

Americans: Too many American kids are ill-equipped educationally to compete successfully in an ever-more competitive global marketplace.

The National Task Force on Public Education makes some recommendations. Here is its outline:

1.   More and Better Use of Learning Time

- Extending the School Day, Lenghtening and/or Reorganizing the School Year, and Making Better Use of Existing Time in School
- Providing Pre-School and Full-Day Kindergarten
- Preparing All High-School Students for Higher Education and Connecting Them to Affordable Post-Secondary Opportunities

2.   High Expectations, Voluntary National Standards, and Accountability for All Students Learning

- Developing voluntary national standards, expanding national accountability measures, and pressing for adequate equitable funding across states.

- Increasing assistance to low-performing schools and districts and promoting school construction and modernization.

3.   Highly Qualified Teachers for Every Classroom and Strong, Effective Leaders for Every School

- Developing better teacher and principal preparation and training, enhanced compensation structures, and a more equitable distribution of highly skilled teachers.

- Connecting Schools with Families and Communities

- Establishing community schools to address out-of-school needs, offering early screening to identify developmental and physical challenges, promoting home visits and support for struggling families, and encouraging greater parental involvement in children's education.

The stakes are high. The European Union and Japan today are formidable advanced industrial competitors. Developing countries such as China and India are offering the world highly educated and sophisticated workers at a far lower cost than we can match. As things stand, by 2050 the three largest economies are likely to be China, the United States and India—in that order.

In order to compete in the 21st century, America must invest in its human capital. We cannot allow the gap between "haves" and "have-nots" to grow in almost every measure of health, income and achievement. Our minority and poor students in rural areas and cities cannot be allowed to continue to fall behind in basic math and reading skills. Students of color are a growing proportion of our population; within the century, they will become our new majority.

Indeed as our world becomes more complex, the skills and critical thinking ability of our citizenry must keep up or the institutions and the leadership necessary to support our democracy will be imperiled.

Here again the mathematical use of average numbers confuses the issue. For instance, as reported by the Organization for Cooperation and Development, the United States ranked at the top of industrial nations in the number of dollars spent per student in all levels of education, $11,152. But to get the true picture we need to look at the component parts of these expenditures. The United States spends vastly more on post-secondary education than any other country, particularly for research expenditures in several world-class universities, but lags significantly behind in ensuring accessibility. We are third in spending for elementary schools and fourth at the secondary level. For pre-school, the United States falls very short. Both the proportion of children in pre-school and those supported by public funds is lower than most European countries.[209]

When it comes to federal funding for K-12 education, the federal government contributes very little; in 2004 of the $395 billion spent, under $30 billion or about 7.5 percent came from federal grants for special purposes; $12 billion went for No Child Left Behind and $9.5 billion for special education students. Amazingly, the feds only contributed 63 cents for each of the 48 million students attending in 2004.

The national average (as reported by NEA) that was spent per student in K-12 ($8,208) is also extremely misleading. Our minority and poor students in rural areas may only be receiving $5,000 in education funding, with those in affluent school districts receiving $13,000. Here are some examples with state ranking:

State	Average Per-Pupil	Rank
District of Columbia	$13,317	1
New York	$12,059	2
Connecticut	$11,773	3
New Jersey	$11,390	4
Mississippi	$6,137	48
Arkansas	$6,005	49
Arizona	$5,347	50
Utah	$5,091	51

The variance in expenditures between states is huge but it often is within the state as well, largely depending on the state's judicial oversight and legislature. It is only the states that have constitutional provisions that variously provide for "sound," "basic," "adequate," or "sufficient" education. The United States Constitution is silent on education and federal courts have no jurisdiction other than to enforce the laws that Congress passes.

The No Child Left Behind Act (NCLB) was supposed to increase federal funding to the highest poverty communities, but Congress and the administration broke their promise. The law was underfunded by $10 billion in 2005 alone, and the cumulative shortfall is projected to total $39 billion by the end of 2006.[210] A lawsuit challenging the under funding of NCLB has been brought by the State of Connecticut.

Our education system in the United States is broken and outdated and we need to do something about it quickly. The system needs more money used to educate *all* our children. We cannot continue to eliminate the poor and the needy. Currently, about $61 billion, less than 3 percent of the federal budget, goes to all levels of education. The National Task Force on Public Education calls for a $325 billion federal investment over 10-years to implement the recommendations in its report. To achieve its full vision, the task force calls for doubling the federal investment in education and increasing the investment from states and localities.

Can we do it? Sure. It is a matter of priorities. We are currently spending about $500 billion annually on defense, even more to service the national debt. The truth is we can't afford not to do it.

But the education we've been discussing is long-term stuff, mostly for the next generation. What do you do if you're in the workforce, have family responsibilities and lose your job?

According to the statistics, in today's labor market the chances are that you don't have a post-graduate degree, and you're a non-supervisory worker who is paid by the hour—over 80 percent of American workers fall into that category. You are not alone; all over America hourly workers are getting shafted, particularly those in manufacturing.

While you may be the victim of globalization, it is more likely that technology and a machine have replaced you. The hard truth is that if a job can be broken down into predictable steps it can be replaced by a computer program. Those programs can run computer-controlled machine tools, allow you to buy your own airline ticket or be your own travel agent or stockbroker.

As former labor secretary Robert Reich put it in his radio broadcast on June 21, 2005, "So if technology – not globalization – is the biggest cause of America's blue-collar blues, what do we do about it? Become neo-Luddities and smash all the machines?

"No. We become smarter."[211]

Reich went on to offer a solution that I think has great merit: To replace our present unemployment insurance system with a re-employment system that gives up to two years of training for the technical jobs of the future. Reich said, "But we have nothing like this. Our paltry job-training system generally pays only for short-term training. And there's no income support."

By way of background, unemployment insurance, which came as part of the Social Security legislation in 1935, never contemplated the need for retraining. Unemployment was then part of an economic downturn—the jobs would come back when business got better. That is no longer the case. The jobs, whether lost to globalization or technology, are never coming back. Our workers have to be retrained or they will be forced into low-paying jobs at Wal-Mart or the like.

The logic behind Reich's proposal is that if machines are replacing jobs why not train technicians to install and repair them? Technicians are in demand. These jobs pay $18 to $25 an hour—a darn sight better than Wal-Mart. The problem is that to qualify for one you need a year or two of training beyond high school.

Unemployment insurance (in all but three states) is paid for by employers, not employees. It pays benefits to workers that qualify for a maximum of 26 weeks, although Congress can extend the benefits for another 26 weeks. During the 2005 jobs crisis, however, Congress refused to do so. The tax rate for employers varies with how many of their workers use the system—the fewer the workers laid off, the lower the tax rate.

Throughout this discussion I have emphasized the need for America to value all work, no matter how seemingly menial the job. The difference between slavery and hourly work is the payment of a livable wage. For that reason it is unconscionable that the minimum wage in the United States stays frozen at $5.15 an hour, when it should be more than twice that. It is unconscionable that so many Americans are unable to find work or are forced to take part-time jobs and it is unconscionable that employers can retool or shut their doors and move to greener pastures without providing for the retraining of their employees. Secretary Reich's un-fleshed-out idea of re-employment insurance is a breath of fresh air in a highly noxious atmosphere.

Note: the Federal Trade Act does provide special retraining benefits to those workers who are laid off or had hours reduced because their employer was adversely affected by increased imports from Mexico or Canada, or because their employer shifted production to either of those countries.[212]

Seventeen

Avoiding the Energy Meltdown

———————◆•◆•◆———————

$E = mc^2$ Albert Einstein, second relativity paper formula, September 1905.

The industrial world is built on cheap energy. Over the past century, we have used the stored energy of millions of years of sunlight—in the form of oil, coal, and natural gas—to create the marvels and miracles essential to modern life. But now the cheap fossil-fuels fiesta is ending, climate change is upon us, and our models of global industry, commerce, food production, and transportation may not survive. Industrial civilization is in big trouble, and the American people are sleepwalking into a future of hardship and turbulence.

The Long Emergency, by James Howard Kunstler, 2005

Two perspectives: The science by Einstein, which I find quite spiritual, established that mass and energy are a different form of the same thing. As Brian Greene, a professor of physics and mathematics at Columbia explained in an April 2005 *New York Times* Op-Ed, $E = mc^2$, an equation as short as it is powerful, told the world that matter can be converted into energy—and a lot of it—since the speed of light squared (c^2) is a huge number (about 100,000,000,000,000,000). Thus a little bit of mass can yield enormous energy. The destruction of Hiroshima and Nagasaki was fueled by converting less than an ounce of matter into energy; the energy consumed by New York City in a month is less than that contained in a newspaper; a baseball contains enough energy to keep an average car running continuously at 65 m.p.h. for about 5,000 years.[213]

So in a world running short of easy-to-find liquid fossil fuel—petroleum—there is actually no shortage of energy; we are in fact surrounded by it in all that we see, including the sorry bag of bones we call humans, who have contained in their molecular make up undoubtedly enough atoms to run a nuclear aircraft carrier.

Greene goes on to explain that the standard illustrations of Einstein's equation—bombs and power stations—have perpetrated a belief that $E = mc^2$ has a special association with nuclear reactions and is thus removed from ordinary activity.

This isn't true. When you drive your car, $E = mc^2$ is at work. As the engine burns gasoline to produce energy in the form of motion, it does so by converting some of the gasoline's mass into energy, in accord with Einstein's formula. When you use your MP3 player, $E = mc^2$ is at work. As the player drains the battery to produce energy in the form of sound waves, it does so by Einstein's formula. As you read this text, $E = mc^2$ is at work. The processes in the eye and brain, underlying perception and thought, rely on chemical reactions that interchange mass and energy, once again in accord with Einstein's formula.

The point is that although $E = mc^2$ expresses the interchangeability of mass and energy, it doesn't single out any particular reaction for executing the conversion. The distinguishing feature of nuclear reactions, compared with the chemical reactions involved in burning gasoline, coal, natural gas or running a battery, is that they generate less waste and thus produce more energy—by a factor of roughly a million. And when it comes to energy, a factor of a million justifiably commands attention.

In the other perspective, author James Howard Kunstler isn't alone in warning that the American people are sleepwalking into a catastrophe caused by the end of cheap fossil fuels. Many geologists, economists, and even a few politicians agree that the damage to our way of life and the world economy will be disastrous and long lasting if we don't act decisively and quickly to mitigate the problem.

Kunstler paints a frightening scenario of global warming, flooding, isolated suburbia, idled transportation, overpopulation, and famine. The simple truth is that oil has become the lifeblood of modern civilization. It fuels most transportation and is the basic stock for pharmaceuticals, agriculture, plastics and a host of other products we use in everyday life.

In light of the events so far in the 21st century—the (oil) war in Iraq, spiking petroleum prices, the despoiling of our environment (massive coal strip mining, repeated attempts to allow oil exploration in our Arctic National Wildlife Refuge in Alaska, the acceptance of global warming, and the contamination of our rivers, streams and water tables—*The Long Emergency* is already upon us. And it shouldn't come as a surprise; we were warned decades ago:

Our ignorance is not so vast as our failure to use what we know.
M. King Hubbert (1903 – 1989)

Sage words. In 1949 M. King Hubbert was probably the best know geophysicist in the world because of his startling prediction that fossil fuel era would be of very short duration.[214]

His prediction in 1956 that U.S. oil production would peak in about 1970 and decline thereafter was scoffed at then, but his analysis proved to be remarkably accurate.[215] It did peak, and unable to cope by increasing domestic oil production, the Arab oil embargo in 1973 was a great shock to the United States.

Figure 2 is from a report by Dr. Robert L. Hirsch in 2005. It charts the peaking of U.S. oil production and the observation that increased pricing didn't result in greater production.

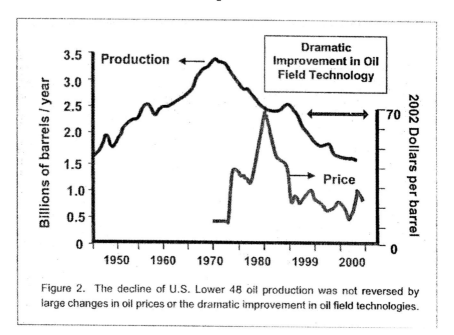

Figure 2. The decline of U.S. Lower 48 oil production was not reversed by large changes in oil prices or the dramatic improvement in oil field technologies.

Eighteen years later, in an article published in *National Geographic* (June 1974), titled "Oil, the Dwindling Treasure," Hubbert predicted, "The End of the Oil Age is in sight…If present trends continue world production will peak in 1995—the deadline for alternative forms of energy that must replace petroleum in the sharp drop-off that follows." Hubbert died in 1989.

The Atlantic Council of the United States, in a bulletin issued in October 2005, titled *The Inevitable Peaking of World Oil Production,* by Robert L. Hirsh, laid out the current situation.[216] It's an excellent work. The following is a brief extrapolation:

- The era of plentiful, low-cost petroleum is approaching an end.
- Without massive mitigation the problem will be pervasive and long lasting.
- World oil production peaking represents a liquid fuels problem, not an "energy crisis."
- Governments will have to take the initiative on a timely basis.

♦ In every crisis, there are always opportunities for those who act decisively.

The concept of the peaking of world oil production follows from the fact that the output of an individual oil field rises after discovery, reaches a peak, and then declines. It is important to recognize that oil production *peaking* is not "running out." Peaking is the maximum oil production rate, which typically occurs after roughly half of the recoverable oil in an oil field has been pumped.

World oil demand is forecast to grow 50 percent by 2025.[217] To meet that demand, ever-larger volumes of oil will have to be produced. Since oil production from individual oil fields grows to a peak and then declines, new fields must be continually discovered and brought into production to compensate for the depletion of older fields and to meet increasing world demand. If large quantities of new oil are not discovered and brought into production somewhere in the world, then world oil production will no longer satisfy demand. Peaking means that the rate of world oil production cannot increase; it does not mean that production will suddenly stop, because there will still be large reserves remaining.

> The world's last super giant oil fields were discovered in the 1960s.

Oil companies and governments have conducted extensive exploration worldwide, but their results have been disappointing for decades. On this basis, there is little reason to expect that future oil discoveries will dramatically increase. The situation is illustrated in Figure 1, which shows the difference between annual world oil reserves additions and annual consumption.[218] The image is one of a world moving from a long period in which reserve additions are falling increasingly short of annual consumption. A related fact is that oil production is in decline in 33 of the world's 48 largest oil-producing countries.[219]

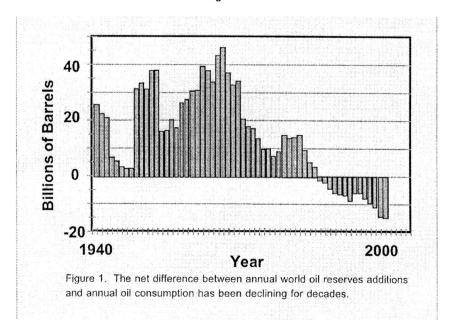

Figure 1. The net difference between annual world oil reserves additions and annual oil consumption has been declining for decades.

Various individuals and groups have used available information and geological tools to develop forecasts for when world oil production might peak. A sampling among experts makes it clear that most believe that peaking is likely within a decade; others think it will peak within the next five years; a few think it is peaking already.

There may be little warning as to when peaking will occur. Examination of actual histories showed that in all cases it was not obvious that production was about to peak a year ahead of the event. In most cases the peaks were sharp, not gentle varying or flat topped, as most forecasters hope. Finally, in some cases post–peak production declines were quite rapid, as in the U.K. for example (figure 3).

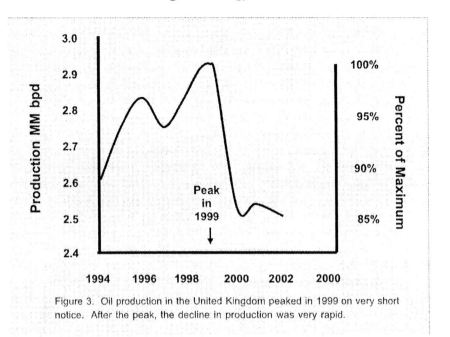

Figure 3. Oil production in the United Kingdom peaked in 1999 on very short notice. After the peak, the decline in production was very rapid.

Mitigation

A recent analysis for the U.S. Department of Energy addressed the question of what might be done to mitigate the peaking of world oil production.[220] Various technologies that are commercial or near commercial were considered:

1. Fuel efficient transportation,
2. Heavy oil/oil sands,
3. Coal liquefaction,
4. Enhanced oil recovery,
5. Gas-to-liquids.

It became abundantly clear early in this study that effective mitigation will be dependant on the implementation of mega-projects and mega-changes at the maximum possible rate. This finding dictated the focus on currently commercial technologies that are ready for implementation. New technology options requiring further research and development will undoubtedly prove very important in the longer-term future, but they are not ready now, so their inclusion would be strictly speculative.

The timing of oil peaking was left open because of the considerable differences of opinion among experts. Consideration of a number of implementation scenarios provided some fundamental insights, as follows:

- Waiting until world oil production peaks before taking crash program action leaves the world with a significant liquid fuel deficit for more than two decades.
- Initiating a mitigation crash program 10 years before world oil peaking helps considerably but still leaves a liquid fuels shortfall roughly a decade after the time that oil would have peaked.
- Initiating a mitigation crash program 20 years before peaking offers the possibility of avoiding a world liquid fuels shortfall for the forecast period.

The reason such long lead times are required is that the worldwide scale of oil consumption is enormous, a fact often lost in a world where oil abundance has been taken for granted for so long. If mitigation is too little, too late, world supply/demand balance will have to be achieved through massive demand destruction (shortages), which would translate to extreme economic hardship. On the other hand, with timely mitigation, economic damage can be minimized.

Dr. Robert L. Hirsch's Concluding Remarks

"Over the past century, world economic development has been fundamentally shaped by the availability of abundant, low-cost oil. Previous energy transitions (wood to coal, coal to oil, etc.) were gradual and evolutionary; oil peaking will be abrupt and revolutionary.

"The world has never faced a problem like this. Without massive mitigation at least a decade before the fact, the problem will be pervasive and long lasting.

"Oil peaking represents a liquid fuels problem, not an 'energy crisis' in the sense that term has been used. Accordingly, mitigation of declining world oil production must be narrowly focused, at least in the near-term.

"A number of technologies are currently available for immediate implementation once there is the requisite determination to act. Governments worldwide will have to take the initiative on a timely basis, and it may already be too late to avoid considerable discomfort or worse. Countries that dawdle will suffer from lost opportunities, because in every crisis, there are always opportunities for those who act decisively."

> "… Most believe that peaking is likely within a decade."
>
> "Without massive mitigation at least a decade before the fact, the problem will be pervasive and long lasting."

The problem is as serious as a heart attack but our government seems oblivious to the threat. Does anyone think that the White House doesn't have access to the historic work of Dr. Hubbert and the current findings of The Atlantic Council of the United States and oil experts such as Dr. Hirsch? Of course it does. The Department of Energy is part of the president's Cabinet; Secretary of Energy Samuel W. Bodman's job is to advise the president. Bodman heads a department with a budget in excess of $23 billion and over 100,000 federal and contract employees. If President Bush, once a major stockholder in a Texas oil company, is unaware of the reality of the oil crisis it is because he chooses to allow the unmitigated profiteering of his oil company buddies at the expense of his country.

In a news conference in the wake of Hurricane Katrina, Bush had the gall to suggest that our nation's "problem" with high gasoline prices was caused by the lack of a national energy policy, and tried to blame it all on Bill Clinton. First, Bush said, "This is a problem that's been a long time in coming. We haven't had an energy policy in this country." This was followed by, "That's exactly what I've been saying to the American people—ten years ago if we'd had an energy strategy, we would be able to diversify away from foreign dependence. And—but we haven't done that. And now we find ourselves in the fix we're in."[221]

And, surprise, surprise, Bush was lying once again.

Actually the United States did have a comprehensive energy policy: President Jimmy Carter gave it to us in 1977—28 years ago. In a famous televised speech to the nation on April 18, 1977, Carter unveiled a plan that would establish the strategic petroleum reserve, initiate the modern solar power industry, lead to the insulation of millions of American homes, and establish America's first national energy policy. (Two months earlier Carter had sent proposed legislation to Congress to reorganize the federal government's energy agencies and programs and to establish the cabinet-level Department of Energy)

"With the exception of preventing war," said Carter, "this is the greatest challenge our nation will face during our lifetimes."

He added: "It is a problem we will not solve in the next few years, and it is likely to get progressively worse through the rest of this century. We must not be selfish or timid if we hope to have a decent world for our children and grandchildren."

"We simply must balance our demand for energy with our rapidly shrinking resources. By acting now, we can control our future instead of letting the future control us. The most important thing about these proposals is that the alternative may be a national catastrophe. Further delay can affect our strength and our power as a nation." He called the new energy policy he was proposing, "The moral equivalent of war—except that we will be uniting our efforts to build and not destroy."

Unfortunately, failure to act decisively in the 1970s and 1980s would inevitably lead to a time when the only way to maintain our lifestyle would be to rape our planet and seize control or oil-rich nations in the Middle East. As Carter pointed out, if we fail to develop alternative sources of renewable energy and conserve what we have, the alternative could be nasty: "We will feel mounting pressure to plunder the environment. We will have a crash program to build more nuclear plants, strip-mine and burn more coal, and drill more offshore wells than we will need if we begin to conserve now. Inflation will soar, production will go down, people will lose their jobs. Intense competition will build up among nations and among the different regions within our own country."

"If we fail to act soon, we will face an economic, social and political crisis that will threaten our free institutions."[222]

Carter knew what was at stake. He not only sought the council of scientists like M. King Hubbert, he was a nuclear engineer and had commanded a nuclear submarine—he was well versed in $E = mc^2$. He was also at the mercy of his political and ideological enemies and they came out in force.

The Saudis and the oil industry ridiculed Carter's speech and his dire warnings. The think tanks that soon emerged in response suggested there really was no energy problem. It wasn't terribly hard for them to sound convincing since by 1977 the oil was again flowing freely from the Middle East; the political embargo was over and there was a glut of oil production because of the opening of the North Sea fields (1975). World oil production was still more than adequate to meet demand. Consequently, although Carter's initiatives did a lot of permanent good, the American people were hoodwinked by vested interests into not taking the seriousness of his visionary message to heart.

Within two years the down and dirty, anything-goes methods of the emerging far right in the United States began to unfold in the campaign tactics of Ronald Reagan and George H. W. Bush.

Saudi citizen and oil baron Salem bin Laden's sole U.S. representative, James Bath, funneled cash into the failing business of H. W. Bush's son, George W. Bush. With that money from the representative of Osama Bin Laden's half-brother, Bush the younger was able to keep afloat his Arbusto ("shrub" in Spanish) Oil Company. And he would be in the pocket of the bin Laden and Saudi interests for the rest of his life.

Carter, on the other hand, was incorruptible and continued his thrust for oil independence. But then came the "Iran/Contra October Surprise," when the Reagan/Bush campaign allegedly promised the oil rich mullahs of Iran that they would sell them missiles and other weapons if only they would keep our hostages until after the 1980 Carter/Reagan presidential election was over. The result was that Carter, who had been leading in the polls over Reagan/Bush, steadily dropped in popularity as the hostage crisis dragged out and lost the election. The hostages were released the very minute that Reagan put his hand on the Bible to take his oath of office. The hostages freed, the Reagan/Bush administration quickly began delivering missiles to Iran.[223]

Ronald Reagan's first official acts of office included removing Jimmy Carter's solar panels from the roof of the White House and reversing most of Carter's conservation and alternative energy policies.

So as Thom Hartmann puts it in his article (footnoted above), "Instead of taking a strong stand to make America energy independent, [George W.] Bush kisses a Saudi crown prince, then holds hands with him as they walk into Bush's hobby ranch in Texas. Our young men and women are daily dying in Iraq—a country with the world's second largest store of underground oil. And we live in fear that another 15 Saudis may hijack more planes to fly into our nation's capitol or into nuclear plants."

" Meanwhile, Bush brings us an energy bill that includes eight billion in welfare payments to the oil business, just as the nation's oil companies report the highest profits in the entire history of the industry. Americans struggle to pay for gasoline, while the Bush administration refuses to increase fleet efficiency standards, stop the $100,000 tax break for buying Hummers, or maintain and build Amtrak. George Bush Jr. is arguably right that gas prices are spiking because we don't have an energy policy. But instead of blaming Clinton, he should be pointing to the Reagan/Bush administration (12 years), and to his own abysmal failures over the past four years."

The Need for Action

Let's pick it up where Dr. Hirsch left off: "Governments worldwide will have to take the initiative on a timely basis, and it may already be too late to avoid considerable discomfort or worse. Countries that dawdle will suffer from lost opportunities, because in every crisis, there are always opportunities for those that act decisively."

Under the Republican administrations of Ronald Reagan, G. H. W. Bush, and now Bush Jr., we will have squandered 20 years that could have been used to mitigate the impeding liquid fuels crisis. The 2005 Energy Bill, crafted by Dick Cheney behind closed doors with oil executives to abrogate longstanding treaties and using the 9/11 attacks as a pretext to invade Iraq, commits the nation to a totally inadequate, corporate welfare energy policy until 2010. The Progressive Report characterized it as "a Bill only Exxon could love."

We're going to have to pay the piper. Even if the far-right ideologues are defeated in the 2006, 2008 election cycles, Americans are very likely in for, as Hirsch put it, "considerable discomfort or worse." I urge Democrats, and those thinking Republicans who remain to make liquid fuels mitigation, energy independence, and global warming the cornerstone of their campaigns. The American people deserve to know the truth and they deserve a government capable of turning the crisis into opportunities for the future. There are no greater issues facing the nation.

What we need is a crash energy program with short and long term goals. As Jimmy Carter said, it must be "The moral equivalent of war— except that we will be uniting our efforts to build and not destroy." It was with that sort of national resolve that John Kennedy launched the space program in the early 1960s.

We currently don't have such a plan, but we do have the science and political templates from which to build one. Bill Clinton's 2001 Climate Change Budget, which Bush Jr. failed to follow up on, allocated funds for a broad spectrum of initiatives to combat global warming, including accelerated efforts to develop clean energy sources both at home and abroad and a new Clean Air Partnership Fund, a five-year package of tax incentives to spur clean energy technologies and increased investment for R&D in energy efficient technology and renewable energy. In addition, Clinton also proposed more than $1.7 billion for global climate change research, for a total package for FY 2001 of over $4 billion.[224] Most of the funding for Clinton's proposed initiatives was not appropriated.

The greatest environmental challenge of the new century is global warming…if we fail to reduce the emission of greenhouse gases, deadly heat waves and droughts will become more frequent, coastal areas will flood, and economies will be disrupted. That is going to happen, unless we act. Many people…still believe you cannot cut greenhouse gas emissions without slowing economic growth. In the Industrial Age that may well have been true. But in this digital economy, it is not true anymore. New technologies make it possible to cut harmful emissions and provide even more growth.

- President Bill Clinton, State of the Union Address, January 27, 2000

President Bill Clinton was an advocate for a sustainable energy plan that would protect our environment, safeguard natural resources, and create new energy technologies and jobs.

The Bush administration, on the other hand, treats our natural resources as assets set aside for big business profit. Its approach to the energy challenges has forsaken our role as leaders in innovating cutting-edge technology in order to pursue an aggressive supply-side plan to drain our nation's remaining oil and gas supplies. Nothing has been done to curb U.S. oil consumption habits or to diversify our energy supply to include domestic renewable sources of energy. In fact, the problem has been made worse. Despite continued declines in automobile fuel economy, the Bush administration granted purchasers of "Hummers," the least efficient vehicles on the road, a new tax break worth more than 10 times the size of the tax break for hybrid cars, the most efficient vehicles.[225] The Bush/Cheney plan to drill and burn our way out of the problem simply will not work. But it will make a lot of their oil company buddies richer in the process, at the expense of our national security and the economic wellbeing of all but a few of America's elite. That is unrestrained capitalism at its very worst.

The Center for American Progress has done some excellent work in developing a series of papers titled, The Progressive Priorities Series: Securing Our Energy Future.[226] It is a plan to, "wean ourselves form oil addiction by transitioning away from oil dependence, enhancing domestic energy supply, prioritizing energy efficiency to enhance supply and improve reliability, and tackling global warming." Following is a synopsis of Progressive Policy's Action Plan:

He [the secretary of energy] should announce an energy security plan that seeks to accomplish the following four broad goals. First, it must dramatically reduce oil consumption by the transportation sector, which accounts for roughly two-thirds of the oil we use. Second, it should enhance domestic energy supplies by making significant investments in clean, renewable energy sources such as biomass, wind, geothermal, and solar energy. Third, it should ensure that we better utilize existing energy sources, adopting efficient technologies and modernizing the energy grid to curb pollution and reduce costs for consumers and business. Research to identify an appropriate future for coal and nuclear energy is an essential component of this, as is a hard look at the infrastructure barriers to tapping existing natural gas supplies. Finally, a new energy security plan should allow us to reassert American leadership on climate change by limiting our own emissions and providing incentives to developing countries to join the effort...

Lester R. Brown, president of the Earth Policy Institute, a nonprofit, interdisciplinary research organization based in Washington, D.C., offers another plan, which is quite similar to the recommendations of The Center for American Progress. Brown is the author of Plan B $_{2.0}$ *Rescuing a Planet Under Stress and a Civilization in Trouble.*

Our global economy is outgrowing the capacity of the earth to support it, moving us ever closer to decline and possible collapse. We have lost sight of how vast the human enterprise has become. A century ago, annual growth in the world economy was measured in billions of dollars. Today it is measured in trillions.

As a result, we are consuming renewable resources faster than they can regenerate. Forests are shrinking, water tables are falling, and fisheries are declining. We are using up oil at a pace that leaves little time to plan beyond peak oil, and we are discharging greenhouse gases into the atmosphere faster than nature can absorb them.

Sustaining progress now depends on replacing the fossil fuel-based, throwaway economy with a new economy, one powered by abundant sources of wind, solar energy, hydropower, and biofuels. The transportation system will be far more diverse, relying more on light-rail, buses, and bicycles and less on cars. And it will be a comprehensive reuse-recycle economy...

Brown's book is an important read for the serious student.[227] For additional information on the topics discussed in the book see www. earthpolicy.org

My Take

We need to stop hiding our heads in the sand and accept the fact that whether it is today or in 10 to 20 years oil production will peak. There is no question. Those of us old enough to remember the 1973 Arab oil embargo know the consequences of finding the country running on "E". As a young airline pilot I was fortunate not to have lost my job before the oil spigot got turned on again. Unlike the embargo, oil peaking will not be temporary and will require massive mitigation over a decade to avoid long-term disruption of our economy and way of life. The question is what are we willing to risk?

So now, thanks to abysmal governmental leadership, the United States is well behind and the stakes are growing higher with every day we lose before taking action.

In a television interview on CNN on December 24, 2005, T. Boone Pickens, a well-known Texas "oil patch" tycoon and geologist, spoke out on the issue of oil peaking saying, "that at 85 million barrels a day (the amount being produced and used at the close of 2005) world oil production has already peaked." He said further, "that the world has been thoroughly explored and there are no other major oil fields to be found." When asked what he thought the result would be, he painted a picture of rising oil prices and disruptions as alternative fuels are developed.

Okay. So let's get back to $E = mc^2$. We are not running out of energy—we're running out of liquid fuel (cheap petroleum).

Much of the following data was either taken or supported from publications provided by the Energy Information Agency (EIA), which is the independent statistical and analytical agency within the Department of Energy (DOE). The information should be attributed to the EIA and should not be construed as advocating or reflecting any policy position of the DOE or of any other organization. The EIA website is: http://www.eia.doe.gov/

Energy Products

In 2004 the energy products used in the United States broke down as follows: Petroleum products contributed the largest amount 40.2 percent. This was followed by natural gas with a 23 percent share; coal with about a 22 percent share, and the combination of nuclear, hydroelectric, geothermal and other sources comprising the remaining 14 percent.

Figure 6 depicts the history and projections of total U.S. production, net imports, and consumption of energy (1980 – 2030).

Figure 7 depicts the history and projections of U.S. production by fuel (1980 – 2030).

The measure used is energy expressed in quadrillion Btu (energy heat value).

Following the graphs, we will focus on each one of the major energy sources, the uses, production limitations, known reserves, and environmental risks. It is a necessary exercise to understand the magnitude of the liquid fuels crisis that our nation is facing. We don't have to understand it all; experts spend their lifetime trying to do that. We just need the basics, and once again, as we did with the GDP and the budget, don't be frightened by the big numbers; it is relationships that are important.

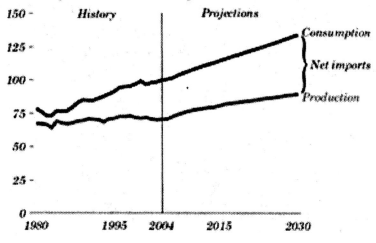

Figure 6. Total energy production and consumption, 1980-2030 (quadrillion Btu)

Figure data

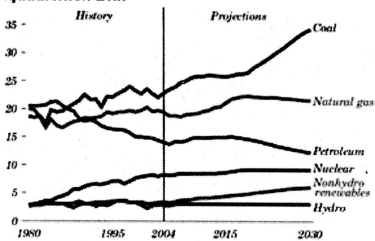

Figure 7. Energy production by fuel, 1980-2030 (quadrillion Btu)

Nuclear

Nuclear electric power plants produce 8.2 percent of the energy consumed in the United States; they generate 20 percent of the nation's electricity. As of October 31, 2005, there were 104 commercial nuclear generating units that were fully licensed by the U.S. Nuclear Regulatory Commission to operate in the United States. The Shippingport Reactor (Pennsylvania, 1957) was the first commercial nuclear generator to become operational in the United States.[228] It was retired in 1982. The last reactor to come on line was the Watt's Bar (Tennessee, 1996). The Brown's Ferry unit in Alabama has been dormant and shut down since 1985—it is expected to come back on line in 2007.

The 1950s marked a time of great expectations for the peaceful use of nuclear power. On December 8, 1953 President Dwight Eisenhower, in an address to the United Nations, characterized our nuclear energy policy as, "Atoms for Peace." Many political historians feel Eisenhower's Atoms for Peace speech embodied his most important initiative as president. It was an uplifting vision; not only could nuclear power be used for weapons of mass destruction, as it had been just eight years earlier, it could be harnessed to benefit mankind.

Lewis L. Strauss, chairman of the Atomic Energy Commission, in a speech to the National Association of Science Writers on September 16, 1954 said, "Our children will enjoy in their homes electrical energy too cheap to meter.... It is not too much to expect that our children will know of great periodic regional famines in the world only as matters of history, will travel effortlessly over the seas and under them and through the air with a minimum of danger and at great speeds, and will experience a lifespan far longer than ours, as disease yields and man comes to understand what causes him to age."[229]

Although U.S. total nuclear generation is the largest in the world at 788,556 million kilowatt hours (2004), its share of national electric generation, at 20 percent, ranks 18th among other nations. By comparison, France generates more than 80 percent, Belgium and Sweden 60 percent, Japan 30 percent, and China scant 2 percent.

Unfortunately, Eisenhower and Strauss' dream for abundant, cheap nuclear electric power has fallen far short of fruition. Electric power generation from nuclear reactors increased rapidly in the 1970s, spurred by the Arab oil embargo in 1973-1974 and the Iranian Revolution in 1979. Both events threatened the flow of Middle Eastern oil. Government policy (with an eye to public opinion) encouraged nuclear power as an alternative.

But that government support fizzled as public opinion turned against nuclear power after the accidents at Three Mile Island in 1979 and Chernobyl in the Soviet Union in 1986. In the United States, anti-nuke environmental groups, such as Greenpeace, filled the daily news with demonstrations and protests against the construction of nuclear generators, increasing the political and monetary cost of building them. Lacking government incentives, the fuel of choice became cheaper natural gas and coal. As a consequence, the last new U.S. nuclear power plant came on line in 1996. U.S. nuclear development screeched to a halt.

As an interesting aside, I made a regularly scheduled flight into Harrisburg Airport on March 29, 1979, the day after the Three Mile Island crash shutdown. The nuclear plant sits about three miles out on the approach to the airport. By the next day it had been determined that there was no radiation hazard and our flight from Washington D.C. remained as scheduled. I learned in the boarding process that Arizona Governor Bruce Babbitt was one of our passengers. He had been appointed by President Carter to the special commission investigating the accident and was on his way to the site.

Knowing we would pass directly abeam Three Mile Island, I got special permission from the president of our airline, Ed Colodny, who coordinated with FAA, to have Babbitt join us in the cockpit jump seat. (Even then access to the cockpit was highly restricted.) As a result, the governor had a first-class view of his new assignment.

Babbitt went on to serve as the U.S. Secretary of the Interior during Bill Clinton's administration (1993-2001). The following is an interesting exchange from a *Los Angeles Times* interview with Babbitt on November 15, 2005, during which he expressed his views on nuclear power.

Q: Didn't it surprise some people a few years ago when you went to work for a law firm representing development interests at the Ahmanson Ranch and the Hearst Ranch in California and the proposed Yucca Mountain storage site for radioactive waste in Nevada?

A: I've always been pro-development. We live in a world that is so polarized that there doesn't seem to be any middle space—if you're an environmentalist, you must oppose everything. That doesn't describe me.

It never has. I believe that nuclear power is the lesser [evil] of the only two alternatives that are on the table right now. One is to fry this planet with continuing use and burning of fossil fuels, and the other is to try to make nuclear power work. That's been my position since 1979, when I served on the Three Mile Island commission. I've endured a lot of hassle over it, but that's my judgment. We've got to get away from fossil fuels fast, or this planet, as we know it, is not going to exist.

As you've guessed by now, I strongly agree with Bruce Babbitt. We can only mitigate the looming liquid fuels problem by not squandering our remaining fossil fuels (oil, natural gas and coal) in the generation of electricity. The share of nuclear generated electricity to that of fossil fuels needs to be inverted. It should be 80 percent nuclear to 20 percent other, and the majority of the "other" should be from renewable fuels (wind, solar, hydro, biomass). The following graph depicts the current outlook for nuclear power generation.

Figure 5. Electricity generation by fuel, 1980-2030 (billion kilowatthours)

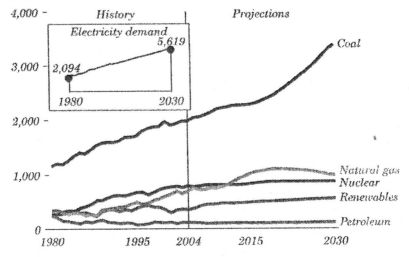

We have the technology to make liquid hydrocarbon fuels from both natural gas and coal.[230] We can also make smaller amounts from agricultural oils (soybeans, peanuts, animal fats, etc.). In fact, everything we can eat can be turned into biodiesel or ethanol.

Yes, we are going to burn the fossil fuels anyway, but over an extended period of time we can greatly reduce the flow of greenhouse gases and climate change. By reducing the use of coal, and greatly limiting the emissions of the coal that is burned, we can all but eliminate acid rain.

Sure, there are problems with the storage of radioactive waste, but they are solvable. Sure, people are frightened of nuclear energy—it is associated with bombs and destruction. And we all know the military has killed and sickened many since the 1940s in testing and developing nuclear weapons. But the truth is commercial reactors have proved to be remarkably safe. There hasn't been a single fatal accident attributed to a U.S. commercial reactor since the first one came on line in 1957. Outside the United States there have been a few. The most deadly was Chernobyl, which killed 46 and sickened an unknown number; Japan also has had a few fatalities.

Radiation is scary stuff. It is used in medicine to see within the body and to cure, but even accumulated low doses can be deadly. However, if we allow the massive burning of fossil fuels to continue to create global warming and climate change, holes in the ozone layer will expand and allow dangerous solar radiation. To say nothing of the increase of the number of violent hurricanes and the coastal flooding caused by a rising sea level.

Everything has a degree of risk and the hazards of using energy and producing fuels are real. China's total death toll from coal mining averages well over 5,000 per year. Coal mining is by its very nature dangerous. While strip mining for coal in the United States is relatively safe, the environmental hazards are horrendous—removing mountaintops, filling valleys with waste, contaminating rivers and water tables, and damaging our eco system overall. Oil tankers sink, hydroelectric dams fail, and liquid natural gas (LNG) blows up. The truth is that the odds are infinitely greater that you will be fried by the gasoline in your car's fuel tank than harmed by a commercial nuclear reactor.

New technologies are also making nuclear reactors safer. It is going to be up to our government to lay all the cards on the table. I think the risk of peaking oil and the destruction of our environment makes a good case for nuclear power. Interestingly, I find, as has Bruce Babbitt, that my fellow progressives find it hard to swallow. But perhaps as fuel prices increase, shortages become more frequent, and concerns about air pollution and global warming increase that will change.

There are already some signs that attitudes are changing. On December 5, 2005, Dr. Patrick Moore, chairman and chief scientist of Greenspirit Strategies Ltd. and co-founder of Greenpeace, attended the UN Climate Change 'Conference of the Parties" in Montreal.[231]

Moore, who broke with Greenpeace in the mid-1980s after spending 15 years in its top committee, says energy decisions must be based more on science, and less on politics and emotion. Moore calls nuclear energy "the only non-greenhouse-gas-emitting power source that can effectively replace fossil fuels and satisfy global demand."

"There is now a great deal of scientific evidence showing nuclear power to be an environmentally sound and safe choice," Moore says. He believes his former colleagues at Greenpeace are unrealistic in their call for a phasing out of both coal and nuclear power worldwide, as Greenpeace called for in Ontario.

"There are simply not enough available forms of alternative energy to replace both of them together. Given a choice between nuclear on the one hand and coal, oil and natural gas on the other, nuclear energy is by far the best option as it emits neither CO_2 nor any other air pollutants."

Thirty-one states now have one or more nuclear power plants. New Hampshire's Seabrook plant came on line in 1983. In 2004 it provided 43 percent of the state's electricity, ranking New Hampshire number five. The Vermont Yankee plant puts our neighboring state in the number one position, providing 73.7 percent of the state's electricity.

What has emission-free electricity meant to the New Hampshire's air quality? Seabrook avoided the emission of 21,600 tons of sulfur dioxide (SO_2), 5,400 tons of nitrogen oxides (NO_x), and 605 million tons of carbon dioxide (CO_2) in the year 2004. Emissions of SO_2 lead to the formation of acid rain. NO_2 is a key precursor of both ground level ozone and smog. Greenhouse gases, like CO_2 contribute to global warming.

For perspective, the 5,400 tons of NO_x avoided by Seabrook is the amount of NO_x released in a year by 284,000 passenger cars. There are only 656,000 cars registered in the state of New Hampshire. Yet New Hampshire suffers from acid rain—it comes with the easterly flow of air from the burning of tremendous amounts of coal and natural gas to the west, used largely to generate electricity.

Nuclear generating capacity is projected to increase from about 100 gigawatts in 2004 to about 109 gigawatts in 2019 and to remain at that level (about 10 percent of total U.S. generating capacity) through 2030. The total projected increase in nuclear capacity between 2004 and 2030 includes three gigawatts expected to come from upgrades of existing plants that continue operating and six gigawatts of capacity at newly constructed power plants, stimulated by the provisions in the Energy Policy Act of 2005 (EPACT2005), that are expected to begin operation between 2014 and 2020.

Note: the EPACT2005 contains numerous tax incentives in order to stimulate supplies of energy in the form of "authorization," it contains no actually "appropriation" of money, so new construction may never happen.

Petroleum

In 2004, the United States used 20.7 million barrels of oil a day, of which about 60 percent was imported. U.S. demand is expected to increase to 26 million barrels a day, and world demand is forecast to increase by 50 percent to over a 120 million barrels a day by the year 2025. The lion's share of the increased demand is expected to be from China.

Although most of us will never purchase a barrel of oil (42 gallons of crude) in our life, we buy petroleum products all the time. We all know oil provides gasoline for our cars, diesel fuel, jet fuel, and home heating oil, but it is all around us in other products such as plastics, pharmaceuticals, fertilizer, lipstick, and vitamins—the list is endless.

The United States, with less than 5 percent of the total number of people on Earth, consumes 25 percent of the global supply of oil, which is followed by the European Union at 18 percent.

The world currently (2005) emits about 28 billion tons of carbon dioxide or its equivalent in other greenhouse gases, know as GHG, each year, according to the United Nations. The United States is responsible for seven billion metric tons, about 25 percent of the world's greenhouse gases, but is not party to the Kyoto protocol's restrictions.

Although the Clinton administration was instrumental in negotiating the Kyoto protocol in 1997, under the leadership of Vice President Al Gore, President Bush rejected it outright in 2001, saying that its mandatory cuts would harm the U.S. economy, and he complained that major developing countries were not covered.

There is a broad scientific consensus that greenhouse gas, byproducts of automobile engines, power plants and fossil fuel-burning industries, contributed significantly to the global temperature rise of one degree in the last century. Continued warming is melting glaciers, shrinking the Arctic icecap and heating the oceans, raising sea levels, and creating significant climate change, which includes more frequent and violent hurricanes.

While everyone was agog at the damage done to the Gulf Coast by Hurricane Katrina and subsequent flooding, few realize that 54 percent of all Americans live within 80 miles of the sea—the world average is about 50 percent. And, as is human nature, the most desirable and expensive properties are at the water's edge.

Petroleum products, especially gasoline, distillate (diesel) fuel, and jet fuel, provide virtually all of the energy consumed in the transportation sector. Transportation is the greatest single use of petroleum, accounting for an estimated 67 percent of all U.S. petroleum consumed in 2004. The industrial sector is the second largest consuming sector and accounts for about 23 percent. Residential/Commercial and the electric utility sectors account for the remaining 8 percent of petroleum consumption. See figure below for world consumption.

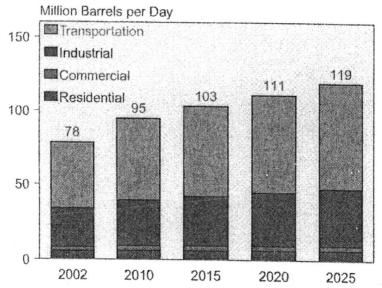

Figure 28. World Oil Consumption by End-Use Sector, 2002-2025

Sources: **History:** Energy Information Administration (EIA), *International Energy Annual 2002*, DOE/EIA-0219(2002) (Washington, DC, March 2004), web site www.eia.doe.gov/iea/. **Projections:** EIA, System for the Analysis of Global Energy Markets (2005).

The numbers are startling. Is America really on the brink of converging catastrophes caused by the world running out of fossil fuel? Because we have wasted so much time, I think we will experience considerable disruptions. But it is also a great opportunity for America to take a leadership role in developing new technologies, if we focus on the fact that the world is not running out of energy. As we have seen, the problem is a shortage of liquid fuels to run the present generation of motor vehicles, aircraft, trains, and ships. Approached from this prospective, the problem is not only manageable, but it is likely that the petroleum reserves we have, about half that ever existed on the planet, will carry us through the rest of the 21st century—even with the increasing demands of China and other emerging industrial nations. It will require both the use of known technologies and those new technologies for great minds to discover in the future.

Every living American has benefited from cheap petroleum pumped from the ground or from under the floor of the sea for a lifetime. As a result, we have grown accustomed to inefficient energy uses and lifestyles that are extraordinarily wasteful. Yet, when push comes to shove, we are capable of conserving fuel. For instance, after the Arab oil embargo in the 1970s the United States cut back its oil use by 17 percent while the GDP increased by 27 percent. Oil imports fell by half and imports from the Persian Gulf declined 87 percent in less than a decade.[232]

Conservation and efficiency are unquestionably our biggest energy resource. By using less we can buy time and the ability to develop new technologies to replace oil. Right now there is no alternative to liquid fuels to power our motor vehicles, aircraft, trains, and ships.

Highway vehicles use more than three-quarters of transportation energy—60 percent by cars and light trucks (including minivans and sport utility vehicles) and 16 percent by heavy trucks. Total transportation energy consumption is increasing by almost 2 percent a year, faster than any other major category of energy use. Consequently, conservation in that sector, particularly by highway vehicles, is extremely important.

In 1975, in response to the 1973-74 Arab oil embargo, Congress passed into law the Energy Policy Conservation Act and established Corporate Average Fuel Economy (CAFÉ) standards for passenger cars and light trucks (vehicles weighing 8,500 lbs. or less). As a result total fleet economy peaked in 1987 at 26.2 miles per gallon (mpg) when light trucks, which include minivans and SUVs, made up only 28.1 percent of the market. By 2001, because of the huge increase of purchases of minivans and SUVs, light trucks made up 46.7 percent of the market and total fleet economy fell to 24.4 mpg. Currently, light trucks make up over 50 percent of vehicle sales (although higher gas prices were edging consumers away from them).[233] The 2004 Hummer H2 SUV, which weighs over 8,500 lbs., is rated at 9.6 mpg.

In August 2004, Norman Mineta, the secretary of the Department of Transportation, proposed a new fuel economy plan for light trucks. It will reform the CAFÉ standards and, he claims, save 10 billion gallons of gasoline in the years to come (whatever that means; he didn't say how many years). After holding hearings, the National Highway Traffic Safety

Administration planned to issue a final ruling in April 2006. Critics were already claiming the result of the plan, if enacted, will do too little too late.

Interestingly, Japanese automakers Toyota and Honda are cleaning up with auto sales of their hybrids as gasoline prices have continued to climb. America's automakers, on the verge of bankruptcy, are finally getting the message.

There is a broad consensus that a truly effective plan would require the government to invest in developing a whole new breed of both light and heavy duty vehicles that would double fuel efficiency and reduce emissions by using technologies such as fuel cells, hybrid-electric drivetrains, and lightweight materials. The overall plan would include implementing much higher market tax incentives than now exist and educational programs to build demand for high-efficiency, cleaner vehicles.

Sadly, only tokenism of an effective gasoline reduction plan is included in the Energy Policy Act of 2005, although there are some incentives for increasing the use of biomass fuels.

Greatly increasing the production of biomass fuels would not only reduce our dependency on petroleum but also introduce a new price support for farm products. As it stands, the government's present price supports not only come out of tax dollars but also are under attack by WTO nations—poorer countries are being locked out of markets because of artificially low prices due to those price supports. Producing biomass is far superior to letting crops rot at our expense.

In the long run, Americans will have to restructure lifestyles that have become extremely energy wasteful. Sprawling suburbia now has commuters spending hours a day locked in traffic, usually with just one person in the car. The United States is going to have to revitalize public transportation. In a world of scarce oil the idea of cheap air travel is just silly. People are going to have to adjust to increased costs. Even simple things such as the plastic packaging of just about all we consume will have to be considered. Petroleum is used to produce plastic. While plastic can be recycled, most of it winds up in landfills, which incidentally can be used (and are to a limited extent) to produce methane gas for small power plants. Simply, there are many energy savings to be had. As a society, if we don't learn, we will be doing without.

The gasoline engines of cars and light trucks can run on biomass fuels but there are limitations. At best, experts say, biomass ethanol (sometimes called grain alcohol) would only produce about 25 percent of the fuel needed, and that is most efficient when blended with gasoline. Most of the ethanol made in the United States is from corn, although it can be made from all kinds agricultural waste. Brazil produces huge quantities of ethanol from sugar cane, a process far less costly than producing it from corn. Its ambitious ethanol program was expected to help that country become energy independent in 2006.

Methanol (sometimes called wood alcohol) can also power gasoline engines; it can be made from various biomass resources such as wood and coal. However, today nearly all methanol is made from natural gas, because it is cheaper. Interestingly, since the 1960s, methanol has been the required fuel for the Indianapolis 500 and other types of racing. The reason is that methanol is made of a single chemical and cannot be doctored. It also is safer in case of accidental fire because it burns cooler. Methanol contains about half the energy of gasoline per gallon.

Car engines can also run on other gases such as propane and natural gas, which are fossil fuels. And most important, hybrid automobiles can be powered by an internal combustion engine and battery power. The Toyota Prius, a hybrid getting 55 mpg, was a hot seller in 2005.

Jet engines, large turbines and diesel engines cannot run on ethanol or methanol; they have too low a flash point and don't contain enough energy when burned. Jets and turbines require the energy and properties of a hydrocarbon fuel oil. Biodiesel, on the other hand, can be made from practically any type of vegetable oil or even animal fat by a process called transesterification, which converts the triglyceride oils into methyl (or ethyl) esters.[234] At the end the process the mono-alkyl esters become the biodiesel, with one-eighth the viscosity of the original vegetable oil and nearly 10 percent oxygen by weight. Ordinary diesels can run on pure biodiesel or a mixture of bio and petroleum diesel, a common mix is 20 percent biodiesel and 80 percent petrodiesel, which is expressed worldwide as B-20.

Pure biodiesel (B-100) and B-20 are Department of Energy (DOE) designated alternative fuels. In 1998 B-20 was designated an "alternative fuel" under the Energy Policy Act, which allows government fleet services to purchase the B-20 blend for operations in normal diesel vehicles and receive credit for those vehicles equivalent to other DOE approved multi-fuel vehicles.

Environmental benefits in comparison to petroleum-based fuels include:

- Biodiesel reduces emission of carbon monoxide (CO) by about 50 percent and carbon dioxide (CO_2) by 78.45 percent on a net lifecycle basis because the carbon in biodiesel emissions is recycled from carbon that was already in the atmosphere, rather than being new carbon from petroleum that was sequestered in the Earth's crust. (Sheehan, 1998)
- Biodiesel contains fewer aromatic hydrocarbons: benzofluranthene: 56 percent reduction, benzopyrenes: 71 percent reduction.
- It also reduces sulfur emissions (SO_2), because biodiesel doesn't include sulfur.
- Biodiesel does produce more NO_x emissions than petrodiesel, but these emissions can be reduced through the use of catalytic converters. Properly designed and tuned engines may eliminate this increase.
- Since biodiesel is biodegradable it is less harmful to the environment if spilled on soil.

Renewable energy sources other than biomass, such as wind, geothermal, hydroelectric dams, solar, and nuclear power can now only produce electricity and heat, not liquid fuels, so their widespread (direct) use in transportation may never come. Indirectly, electricity can be used to charge batteries or produce hydrogen.

Nuclear reactors have been used in military ships since the 1960s but it is tremendously expensive and beyond commercial application. In 1955 there was even an effort to develop a nuclear power aircraft; the engine was dubbed the X-39. The original X-39 engine was too heavy to lift by aircraft. The only way it could be made light enough was to remove the radiation shield and be flown by a suicide pilot, and even then it would have required a runway eight miles long to get off the ground. President Kennedy cancelled the project in 1961. The aircraft was never built but the twin X-39 engines are on display at Idaho National Energy and Environmental Laboratory.

The United States has just about 2 percent of the world's remaining oil reserves to accommodate what amounts to a quarter of global demand. The DOE predicts that by 2025, more than two thirds of our petroleum will have to be imported to meet our oil needs.

Natural Gas

In 2003, the United States consumed 22.3 trillion cubic feet (Tcf) of natural gas, 2.08 percent more than in 2002—about 15 percent of it imported. By the year 2025, U.S. natural gas consumption is projected to increase to between 27 Tcf and 33 Tcf; most of the increase used to generate electricity.

Natural gas is a fossil fuel that was formed millions of years ago by the remains of plants and animals (organic material). Over time, the mud and soil changed into rock, covered the organic material and trapped it beneath the rock. Pressure and heat changed some of this organic material into coal, some into oil (petroleum), and some into natural gas. The major ingredient in natural gas is methane, a gas (or compound) composed of one carbon atom and four hydrogen atoms.

Natural gas provides about 23 percent of the total energy used in the United States, second to petroleum. The uses are broken down as follows.

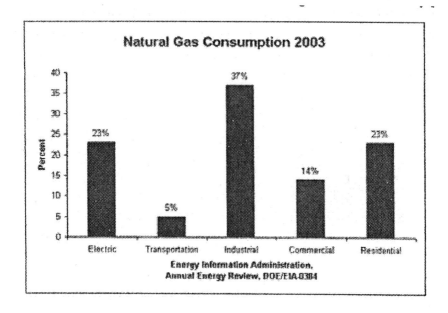

Like oil, natural gas is described as sweet (low) or sour (high), depending on its sulfur content. It is also described as wet or dry, depending on the presence of natural gas liquids and other energy gases. Natural gas that is greater than 90 percent methane is referred to as dry. Finally, natural gas is described as associated or non-associated, depending upon whether it is associated with significant oil production. Contrary to popular belief, most natural gas is not associated with oil. In the United States, only 20 percent of the natural gas reserves are believed to be oil associate.

Okay. We know oil production peaked in the United States in 1970, and we are scared stiff that it has or will peak in the world in the very near future. How about natural gas? Sorry, I'm afraid that is bad news again. U.S. production of natural gas peaked in 2003 at about 24 Tcf and has been dropping ever since in the face of sharply increasing domestic demands. The shortfall has been made up by imported natural gas; 14 percent from Canada by pipeline (natural gas under pressure), using 60 percent of the Canadian natural gas produced; and 1 percent by Liquid Natural Gas (LNG) super tanker ship.

At the Reuters Energy Summit in June 2005, Exxon Mobil's chief executive, Lee R Raymond, told reporters, "Gas production has peaked in North America." Asked whether production would continue to decline even if two huge arctic gas pipeline projects were built, Raymond said, " I think that's a fair statement, unless there's some huge find that nobody has any idea where it would be." When pressed further on the need for the pipeline projects he said, "The facts are that gas production continues to decline, and will start to decline even more rapidly. By the time we get to that period (2010-2012), we'll need it badly."

Unlike oil field production, which tends to peak on a bell curve, gas wells by nature tend to just quite producing requiring new finds and wells to be drilled to meet demands. Here is the way world gas consumption shapes up.

Figure 34. World Natural Gas Consumption, 1980-2025

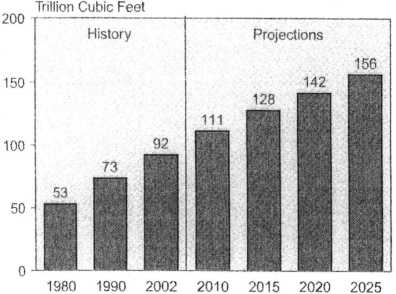

Sources: **History:** Energy Information Administration (EIA), *International Energy Annual 2002*, DOE/EIA-0219(2002) (Washington, DC, March 2004), web site www.eia.doe.gov/ iea/. **Projections:** EIA, System for the Analysis of Global Energy Markets (2005).

Figure 35. Natural Gas Consumption by Region, 1980-2025

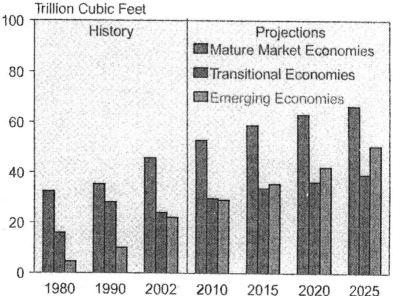

Sources: **History**: Energy Information Administration (EIA), *International Energy Annual 2002*, DOE/EIA-0219(2002) (Washington, DC. March 2004), web site www.eia.doe.gov/iea/. **Projections**: EIA, System for the Analysis of Global Energy Markets (2005).

As you can see the largest increase in gas demand, as with oil, will be from the emerging economies, China, India and other former Soviet Union nations (FSU).

The proved world natural gas reserves, as reported by *Oil & Gas Journal*, were estimated at 6,040 trillion cubic feet (January 1, 2005). Almost three-quarters of the world's natural gas reserves are located in the Middle East and in the transitional economies of Eastern Europe (EE) and the FSU. (Figure 40) Russia (27 percent), Iran (16 percent), and Qatar (15 percent) account for about 58 percent of the world's natural gas reserves; North America about 5 percent (the United States 3.1 percent and Canada 1.0 percent). At current projections, the world has about a 60-year supply of natural gas, although production is expected to peak globally around 2020, leading to serious global conflicts as China and other large and growing economies continue down the path of increased dependence on fossil fuels.[235]

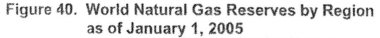

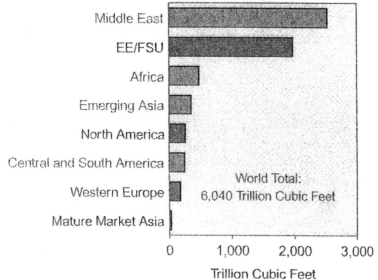

Figure 40. World Natural Gas Reserves by Region as of January 1, 2005

World Total: 6,040 Trillion Cubic Feet

Trillion Cubic Feet

Source: "Worldwide Look at Reserves and Production," *Oil & Gas Journal*, Vol. 102, No. 47 (December 20, 2004), pp. 22-23.

With no way to meet growing demand with domestic natural gas production, the United States is left with no alternative but to import it. While gas from Canada (and Alaska) come into our domestic pipeline network by pressurized, very specially outfitted long distance pipelines, natural gas from overseas comes as Liquefied Natural Gas (LNG).

LNG is made by cooling natural gas to about -260°F, which condenses it into a liquid form that takes up about one six hundredth the volume of gaseous natural gas. Liquification also has the environmental advantage of removing oxygen, carbon dioxide, sulfur, and water from the natural gas, resulting in LNG that is almost pure methane. On the down side, the process itself uses 25 percent of the gas.

LNG is typically transported by specialized tanker with insulated walls, and is kept in liquid form by autorefrigeration, a process in which the LNG is kept at its boiling point, so that any heat additions are countered by the energy lost from LNG vapor that is vented out of storage and used to power the vessel.

The United States gets a majority of its LNG from Trinidad and Tobago, Qatar, and Algeria, and receives shipments from Nigeria, Oman, Australia, Indonesia and the United Arab Emirates.

There are currently four LNG import terminals in the continental United States: Cove Point, Maryland; Elba Island, Georgia; Everett, Massachusetts; and Lake Charles, Louisiana. The first new U.S. LNG terminal in more than 20 years is expected to open on the Gulf Coast in 2007. There are at least two-dozen proposals to build new LNG regasification terminals in North America over the next several years.

While the experts say that LNG, when vaporized to a gaseous form, will only burn in concentrations of between 5 and 15 percent mixed with air, there is little said of the potential result of one those behemoth supertankers colliding with another ship or being struck by an aircraft in a terrorist attack. I used to see them in Boston harbor on their way to the Everett terminal—the Port Authority used to close the harbor to other shipping! As with conventional giant oil tankers, it is idiotic not to recognize them as inherently dangerous.

The following graph depicts the net U.S. import and export of natural gas. (Note the U.S. exports a small amount of gas to Mexico.)

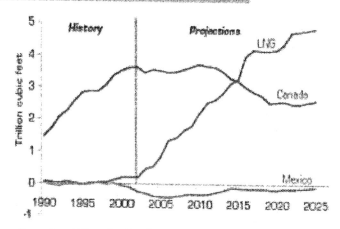

Source: Energy Information Administration, Annual Energy Outlook 2004 Reference Case

When Dr. Hirsch listed Gas-to-Liquids as one of the proven technologies that could be used to mitigate peaking oil, it wasn't LNG he was talking about; LNG is not an end product or fuel, its just a way to transport it. The other technology called "gas to liquids" (GTL) actually converts natural gas into petroleum liquid substitutes, such as diesel, naphtha, gasoline, or other products (such as lubricants and waxes).

The economics of GTL continue to improve as the price of oil rises but conversely hinges on the price of natural gas. In the natural gas rich countries the numbers are beginning to add up; consequently, projects are being initiated in Qatar, Iran, Russia, Nigeria, Australia, and Algeria, where natural gas can be developed at a cost of less than $1.00 per million Btu.

The world demand for oil in the transportation sector is projected to grow by 2.1 percent per year, from 41.7 million barrels per day in 2002 to 67.3 million barrels per day in 2025. Even if all the proposed GTL projects worldwide materialized by 2025, assuming a 70 percent yield for diesel from the natural gas stock, the expected GTL diesel supply of 1.2 million barrels per day in 2025 would represent only a fraction of total world transportation sector demand.

The question is how can the United States best use its domestic and imported natural gas resources to mitigate our looming liquid fuels crisis? The answer is astonishingly simple; quit using this valuable resource to heat water! In 2003 we used 23 percent of our natural gas to generate electricity, and another 23 percent to heat residential homes. Consumption for both sectors is going up exponentially, as over 1,000 proposals for new natural gas power plants (90 percent) have poured in since the late 1990s, and gas heat continues to be put into any new home built near a gas line.

It is ludicrous. Natural gas is far too precious to waste. Nuclear reactors can produce all the steam we want to power turbines, and the electricity produced can heat our homes. Plus, how dependent do we want to be on other nations to supply our fossil fuels other than coal (fortunately, the United States still has vast coal reserves)? Are we willing to risk our sons and daughters and potentially nuclear war to fight for them?

At the end of 2005 there was a raging dispute between Russia and Ukraine over a huge price increase that Russia threatened to impose on natural gas. Russia, a large exporter of natural gas, supplies Ukraine and Europe by a pipeline that crosses Ukraine—if they shut off Ukraine they shut off Europe. The dispute was settled by a modest increase in price, which remains far below that charged other countries.

Global demand for natural gas is soaring. We know the risks of global oil markets very well; can anyone doubt the risks of politically unpredictable gas producing countries on global gas markets?

Finland, which shares a border with Russia, has weighed these risks very carefully. The Finns are moving ahead with plans to build the world's largest nuclear reactor that would lessen its reliance on imported Russian natural gas.

Despite the risk, according to the EIA's *Annual Outlook* 2005, the U.S. importation of LNG will increase from 1 percent of total consumption to 21 percent by 2025, bringing our total reliance on imported natural gas to 35 percent of anticipated demand.

Coal

Coal represented about 22.53 percent of the energy consumed in the United States in 2004. The amount of coal used was over 1,104 million (short tons); that is expected to increase 1.9 percent a year (39 percent total) to 1,784 million tons by 2030.While the bulk of the increase will be in the electric power sector, it is expected that 62 million tons in 2020 and 190 million tons in 2030 will be used in coal-to-liquid (CLT) production—a little over 10 percent.

As with buying a barrel of petroleum, very few people will ever buy a ton of coal. That wasn't so in the latter part of the 19th century and the first half of the 20th century, when coal was the primary home heating fuel, both in the United States and Europe. As a child, I remember my dad stoking up the coal-burning furnace in our basement that produced steam heat for our home (circa 1940s). Now most homes are heated with natural gas or oil. In the 1960s and 70s electric heat was highly popular, but it was largely replaced by gas or oil when the price of electricity skyrocketed in the 1980s and 1990s. In the winter of 2005-6, with the price of gas and oil sharply higher, electric heat has once again become competitive in some markets.

In 2005, 88 percent of the coal burned in the nation was used for electric power generation or in some combined-heat-and-power (CHP) plants whose primary business is to sell electricity, or electricity and heat to the public (Re: NACIS 22 plants). Coal is used to generate over 50 percent of the nation's electricity. Uranium, the current fuel of nuclear power plants, is the basis for 20 percent of the U.S. electricity supply.

The remainder of the coal is used in other industries, such as iron and steel, concrete, and paper.

Almost any petroleum or natural gas product can also be made from coal, but at a greater expense—these include liquid fuels, agricultural products, pharmaceutical products and plastics. That is because coal, natural gas and petroleum, the world's fossil fuels, share a similar (not identical) carbon/hydrogen based molecular structure.

In 2004, the United States had a net export of 21 million tons of coal. It is predicted that we will have a net import five million tons of coal in 2015, and that net imports will increase to 83 million tons by 2030.

Okay. We know we are dependant on a limited supply of imported petroleum and natural gas, but how much coal do we have? The answer, to risk a pun, is a ton. According to John E. Shelk, senior vice president, government affairs, of the National Mining Association, coal is the only domestic source of energy that is expected to increase production to meet demand over the next two decades. The demonstrated U.S. coal reserve is over 500 billion tons with economical recoverable reserves of over 275 tons. This is a reserve large enough to support coal demand for well over 200 years at the current rate of use.[236]

The United States has the largest recoverable coal reserves in the world. (See bar graph below)

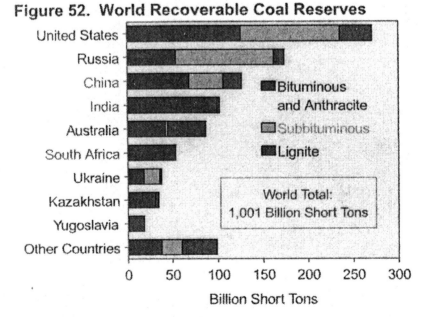

Figure 52. World Recoverable Coal Reserves

Shelk went on to say that while NMA was asked to speak primarily about coal, we would be remiss if we did not point out that the United States uranium recovery industry is also essential in the nation's energy supply mix. Today, nearly 20 percent of America's electricity comes from nuclear power, which translates into the consumption of about 45 million pounds of uranium each year. However, the collapse in uranium prices since 1980 has produced a sharp decline in the viability of the U.S. uranium mining industry. America's remaining uranium miners produce only about three million pounds—or just 6 percent of nuclear utilities annual uranium requirement. The balance of the uranium comes from rapidly declining inventories in the hands of the utilities, the federal government, and foreign entities.

Historically, the United States was the world's leading producer of uranium and still has extensive proven reserves of natural uranium that offer the potential for secure sources of future supply. Only a strong domestic uranium recovery industry can assure an adequate long-term supply to preclude threats of foreign supply disruptions or price controls that could adversely affect the nation's security.

There is no question that coal is an extremely valuable and important resource for the United States. It is a resource that we are very fortunate to have; one that can ease our transition into a future weaned of fossil fuel dependence.

In Shelk's remarks to Congress, he was glowingly complimentary of the proposed legislation that would become the Energy Act Of 2005 (EAO2005). It is easy to understand why, given the Bush administration's love affair with the oil, coal and natural gas producers and the resulting regulatory weaknesses of the act. But make no mistake, mining interests and coal have a dark and deadly past, and EAO2005 falls far short of protecting miners and our environment in the future. Yet, despite the act's shortcomings, it is now our national policy to encourage increasing the use of coal by about 40 percent over the next 25 years.

There is a lot at risk. While the Clean Air Act, passed in 1967 and reinforced in 1977 and 1990, has proved to be a powerful tool to reduce pollution, it is under attack by the Bush administration and the Republican majority in Congress. Today some of the biggest polluters are being permitted not to clean up the emissions coming out of their smokestacks. The toll of death, disease and environmental destruction caused by coal-fired power plant pollution continues to mount. An analysis released in 2004 attributed 24,000 premature deaths *each year* to power plant pollution. In addition, the research estimates over 550,000 asthma attacks, 38,000 heart attacks and 12,000 hospital admissions are caused annually by power plant pollution.[237] We can add to that a steady rate of about 1,500 coal miners dying from black lung disease (coal workers' pneumoconiosis) annually.[238]

While many old coal-fired power plants continue to get a pass from the Environmental Protection Agency (EPA) on cleaning up, newly constructed plants will be substantially cleaner—except, and it is a big except, the Bush administration has refused to make any restrictions on CO_2 emissions. To sequester (capture and store) carbon dioxide from the gases of most conventional power plants is difficult and expensive, but new Integrated Gasification Combined Cycle (IGCC) plants offer much lower incremental costs for capture. Currently, no fully commercial IGCC plants are in use, because they are more expensive than conventional plants. However, if the government were to invest in the constructions of IGCC plants and limit the emissions of CO_2, the relative cost would be reduced and their widespread deployment encouraged.

How important is it that we control the release of carbon dioxide? The answer is, extremely important, and at this time the United States is the world's largest emitter of CO_2. In the early 19th century (with the advent of the industrial revolution), coal burning began to drive up CO_2 levels. They rose gradually at first—it took more than a century to reach 300 parts per million—and later, following the Second World War, much more rapidly. By 1965, CO_2 concentrations had reached 320 parts per million; by 1985, 345 parts per million; and by 2005, 378 parts per million.

If current trends continue, it will reach 500 parts per million (nearly double pre-industrial levels) by the middle of this century, and could reach as much as 750 parts per million by 2100. The equilibrium warming associated with double CO_2 is estimated to be between three and a half and seven degrees, and with tripled CO_2 between six and 11degrees. A global temperature rise of just three degrees would render the Earth hotter than it has been at any point in the past two million years.[239]

Yes, global warming is a serious threat, one that the Bush administration and the far-right nitwits ruling our country ignore as "egg head," lefty concerns of no merit, as they have with stem cell research, and other basic science that conflicts with their fundamentalist ideology. But the signs of climate change are already evident. They are to be seen in the increased violent weather experienced in 2005; in the melting glaciers of the Antarctic and receding glaciers in Greenland; in the softening of Arctic Ocean ice cap that now makes trekking to the North Pole impossible; and in the dying or migrating of plant and animal species that inhabit the Earth. We are in a situation where a quarter of the terrestrial species might be at risk of extinction from climate change. Remember, the dinosaurs are thought to have died out suddenly because of climate change; perhaps Homo sapiens will be another species not to survive into the 22nd century.

The global landscape will also change as islands vanish under the sea and coastal areas flood. If enough cold, fresh water coming from the melting polar ice caps and the melting glaciers of Greenland flows into the northern Atlantic, it will shut down the Gulf Stream, which keeps Europe and northeastern North America warm. The worst-case scenario would be a full-blown return of the last ice age—in a period as short as two to three years from onset—and the mid-case scenario would be a period like the "little ice age" of a few centuries ago that disturbed worldwide weather patterns, leading to extremely harsh winters, droughts, worldwide desertification, crop failures, and wars around the world.[240]

Sure, most adults living today will not live long enough to see more than disruptions. Nonetheless, climate disruptions combined with liquid fuels shortages and spiking prices may very well be in our future. Unless we change direction, as a nation and as a member of the world community of nations, most surely our legacy to our children, grandchildren and great-grandchildren will be sadly grim.

Let's look at some other visuals to understand carbon dioxide emissions.

Figure 68. World Carbon Dioxide Emissions by Fuel Type, 1970-2025

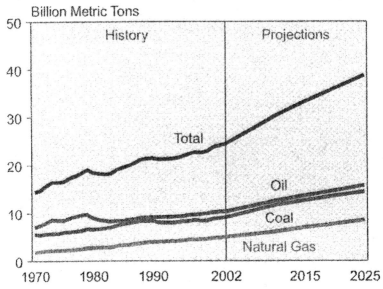

Sources: **History:** Energy Information Administration (EIA), *International Energy Annual 2002*, DOE/EIA-0219(2002) (Washington, DC, March 2004), web site www.eia.doe.gov/ iea/. **Projections:** EIA, System for the Analysis of Global Energy Markets (2005).

Figure 67. World Carbon Dioxide Emissions by Region, 1990-2025

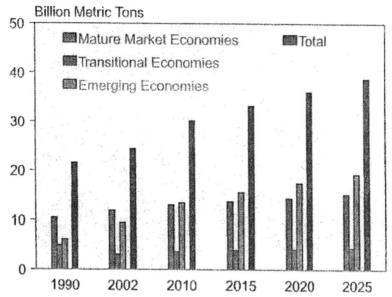

Sources: **1990 and 2002:** Energy Information Administration (EIA), *International Energy Annual 2002*, DOE/EIA-0219 (2002) (Washington, DC, March 2004), web site www.eia.doe.gov/iea/. **Projections:** EIA, System for the Analysis of Global Energy Markets (2005).

Another factor in the accumulation of carbon dioxide in the atmosphere is deforestation. Forests are being felled for lumber, paper, and fuel around the world, in the South American Amazon, in the Philippines, in Africa, in North America, and on and on. The CO_2 produced by the chemical process of burning (carbon plus oxygen) and by all living animals is used by green-leafed plants in a process called photosynthesis—the plants absorb carbon dioxide and in turn emit oxygen. As we pave over more and more acres for roads and parking automobiles at the Wal-Marts of the world, and chop down our trees, we are literally choking ourselves to death, and losing our most important means of limiting CO_2 accumulations. It is crazy, and we should be providing world leadership to stop doing it. Instead the Bush administration considers clear-cut forestry in our national forests as a way to limit forest fires. If the logic were not so pathetic it would be funny.

Incidentally, because of photosynthesis biomass fuels are almost a wash when it comes to carbon dioxide emissions; burning only returns the CO_2 back into the atmosphere that was used by the plant during its lifecycle. Fossil fuels, on the other hand, when burned release CO_2 that had been sequestered in the Earth for millions of years.

Two-thirds of coal mined is from strip or open-pit mining, instead of tunneling. If coal is within a couple of hundred feet from the surface, the earth is just stripped away to uncover the coal. Giant shovels and earthmovers are used. Mountains are flattened and valleys and streams filled and polluted. I have flown over some of these sites in Appalachia, and let me tell you it is ugly to see. Of course the National Mining Association will tell you that the land is brought back to a pristine state suitable for parks, but that is pure bull. The destruction to our water tables and environment is permanent, and it is essential that our anti-regulation, pro-big business get a grip on it before it is too late.

The other third of coal comes from tunneled mines. Here again, the industry would have you believe that it is an antiseptic process now, with nicely dressed workers merely pushing buttons on equipment while breathing clean air. And again it is bull. In many mines the tunnels are only three feet high, rarely more than five feet, and the black lung statistics are lethally real. So are the accident rates and deaths in mines. In early January 2006, the public was shocked when 12 miners were killed in the Sago coalmine in West Virginia. We shouldn't have been. Since the mine reopened in February 2004, two-dozen miners had been hurt in a string of accidents, some of them caused by rock chunks falling from the mine ceilings. Federal safety inspectors slapped the mine with citations 273 times, or an average of once every 2-½ days.

Despite this record, the price paid by Sago's operators was light. Government regulators never publicly discussed shutting down the mine and never sought criminal sanctions. The biggest single fine was $440, about 0.0004 percent of the $110 million net profit reported last year by the mine's current owner, International Coal Group Inc.[241]

Critics, including several former Mine Safety and Health Administration (MSHA) officials, say relatively light sanctions, coupled with the current administration's more collegial approach to regulation, make it harder for inspectors to force noncompliant companies to change.

"There was a dramatic shift in MSHA's philosophy in 2001, with a new emphasis on cooperation by the enforcers," said J. Davitt McAteer, who headed the agency under the Clinton administration, "and it came at a cost of less enforcement of the statute."

Sago, and lots of other small, less productive mines are non-union.

Coal mining is rated as the second most dangerous job on the planet, second only to fishing in the Bering Sea.

So all in all, coal comes at a very high price indeed. Coal mining and the burning of coal absolutely has to be regulated more strictly, particularly as the tonnage used goes up over the next 25 years. And, as with natural gas, coal is far too valuable a resource to be wasted boiling water to turn turbines to make electricity. While it is encouraging to see a small percentage of coal used by 2030 to coal-to-liquid production (10 percent), I feel that long before the passage of 25 years liquid fuel shortages will be acute, and the amount now expected to be produced will do little to mitigate the problem.

Without question, energy independence and climate change are the two major, interrelated issues of our time. If the United States fails to come quickly to terms with them, we will face crisis after crisis that will result in major dislocations, economic decline, and war as we struggle to control diminishing world supplies of fossil fuels.

The glaring truth is that our country is now ruled by an administration and Congress that have relinquished governing to big business and special interests. As a result we have no energy policy; the Energy Policy Act of 2005 is largely an $8 billion incentive program for the energy industries to essentially keep doing the same thing, making outrageous sums of money, with hopes that along the way they will come up with some long-range solutions.

If we fail to rid ourselves of the far right in the 2006, 2008 elections, I fear our country will experience a downward spiral unprecedented in American history. To make the change, it will take candidates who have the courage to tell the truth, candidates able to rally the people by framing energy independence and climate control as a national opportunity rather than a great sacrifice. And more than anything, it will take educated voters. The purpose of this book is to encourage both.

Eighteen

Bush's Foreign Policy Fiasco

———————◆•◆•◆———————

I know not with what weapons World War III will be fought, but World War IV will be fought with sticks and stones.

Albert Einstein

Every gun that is made, every warship launched, every rocket fired signifies, in the final sense, a theft from those who hunger and are not fed, those who are cold and not clothed.

Dwight D. Eisenhower

Today, every inhabitant of this planet must contemplate a day when this planet may no longer be habitable. Every man, woman and child lives under a nuclear sword of Damocles, hanging by the slenderest of threads, capable of being cut at any moment by accident or miscalculation or by madness. The weapons of war must be abolished before they abolish us.

John F. Kennedy

As someone who has lived through World War II, the bombing of Hiroshima and Nagasaki, the Cold War, and regional wars too numerous to count, it is mind boggling to be lectured by President Bush about the "war on terror," and "weapons of mass destruction" (WMD). Bush's "Rambo" attitude and hawkish foreign policy may play well to his neoconservative base, but it plays poorly on the world stage and makes the United States more vulnerable, not less. Rather than support the Nuclear Proliferation Treaty (NPT), and work to eliminate the possibility of "loose nukes," Bush has turned his back of the NPT, and diverted our energy and resources to fighting an ill-advised oil war in Iraq. He used the terrorist attacks on 9/11 (which he says defined his presidency) to keep the populace in a perpetual state of fear in order to win elections and feed the military-industrial complex at the expense of the rest of the nation's needs. He claims that to fight the enemy, we must give the president (him) unprecedented war powers, surrender civil liberties, and pursue a militaristic (imperialistic) foreign policy. What Bush means when he talks about the "war on terror," is not so much about stopping terrorism where it exists, as it is about entering a state of perpetual war.

The preemptive war with Iraq has backfired, putting American troops in the middle of a civil war between the Shiites, Kurds, and the Sunnis. Iraq has now become a cauldron of terrorism, which didn't exist before we invaded. In January 2006, terrorist attacks averaged over 500 a week in Iraq. In the week following the February 22, 2006 insurgent bombing of the gold-domed Askariya Shiite shrine, Shiite militiamen killed over 1,300 Sunnis. By May 2006, a so-called unity government had been cobbled together, but three key ministries were left vacant (defense, interior and national security) and the violence was accelerating.

The number of global terrorist attacks increased tremendously as well. In 2005 there were 3991, up 51 percent from the previous year. By June 2006, American servicemen and women killed in Iraq stood at nearly 2,500; about 17,000 were wounded, many very severely. It is estimated that more than a hundred thousand Iraqis have died.

It is a mess, yet three years after the invasion on March 20, 2003, there was no definitive plan to withdraw the 130,000-plus American troops who remained in Iraq. Bush said that we had to "stay the course," and continue to bear the loss of life and treasure until the job is done.[242] Those who question the conduct of the war and our overall Middle East policies are castigated by the administration and branded as weak and unpatriotic.

In a rare public address in January 2006, White House political adviser Karl Rove called Democratic senators on the Senate Judicial Committee "mean-spirited and small-minded" in their questioning of Supreme Court nominee Samuel Alito. (Alito is an advocate of a concept called the "unitary executive," which favors an imperial presidency—that's what the Democrats were demanding answers about, answers that were never given.) Alito was later confirmed by a narrow margin and took the oath of office as a justice of the U.S. Supreme Court on January 31, 2006.

Rove then drove home the White House's party line to the Republican audience: "Republicans have a post-9/11 worldview of the world. And Democrats have a pre-9/11 worldview of the world. That doesn't make them unpatriotic, not at all. But it does make them wrong—deeply and profoundly and consistently wrong."

What utter nonsense. Although 9/11 was horrific (the death toll of about 3,000 surpassed that at Pearl Harbor), the attacks did not put the nation in mortal jeopardy; there was no invading force approaching our shores or nuclear missiles coming over the horizon. Osama bin Laden's Al Qaeda and other Islamist extremist groups existed a decade before 9/11. The truth is we were vulnerable to a terrorist attack largely because of the negligence of the Bush administration. The independent, bipartisan 9/11 Commission (The National Commission on Terrorist Attacks Upon the United States) found that the attacks could and should have been prevented.[243] The following statement is from the executive summary of the commission's final report:

A Shock, Not a Surprise

The 9/11 attacks were a shock, but they should not have come as a surprise. Islamist extremists had given plenty of warning that they meant to kill Americans indiscriminately and in large numbers. Although Usama Bin Ladin himself would not emerge as a signal threat until the late 1990s, the threat of Islamist terrorism grew over the decade.

In testimony, Richard Clarke, a former senior counterterrorism adviser, told the 9/11 Commission:[244]

> At the senior policy levels in the Clinton Administration, there was an acute understanding of the terrorist threat, particularly al Qida. That understanding resulted in a vigorous program to counter al Qida including lethal covert action, but it did not include a willingness to resume bombing of Afghanistan. Events in the Balkans, Iraq, the Peace Process, and domestic politics occurring at the same time as the anti-terrorism effort played a role.
>
> The Bush Administration saw terrorism policy as important but not urgent, prior to 9/11. The difficulty in obtaining the first Cabinet level (Principals) policy meeting on terrorism and the limited Principals' involvement sent unfortunate signals to the bureaucracy about the Administration's attitude toward the al Qida threat.

No link has ever been established between Al Qaeda, and Iraq. Fifteen of the 19 hijackers who crashed the four airliners that day were Saudi Arabians. Osama bin Laden, who claimed credit for Al Qaeda for planning and executing the attacks, is the son of a wealthy, prominent Saudi Arabian family. While WMD were used as justification to invade Iraq, only chemical weapons given to them by the United States, and others through the 1980s (during the Iraq-Iran war), were ever found. These weapons were under control of U.N. inspectors and were being dismantled when the United States invaded. The inspectors were kicked out weeks before the war started. No U.S. troops were assigned to guard the sites and they were subsequently systematically looted. Where the weapons wound up is anybody's guess, but many believe they are arming the insurgency.

The simple fact is the United States invaded Iraq on the basis of lies from President Bush and his war cabinet, which continues to claim it was because they had faulty intelligence. Baloney! Paul Pillar, who was the CIA's national intelligence officer for the Middle East at the time, tells us "intelligence was publicly misused to justify the decision that the administration had already made, to topple Saddam Hussein." In fact,

Pillar wrote, "If the entire body of official intelligence analysis on Iraq had a policy implication, it was to avoid war—or, if war was going to be launched, to prepare for a messy aftermath."[245]

Despite the fact that President Bush assures us day after day that the United States is engaged in a "war on terror," others feel differently. In a December 2005 interview by Geov Parrish, Noam Chomsky, an MIT professor for over 40 years and one of the world's leading critics of U.S. foreign policy, said, "As a matter of fact there is no War on Terror. It's a minor consideration. So invading Iraq and taking control of the world's energy resources was *way* more important than the threat of terror. And the same with other things. Take, say, nuclear terror. The American intelligence systems estimate that the likelihood of a "dirty bomb," a dirty nuclear bomb attack in the United States in the next ten years, is about 50 percent. Are they doing anything about it? Yeah. They're increasing the threat, by increasing nuclear proliferation, by compelling potential adversaries to take very dangerous measures to try to counter rising American threats."

Chomsky later said in the interview, "Well, the first thing that should be done in Iraq is for us to be serious about what's going on. There is almost no serious discussion, I'm sorry to say, across the spectrum, of the question of withdrawal. The reason for that is that we are under a rigid doctrine in the West, a religious fanaticism, that says we must believe that the United States would have invaded Iraq even if its main product was lettuce and pickles, and the oil resources of the world were in Central Africa. Anyone who doesn't believe that is condemned as a conspiracy theorist, a Marxist, a madman, or something. Well, you know, if you have three gray cells functioning, you know that's perfect nonsense. The U.S. invaded Iraq because it has enormous oil resources, mostly untapped, and it's right in the heart of the world's energy system. Which means that if the U.S. manages to control Iraq, it extends enormously its strategic power, what Zbigniew Brzezinski calls its critical leverage over Europe and Asia. Yeah, that's a major reason for controlling the oil resources—it gives you strategic power. Even if you're on renewable energy you want to do that. So that's the reason for invading Iraq, the fundamental reason."[246]

Terrorist groups like Al Qaeda are not nation-states. Consequently, there really cannot be a "war on terror" anymore than there can be a war on crime or drugs—using the word "war" metaphorically is deliberately misleading. The Bush administration continues to use the word precisely to give itself the extraordinary powers enjoyed by a wartime government without the nation actually being engaged in a war, declared or otherwise.

In fact, in its entire history the United States has only formally declared war 11 times; the first was against Great Britain in the War of 1812. The last six times were during World War II against Japan, Germany, Italy, Bulgaria, Hungary, and Romania. Regarding the Korean Conflict, Congress didn't declare it to have been a war until well after the ceasefire in 1958, thereby allowing the Korean veterans the same benefits as the WWII vets. President Johnson committed troops to fight in Vietnam on the basis of the Congressional Gulf of Tonkin Resolution (August 7, 1964). War was never declared.

In 1973, following the withdrawal of troops from Vietnam, a heated debate emerged in Congress about the extent of presidential power in deploying troops, or to engage in war, without a formal declaration of war, as required by the Constitution. A compromise was reached with Congressional passage of the War Powers Resolution (passed over the veto of President Nixon on November 7, 1973). The law prescribes the balance of power between the president and Congress to wage war, and established presidential reporting requirements to Congress.

Section 2 (c) of the War Powers Act states, "the constitutional powers of the President as Commander-in-Chief to introduce United States Armed Forces into hostilities, or into situations where imminent involvement in hostilities is clearly indicated by the circumstances, are exercised only pursuant to (1) a declaration of war, (2) specific statutory authorization, or (3) a national emergency created by attack upon the United States, its territories or possessions, or armed forces." [247]

Although the constitutionality of "specific statutory authorization" has never been tested, it has been used, most notably during the Grenada conflict, the Panama conflict, the Somalia conflict, the first Gulf War, the attack on Afghanistan, and the invasion of Iraq. In each case the president received Congressional authorization for troop deployment.

All of which doesn't make stopping terrorism any less important; we just shouldn't allow President Bush to parley his "war on terror" into a perpetual state of war. Congress has never given him a blank check to be a wartime dictator. This is a deeply significant when one considers the potential of future undeclared preemptive wars against nation-states such as Iran, North Korea, and Syria; and when one considers the power the Bush administration claims for itself in order to mistreat and detain so-called enemy combatants indefinitely. In his State of the Union address following 9/11, in January 2002, the comments of President Bush were extremely disquieting in this regard. He said:[248]

But some governments will be timid in the face of terror. And make no mistake about it: If they do not act, America will.

Our second goal is to prevent regimes that sponsor terror from threatening America or our friends and allies with weapons of mass destruction. Some of these regimes have been pretty quite since September 11th. But we know their true nature. North Korea is a regime arming with missiles and weapons of mass destruction, while starving its citizens.

Iran aggressively pursues these weapons and exports terror. While an unelected few repress the Iranian people's hope for freedom.

Iraq continues to flaunt its hostility toward America and to support terror. The Iraqi regime has plotted to develop anthrax, and nerve gas, and nuclear weapons for over a decade. This is a regime that has used poison gas to murder thousands of its own citizens—leaving the bodies of mothers huddled over their dead children. This is a regime that agreed to international inspections—then kicked out the inspectors. This is a regime that has something to hide from the civilized world.

States like these, and their terrorist allies, constitute an axis of evil, arming to threaten the peace of the world. By seeking weapons of mass destruction, these regimes pose a grave and growing danger. They could provide these arms to terrorists, giving them the means to match their hatred. They could attack our allies or attempt to blackmail the United States. In any of these cases, the price of indifference would be catastrophic.

Little more than a year after he gave the speech, the United States launched a preemptive war against Iraq. After about a year of searching for WMD with no success, Bush shifted gears, claiming the war was justified to topple Saddam Hussein and to "spread democracy" in the Middle East. Thereafter, democratization became the noble smokescreen to cover the administration's failure to provide the necessary security to rebuild Iraq in order to form a stable government. Apparently no realistic thought was given to what sort of government would emerge from such instability. We might have had a clue from the relatively recent history of Iran, which thanks to failed U.S. and Western foreign misadventures, has continued to elect extreme Islamists to govern their theocracy since 1979. The United States also encouraged the Palestinian Authority to allow Hamas party candidates on the ballot—they did and in February 2006 Hamas won the majority of seats in parliament, wresting control from the President Abbas and the Fatah party, which had the support of the United States and Israel. (Washington and the European Union list Hamas as a terrorist organization). In their first free election in December 2005, Iraqis voted in a fundamentalist Shiite majority government, giving power to Shiite religious leaders with close ties to Iran.[249]

Thus a war based upon lies has deteriorated into a quagmire that seriously threatens U.S. and Western interests in the Persian Gulf. These interests include preventing Iran from acquiring nuclear weapons, and maintaining the flow of oil from both Iran and Iraq. While oil production in Iraq remains below pre-war levels because of the insurgency, the continued flow of oil and natural gas from Iran is essential to the economy of the world. Today the world's oil producers pump about 80 million barrels of oil a day, and 80 million barrels a day are purchased. Any disruption in the flow of oil from the Persian Gulf because of civil war in Iraq, the freezing of Iranian sales, or political instability in Saudi Arabia caused by terrorism would have serious ramifications. As I said in the previous chapter, world oil production has peaked and a liquid fuels crisis is upon us. These are serious questions that require U.S. leadership, and a new post Cold War world dialogue between nations. Unfortunately, it is a dialogue the Bush administration seems to have no interest in having, betting instead that the oil industry will miraculously save us. It is a bet I hope the American people reject at the polls.

Do the terrorists have WMD? I think if they did they would have used them already. They certainly have the capability to make or acquire limited chemical or biological weapons. On a relatively small scale, it doesn't take that much to harm people. For instance, Aum Shinrikyo, a terrorist group in Japan, flooded the Tokyo subway system with sarin (a nerve gas) in 1995, killing 12 and hospitalizing hundreds. Also, after 9/11 there were a few fatalities in the United States from mail containing anthrax; some letters containing it were even sent to member of Congress but were intercepted before causing harm. That mystery is still unsolved, however. No terrorist group has claimed responsibility. Then, the arms and chemical weapons apparatus that vanished from Iraq remain at large. As I indicated earlier, these are likely in the hands of anti-American forces.

What are the odds of terrorist groups acquiring a nuclear weapon? As Chomsky pointed out, the odds of terrorists and or rogue states acquiring nuclear material or weapons are far from acceptable. Which leads to the most serious question of all: Has the foreign policy, war policy, nuclear policy, energy policy, and anti-terrorism strategy of the Bush administration made our country safer? The answer is resoundingly no. They have placed our country in great peril by hiding the truth, playing politics with national security, making security decisions based upon the financial interests of big business, and failing miserably with diplomacy.

Before going on to learn what the White House will never tell us, I'd like to revisit another famous quote mentioned earlier in the book. It will help us stay focused on the Bush administration's strategy to scare the people into accepting the neoconservative agenda of massive defense spending, and their goal of global dominance.[250]

Naturally, the common people don't want war...but after all it is the leaders of a country who determine the policy, and it is always a simple matter to drag the people along, whether it is a democracy, or a fascist dictatorship, or a parliament, or a communist dictatorship. Voice or no voice, the people can always be brought to the bidding of the leaders. That is easy. All you have to do is to tell them they are being attacked, and denounce the pacifists for lack of patriotism and exposing the country to danger. It works the same in every country.

Hermann Goering

The reality is that the foreign policy of the United States is now governed by neo-conservatives who share the goal of asserting U.S. military power worldwide.[251] *Adbuster* magazine summed up American neoconservatism as:

The belief that democracy, however flawed, was best defended by an ignorant public pumped on nationalism and religion. Only a militantly nationalist state could deter human aggression…Such nationalism requires an external threat and if on cannot be found it must be manufactured.

Karl Rove and his neocon masters used 9/11 and Al Qaeda, a real but limited threat, to create an imaginary axis of evil threatening America. They now predict decades of a war on terror, drawing a similarity to the 40-year Cold War against communism.

Motives? Here's my take: I believe there are basically two motives that define the Bush administration's policies: line the pockets of their rich friends with dollars, and increase their control over the world for big business—Capitalism with a capital C. If the world drowns in the aftermath of global warming, experiences severe economic disruptions because of fuel shortages or blows up, I am convinced these guys don't care. It will be years away and it will be on somebody else's watch. As Secretary of Defense Rumsfeld frequently says, "stuff happens." That is why they have done such a terrible job of governing: They don't give a fig about the United States or its people. The almighty dollar is their god, despite the Christian chevrons Bush wears on his sleeve. Bush may be an incompetent dullard, but the driving forces behind this administration are not stupid; they are diabolically clever, manipulative, and committed to an ideology that, in fusing government and corporate power, fits the definition of fascism.

Consider Bush the man: He is unique in that, like his evangelical base, he believes he is on a mission from God and that faith trumps empirical evidence. We can learn a lot about this from *Dark Ages America: the Final Phase of Empire*, by Morris Berman, a professor of sociology at the Catholic University of America in Washington, D.C.[252]

As Berman puts it:

We were already in our twilight phase when Ronald Reagan, with all the insight of an ostrich, declared it to be "morning in America"; twenty-odd years later, under the "boy emperor" George W. Bush (as Chalmers Johnson refers to him), we have entered the Dark Ages in earnest, pursuing a short-sighted path that can only accelerate our decline. For what we are now seeing are the obvious characteristics of the West after the fall of Rome: the triumph of religion over reason; the atrophy of education and critical thinking; the integration of religion, state, and the apparatus of torture—a troika that was for Voltaire the central horror of the pre-Enlightenment world; and the political and economic marginalization of our culture...

Berman quotes a senior White House adviser who disdains what he calls the "reality-based community," to which Berman sensibly responds: "If a nation is unable to perceive reality correctly, and persists in operating on the basis of faith-based delusions, its ability to hold its own in the world is pretty much foreclosed."

A man such as George W. Bush scares the world for good reason; as commander-and-chief, his finger is on the trigger of the largest arsenal of ready-to-launch nuclear weapons on Earth. Hands down, the United States is the largest holder of WMD. Is it any wonder that nuclear proliferation has once again become a major problem? In a mere decade, we have moved from optimism at the end of the Cold War back into great uncertainty. The Bush administration's unilateral cowboy tactics and distain of the United Nations makes it hard to solve problems by diplomacy. In the eyes of many, as the world superpower we have become a dangerous adversary.

Weapons of mass destruction

The term was first used in a *Times* article on December 28, 1937 about the bombing of Guernica, Spain, by the German Luftwaffe during the Spanish Civil War:

Who can think without horror of what another widespread war would mean, waged as it would be with all the new weapons of mass destruction.

The bombing by the Luftwaffe destroyed about 70 percent of Guernica.

What differentiates WMD from other weapons is the scale of destruction and the targeting of noncombatants. In the 1920s and 1930s, military aviators in the United States and the rest of the world became enamored with the possibilities of strategic bombing. Rather than the trench warfare of WWI, potentially nations could be brought to their knees by destroying their industrial base, causing panic, destruction of infrastructure, and deprivations. Protagonists believed that the population would rise up against the government and force it to sue for peace. In this regard, the Spanish Civil War was a training ground for Nazi Germany. The Germans would use that strategy a few years later in their Blitzkrieg attacks across Europe and during the Battle of Britain with the bombing of London.[253] (In preparing to invade Britain in August of 1940, Hermann Goering's Luftwaffe began by cleverly destroying British airfields. When Hitler ordered them to bomb London instead of the airfields, the tide turned because the Brits were again able to keep their defending fighters in the air. After suffering heavy loses, Hitler abandoned the "Blitz" and called off the invasion.) In August 1940, Winston Churchill made this famous statement about the British pilots who single-handedly fought the battle: "Never in the field of human conflict was so much owed by so many to so few."

World War II put all theories about strategic bombing to the test. Proponents argued that the destruction of German and Japanese industrial societies was "decisive." Many analysts disagree, claiming that despite the sacrifices of aircrews, and cost in material and morale, strategic bombing never came close to prewar predictions.[254] They point out that strategic bombing, while causing destruction, also hardened resolve and increased resistance. This was certainly the case with the bombing of Pearl Harbor and London. The fire bombing of Dresden and Tokyo are other examples. It is estimated that between 25,000 and 35,000 died in the Dresden raid and 80,000 to 100,000 in the Tokyo raid, more than died in Nagasaki (70,000 to 80,000), and more than half the number who died in Hiroshima (120,000 to 150,000). Yet despite the massive loss of life the citizenry in Germany and Japan didn't rebel against the government.

While no one can say that Germany was bombed into submission, some argue that atomic bombs forced the surrender of Japan. Others say that what actually forced Japan to surrender was the cumulative weight of Allied land, sea, and airpower, which cost the military and the government their credibility—that the atomic bombs were a face-saving excuse for the Japanese military and a way for Emperor Hirohito and his family to avoid death at the hands of the Chinese.[255]

Strategic bombing with "conventional" weapons continued after nuclear weapons came on the scene in 1945, and the arguments still go on as to its value. Did the 1972 Christmas bombing of North Vietnam force the Communists to finally accept peace proposals to end the war in Vietnam? Not really. North Vietnam was never deterred; the bombings only added to its resolve. The only real effect of massive carpet-bombing by U.S. B-52s, some say, was to allow the United States to leave with honor. Others say the needless killing was far from honorable; it was a national disgrace.

The same questionable results could be attributed to our bombing of Iraq during the first Gulf War and during the more recent invasion of Iraq. While there is no question that our tactical bombing was devastatingly effective, it didn't drive Saddam Hussein out of power. It took boots on the ground to do that. And as "smart" as our smart bombs have become, thousands of noncombatants have been killed or maimed, leaving the United States as a hated invader in the eyes of many Iraqis. Calling those deaths unintentional "collateral damage" does little to assuage their hatred or improve our image.

In 1946, the term "weapons of mass destruction" took on a narrower meaning when the United Nations created the Atomic Energy Commission (forerunner of the International Atomic Energy Agency (IAEA). They used the wording: "...Atomic weapons and of all other weapons adaptable to mass destruction."

While WMD means different things to different people, the term has been used widely in the arms control community to mean nuclear, biological, and chemical weapons. More recently, radiological weapons have been lumped with them. (These are weapons that use a low-tech conventional explosive to spread lethal radioactive material, those so-called "dirty bombs.")

Following WWII, the United States and the Soviet Union began the most expensive and dangerous arms race in the history of humankind. Nuclear weapons and delivery systems of all sorts were developed and added to the military arsenals on both sides. They included aircraft, intercontinental and shorter-range missiles launched from beneath and above the land and sea, cruise missiles, cannons and God knows what else. Biological and chemical weapons were developed and stockpiled as well—combined there were, and still are, more than enough WMD to annihilate most of the living organisms on the planet. A Brookings Institute report titled "Atomic Audit" estimated the cost of the 70,000 U.S. nuclear weapons built between 1940 and 1995 at a minimum of $5 trillion—or nearly equal to the national debt (at the time of the audit).[256] It was a prophetically highly profitable time for the military/industrial complex that President Eisenhower was deeply concerned about.

The race to produce the first nuclear weapon began during WWII, when the United States learned that Nazi scientists were working on developing the atom bomb. The United States realized that such a weapon could make Germany unstoppable and we launched our own massive development program, called the Manhattan Project. The first weapon was tested on the Alamogordo bombing range in New Mexico on July 16, 1945. Within weeks, the only two nuclear weapons ever actually used during war were dropped on Hiroshima and Nagasaki by the United States on August 6 and 9 1945.

During WWII, the USSR and the USA were allies, but had little trust in one another. The United States didn't share information or seek assistance from the Soviet Union for the Manhattan Project but did coordinate with Great Britain. The Soviets became aware of the project as a result of espionage penetrations. Long after the war, it was discovered that Klaus Fuchs, a German refugee theoretical physicist working for the British mission in the Manhattan Project, had given key documents to the Russians throughout the war. Theodore Hall, a young physicist at Los Alamos during the 1940s, was also shown to have provided important data to the Soviets. Julius and Ethel Rosenberg were caught relaying messages in the espionage effort. Their apprehension and trial was front-page news.

Although a small cog, the Rosenbergs were convicted on March 29, 1951, and sentenced to death in the electric chair under the Espionage Act.[257] They were the only two American civilians to be executed for espionage-related activities during the Cold War. At the time the United States was at war in Korea (1950-1953). In imposing the death penalty, Judge Irving Kaufman on April 5, 1951, held them responsible not only for espionage but also for the deaths of the Korean War: "I believe your conduct in putting into the hands of the Russians the A-bomb [...] has already caused, in my opinion, the communist aggression in Korea, with the resultant casualties exceeding 50,000 and who knows but that millions more of innocent people may pay the price of your treason."

Some still ask just how responsible the Rosenbergs were. Many viewed them as a rather pathetic couple who may well have been duped. Kaufman's severity may have been a result of the "Red scare" that was gripping the nation at the time, a witch-hunt mentality that produced the likes of Sen. Joseph McCarthy.

Whatever the case, it is interesting to note that when China's People's Liberation Army (backed by the Soviet Union) attacked across the Yalu River on October 25, 1950, General Douglas MacArthur repeatedly requested permission (and publicly threatened) to strike Manchuria and major Chinese cities with [30 to 50] nuclear weapons. Overriding him, President Harry Truman, as commander and chief, relieved him of command April 11, 1951 (just days after the Rosenbergs were sentenced to death), replacing him with General Matthew Ridgeway. Because of stolen secrets, some transmitted by the Rosenbergs, the Soviet Union had already tested their first nuclear weapon in August 1949. One can only guess what Truman's decision would have been about using nukes against the Chinese if the Russians hadn't established a nuclear counter threat. As it was, many in Congress denounced Truman and supported MacArthur. On the other hand, unsupported by Russian nukes, China might have never invaded. As it worked out, Ridgeway was able to force a "ceasefire" along the 38th parallel in 1953. The war has never been officially declared over.

After Russia's first successful test, the nuclear race was on. The Americans responded with the development of the hydrogen bomb—weapons that can be thousands of times more powerful than those dropped on Japan. The United States tested its first hydrogen bomb in March of 1954, obliterating a small island in the South Pacific Ocean.[258] The Soviets tested their first thermonuclear device in 1955. A neutron bomb was also developed—weapons that have a smaller explosion than atom or hydrogen bombs, but emit large amounts of radiation, killing soldiers but doing less material damage. (A large number of low-yield nukes were deployed as tactical battlefield weapons during the European standoff between the USSR and NATO.)

The number of nuclear weapons held by the two superpowers during the Cold War increased drastically because of the concept of a first strike and later a second strike force. The highest number of nuclear warheads held was about 12,000 for the USSR and 10,000 by the United States. That many nuclear weapons had the potential to destroy life on Earth more than 1,500 times over.[259] Thus was born the concept—never stated as policy—of mutually assured destruction (MAD), or the "Dr. Strangelove" scenario.

Control of WMD

The development and use of WMD is governed by international conventions and treaties, although not all countries have signed and ratified them:[260]

- Nuclear Non-Proliferation Treaty (NPT).

The NPT was open for signatures on July 1, 1968, and signed on that date by the United States, the Soviet Union, the United Kingdom, and 59 other countries. China and France acceded to the NPT in 1992. As of 2000, a total of 187 states were parties to the NPT. Cuba, Israel, India, and Pakistan were the only states that were not members of the NPT; the latter three states are known to have nuclear weapons.[261]

The NPT obligates the five known nuclear-weapons states (the United States, Russian Federation, United Kingdom, France, and China) not to transfer nuclear weapons, other nuclear explosive devices, or technology to any non-nuclear-weapon state. Non-nuclear–weapon-state parties undertake not to acquire or produce nuclear weapons or nuclear explosive devices. They are required also to accept safeguards to detect diversions of nuclear materials from peaceful activities, such as power generation, to the production of nuclear weapons or other nuclear explosive devices. This must be done in accordance with an individual safeguards agreement, concluded between each non-nuclear-weapon-state party and the International Atomic Energy Agency (IAEA). Under these agreements, all nuclear materials in peaceful civil facilities under the jurisdiction of the state must be declared to the IAEA, whose inspectors have routine access to the facilities for periodic monitoring and inspections. If information from routine inspections is not sufficient to fulfill its responsibilities, the IAEA may consult with the state regarding special inspections within or outside declared facilities.[262]

- Comprehensive Test Ban Treaty (CTBT).

The CTBT was adopted by the United Nations General Assembly and open for signature in September of 1996. Seventy-one states, including the five nuclear-weapon states, initially signed the CTBT, which prohibits all nuclear test explosions. Although China, Israel, and the United States signed the treaty, they never ratified it. On October 13, 1999, the U.S. Senate rejected ratification of the CTBT, having previously ratified the Partial Test Ban Treaty in 1963.

The CTBT obligates countries that sign and ratify "not to carry out any nuclear weapons test explosion or any other nuclear explosion." It provides for an extensive verification regime including an International Monitoring System (IMS) to detect nuclear explosions, a global infrastructure for satellite communications from the IMS stations to an International Data Center (IDC) that processes and distributes data to state parties, and for onsite inspections, which may be requested by any state party to determine whether suspected cheating has occurred. To implement these verification arrangements, the treaty establishes a Comprehensive Test Ban Organization (CTBTO) located in Vienna.[263]

The Bush administration, which doesn't place great value in arms control treaties, has said that it will not seek Senate reconsideration of the treaty. However, it supports the continuation by states of the voluntary moratorium that is in place, as well as maintaining and completing the IMS, which is seen as value added to U.S. national technical means of detection. But the administration does not support funding for or participation in onsite inspection related activities that would be used as part of challenge inspections after the treaty entered into force.

As of September 2005, 176 states had signed the CTBT and 125 had ratified it. However, the treaty will not enter into force until 44 named nuclear-capable states (including the United States, India, Pakistan, and North Korea) ratify the treaty. Only 33 have done so.

The United States has not tested a nuclear weapon since 1992.[264] The total number of U.S. nuclear weapons tests, 1945-1992 was

1,030 (1,125 nuclear devices detonated; 24 additional joint tests with Great Britain).

The Bush administration decided in 2003 to engage in research about a new generation of small tactical nuclear weapons, especially "earth-penetrators." The budget passed by the United States Congress in 2004 eliminated funding for some of this research, including the "bunker-busting or earth-penetrating" weapons, but research on small tactical weapons continues nonetheless. In these days of supercomputers the need for actual testing is greatly reduced.

- Biological and Toxin Weapons Convention (BWC).

The BWC was opened for signatures on April 10, 1972, and took effect on March 26, 1975 after 22 states had joined the convention, including its three depositary governments: the Soviet Union (now the Russian Federation), the United Kingdom, and the United States. The convention is of unlimited duration. As of December 2002, more than 30 years after it opened for signature, the BWC has 147 members. An additional 16 countries have signed the convention but have not yet ratified it, including Egypt and Syria. Some 30 countries still remain outside the BWC, including Azerbaijan, Israel, Kazakhstan, Kyrgyzstan, Sudan, and Tajikistan.[265]

The Bush administration's decision to walk away from the BWC Protocol in December 2001 is an example of current U.S. policy weakening WMD treaties, international ability to verify compliance, and overall international support. While the protocol, as written, may have been flawed, Under Secretary of State John Bolton alienated other members by the rude manner with which he left.[266] More important, the United States failed to follow up with other mechanisms that might have addressed the weaknesses in the draft protocol. Thus, the net effect was to weaken U.S. security and slow the momentum against biological weapons proliferation.

- Chemical Weapons Convention (CWC).

  The CWC entered into force on April 29, 1997 and its membership has since increased from 87 to the current number of 153 States. The CWC has strengthened international efforts to eliminate the threat of a chemical weapons attack. This has been accomplished through the work of its own verification regime, the Organization for the Prohibition of Chemical Weapons (OPCW).[267]

The United States and the Soviet Union (now Russia) entered into several bilateral treaties and agreements limiting the size and configuration of their nuclear forces, as well as banning certain nuclear tests and weapons systems. They also implemented a number of confidence-building measures to reduce the threat of nuclear confrontation between them. There was Strategic Arms Limitation Talks (SALT I, 1969-1972), which lead to the Anti-Ballistic Missile Treaty (ABM Treaty, 1972). The 1991 Strategic Arms Reduction Treaty (START I) and the 1993 START II codified deep reductions in the arsenals of both countries. START II did not enter into force, however. Russia linked the entry into force of this agreement to the continued existence of the 1972 ABM Treaty. When the President Bush withdrew from the ABM Treaty in June 2002, Russia terminated participation in START II.[268]

What remains is the 2002 Treaty on Offensive Reductions (SORT). Russian President Vladimir Putin and U.S. President George W. Bush signed this treaty on May 24, 2002. The very short (approximately 475-word) treaty states that both the United States and Russia will reduce their number of *operationally deployed warheads* to between 1,700-2,200 within the next 10 years. The treaty will remain in force until December 31, 2012, at which time the parties have the option of extending or terminating the agreement. Either party can withdraw from the treaty upon giving three months notice to the other. The document does not require the destruction of strategic delivery systems, specify what is to be done with the warheads once they have been removed from launchers, *or constrain the development of ballistic missile defense.*

Two other agreements are noteworthy: 1991. The Cooperative Threat Reduction (CTR) Program of the United States assists the states of the former Soviet Union in controlling and protecting their nuclear weapons, weapons-usable materials, and delivery systems. The CTR program was sponsored in the Senators Sam Nunn (D-GA) and Richard Lugar (R-IN) as a result of a request from Soviet President Mikhail Gorbachev for assistance.[269] 2003. Proliferation Security Initiative (PSI) is a voluntary international arrangement between states that seek to strengthen existing export control laws by interdicting suspected transfers and shipments of WMD-related materials.

For further information concerning the history of nuclear arms control and WMD I recommend the Nuclear Threat Initiative website: http://www. nti.org/ much of the research for this section has come from that source.

Today, there are eight countries that are known to have nuclear weapons, only five of which are members of the Nuclear Non-Proliferation Treaty. Following is a short nuclear profile of those countries:

United States

The United States has a substantial nuclear weapons arsenal and associated weapons systems. The Bush administration's refusal to seek Senate ratification of the Comprehensive Test Ban Treaty, its withdrawal from the Anti-Ballistic Missile Treaty, the loosened parameters of the Strategic Offensive Reduction Treaty (SORT), and recent budget requests from the Secretary of Defense indicate that the United States may develop and test new types of nuclear weapons in the future.

As one of the five recognized nuclear weapons states under the Nuclear Non-Proliferation Treaty (NPT), the United States maintains an arsenal of 10,000 nuclear warheads, of which nearly 6,000 are operational and the remainder in reserve or active stockpiles. About 1,700 warheads are deployed on land-based systems, 1,098 on bombers, and 3,168 on (Ohio-class) submarines. Approximately 800 are tactical nuclear weapons (TNWs), and consist of Tomahawk land attack cruise missiles and B61 bombs. The remaining warheads are stockpiled.

Russian Federation

The collapse of the Soviet Union in 1991 left the Russian Federation with the bulk of the massive soviet weapons of mass destruction complex. This legacy has allowed Russia to retain its great-power status even as its economy collapsed, but the burden of supporting this oversized complex has strained the Russian political and economic system. The goal of The Cooperative Threat Reduction Program is to reduce the threat of "loose nukes" falling into the hands of terrorists.

Russia is a nuclear weapons state as party to the NPT. According to the Natural Resource Defense Council, in 1991 the Soviet Union had about 35,000 nuclear weapons in its stockpile, down from a peak in 1986 of about 45,000. Russia is estimated to have around 20,000 nuclear weapons, although the total stockpile size is uncertain because there is no accurate count of tactical weapons. It is thought that Russia now has about 5,000 strategic operational weapons.

Russia also inherited a massive nuclear weapons production complex and large stocks of weapons grade fissile material. It is estimated that Russia has between 735 and 1,365 metric tons (t) of weapons grade-equivalent highly enriched uranium (HEU) and between 106 and 156 t of military-use plutonium.

China

China possesses nuclear weapons and a range of ballistic missile capabilities. A key uncertainty is how ongoing military modernization efforts will ultimately reshape China's strategic nuclear capabilities. U.S. deployments of missile defenses are likely to be a key variable.

China's nuclear weapons program began in 1955 and culminated in a successful nuclear test in 1964. Since then, China has conducted 45 nuclear tests, including tests of thermonuclear weapons and a neutron bomb. China is a signatory to the CTBT and acceded to the NPT in 1992 as a nuclear weapons state. China is thought to have between 400 and 430 (strategic and tactical) operational nuclear weapons.

France

France is a nuclear weapons state party to the NPT and a signatory to the CTBT. France maintains about 350 nuclear warheads on 60 Mirage 2000N bombers, four nuclear-powered ballistic missile submarines, and on carrier-based aircraft.

United Kingdom

The United Kingdom is a nuclear weapons state party to the NPT and a signatory to the CTBT. The UK's current stockpile is thought to be less than 200 strategic and "sub-strategic" warheads on Vanguard-class nuclear-powered submarines.

Israel

It is easily understood why Israel, forged out of the Holocaust and surrounded by hostile neighbors, has developed a range of weapons systems to ensure its security. Israel maintains a highly advanced military, a nuclear weapons program, and offensive and defensive missiles.

Israel has not signed the NPT, but has declared it will not be the first to use nuclear weapons in the Middle East. Its nuclear program allegedly is centered at the Negev Nuclear Research Center, outside the town of Dimona. Based on estimates of the plutonium production capacity of the Dimona reactor, Israel has about 100-200 nuclear weapons.

India

India regards its nuclear and long-range power projection programs as instruments for maintaining strategic stability in the Asia-Pacific region. India rejects the distinction between a small group of states that are allowed nuclear weapons and the rest of the world's states that are denied this right. India has also been highly critical of the nuclear weapons states' failure to meet their nuclear disarmament commitments.

India embarked on a nuclear power program in 1958 and a nuclear explosives program in 1968. Following a test of a nuclear device in May 1974, and five additional nuclear weapon-related tests in May 1998, India formally declared itself a nuclear weapons state. New Delhi's stock of weapons-grade plutonium is estimated to be between 240-395kg, which could be used to manufacture between 40 and 90 simple fission weapons. India is not a member of the NPT.

Pakistan

Pakistan embarked on a nuclear weapons program in the early 1970s, after its defeat and break up in the Indo-Bangladesh war of 1971. Islamabad regards nuclear weapons as essential to safeguard the South Asian balance of power and offset its conventional inferiority and lack of strategic dept against India. The technological complexity associated with nuclear weapons and their systems of delivery is also closely tied to Pakistan's post-colonial identity as the first Muslim nation to have acquired such a capability.

In the mid-1970s, Pakistan embarked upon the uranium enrichment route to acquiring a nuclear weapons capacity. Since than Pakistan is believed to have stockpiled about 580-800kg of HEU, sufficient to build 30-50 fission bombs. Shortly after India conducted its first nuclear test in May 1998, Pakistan conducted its own and declared itself a nuclear weapons state. Pakistan is not a member of the NPT.

As already expressed on these pages, most analysts agree that it was ultimately the escalating cost of the arms race that led to the collapse of the Soviet Union (although there is much to be said for the view that, with a few sharp nudges from Mikhail Gorbachev, an unworkable system simply imploded). Thankfully, the Cold War never resulted in the use of nuclear weapons, although it came perilously close during the Cuban missile crisis. Did the fear of WMD prevent war? Not at all—the balance of nuclear capability, or what wags termed mutually assured destruction or MAD, prevented only nuclear war. By one estimate, 125 million people have died in 149 wars since 1945.[270] There is an excellent paper advocating the elimination of all WMD (nuclear, biological and chemical) that was published in the *Aerospace Power Journal* – <u>winter 1997</u>, titled "Mutually Assured Destruction Revisited," by Col. Alan J. Parrington, USAF.[271] After making his case, the author says:

> Of course, this may require that we abandon strategic warfare altogether, for it goes to the very heart of the question of what war is really about. The truth is we would be better off militarily and economically, for there are far more productive ways of convincing opponents to accept our political will than by attacking their passions. We might even find it more civilized.

> Since the seventeenth century, wars have progressively become more destructive and inhuman, no doubt the result of an industrial revolution that put a weapon in every peasant's hand. Democracy has been no cure, and in fact may have added to the inhumanity by fomenting intense nationalism and partisanship as in the American Civil War, when six hundred thousand fellow countrymen lost their lives over the democratic question of states' rights. World War I saw 10 million men killed in the trenches of a senseless stalemate egged on by nationalistic pride. World War II saw another 50 million perish, most of them civilians in bombed-out cities and concentration camps, justified in the name of "total war" that was started by a free and democratically elected chancellor of the German Third Reich. If the world is to reverse the tide of history and survive the atomic age, we must soon recognize the incompatibility of weapons of mass destruction with the political nature of warfare. Only then will we begin to change the counterproductive strategies that threaten us all.

Bush's war on terror

Both ends of President Bush's use of the term "war on terror" are problematic. We've already talked about why he wants to be a wartime president; it wins elections and provides the rationale for him to flout the law under cover of an endless war. But the other end of the term is problematic as well. As Hendrik Hertzberg put it in a *New Yorker* commentary titled "War And Words" on February 13, 2006:

> "Terror" is not a conquerable enemy, or an end in itself. It is a method of achieving some political goal, however outlandish or unrealistic—an ugly and frightening method, as was the bombing of civilian populations in the Second World War. But "war on terror" is a chimerical circle, like "war to end all wars." Woodrow Wilson's war to end all wars defeated imperial Germany, but it did not, and could not, defeat war. Nor can a war on terror defeat terror.

There is no universally accepted definition of terrorism under international law. The United Nations has refused to adopt one, because, as an old saying goes, "one person's terrorist is another person's freedom fighter." European countries and the United States tend to define terrorism narrowly, making sure it only applies to acts of non-government organizations. While there are countless definitions, the one used usually depends on the side from which the action is viewed: "we" are always "non-terrorists" and "good"; "they" are always "terrorists" and "bad."

The U.S. Department of Defense definition of terrorism is "the calculated use of violence or the threat of violence to inculcate fear; intended to coerce or to intimidate governments or societies in the pursuit of goals that are generally *political, religious, or ideological."*

Although terrorism has occurred throughout history, the term dates from the French Revolution of the 18th century. Maximilien Robespierre is recognized as the man who gave birth to the political term when he instituted his Reign of Terror in 1793. Today it involves acts such as assassinations, bombings, random killings, and hijackings.

An interesting side note to the origins of the word *assassination* is that it came from the drug hashish used by suicide terrorists to screw up their courage before they committed their terrible acts. According to Professor Emeritus Sol Encel,

> The Assassins were actually agents of the Ismaili sect, a schismatic branch of Shi-ite Islam, whose activities were directed partly against the

established Sunni sultanates, but mainly against the Crusaders. There's a considerable historic irony in George W. Bush's use of the term "crusade" against the latter-day assassins.[272]

Terrorism by radicals of both the left and the right, and by nationalists, flourished after World War II. Acts of terror have been associated with the Italian Red Brigades, the Irish Republican Army, the Palestine Liberation Organization, Peru's Shining Path, Sri Lanka's Liberation Tigers of Tamil Eelam, the Weathermen and some members of U.S. "militia" organizations, among many other groups. Religious inspired terrorism has also occurred, such as that of extremist Christian opponents of abortion in the United States; of extremist Muslims associated with Hamas, Osama bi Laden's Al Qaeda, and other organizations; of extreme Sikhs in India; and of Japan's Aum Shinrikyo, which released the nerve gas in Tokyo's subway system in 1995.

However, in all instances prior to 9/11, the United States spoke of terrorist attacks, from whatever source, home or abroad, as crimes, not acts of war. By using the rhetoric of a war, Bush painted the world in black and white, which is exactly what the terrorists want. He has also granted its criminal perpetrators the questionable dignity of warriors.

Immediately after 9/11, Bush was talking about a "crusade" against terrorism. Thankfully his spin-doctors got him off that kick. By implication, that would have put us at war with over a billion Muslims! One of Al Qaeda's goals has been to frame the conflict as a holy war between Muslims and infidels. The problem is that while Bush wants to be a wartime president, the question remains, the United States is at war with whom?

Over the past couple of years the administration has tried to shed the confines of its beloved slogan but always returns to it. Bush mused about naming the "focused ideology" that brought about 9/11 in a speech to the National Endowment for Democracy in October 2005.[273] "Some call this evil Islamic radicalism," he said. " Others, militant jihadism; still others, Islamo-fascism." As of February 2006 he seemed to have settled on the poor choice of "radical-Islam." It is a poor choice because Islam is not our enemy, radical or otherwise. While certainly the suicide bombers of the Al Qaeda ilk come from the ranks of radical or fundamentalist Islam, radical

Islam is a far broader and more variegated phenomenon than the terrorist disease that infects it. The same could be said of the radical mutants of our domestic Christian fundamentalist groups or extremists in fundamentalist Jewish sects.

There is good reason for America to oppose radical religious fundamentalism of any type. In its various incarnations it demands the subordination of women, stunts education, and curbs freedom of speech, of the press, and other religions. But it is not something that can be opposed by war, not in the Middle East, not in Israel, and not in America's heartland.

Al Qaeda and their fellow travelers don't simply wish to kill Americans, or Russians in Chechnya, or Israelis, they have a goal; they want to establish their hateful form of Islamist fundamentalism throughout the world of Islam. To do this they have to topple the democratic governments and authoritarian regimes that the United States and the West support, and replace them with a theocracy.

In 1993, Samuel Huntington, a Harvard political scientist, published a Foreign Affairs essay (later adapted into a book) titled "The Clash of Civilizations," which attempted to predict the shape of international relations following the end of the Cold War and the collapse of the Soviet Union. His hypothesis is, "that the fundamental source of conflict in the new world will not be primarily ideological or economic. The great divisions among humankind and the dominating source of conflict will be cultural. Nation-states will remain the most powerful actors in world affairs, but the principal conflicts of global politics will occur between nations and groups of different civilizations. The clash of civilizations will be the battle lines of the future." Pulling no punches he observes, "the West is using international institutions, military power and economic resources to run the world in ways that will maintain Western predominance, protect Western interests and promote Western political and economic values."[274]

Huntington's book became a best seller in the United States after 9/11. One critic described his message as the "the West versus the Rest." It is this conflict, Huntington argues, which has become "the central axis of world politics." The Bush administration picked up the term 'axis' to describe "the axis of evil." Bush's rhetoric of war, including "you're either with us or against us" and 'bring them on" and the use of words such "evil" and "crusade," is an absurd oversimplification of complex issues. But Bush had a good teacher for simplistic absurdity in Ronald Reagan, as Professor Encel reminds us:

> In July 1985, former United States President Ronald Reagan addressed the American Bar Association on the subject of terrorism. He described terrorists as a "bunch of misfits, Looney tunes, and criminals," comparable with Murder Incorporated and Nazi Germany, and identified Libya, Iran and North Korea as supporters and funders of terrorist groups.
>
> President Reagan's tirade was provoked by a spectacular plane hijack at Beirut Airport, which had occurred a few days earlier.
>
> Ronald Reagan told his audience that he had been to the cinema on the previous evening to watch Sylvester Stallone as Rambo. Now, he declared, he knew what to do.

There's an old adage that goes "to know your enemy you have to be able to walk in his shoes." So let's look at some history and try to understand what drives the 21st century Islamist terrorist. Professor Huntington provides an interesting timeline. He writes:

> The conflict along the fault line between Western and Islamic civilizations has been going on for 1,300 years. After the founding of Islam, the Arab and Moorish surge west and north only ended at Tours in 732. From the eleventh to the thirteenth century the Crusaders attempted with temporary success to bring Christianity and Christian rule to the Holy Land. From the fourteenth to the seventeenth century, the Ottoman Turks reversed the balance, extended their sway over the Middle East and the Balkans, captured Constantinople, and twice laid siege to Vienna. In the nineteenth and early twentieth centuries as Ottoman power declined, Britain, France, and Italy established Western control over most of North Africa and the Middle East.
>
> After World War II, the West, in turn, began to retreat; the colonial empires disappeared; first Arab nationalism and then Islamic fundamentalism

manifested themselves; the West became heavily dependent on the Persian Gulf countries for its energy; the oil-rich Muslim countries became money-rich and, when they wished to, weapons-rich. Several wars occurred between Arabs and Israel (created by the West). France fought a bloody and ruthless war in Algeria for most of the 1950s; British and French forces invaded Egypt in 1956; American forces returned to Lebanon, attacked Libya, and engaged in various military encounters with Iran; Arab and Islamic terrorists, supported by at least three Middle Eastern governments, employed the weapons of the weak and bombed Western planes and installations and seized Western hostages. This warfare between Arabs and the West culminated in 1990, when the United States sent a massive army to the Persian Gulf to defend some Arab countries against aggression by another...

Perhaps Dr. Wafa Sultan, an Arab-American psychiatrist, in an interview with Al Jazeera, spelled out the best insights I have read concerning the cultural challenges of the Arab-Muslim world. She said: "The clash we are witnessing...is not a clash of religions, or a clash of civilizations. It is a clash between two opposites, between two eras. It is a clash between a mentality that belongs to the Middle Ages and another that belongs to the 21st century. It is a clash between civilization and backwardness, between the civilized and the primitive, between barbarity and rationality. It is a clash between freedom and oppression, between democracy and dictatorship. It is a clash between human rights, on the one hand, and the violation of these rights, on the other hand. It is a clash between those who treat women like beasts, and those who treat them like human beings."

When asked by the Al Jazeera host: "I understand from your words that what is happening today is a clash between the cultures of the West, and the backwardness and ignorance of the Muslims?" Dr. Sultan replied: "Yes, that is what I mean."

Resource wars

For over a half-century the United States' interest in the Middle East and North Africa – apart from the Suez Channel and Israel - has been oil.

In order to keep that oil flowing we have supported and made fabulously wealthy those who rule—and they have ruled with an iron hand. Under America's tolerant eye, mullahs, monarchs and dictators got rich, and the poor grew poorer. Under such conditions Islamic fundamentalism flourished, creating a fertile breeding ground for radical Muslims. People with a job, families, and a future don't become suicide bombers.

Although world leaders never publicly speak of it, the terrorist organizations also covet the wealth and the power that oil and natural gas resources provide. Saudi Arabia is Osama bin Laden's number one target, not the United States. He has long made it clear that his ultimate goal is more than wreaking havoc in the West; it is to topple the Saud family, and gain control of the oil and the Persian Gulf.

Energy resources shaped the foreign policies of industrial nations, including the United States, for a large part of the 20th century. After the Japanese occupation of Indochina in July 1941, President Roosevelt embargoed oil shipments to Japan and the Japanese navy and air force struck back. Not just south to occupy Dutch-ruled Indonesia and acquire an alternative source of oil, but everywhere else in the Southwest Pacific—including Pearl Harbor. Oil was a tremendous factor for the mechanized armies of WW II. The lack of it caused Germany to pioneer coal-to-liquid fuels technology. All together "black gold" – crude oil, has an ugly, bloody history.

In 1953, British and American intelligence officers helped bring about the overthrow of Iran's prime minister, Mohammed Mossadegh. The Cold War was in full swing and Mossadegh was thought much too close to Iran's communists, the Tudeh Party. He had plans to nationalize the oil industry, which was owned and controlled by British interests. The West conspired to take him out rather than risk Soviet influence over Iranian oil. Following a military coup, power was given to Shah Mohammed Reza Pahlavi. The shah was good to his word and the oil flowed freely from Iran to the West. By the end of the 1960s, the Shah of Iran became a pillar of the so-called Nixon Doctrine, in which American allies became regional surrogates to maintain peace and stability. Serving both purposes, the United States sold billions of dollars of sophisticated weapons to Iran, sopping up what became known as "petro-dollars," while equipping the shah's air force.[275]

The reliance on Iran to maintain stability in the Persian Gulf had bipartisan support. In 1977, President Jimmy Carter, visiting the shah in Tehran, toasted his great leadership, which he said had made Iran "an island of stability in one of the more troubled areas of the world."

Shortly after Carter's visit, Shiite fundamentalists, be they called freedom fighters or terrorists, rebelled, both against the shah, and the United States. On January 16, 1979, after months of violent protests the shah was forced into exile and flown to the United States. On February 1, Ayatollah Ruholla Khomeini returned to Iran after 14 years in exile in France. Khomeini declared the country an Islamic Republic on April 1 and ruled the country until his death in 1989. Khomeini was fiercely anti-American.

On November 4, 1979, Iranian militants attacked the U.S. Embassy in Tehran, taking over 90 hostages. Forty-four remained in captivity for 444 days and, as we have seen, were released "coincidentally" at the exact time that Ronald Reagan was sworn into office on January 20, 1981.

In his final State of the Union address to the nation on January 23, 1980, President Carter laid it on the line: "An attempt by any outside force to gain control of the Persian Gulf region will be regarded as an assault on the vital interests of the United States of America, and such an assault will be repelled by any means necessary, including military force."

Later in the address Carter went on to say, "The crises in Iran and Afghanistan have dramatized a very important lesson: Our excessive dependence on foreign oil is a clear and present danger to our nation's national security. The need has never been more urgent. At long last, we must have a clear, comprehensive energy policy for the United States." Unfortunately, it was a lesson we didn't heed, and any progress being made under the Carter administration was quickly abandoned when President Reagan took office.

On July 16, 1980, Saddam Hussein, who had taken control of the Ba'ath Party, forced Iraq President Al-Bakr out of office. Within two months, long-standing territorial disputes and border skirmishes result in the outbreak of formal war between Iran and Iraq. The United States supplied weapons to both countries;[276] China and North Korea backed Iran, while the Soviet Union and France backed Iraq. The war, which ran between 1980 and 1988, would eventually result in the death of more than one million people over a period of eight years, making it the longest conventional war of the 20th century.

With war raging between Iran and Iraq in 1981, Defense Secretary Casper Weinberger signaled that the United States was seeking a new base of operations in the Persian Gulf: "We need some facilities and additional men and material there or nearby, to act as a deterrent to any Soviet hopes of seizing the oil fields or interdicting the line." Subsequently, the United States began establishing military bases in Saudi Arabia and selling that country vast amounts of aircraft and other military equipment in return for petro-dollars. Since 1979, the kingdom has spent more than $50 billion on U.S. military purchases, including five airborne warning and control systems (AWACS) and a $5.6 billion "peace shield"—a state-of-the-art command and control system for the Royal Saudi Air Force with six underground command centers linking 147 defense-related sites.

Following Iraq's surprise invasion of Kuwait on August 2, 1990, King Fahd authorized the deployment of U.S. forces to aid in his border defense. (Saddam Hussein justified the invasion by claiming that the overproduction of oil by Kuwait and the United Arab Emirates amounted to economic warfare against Iraq.) The kingdom hosted over 600,000 allied forces during the first Gulf War. The United States retained a robust military presence in Saudi Arabia until after the Sept. 11 attacks and the discovery of evidence linking Saudi citizens to Al Qaeda. Though a long-term ally, Saudi Arabia refused to allow U.S. aircraft to use bases during the war with Iraq. For over a decade following the first Gulf War those bases were used to launch U.S. sorties enforcing the Iraqi no-fly zone. A month after the U.S. invasion of Iraq all but a few hundred U.S. military personnel used to train Saudi troops were withdrawn from Saudi Arabia.

The Gulf War differed from the 2003 invasion of Iraq in several important ways:

- Iraq was the aggressor. When President Bush (senior) drew his line in the sand over Kuwait, the world knew the United States was going to war to protect the vital interests of the United States and the West—the unimpeded flow of oil from the Persian Gulf.

Consequently, the United States had allies in the first Gulf War who contributed major military forces and largely financed the war. In 2003, the United States invaded Iraq with only token forces from some of our allies; others opposed the invasion. There was no financial assistance.

- Overwhelming military force was used; enormous air power, over a half million troops, and more tanks and heavy armor than had ever been on a field of battle before. Bush the younger invaded Iraq with less than half the troops used for the first Gulf War, sufficient force to overcome the Iraqi military but not enough to provide security after hostilities ceased.

- The air war lasted only 40 days, the ground war merely 72-hours. The United States and its allies did not choose to occupy Iraq, a land of 26 million people, a nation that was artificially contrived by the British in 1921, and a land deeply divided between three hostel ethnic groups, the Kurds, the Shiites, and the Sunnis—a land that was being held together by the iron fist of Saddam. Under Bush the younger, after three years of occupation, more than 130,000 troops remained in Iraq, with no definitive plan for withdrawal.

In Afghanistan during the 1980s, the Soviet Union got its butt kicked by an ultimately unbeatable Afghan guerrilla force called the mujahideen, to which the United States supplied arms and support. The Soviet-Afghan War (1979-1989) has been called the Soviet Union's Vietnam. It resulted in more than 25,000 dead Soviet soldiers plus many more casualties and further demoralized a USSR on the verge of disintegration.

Here again, why were the USSR and the United States interested in Afghanistan? Easy. Because of fossil fuel resources (oil and natural gas): 1) Afghanistan's proven natural gas reserve is about five trillion cubic feet. In the 1970s, Afghan natural gas production reached 275 million cubic feet per day. Most of it went to the Soviet Union's natural gas grid via a link through Uzbekistan. And even more valuable, 2) Afghanistan makes an ideal energy transit route that avoids either Iran or the Persian

Gulf, because of its location between the oil and natural gas reserves of the Caspian Basin, which is landlocked, and the Arabian Sea, which opens to the Indian Ocean.[277]

During the mid-1990s, Unocal, a U.S. based oil industry giant with roots going back to 1890, and the Union Oil Company of California pursued possible oil and natural gas pipelines from Turkmenistan's Dauletabad-Donmez gas basin via Afghanistan to Pakistan, but withdrew from the deal after the U.S. missile strikes against Al Qaeda training camps in Afghanistan in August 1998.

Unocal, which spearheaded the Afghan project, was to have built a 1,005-mile oil pipeline and a companion 918-mile natural gas pipeline, in addition to a tanker-loading terminal in Pakistan's Arabian sea port of Gwadan. Unocal opened offices in Kazakhstan, Uzbekistan, Pakistan and Turkmenistan and got every faction of the Afghan Northern Alliance to sign on. This deal was brokered by some prominent political figures, including former Secretary of State Henry Kissinger, and former Secretary of Defense Dick Cheney, who, as CEO of Halliburton, was successful in winning contracts from Caspian Sea states to be part of any future development. In 1994, Cheney helped to broker a deal between the oil company Chevron, which in 2005 merged into Unocal, and the state of Kazakhstan when he sat on the Oil Advisory Board of that former Soviet state.

The *Amarillo Globe-News* reported on a 1998 talk to oil executives at the Cato Institute in which Cheney said, "the current hot spots for major oil companies are the oil reserves in the Caspian Sea region. Former Soviet states Azerbaijan, Kazakhstan and Turkmenistan all are seeking to quickly develop their oil reserves, which languished during the years of Russian domination." The stakes in that region could be as much as 200 billion barrels of oil and natural gas, he told the crowd.

"The potential for this region turning as volatile as the Persian Gulf, though, does not concern Cheney," the article continued. "You've got to go where the oil is," he said. " I don't worry about it a lot."[278]

Map: Asia

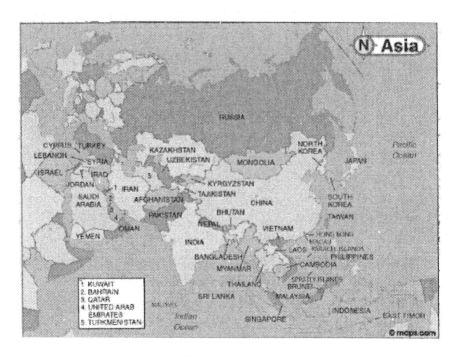

After the withdrawal of Soviet forces in 1989, the Soviet-backed communist government lost control, and an alliance of mujahideen ("holy warriors" or "freedom fighters") that included the Taliban, set up a new government. Afghanistan was reduced to a collection of territories held by competing warlords. In 1994, a group of well-trained Taliban ("religious students") was chosen by Pakistan to protect a convoy connected with Unocal trying to open an oil and natural gas trade route from Pakistan to Central Asia. They proved an able force, fighting off rival mujahideen and warlords. The Taliban went on to take the city of Kandahar, and then Kabul, the capital, in September 1996.[279]

Although civil war never ended under the Taliban, they did ultimately control about 90 percent of the country. Their strongest opposition came from the Northern Alliance, which held the northeast corner of the country. Over 80 percent of Afghanis and all of the Taliban are Sunni Muslims. The Taliban, under the direction of Mullah Muhammad Omar, instituted a strict interpretation of Sharia, or Islamic law. (The Taliban are followers of the Deobandi school of Sunni Islam, an extreme form of the faith closely related to Wahhabism.) Under their rule, public executions and punishments such as floggings became regular events at Afghan soccer stadiums. Frivolous activities were outlawed, television, music and the Internet were banned, men were required to wear beards and were subject to beatings if they didn't.

Most shocking to the West was the Taliban's treatment of women. After the Taliban took Kabul in 1996, they immediately forbade girls to go to school, nor could women work outside the home. Women were also prohibited from leaving the home without a male relative. Those who did risked being beaten, even shot, by officers of the "ministry for the protection of virtue and prevention of vice."

Coincident with the rise of the Taliban mujahideen in Afghanistan was the rise of another charmer in Saudi Arabia, Osama bin Laden. Since the fall of the Taliban at the hands of United States and Northern Alliance forces in early 2002, Osama, Muhammad Omar, and elements of the Taliban are thought to be hiding out in the Northern Tribal-Area of Pakistan. Bin Laden remains America's most wanted criminal, with a total of $27million in reward money on his head. Research from shadowy and not totally reliable sources enables us to piece together a short biography of Osama bin Laden.

Map: Pakistan – the Northern Tribal-Area where Osama is
thought to be hiding.

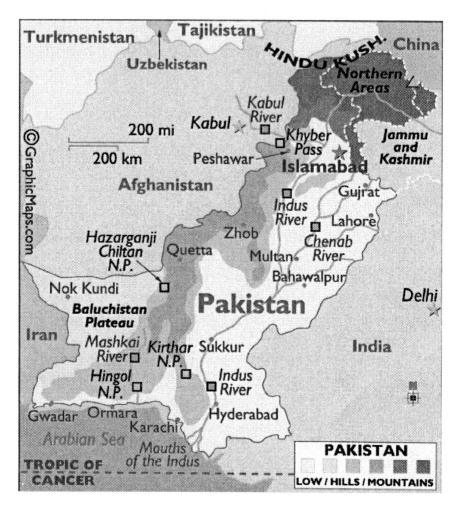

[Note: the Northern Tribal-Area has some of the roughest terrain in
the world. Stretching in the north, from east to west, are a series of high
mountain ranges that separate Pakistan from China, Russia and Afghanistan.
They include the Himalayas, the Karakoram, and the Hindukush. These
contain 40 of the world's 50 highest mountains, including K-2, being just
some "ropes" short of Everest in Nepal.]

Born in 1957, Osama was the son of a Yemen born billionaire, who built a construction business empire based in Saudi Arabia. Osama's mother, a Syrian, was his father's fourth wife. One family friend said of bin Laden, "In a country that is obsessed with parentage, with who your great-grandfather was, Osama was almost a double outsider."

According to his half brother Yeslam bin Laden, now a Swiss citizen, there are 54 siblings within the family, which ultimately included 20 different mothers. Each wife was given a separate house. And because Osama was the only child of his mother, he had very little contact with his extended family.[280]

In 1970 bin Laden's father died, leaving his 13-year-old son $80 million dollars. Eleven years later, in 1981, Osama graduated from King Abdul-Aziz University in Jeddah with a degree in either civil engineering or public administration (the information varies with the source). Like his father, Osama embraced the Saudi Arabian government's strictly conservative Wahhabi sect of Sunni Islam. Muslims who do not adhere to the officially sanctioned Sharia (Islamic law) can face severe repercussions at the hands of the Mutawwa'in (religious police).[281] The only difference in Taliban and Saudi Arabian religious practices is the degree of oppression, although both suppress the Shia minorities, and oppose the Shiite theocracy in Iran.

Two weeks after the Soviet invasion of Afghanistan (1979) bin Laden went to Pakistan, which is almost totally Muslim, and was taken to Peshawar, a city in the Tribal-Areas, to see Afghan refugees and meet some leaders. Taken with their cause, he went back to the kingdom and started lobbying his brothers, relatives and friends at school to support the mujahideen. He succeeded in raising huge amounts of money and material as donations to jihad.[282]

In 1982, he went inside Afghanistan, bringing with him a substantial amount of construction equipment, which he put at the disposal of the mujahideen. Thereafter, the frequency of his trips increased, and he even joined some actual battles with the Soviets—but reports indicate that he didn't amount to much as a fighter. His presence encouraged other Saudis to join the mujahideen but only in small numbers.

He went one step further in 1984 by establishing a guesthouse in Peshawar. It served as the first station for Arab recruits going to the Afghan front or training camps. The guesthouse was coincident with the Jihad Service Bureau in Peshawar to attract Saudis and Arabs to Afghanistan.

In 1986, after seven years of war in Afghanistan, bin Laden opened his own camps and within two years had six camps in that country. Mujahideen from his camps fought in five major battles and hundreds of small operations. Between 1984 and 1989 Osama spent eight months a year or more in Afghanistan.

By 1988, bin Laden found the organization he had set up needed an identity. He named the operation Al-Qa'edah, which is an Arabic word meaning "The Base."

By the time the Soviet Union withdrew from Afghanistan in 1989, bin Laden had become a sizable pain in the royal butt for the Saudi monarchy. With the Afghan war over, bin Laden's Al Qaeda needed a new enemy on which to wage jihad lest the organization fade away. He first spoke of starting a new "front" of jihad in South Yemen. In addition, he embarrassed the monarchy with lectures and speeches warning of an impending invasion by Saddam Hussein. As a result, bin Laden was banned from travel and trapped in the kingdom, and warned to keep silent. Despite the warnings, he was not hostile to the regime at that point, even writing detailed letters to the king suggesting how to protect the country from potentially advancing Iraqi forces. In addition to many military tactics suggested, he volunteered to bring all the Arab mujahideen to defend the kingdom.

Understandably, the king chose instead to invite the huge U.S. led armada to defend the nation. Osama describes the moment he learned of this as shocking—infidels were being invited by the king to defend Islam's most holy places. The House of Saud would later become bin Laden's number one target.

Osama managed to get out of the kingdom sometime in April 1991, going first to Pakistan, and then on to Afghanistan, knowing that Pakistani intelligence would hand him back to the Saudis. There, he fell into the collapse of the communist regime and the consequent dispute between the Afghan parties. Apparently he tried to arbitrate between them with no success, ordering his followers to avoid any involvement in the conflict and told them it was a sin to side with any faction.

By late 1991, with Saudi and Pakistani intelligence on his tail, he left Afghanistan and fled to the Sudan. In that Islamic country he was treated as a special guest. In Sudan he again escaped an assassination attempt, which turned out later to be the plan of Saudi intelligence. Only well informed people knew that he was classified as an enemy to the Saudi regime. His assets were frozen sometime between 1992 and 1994 but that was not published. The Saudis decided to announce the hostility in early 1994, when they publicized withdrawing his citizenship.[283]

By 1996, bin Laden had outlived his welcome in the Sudan, and the Taliban, friendly to bin Laden, had taken control of most of Afghanistan. Early in the year he fled Sudan in a well-planned trip with many of his followers to go straight to Jalalabad in eastern Afghanistan.

Map: Afghanistan

The Taliban allowed terrorist organizations to run training camps in their territory and, from 1994 to at least 2001, provided refuge for Osama bin Laden and his Al Qaeda organization. The relationship between the Taliban and bin Laden is close, even familial—bin Laden fought with the mujahideen, financed the Taliban, and reportedly married one of his daughters to Mullah Omar.

Fast forward to the spring of 2006...

In five short years George Bush's White House, Inc., with the support of a Republican Congress bought and paid for by the big business lobby, has made a mess of America's foreign policy. Which is ironic considering the great lengths the far right has gone to portraying Bush as a national security president. The "wars" have mostly served as a smokescreen for the administration's agenda of tax cuts for the rich, cuts in social entitlements, and the globalization of the nation's economy. The result is an extremely dangerous, befuddled strategy for our national security. A foreign policy built on lies and propaganda lacks clearly defined national goals. Which begs the question, what are the policies and goals that the United States is trying to achieve with the use of military force (war) under President George W. Bush? I don't think anybody really knows the whole story for sure.

We can learn a lot about "war", and war's role in foreign policy from Carl von Clausewitz, whose writings have been taught at the U.S. War Colleges for years. Two of his more commonly known definitions of war are:[284]

"War is...an act of force to compel our enemy to do our will," and "War is nothing but the continuation of policy with other means."

If Clausewitz's definitions were correct, and most people believe they were, the war on terror, the forgotten Afghan war, and the Iraq war have thus far been failures; we have not defeated the terrorists, nor have we compelled those on whom we waged preemptive war to do our will. Of course to change our strategic goals the administration would tacitly be admitting error, which is something the Bush administration never does. For example:

In a January 10, 2006 Address to Veterans of Foreign Wars on the war on terror,[285] President Bush said:

"The American people know the difference between responsible and irresponsible debate when they see it. They know the difference between honest critics who question the way the war is being prosecuted and partisan critics who claim that we acted in Iraq because of oil, or because of Israel, or because we misled the American people. And they know the difference between a loyal opposition that points out what is wrong, and defeatists who refuse to see that anything is right."

Bush's asinine comments validate Noam Chomsky's observation made early in this chapter that before the United States can safely withdraw our troops from Iraq there must be a serious domestic and international discussion of essential national priorities.

The United States only stands alone if we continue to isolate ourselves behind the mantle of being the world's only "superpower." It is a mantle I would gladly trade for reducing military expenditures and increasing national security. It is high time for a serious dialogue that must center on the following priorities:

First, the United States, and the industrial nations of the world have a vital interest in the availability of the energy resources of the world. To say that is not a major factor in U.S. foreign policy decisions is just plain stupid. Oil and natural gas production from the troubled areas of the Middle East, North Africa, and the Caspian Sea Basin will remain important to mitigating the peaking of world oil production for at least the next 20 to 30 years—and even at that, mitigation will be dependant on serious conservation efforts and the expenditure of substantial amounts of money to develop alternatives for liquid fossil fuels.

Second, at its root, Islamist terrorism is an internal dispute within the world of Islam. Whether Islamic, Christian, or Jewish, extreme fundamentalists are at odds with mainstream modernists. They want to turn the clock back, control others, and block progress. If modernists and progressives are going to prevail in the 21st century, and I am certain they will, it will be by example, and by providing models to follow, not force of arms. The international community must focus on the economic injustice endemic throughout the Muslim world in the Middle East, Africa, and Europe. In many places the jobless rate exceeds 30 percent and the majority of the population is below 24 years of age.

Third, Asian nuclear proliferation and "loose nukes" are the 21st century's major threat. There is no choice; we either achieve the goals of the Nuclear Proliferation Treaty or risk annihilation. This is not an American problem, a European problem, or an Asian problem—it is a world problem, with the survival of humankind at stake.

Suggestions

The Bushies say Democrats are defeatists who just criticize with no solutions of their own. Well here are a few suggestions from this Democrat, suggestions that are shared by others who are speaking up loud and clear:

Afghanistan

It was common knowledge that Al Qaeda was allowed camps within Afghanistan by the ruling Taliban. Consequently, after the September 11th attacks the world sympathized with the United States in striking back, although the nation of Afghanistan never attacked us. And strike back we did; with overwhelming U.S. air power and amazing swiftness the Taliban were defeated and the Afghan government turned over to our Northern Alliance allies. The only trouble was that bin Laden, who did attack us, escaped into the Tribal-Areas of Pakistan with many of his followers. Given the facts, I skeptically wonder what our real goals were, making it difficult to judge success or failure.

Did the United States wage a successful war and "compel our enemy to do our will"? I don't think so. Hamid Karzai, an expatriate, was installed as president, but rules only the immediate area surrounding the capital city of Kabul, while most of the country is still run by warlords dealing in the growth and trade of opium.[286] About 21,000 North Atlantic Treaty Organization (NATO) personnel from 36 countries, including the United

States, are responsible for stability and security operations in southern and eastern Afghanistan. U.S. troops operating independently are concentrated along the Pakistan border, where Taliban, Al Qaeda and other anti-government groups remain active and where bin Laden is believed to be hiding.

Aside from getting bin Laden, if U.S. interest was to secure an energy route from the Caspian Basin across Afghanistan to Pakistan and the Arabian Sea, we also failed in that. Afghan security is far too fragile to allow such an undertaking.

As for liberating the Afghan people, we succeeded in certain places where there are sufficient NATO or U.S. forces—other areas remain the same, under strict Islamic fundamentalist law. Very little of the touted "rebuilding of Afghanistan" has actually occurred. In June 2006, anti-American riots lashed Kabul, which was considered the most secure area. Reports said the underlying anger was against the United States for not delivering on the promised rebuilding and against the Karzai government because of its corruption. There was even nostalgia for the Taliban regime, which, for all its faults, was at least not corrupt.

If it is the foreign policy of the United States to open an energy route across Afghanistan, and create a stable democracy free of religious repression, a much larger commitment in personnel and money is needed, a commitment far in excess of what the United States can provide alone. For it to happen, a coalition of nations formed around mutual self-interest, with clearly stated goals, would have to be formed, which far exceeds the capabilities of the limited NATO forces now committed.

Iraq

If it was the United States' national will to create a "democracy" in Iraq, I guess we have succeeded. The only trouble is the will of the Iraqi people seems to be to separate the country into three different parts, with the Kurds controlling the north and the Kirkuk oil field, the Shiites the southeast and the Rumaila, Zubair, West Qurnaand, and Bin Umar oil fields, and the Sunni minority left out in the cold with no natural resources. According to Saddam's inner circle, this is what he feared most, not the United States, which he didn't believe would actually attack and upset the apple cart. Cutting through U.S. propaganda, if our real goal was to control Iraqi oil, and enhance Middle Eastern stability, we are failing miserably, where we could yet succeed.

The United States easily toppled Saddam but lacked the troops and international support to enforce security. It is a mess with no easy way out—but it could get worse if America continues to use muscle instead of brainpower.

If the 130,000-plus U.S. troops stay in Iraq, they will remain unwelcome occupiers in the middle of a civil war, and U.S. casualties will continue. Even if a miracle happens and the "unity" Iraqi government endures, why in the world would we leave our troops in a shooting gallery?

On the other hand, if we redeploy our troops out of Iraq on a timetable (six months to a year), keeping sizable contingents in nearby friendly countries, as Congressman John Murtha, (D-PA), Senator Joe Biden (D-DE), and others, suggested, we may be able to engage an international response from those countries doing business with Iran that are dependant on Iranian oil, to defuse the potential of projected Iranian power into Shia controlled Iraq. These counties include France, Russia, and China—they have influence with Iran that the United States has not had since the fall of the Shah in 1979.

In short, having done the peoples' job and overthrown Saddam, it is time for the United States to leave, find other ways to look after our vital interests, and let the people of that land decide their own future. That, at any rate, is the way it looked in the spring of 2006. (By the way, that's pretty much what we did in South Vietnam.[287])

Iran

The situation in Iran remains challenging. Since Iran became an Islamic Republic in 1979, the ultimate power in the country has rested with the supreme leader, who at present is Ayatollah Ali Khamenei. The president of Iran, originally a figurehead position in the theocracy, has become an increasingly important office. As the highest elected official in Iran, the president is responsive and responsible to public opinion in a way that the supreme leader is not. In June 2005, an overwhelming majority of the Iranian people elected Mahmoud Ahmadinejad president. Ahmadinejad, an ultraconservative ally of Khamenei, is outspokenly anti-American, has called for the "removal" of Israel, said that the Holocaust was a hoax, and seems determined to make Iran a nuclear weapons state—from the standpoint of U.S. foreign policy, not good.

Iran's nuclear ambitions go back over 40 years to the days of the Shah. As the Shah put it in 1974, "Petroleum is a noble material, much to valuable to burn...we envision producing, as soon as possible, 23,000 megawatts of electricity using nuclear plants." Iran was one of the first to sign the Nuclear Nonproliferation Treaty (NPT) in 1968 and plans were drawn to construct (together with the United States) up to 23 nuclear power stations across the country by the year 2000. That never happened, but the Russians have essentially completed a 1,000 megawatt-electrical light-water reactor at Bushehr. It will use low enriched (about 3.5 percent in uranium-235) as fuel. Under the contract Iran has with Russia, Russia will provide fuel for the lifetime of the reactor and will take back to Russia the spent fuel for storage and possible reprocessing.

Iran wants to develop five additional reactors and enrich its own uranium. Iran explains that it is interested in establishing a capability to produce low-enriched uranium so that it has an indigenous supply of nuclear reactor fuel for its reactors and possibly to export to other countries. Observers question the need for extensive nuclear power infrastructure, given Iran's huge fossil fuel reserves and rather limited uranium ore fields.

The red lights started flashing in 2003, when clandestine nuclear sites were uncovered in Iran by IAEA. A major enrichment capability would also allow the production of weapons grade nuclear material, which is prohibited by the NPT. In February 2006, Iran's refusal to allow IAEA inspectors full access to all Iranian research reactors resulted in the IAEA putting the matter before the U.N. Security Council, which could, although unlikely, impose sanctions.

Given the nuclear balance of power in Asia, it would not be surprising if Iran wanted to join the nuclear weapons club. Israel, India, Pakistan, and very likely North Korea have nuclear weapons. And all are nuclear weapons states that are not part of the NPT, bound by its restrictions, and subject to inspection by the IAEA. North Korea had been a signatory to the NPT but withdrew in 2003 to be free to develop its nuclear weapons program.

Yet, despite the controversy, when commenting to the press on the country's foreign policy, Ahmadinejad said, "Iran is interested in friendly ties with all world states and nations. Tehran is ready to cooperate with any government which has no hostile attitude toward the Iranian nation."

The bottom line is, aside from the saber rattling, without the West's petro-dollars Iran would be broke. One would think that U.S. capitalists would understand Iran's economic reality and find a way to negotiate solutions through friends. But no, instead the White House is calling for a regime change, and Vice President Cheney, one of the strongest advocates of the war to overthrow Saddam Hussein in Iraq, is promoting a drive to blanket Iran with radio and television broadcasts and support Iranian political dissidents.

Elizabeth Cheney, a principal deputy assistant secretary of state for Near Eastern affairs, who is also the vice president's daughter, is overseeing that $85 million State Department program.[288]

In a familiar pattern the White House is ratcheting up the rhetoric:

As a backdrop to the nuclear issue, Secretary of State Condoleezza Rice said to Senate Appropriations Committee, "We may face no greater challenge from a single country than from Iran, whose policies are directed at developing a Middle East that would be 180 degrees different than the Middle East we would like to see developed."

She said Iran is not only the "central banker for terrorism" but is also blocking democracy in the region. In fact, Iran welcomed elections in Lebanon, Iraq and the Palestinian Occupied Territories, where its surrogates won, much to the chagrin of the United States.

With Cheney threatening Iran with "meaningful consequences," the clerics responded right back that the United States, too, is "susceptible to harm and pain. So…let the ball roll."

It's a dangerous strategy, smacking of threats of preemptive war. True to form, the Bush White House is going down a familiar path that will achieve exactly the opposite of what is in our national best interest. There were reports in April 2006 that the United States was planning extensive air strikes on Iran, possibly including the use of tactical nuclear weapons. (In an abrupt turnabout, the Bush administration said in June 2006 that it was open to direct talks with Iran, provided Iran ceased enriching uranium before the talks began. Many saw that as an ultimatum leading to sanctions, and possible military action, rather than a good-faith invitation to genuine talks.)

On March 16, 2006 the White House released a 49-page national security report titled "National Security Strategy." In the report Bush summarizes his plan for protecting America and directing U.S. relations with other nations. It is an updated version of a report issued in 2002.

With no reference to the difficult war in Iraq, Bush reaffirmed his strike-first policy against terrorist and enemy nations and said Iran may pose the biggest challenge for America.

Bush wrote, "If necessary, however, under longstanding principles of self-defense, we do not rule out the use of force before attacks occur—even if uncertainty remains as to the time and place of the enemy's attack."

In a report, and State of the Union Address following the September 11 attacks, Bush underscored his administration's adoption of a pre-emptive policy, marking the end of a deterrent military strategy that existed throughout the Cold War.

The latest report makes it crystal clear that Bush hasn't changed his mind, even though no weapons of mass destruction were found in Iraq.

India

The mission of the Nuclear Nonproliferation Treaty was to limit nuclear weapons to the five known nuclear weapons states; the United States, Russian Federation, United Kingdom, France, and China, and further to work toward eliminating such weapons altogether. As we have seen, the five states with nuclear weapons are obligated not to transfer nuclear weapons, other nuclear explosive devices, or technology to any non-nuclear weapon state. Members that are not nuclear weapons states are obligated not to acquire or produce nuclear weapons or nuclear explosive devices. They are also required to accept safeguards to detect diversions of nuclear materials from peaceful activities, such as nuclear reactors for electricity generation, to the production of nuclear weapons. This is done through individual agreements with IAEA.

As one can see, the five nuclear weapons nations form quite an elite, if not bankrupting and terribly dangerous club.

North Korea signed the NPT and reached an Agreed Framework with the IAEA in 1994, went on to develop a nuclear program for electricity generation, and then, once they had the technology, dropped out of the NPT in 2003 to pursue a weapons program. Ever since Kim Jong-il's regime has been using the threat to blackmail the United States and the nuclear weapons club of nations for financial aid and military assurances of protection.

Israel, Pakistan, and India never became a signatory to the NPT, but are simply developing their own nuclear capability for nuclear power generation and weapons. It has been proven that Pakistani scientists have helped Iran travel along the same road. These countries are not subject to the limitations and inspections of IAEA.

India set off its first nuclear blast in 1974. As the world's largest democracy, it has sought "special status" to receive nuclear materials and technology from the United States for over three decades—from Richard Nixon through Bill Clinton—but all refused to make a deal with India in violation of the NPT.

Then came Mr. Bush's Asian road trip in March 2006. This is the same president who used claims against Iraq of a nuclear threat (Iraq is a signatory to the NPT) to launch an invasion. What does he do while visiting India? He makes a deal, under which India would designate 14 of its 22 nuclear power reactors as "civilian," to be put under control of the IAEA, leaving the other eight free from inspection and able to produce as much bomb-grade plutonium as India wanted. In return, U.S. companies would be able to sell India civilian-use nuclear reactors and technology.

The Bush-India deal threatens to blast a loophole through the NPT. If the U.S. Congress okays this deal, which I dearly hope it will not, the treaty basically becomes worthless. But, as we well know, the Bush administration doesn't believe in regulations and treaties—selling anything to anybody is what America is all about under our far- right rulers. Never mind that America needs a massive nuclear power program at home to deal with the liquid fossil fuels crisis; never mind that China may well respond by making similar bilateral deals with Pakistan or Iran, or that Turkey may decide it needs to join the Asian nuclear arms race; and never mind that the original nuclear powers—U.S., U.K., France, Russia and China—have all stopped producing fissile material for weapons.

"It's a terrible deal, a disaster," said Joseph Cirincione, the director for nonproliferation at the Carnegie Endowment. "The Indians are free to make as much nuclear material as they want. Meanwhile, we're going to sell them fuel for their civilian reactors. That frees up their resources for the military side, and that stinks."

"We can't break the rules for India and then expect other countries to play by them," said Representative Edward Markey, a Massachusetts Democrat, who was one of the leading opponents of the deal.[289]

On June 7, 2005, former Senator Sam Nunn, co-chair of the Nuclear Threat Initiative, gave a speech in Tokyo titled "The Race Between Cooperation and Catastrophe." He said, "The gravest danger in the world today is the threat of nuclear and other weapons of mass destruction. We will prevent this danger only if every country accepts that it is the number one threat, and every country makes it a priority to cooperate for our common security."

Nunn then went on to describe the "four nuclear-related threats we face today":

1) A terrorist attack on a major city with a nuclear weapon smuggled across a border under a thin lead shield;

2) A terrorist attack with a dirty bomb that uses conventional explosives to spread deadly cesium isotope across a 60-block area of New York or some other major city. Millions flee. "Billions of dollars of real estate is declared uninhabitable. Cleanup is estimated to take years and cost additional billions";

3) A sharp increase in the number of nuclear weapon states, causing the Nuclear
Non-Proliferation Treaty to become " an artifact of history." We have seen this happening in the Bush-India nuclear deal;

4) An accidental or unauthorized nuclear missile strike after the relationship between Russia and the United States deteriorates and those two nuclear powers revert to a Cold War scenario. There is no doubt that U.S./Russian relations are steadily deteriorating.

The Nuclear Threat Initiative has also produced a film that dramatizes the vulnerability of America to nuclear terrorist attack. It is called "Last Best Chance."* In the cast is actor and former U.S. senator from Tennessee Fred Thompson. It opened at the New York Film Festival in September 2003.

Commenting on the film for *The New Yorker* magazine, Hendrik Hertzberg wrote:

"'Last Best Chance' is entertaining, in a grim sort of way, but entertainment is not its raison d'être. Its purpose is to stimulate public support and political pressure on the Bush Administration and Congress to do something serious about the terrifying danger of nuclear terrorism. And this is a scandal. It is scandalous that at this late date, four years after the attacks on New York and Washington, people like Nunn, [Sen. Richard] Lugar, and [Warren] Buffet feel it necessary to go to such unorthodox lengths to get the attention of Washington's responsibles. 'Last Best Chance' is a symptom of an immense failure of national, and especially Presidential, leadership."

One of the attendees at the screening was Graham Allison, the founding dean of Harvard's Kennedy School of Government and the director of its Belfer Center for Science and International Affairs, who held high Pentagon posts under Reagan and Clinton. Allison's *Nuclear Terrorism: The Ultimate Preventable Catastrophe*, which has just been published in an expanded paperback edition, is the indispensable text on the subject. "Americans are no safer from a nuclear terrorist attack today than we were on September 10, 2001," he writes. "A central reason for that can be summed up in one word: Iraq. The invasion and occupation have diverted essential resources from the fight against Al Qaeda; allowed the Taliban to regroup in Afghanistan; fostered neglect of the Iranian nuclear threat; undermined alliances critical to preventing terrorism; devastated America's standing with the public in every country in Europe and destroyed it in the Muslim world; monopolized the time and attention of the president and his security team (for simple human reasons, an extraordinary important factor); and thanks to the cry-wolf falsity of the claims about Iraqi weapons systems, discredited the larger case for a serious campaign to prevent nuclear terrorism."

In the spring of 2006, with the possibility of Bush's war spreading to Iran, it sometimes seemed that the nuclear winter was already upon us.

*"Last Best Chance" is available free of charge on DVD and can be ordered at: http://www.lastbestchance.org/film/

Part Four

Taking Back America

Nineteen

Facing the Threat; Finding the Solution

————•◆•◆•————

Fascism:

A political system in which all power of government is vested in a person or group with no other power to balance and limit the activities of the government. Fascist governments are often closely associated with large corporations and sometimes with extreme nationalism and racist activities. Modern fascism is often called "Corporatism".

Adrian Adamson,
Canadian educator.

The 14 Characteristics of Fascism
By Lawrence Britt
Spring 2003

Free Inquiry magazine

Political scientist Dr. Lawrence Britt wrote an article about fascism ("Fascism Anyone?" *Free Inquiry,* Spring 2003, page 20). Studying the fascist regimes of Hitler (Germany), Mussolini (Italy), Franco (Spain), Suharto (Indonesia), and Pinochet (Chile), Britt found all had 14 elements in common. He calls these the identifying characteristics of fascism. The excerpt is in accordance with the magazine's policy.

The 14 characteristics are:

1. Powerful and Continuing Nationalism

Fascist regimes tend to make constant use of patriotic mottos, slogans, symbols, songs, and other paraphernalia. Flags are seen everywhere, as are flag symbols on clothing and in public displays

2. Disdain for the Recognition of Human Rights

Because of fear of enemies and the need for security, the people in fascist regimes are persuaded that human rights can be ignored in certain cases because of "need." The people tend to look the other way or even approve of torture, summary executions, assassinations, long incarcerations of prisoners, etc.

3. Identification of Enemies/Scapegoats as a Unifying Cause

The people are rallied into a unifying patriotic frenzy over the need to eliminate a perceived threat or foe: racial, ethnic or religious minorities; liberals; communists; socialists, terrorists, etc.

4. Supremacy of the Military

Even when there are widespread domestic problems, the military is given a disproportionate amount of government funding, and the domestic agenda is neglected. Soldiers and military service are glamorized.

5. Rampant Sexism

The governments of fascist nations tend to be almost exclusively male-dominated. Under fascist regimes, traditional gender roles are made more rigid. Opposition to abortion is high, as is homophobia and anti-gay legislation and policy.

6. Controlled Media

Sometimes the media is directly controlled by the government, but in other cases, the media is indirectly controlled by government regulation, or sympathetic media spokespeople and executives. Censorship, especially in wartime, is very common.

7. Obsession with National Security

Fear is used as a motivational tool by the government over the masses.

8. Religion and Government are Intertwined

Governments in fascist nations tend to use the most common religion in the nation as a tool to manipulate public opinion. Religious rhetoric and terminology is common from government leaders, even when the major tenets of the religion are diametrically opposed to the government's policies or actions.

9.   Corporate Power is Protected

The industrial and business aristocracy of a fascist nation often are the ones who put the government leaders into power, creating a mutually beneficial business/government relationship and power elite.

10.   Labor Power is Suppressed

Because the organizing power of labor is the only real threat to a fascist government, labor unions are either eliminated entirely, or are severely suppressed.

11.   Disdain for Intellectuals and the Arts

Fascist nations tend to promote and tolerate open hostility to higher education, and academia. It is not uncommon for professors and other academics to be censored or even arrested. Free expression in the arts is openly attacked, and governments often refuse to fund the arts.

12.   Obsession with Crime and Punishment

Under fascist regimes, the police are given almost limitless power to enforce laws. The people are often willing to overlook police abuses and even forego civil liberties in the name of patriotism. There is often a national police force with virtually unlimited power in fascist nations.

13.   Rampant Cronyism and Corruption

Fascist regimes almost always are governed by groups of friends and associates who appoint each other to government positions and use governmental power and authority to protect their friends from accountability. It is not uncommon in fascist regimes for national resources and even treasures to be appropriated or even outright stolen by government leaders.

14. Fraudulent Elections

Sometimes elections in fascist nations are a complete sham. Other times elections are manipulated by smear campaigns against or even assassinations of opposition candidates, use of legislation to control voting numbers or political district boundaries, and their judiciaries to manipulate or control elections.

Truth is, when I began writing this book coming off the 2004 campaign, I never realized that my research would take me so far into the dark side of what is going on in our country. It has been both an education and a chilling experience. What began as a rather simple political primer quickly turned out to be something much more than expected. In every area that I delved into I found an America deeply divided between the few ultra-privileged and the rest of us. Be it the tax cuts for the rich, corporate welfare, the nation's structural budget deficits, globalization, deregulation, poverty, education, health care, energy dependence, religious and racial intolerance, women's rights, the environment, nuclear proliferation, military spending, the wars, and on and on, there was the unmistakable stench of fascism. It surfaces in Worldview, Part 2, Chapter 8.

As a child during World War II, I grew up with the word "fascism"; it was commonly used back then. As a history student, I learned that fascism is far more complex than the cartoon characters shown by American propagandists during the war. Today the word is rarely heard—it is apparently too frightening for our sheltered ears. Anyone who uses it is labeled a conspiracy fanatic or a slanderer. I am neither, but be that as it may, when viewed as a body of evidence in its historical context, the threat to American democracy in the 21st century is "fascism." And as we learned in Worldview, fascism, in its variant forms, is not new in the United States. I think of the current threat as the reemergence of unrestricted capitalism that has found structure in a world of huge international business empires, and regained strength to form the mutations of America's current elite—all the while being applauded by the religious fanatics who want to take our culture back into the caves. Given the immense power of today's industrial-military complex, and today's national priorities, there is little question that the United States has developed the characteristics of a fascist state.

Al Meyeroff, a Los Angeles attorney who led a class-action suit on behalf of the workers on the Marianas, in describing what his constituents were up against, said, "a society run by the powerful, oblivious to the weak, free of accountability, enjoying a cozy relationship with government, thriving on crony capitalism." Unfortunately, that description fits across a broad spectrum of present day America.

The Northern Marianas Islands in the Pacific became a trusteeship of the UN, administered by the U.S. government, after World War II. The islands are exempt from U.S. labor and immigration laws, and over the years tens of thousands of people, primarily Chinese, mostly women, were brought there as garment workers to live in crowded barracks in miserable conditions. The main island, Saipan, became known as America's biggest sweatshop.

The moguls of the Marianas, fighting all efforts at reform, hired lobbyist Jack Abramoff, knowing of his close ties with Tom DeLay, who was then Republican House majority leader. At stake is a cash cow industry because the biggest retailers in the clothing industry are able to label their clothes "made in the USA" while paying their workers practically nothing.

Abramoff made millions off the Marianas, and DeLay's Political Action Committees benefited handsomely as he protected the clothing industry's business practices in Congress. DeLay said the Marianas "represented what is best about America." He called them "my Galapagos" – "a perfect Petri dish of capitalism."[290]

It is imperative that thinking Americans wake up to the fact that the fascist threat to our democracy is real. Patriotic Americans shouldn't shy from the word; they should use it in its proper context to identify the danger. I have no doubt that if the corporate, political, and religious far right have their way, we will revert to a modern version of the first Gilded Age, an age when privilege controlled politics, votes were purchased, legislatures were bribed, bills were bought, and laws flagrantly disregarded—all as God's will. It will be a day when income on wealth will not be taxed at all, and public expenditures for social programs would come exclusively from taxes on salaries and wages. Burdened with debt caused by structural deficits and stripped of power, over time, the government of the United States will do little more than wage war and reward privilege.

This book has not been easy to write. I know it hasn't been an easy or pleasant read—but I didn't make this stuff up. No one could. I found, read, and compiled information that is available to all of us—if you dig. And I dug and dug for about a year and a half. As tough as it was to stomach, I am glad that I stuck it out, because if "we the people" hope to recapture the American dream we are going to have to be damned sure we know what we are talking about. Our beloved country is in great peril. The fascist leaning government that has emerged in the United States in the 21st century must be stopped from planting its roots deeper and destroying our national soul.

It didn't happen overnight. The far right launched its campaign over a quarter century ago to dismantle the institutions, laws, and the intellectual, cultural, and religious infrastructure that made up America's social contract as a nation. The convergence of the corporate, political and religious far right went largely unnoticed for a long time as they cleverly manipulated the nation's worldview, accumulated power, and waited for the right moment to exercise that power. That moment came with the presidency of George W. Bush in 2001, Republican control of Congress, and the terrorist attacks on September 11, 2001. It was then that American fascism emerged from the shadows—they had the power, and the cover of "war" to use that power to effect fundamental structural changes in our society.

To win elections and influence legislation, the movement, led by some of the wealthiest men in the world, zeroed in on the deep flaw in America's political system: the power of big money.

Elected officials need enormous sums of money to finance their campaigns, most of it going to buy television ads. In 2006, the average cost of running for a seat in the House of Representatives—the "people's house"—will top one million dollars. A run for the U.S. Senate will cost many times that amount. The chairman of the Federal Election Commission has said that anyone who expects to run for the nomination for president— just the *nomination*—will have to raise $100 million by the end of 2007.

It is expected that each of the two major party presidential candidates will spend between $300 and $500 million in the 2008 race.

Given the fact that less than one half of one percent of all Americans made a contribution of $200 or more to a federal candidate in 2004, most of that money will come from those special interests who have mastered the money game and taken advantage of this fundamental weakness in our system. It has made democracy for sale to the highest bidder. While both Republicans and Democrats feed at the trough, the Republicans have far greater access to money because of their closer links to big business.

The number of lobbyists has more than doubled since the turn of the century, from 16,342 in 2000 to 34,785 in 2005. That means 65 lobbyists for every member of Congress! And they spend money lavishly, wining, dining, and courting federal officials—to the tune of nearly $200 million *per month*. But it is a small price when one considers the return on investment in legislation passed. Here, to recapitulate, is some of what the Bush administration has pulled off:

Hundreds of billions in tax breaks for the rich.

Corporate welfare, with congress blocking even the smallest attempts to prevent American corporations from dodging more than $50 billion a year in taxes by opening a P.O. box in off-shore tax havens such as Bermuda or the Cayman Islands. In 2005, the Bush administration's largess permitted the repatriation of billions earned by corporations offshore for pennies on the tax dollar.

An energy bill that gave oil companies huge tax breaks at the same time Exxon/ Mobil posted the largest profits in U.S. corporate history— $36 billion in 2005, while the price of gasoline and home heating bills were at an all-time high for American families. In the Gulf of Mexico, "royalty relief" as an incentive for exploration has cost the U.S. Treasury $7 billion, which is likely to rise to $28 billion by 2010.

A transportation bill loaded with so much pork it earmarked money for $100 million bridges and roads leading to nowhere.

A bankruptcy "reform" bill crafted by the credit card industry to make it almost impossible for poor debtors to get relief from the burdens of divorce or medical catastrophe.

Further deregulation of the banking, securities, and insurance industries, which permitted rampant corporate malfeasance and greed and led to the destruction of retirement plans of millions of small investors.

Deregulation of the telecommunications sector, which led to cable industry price gouging and the abandonment of extensive news coverage by the big media companies.

And to top it off, the oil war in Iraq with the attendant huge increase in military spending that has been a bonanza for the defense industry and private contractors, such as Halliburton.

Life has been very good for the ultra-rich under the Bush administration. While times are tough for the average Joe, top executive salaries and business profits have never been as high.

The question is how can "we the people" turn this around and take America back? It is ultimately a matter of power, which brings us back to the Grassroots Policy Project and Richard Healy's *"The 3 Faces of Power"* discussed briefly in Part 2 – Worldview.

The First Face of Power – Immediate Political Gains

In order to win on the issues, progressives have to win elections; it is just that simple. As we have seen, there was a time when the middle class flourished in America, a time when true debate could occur within the committees and halls of Congress. Unfortunately, that time has passed. As the Republican far right gained control of the White House and both houses of Congress, it also demanded complete party fealty. In the House, under the reign of former Majority Leader Tom DeLay, those who fell in line reaped huge rewards (financial and otherwise), while those who didn't got hammered.[291] In the Senate, party fealty was rewarded with exorbitant pork for projects in the senator's state, and, of course large campaign contributions to already bursting war chests.

As I said in Part 1, I believe the outcomes of the 2002 (mid-term) and 2004 (presidential) federal elections were a major setback for America. But that is water under the bridge. What matters now are the 2006 and 2008 elections. Of these I am convinced that if we wake up on November 5, 2008 with Republicans still in control of the White House and Congress, given a Supreme Court weighted heavily with ultraconservative justices (thanks to George Bush), many of us won't live long enough to see a socially responsible government in the United States again. And the world will share our pain.

That said, there is a part of me that is guardedly optimistic. I believe that Americans on the whole are a good and generous people. That despite all the B.S. the spin-doctors have fed them about being rough and tough and all that stuff, Americans are not stupid. Once they figure it out, the tide will turn. The question is, when?

In the spring of 2006 President Bush's approval ratings were at an all-time low for any sitting president, in the 32-percentile range, echoing that of Richard Nixon before he was forced to resign. Congress' ratings (Democrats and Republicans) were at 30 percent. Seventy percent felt we should throw the bums out!

Iraq was at the 11th (if not later) hour before civil war and the so-called unity government seemed incapable of keeping the country from plunging deeper into chaos. Bush now told us it may be up to "future" presidents to decide when American troops will be withdrawn from Iraq, and Rumsfeld said that history would exonerate the war. In the meantime, about 140 thousand G.I.s were caught in the middle while their incompetent government lived a fantasy.[292]

The issue of what was estimated to be 11-12 million illegal immigrants had driven a wedge in the Republican Party, which is divided between those who want to expel and those that want to exploit. The far right was urging a get-tough policy that would make illegal immigrants, their children born in the United States, and employers or caregivers felons, and deport them. Such a bill had passed in the House. On the other side, Bush, joining most Democrats, was urging a get-tough boarder policy while allowing the illegal immigrants to stay and work for a period of time while seeking legal status.[293] It was a difficult issue for the Republicans, who, I am pleased to say, had more to lose than the Democrats.

Despite the increased Gross Domestic Product and low unemployment numbers game, and the Bush administration's protestations that the economy is doing great, most Americans only had to look at their own financial situation to know it simply was not so. Piddling tax cuts of a few hundred dollars for most families had been more than offset by the increased cost of health care, skyrocketing fuel prices, and stagnant wages. And that's if you were lucky and still had a job that hadn't been outsourced.

Given all that, I think most Americans had "had enough" and had come to the conclusion that the Bush administration was hopelessly incompetent in governing.[294]

Democrats will not be running against Tom Delay in 2006 or George Bush in 2008. Those two will fade into history. We will be running to end the Republican culture of corruption and restore competence and integrity to our government.

DeLay is merely a symptom of a much larger disease—a sick Republican culture of corruption that touched everyone who took his dirty money, voted for his corrupt leadership, or sat silently while their party sold our government to the highest bidder. The corruption extends to the House, the Senate, and the Bush administration. On Election Day in 2006 and 2008 it is imperative that accountability reach just as wide. Regaining Democratic control of the Senate will take five seats, in the House 15.

Playing against us is that statistically the vast majority of congressional incumbents win, largely because they are able to raise far more money than challengers. It will be up to us to negate the power of that money with an effective grassroots campaign. I am convinced that the day when campaigns can be won by spending vast sums on television advertising has passed. People are sick of it.

Advice to candidates: At the federal and top state level candidates need professional help to organize and run campaigns. Get that help. But do not, I repeat, do not allow the "professional" advisers to steal your voice or micromanage your campaign. You might compare them to stockbrokers: If stockbrokers had all the answers they would be far richer. As the candidate, the voters need to know you and you can't let anyone dilute your voice.

The political myth inspired by Bill Clinton's success is that to win a candidate must pander to the "center" and court the independent voter. Clinton's political acumen has been misinterpreted; a gifted speaker, he was able to appeal to independents, not pander. As has been said by others, the only thing in the center of the road is the yellow line and road kill. People want a passionate candidate with the courage to tell the truth. Anything less is like stale beer, flat. Yet in recent years the Democratic Party powerful have not supported those with too much passion or those who don't fit the "centrist" mold—and we have been losing. Trying to be all things to all people also prevents Democrats from playing as a team with a strong message behind which people can rally.

Howard Dean's run in the 2004 Democratic primary was an example. He didn't fit the mold. When he was ostracized by the press for a televised middle-of-the-night scream to supporters after losing the Iowa Caucus, the Democratic Party didn't lift a finger. No sir. They let him go down like a stone. It is true that the party couldn't, and shouldn't, take sides in a primary, but it certainly could have defended a Democrat's right to passionate expression. So should have the other candidates. Throughout his campaign, Dean was also brutally truthful, which didn't sit well with the obfuscators and spin-doctors. I worked for Dean as a North Country volunteer and got to spend some one-on-one time with him. He is a great guy, whom I hope (for all of us) enjoys success as head of the Democratic National Committee. He certainly continues to have my support.

John Kerry, who won the primary but lost the election, was on the opposite side of that spectrum. He followed the professional advice and tried to walk the yellow line as a wartime hero and Iraq war critic. It didn't work. Being a war hero was a difficult sell for an aristocrat in any case: Had he said, yes I served my country in Vietnam and yes, I am proud of my medals, although others (unsaid: less rich and connected) were equally deserving. I think people, particularly military people, would have empathized. Had he also claimed pride for having spoken against that ill-advised war when he came home from Vietnam, he would have come off far better than he did trying to be cagy. Ditto on his vote to give Bush statutory war authority in the Senate. By saying he would still vote the same way (knowing of Bush's lies for going to war), he came across as a flip-flopper for criticizing the war. Mind, I worked and voted for Kerry, but I think had he spoken his heart, instead of the "politically correct" words of others, he might have won. It was a close race after all, and he did receive more votes than any other Democratic presidential candidate in history.

Although as yet (spring 2006) nobody has publicly announced as a 2008 Democratic presidential candidate—that won't happen until after 2006 mid-term election—there is quite a field already sniffing the air, and there is no better air than in the first-in-the-nation primary State of New Hampshire. One of these was General Wesley Clark.

In 2004, Clark entered the Democratic presidential primary late, stepped in a lot of self-admitted potholes, and dropped out relatively early. During his run, I heard him speak at the annual New Hampshire Democratic Party Jefferson-Jackson Dinner in Manchester. I sat at a table way in the back of a huge room with my wife Sue and other North Country party officials and state candidates. Hardly a one-on-one encounter with several hundred people between us. Nonetheless, he sounded a capable and good candidate.

In mid-March 2006, as chair of the North Country Democratic Committee, I was both shocked and delighted to get a call from state party headquarters asking if I would be interested in hosting a reception for General Clark—like in four days! Well I certainly was interested, but four days isn't much notice, and Clark is quite a dignitary. He not only ran in the 2004 presidential primary, he is a retired four-star general and former head of NATO. We couldn't very well just take him to the local dinner for coffee and doughnuts.

To make a long story short, we—meaning mostly my wife Sue and some wonderful volunteers—pulled it off by having the reception at our home, which is large and can accommodate quite a few people.

General Clark arrived in New Hampshire on a Friday evening with his brother-in-law Gene Caufield, and had events scheduled throughout the weekend, ending with our reception on Sunday in Littleton at 1 p.m. Following our event, he and Gene had to beat it back to Manchester Airport (an hour-and-a-half drive) to catch their return flights. To make it work, we coordinated a pickup at a rest area about an hour and 15 minutes south of Littleton on Interstate 93. I was to pick the general and Gene up; another volunteer from the North Country group would drive them back to the airport.

I share this with you because it was such a personally inspiring visit. On the drive north, Clark sat in the right seat and we had this wonderfully intense conversation. Clark is a brilliant guy. It was easy to see why he graduated first in his class at West Point and was a Rhodes scholar. He is also very good company. We talked about a wide range of subjects; I'd like to share a few snippets of what he had to say:

About another presidential run in 2008, he said, yes, he is considering it but wouldn't make a decision until after the 2006 mid-term election. He said people run for the presidency for two reasons, the glory and prestige or to serve their country. He said he has more medals than can fit on his uniform, and as commander of NATO lived in a grand mansion with a government staff and a jet aircraft at his disposal. So he has done all of that.

After 34 years in the military, Clark said he was drawn to politics because something is wrong in America. We are in a desperate situation, he said, adding that much of the world now thinks the United States' day is over. The Bush administration is "wrecking America's future," he said.

He cited spying on American citizens without a judicial warrant as an example. It should be investigated, he said; instead, congress is passing measures to legalize it. Special prosecutors should be investigating the whole lobbyist scandal and the legislators it has corrupted, Clark said. "We need to clear it out, air it out," he said. "We have got to help fix America before it's too late, before our freedoms are lost."

Clark is also a prolific reader and history student. His voice taking on a passionate tone, he said that he'd just read a book titled *Washington's*

Crossing, by David Hackett Fisher. What touched him deeply were eyewitness accounts written of General Washington's appeal to the troops on December 31, 1776.

The ragged army of 2,400 colonials had crossed the ice-choked Delaware River in the face of a nor'easter on Christmas and defeated a Hessian garrison of 1,500 at Trenton. In the previous five months following the Declaration of Independence the American rebels had lost every battle. They had been driven from Long Island to Westchester and across the Hudson and Delaware Rivers to Pennsylvania. General Washington's army had lost 90 percent of its strength, and many of the remaining troops intended to go home when their enlistments expired at the end of the year; that night. The American Revolution was in danger of collapse.

Against that background, Clark told the story from memory. Here it's repeated from the book:

He [Washington] mustered the New England regiments and begged them to serve for another six weeks. A sergeant remembered that the general "personally addressed us...told us our services were greatly needed, and that we could do more for our country than we could at any future date, and in the most affectionate manner entreated us to stay." Then the regimental commanders asked all who would stay to step forward. "The drums beat for volunteers," one remembered, "but not a man turned out." One explained that his comrades were "worn down with fatigue and privations, had their hearts fixed on home and comforts of the domestic circle." The men watched as Washington "wheeled his horse about, rode in front of the regiment," and spoke to them again. Long afterwards, a sergeant still remembered his words:

"My brave fellows," Washington began, "you have done all I asked you to do, and more than could be reasonably expected; but your country is at stake, your wives, your houses, and all that you hold dear. You have worn yourselves out with the fatigues and hardships, but we know not how to spare you. If you will consent to stay one month longer; you will render that service to the cause of liberty, and your country, which you probably can never do under any other circumstances."

The drums rolled again. The sergeant recalled that "the soldiers felt the force of the appeal" and began to talk among themselves. One said, "I will remain if you will." Another said, "We cannot go home under such circumstances." A few men stepped forward, then several others, then many more, and "their example was [followed] by nearly all who were fit for duty in the regiment, amounting to about two hundred volunteers." These were veterans who understood what they were being asked to do. They knew well what the cost might be. One of them remembered later that nearly half of the men who stepped forward would be killed in the fighting or dead of disease "soon after."

Clearly Clark views America's freedoms in a crisis of such magnitude that he is willing to step forward. After the depressing work on this book, it was an uplifting experience to be in the presence of a truly patriotic national leader. I think Clark would be a great president, particularly given the threats to our national security.

General Clark was greeted by the resounding applause of about 65 people when he stepped through the door of our home. He then spoke for about an hour to a rapt audience. And I thought, if we have people like Wesley Clark, and people like these friends and neighbors assembled, perhaps, just perhaps American democracy is resilient enough to survive the nut jobs that are ruling our country now.

Other potential Democratic presidential candidates with feelers out are: Sen. Joe Biden (DE), Sen. Evan Bayh (IN), Sen. Hillary Rodham Clinton (NY), former Sen. Tom Daschle (SD), former senator and vice presidential candidate John Edwards (TN), Sen. Russ Feingold (WI), former presidential candidate Sen. John Kerry (MA), Gov. Bill Richardson (NM), and former Gov. Mark Warner (VA). It is quite an impressive field. And, being an activist in New Hampshire, I know I will get to hear and meet most of them again, and rather expect to be asked to escort one or the other of them on a Littleton Main Street walk. New Hampshire offers retail politics at its finest.

The New Hampshire 2006 Democratic Candidates – spring

For Congress, we have a better-than-usual chance of unhorsing both Jeb Bradley (District 1) and Charlie Bass (District 2). Paul Hodes is running again in District 2 with much stronger name recognition than he had two years ago and Bass' dismal lockstep voting record going for him. Lined up against Jeb Bradley are four candidates who will face a primary election. These are: Jim Craig, Gary Dodds, and Carol Shea-Porter.

There is no U.S. Senate race in 2006. In 2008, we will get another shot at John Sununu, who won over former Governor Jeanne Shaheen in 2002.

Governor John Lynch, who will enter the 2006 election with a record breaking 70 percent-plus approval rating, is pretty much a shoe in. On the Republican side is NH House Rep. Jim Coburn.

The breakdown in the state Senate remains 16 Republicans and eight Democrats, with Democrats standing a good chance of picking up some seats in 2006. My former opponent, John Gallus, is opposed by Lincoln attorney Norman Jackman, who earlier tried unsuccessfully to unseat Congressman Charlie Bass.

In 2006, the prospects for the NH House are particularly encouraging. Since 2004, Democrats have won seven out of eight special elections, bringing our total number to 157. Of the 243 Republicans, a significant number are voting on the Democratic side of issues. This is quite a departure from the previous legislature, in which few Republicans crossed over. In fact, the Democratic leaders in the House figure that if we pick up 25 more seats, Democrats will have a working majority. That is pretty exciting considering Republicans have controlled the NH House since the Civil War.

And I have decided to step forward once again and run for the NH House for my district, which includes the towns of Littleton and Lyman (population more than 6,000).

Second Face – Building Infrastructure to Shape Political Agendas

How do we do it? It is here that progressives have had their butts kicked by the far right. And it is here, despite all the reasons that the far right should be blown out of office, that we could lose again.

While relatively few people will run for or hold public office, it is the deeper infrastructure among organizations and their grassroots members that shape public policy and get candidates elected. These include political parties, think tanks, advocacy groups, and just about any group of two people or more. On the Right, both corporations and social conservatives have active networks and organizations that can and do unite around a shared agenda.

We have had plenty of super candidates go down in flames because progressives haven't had the infrastructure to get them elected or to form a consensus to shape public policy. Throughout this book plenty has been said about how this happened over the past 25 years. It is now time to talk about solutions.

Political parties have a fundamental role in a democracy. In a parliamentary system it is up to the majority party, or a coalition of parties, to create a majority that forms the government. In the American system, it is the majority party in Congress and in most state legislatures that gains the chairmanship of committees, which represents enormous power. And of course, voting as a block, the majority party can bring bills out of committee and pass legislation.

There is no such thing as an independent political party in the United States. To run as an Independent, a candidate must serve up a petition with a specified number of signatures, depending upon the office, to win a place on the ballot. That person runs as an *individual,* without party affiliation. In all of the federal government there are only two independent office holders, both from Vermont—Sen. Jim Jeffords, who left the Republican Party, and Congressman Bernie Sanders. *Yet the largest block, over one-third of America's voters, is registered as Independents.* In this the United States is unique in the world and the question is why? From my experience there are several reasons:

- American's take pride of their independence, why not registers as one?
- Political party affiliation is public information; in certain communities, particularly small towns, a business or professional person may suffer financial loss if out of step with the pack.
- Displeasure with both major parties and not wishing to be identified with either.
- Compared to many other countries, everyday American's are amazingly politically naive and don't know how political parties work. Consequently, they don't get involved.
- And that good old stand-by that drives me nuts, "Whatever I do it won't make a difference, why should I bother?"

There are also about 53 so-called third parties in the United States. They run the gamut from Libertarian, to Socialist, to Nazi. While a third party hasn't won the presidency since Teddy Roosevelt, they have been a swing factor between the Republicans and Democrats in a few close elections. Very notable was Bill Clinton's first presidential victory, largely because Ross Perot stole votes from George H. W. Bush.

For the good of our country, all this stuff must be put aside and Americans must unite behind our Democratic candidates. The stakes are high and there is no other party or "individual" that can defeat the Republican far right now in power.

I was a Republican for much of my life. But it was a different Republican Party, one that was fiscally conservative (in a traditional way) and strong on national security, with leaders such as Nelson Rockefeller and Dwight Eisenhower. I sincerely hope that mainstream responsible Republicans will take back their party. America needs a strong two-party system. But it is not possible for that to happen soon enough to prevent an American disaster.

There isn't enough time. If the far right remains in power beyond 2008, the fundamental changes made to America's institutions and infrastructure will make future elections a ruse. Oh we will have them, but with unrestricted money coming out of K Street, gerrymandering and all the rest, only those they choose will win, and they will be controlled with an iron fist.

Now is the moment—as Washington said to the troops on that dark night in 1776—that you could do more for our country than at any future date. And at this point you don't (yet) have to risk your life to do it. It is time for you to "step forward" and be an activist for American democracy, because only you can save your country from the threat from within. What can you do?

- Being an activist starts out around the dinner table and with friends and neighbors. As former Speaker of the House Tip O'Neill said, "All politics is local." What carries more weight, being bombarded with 30-second television commercials or the opinion of a trusted person you know? All the campaign money in the world can't buy the latter.

- As an activist you can be that trusted person. Think of all the people you know, groups you may belong to, your church, school, union, service club, or whatever. That is the grassroots campaign; it is networking to make coalitions, alliances, and other forms of collaboration work for us.

- Get involved. If you are a registered Democrat or thinking of becoming one, attend town or regional meetings of the Democratic Party. They are your friends and neighbors and they are anxious to have you participate. It is the best way to meet the candidates, learn the issues, and have your voice heard. If you are a registered Republican, either change over or go to their meetings and raise hell.

- As explained in Part 1, the Bipartisan Campaign Reform Act (BCRA) of 2002 prohibited political party committees from receiving "soft money" for federal elections. In a very complicated set of regulations, BCRA greatly limited the way a political party can support a federal candidate or advocate for or against issues. This resulted in the emergence of powerful, well-financed 527 and 501 (c) groups in the 2004 election. These have become sort of phantom parties, which will be out in force again in 2006 and 2008. While some are progressive groups, such as America Coming Together (ACT), and MoveOn, others, such as Swift Vets and POWs, are far-right attack dogs.

Under BCRA in 2004 the top (50) 527 organizations spent over $500 million dollars—roughly the equivalent of what was spent in "soft money" in 2002. What changed was the way it was spent. Though the 527s enjoy freedom of speech, they can't engage in "federal campaign activity." Huh? In other words they can say Joe Blow sucks eggs but cannot say vote for Mr. Good Guy. With soft money political parties had a greater ability to promote and build party values, which not only benefited the candidates but also raised a banner for people to rally behind.

501(c) issues groups existed long before BCRA and the new law didn't change the rules for them. I sit on the board of the New Hampshire Citizens Alliance; it has been around for about 25 years as a progressive advocacy group with interests in health care, women's rights, and immigration, to name a few. There have been tons of them—but the mission traditionally was to influence political parties by swaying public opinion and lobbying, not replace them. The new generation of 501(c)s has clouded the distinction. They have formed the second leg of the three-legged stool to get around BCRA—with them groups and individuals can spend unlimited money to campaign for issues.

The third leg of the stool is 501(c)4s and PACs. BCRA didn't change them either. Within FEC and state limitations they can still identify and support candidates. By using all three, 527s, 501(c)s, and 501(c)4s and PACs you have the makings of a shadow political party. Big organizations like MoveOn do exactly that.

I think BCRA is bad law. At a time when America needs the people's Democratic Party, its voice has been muted and people are confused. I hear this question all the time: I support MoveOn or ACT or Democracy for America or Democracy for New Hampshire, do I need to support and join that old-fashioned relic called the Democratic Party? The party doesn't seem to do anything. The answer is resoundingly "yes." (And you need to directly support Democratic candidates as well.) Political parties play an essential role in the way our government works. None of these other groups can replace them. As for the progressive 527s, sure if you have the money, time and energy, support them—that collaborative effort has become essential under today's law. Just understand that one is not a substitute for the other.

- Be visible. Stand up for what you believe! Some of the greatest success we had in the North Country was with parades, county fairs and dancing and waving with signs on street corners. It's fun and it works!

So do public demonstrations. Without them the civil rights movement in the 1960s would have been dead in the water. On April 10, 2006, an estimated 180,000 Latinos demonstrated in Washington, 100,000 each in Phoenix and in New York City, and tens of thousands more on the streets of nearly 70 U.S. cities in support of what is estimated to be 11-12 million illegal immigrants. They were protesting against the bill (mentioned earlier) the House passed that would lock our borders, treat illegal immigrants as felons, and export them. Good for them! If they didn't demonstrate nothing would change. In France, after weeks of demonstrations by young workers, the government has withdrawn a change in labor law that would allow young workers to be terminated without cause. Good for them! We don't have that protection for workers in the United States. Last March, in cities around the world, people demonstrated against the War in Iraq on its third anniversary. Was anyone at the White House listening? Apparently not.

Third Face – Shifting Worldview

The Grassroots Policy Project describes the third face of power as about using cultural beliefs, norms, traditions, histories and practices to shape political meaning. Following Barry Goldwater's defeat in the 1960s, the mega-millionaires and billionaires of the far right spent lavishly on their think tanks to do exactly that. They learned to frame the issues that advanced their ultraconservative agenda around the dominant worldview that reinforces an American notion of rugged individualism—a go-it-alone, lift yourself up by your own bootstraps approach—an approach that discourages involvement in collective action. They have been very good at it. They got Ronald Reagan, George H. W. Bush, and George W. Bush elected president; control both houses of Congress; have established a conservative Supreme Court; and have substantially advanced their far-right agenda. In the process, the neoconservatives also hijacked the Republican Party.

To challenge the dominant worldview, progressives have to learn to frame issues to reflect their broader goals for social change and economic justice. That has been a major goal of this book—to shed light on the various forces that have shaped (or misshaped) our own worldview, and to acquire the ability to frame our issues with progressive themes. I am pleased to say, in this regard, the ultraconservative think tanks no longer dominate the playing field. In my research I found fantastic progressive research and analysis groups and used their work extensively. We now have the meat and potatoes of what we need to know.[295]

Nonetheless, shifting worldview is a slow, never-ending process. Life isn't a snapshot; it is a motion picture. Today's current events are tomorrow's history. In order to influence the way others look at the world you essentially need to be a student of both history and current events. Mindful of Dr. Mindich's findings in his work *"Tuned Out"* (talked about in Chapter 6), I think *Facing Fascism* could be useful as a guide for students of all ages to learn how to research today's news and information. High-speed Internet access has literally put the world at our fingertips.

Combined with books, newspapers, radio, and television news—many of which are available online—there is no reason for our citizenry to be led around by the nose with the misrepresentations of spin-doctors, at least not until an authoritarian government succeeds in muting these resources.

The big question is: okay, "we got the message; who gets to sing?" The answer, for the sake of our country, is that we all do. And, with hard work and a little luck, it will be a thunderous chorus heard around the world, a hymn to the common good.

That is the grassroots campaign.

In this book, you get to write the ending....

Notes

Chapter Two

[1] Volunteers and contributors that must be mentioned: Larry & Jeanne Boisseau, Pat Bonardi, Paula & Bill Bradley, Charles Buckley, Helen Collings, William Cowie, Victor Dahar, Ned Densmore, Elise Drake, Debby Erb, Barbara Farrell, Bob Fink, Linda Frank, Gina & Beth Funicella, Ellen & Andrew Gallagher, Warren & Barbara Geissinger, Doug Grant, Brien Hardy, Tony Ilacqua, Rhonda Jenness, Terri & Dan Jones, Larry Kelly, Carol & Tim MacIver, George Manupelli, John McIlwane, Martha McLeod, Don Merrill, Lars & Cynthia Nielson, Bob O'Connor, Janet Parker, Bob Peraino, Michael Reed, George Roorbach, Carl & Mary Lu Schaller, Sally & Jim Sherrard, Arnold Shields, Loretta & Bill Silver, Terry St. Germain, Art Tighe, Irene Valliere, Wilber Willey, David Wood, Natalie Woodroofe, Irene & Warren Yeargle, and Walter & Priscilla Zandi. They have my sincerest thanks and appreciation.

Chapter Four

[2] The Center for Responsive Politics is a nonpartisan, nonprofit research group based in Washington, D.C. that tracks money in politics, and its effect on elections and public policy. Major foundation funders are The Ford Foundation, The Pew Charitable Trusts, The Carnegie Corporation and The Joyce Foundation. Much of the data on election money in this book comes from the center's website, opensecrets.org, and from direct research from the FEC.

Chapter Five

[3] dkosopedia.com FEC June 1, 2003

[4] John Lott, a resident scholar at the American Enterprise Institute.

[5] Stealth PACs are numerous nonprofit groups with 501(c) tax status that spend millions to influence elections without revealing the identities of their donors or how they spend their money.

[6] Common Cause

[7] "Soft money" is actually a colloquial term for nonfederal funds that cannot be used in connection with federal elections, but can be used for other purposes.

[8] See "A Party Inverted," by Bill Bradley, *New York Times*, 30 March 2005.

Chapter Six

[9] United States Election Assistance Commission

[10] *Now*, with Bill Moyers, Election 2004

[11] John W. Dean, Find Laws Legal Commentary

[12] Mr. Gates and his wife Melinda have established the Bill & Melinda Gates Foundation, endowed with $1 billion dollars for education scholarships.

[13] The full text of Mr. Gate's speech is available at gatesfoundation. org

[14] The NIFL is administered by the Secretaries of Education, Labor, and Health and Human Services, who make up the governing Interagency Group. More information is available at nifl.gov

[15] Definition from wipedia.org

[16] Published on Friday, April 1, 2005 by the Hearst Newspapers.

[17] Description of the organization at nrb.org/whoweare

[18] *Tuned Out* is published by the Oxford University Press. David T.Z. Mindich is the chair of the Journalism and Mass Communications Department at Saint Michael's College in Vermont.

Chapter Seven

[19] The Grassroots Policy Project describes itself as "an educational and research organization working in partnership with grassroots community groups, activist networks, statewide coalitions and other training organizations to encourage strategic approaches to issues of social and economic justice. Since GPP's inception in 1993, we have been exploring ways to provide grassroots organizations with the tools to further their long-term social change goals. GPP's home page and research papers can be found at grassrootspolicy.org (2040 S Street NW, Washington, DC 20009)."

[20] The NHCA is an organization whose mission is to promote social and economic justice. nhcitizensalliance.org (4 Park St., Suite 403, Concord, NH 03301).

[21] This saying is attributed to John Raye and Erasmus—it is also used expansively by Dave Phipps, an old union buddy.

[22] CIA – The World Factbook – United States

[23] U.S. and World Population Clocks www.census.gov/www/popclock.html

[24] U.S. Census Bureau

[25] BBC News published 2004/10/19

[26] *The New York Times,* April 9, 2005, "Nukes Are Green," by Nicholas D. Kristof

[27] American Samoa, Baker Island, Guam, Howland Island, Jarvis Island, Johnson Atoll, Kingman Reef, Midway Islands, Navassa, Island, Northern Mariana Islands, Palmyra Atoll, Puerto Rico, Virgin Islands, and Wake Island.

[28] The IMF is an organization of 184 countries. www.imf.org

[29] State of the World's Children www.unicefusa.org

[30] Press release August 26, 2004 www.census.gov/Press-Release

Chapter Eight

[31] *The New York Times*, March 30, 2005.

[32] All Barma Research studies define "evangelicals" as "individuals who meet the born again criteria; say their faith is very important in their life today; believe they have a personal responsibility to share their religious beliefs about Christ with non-Christians; acknowledge and describe God as the all-knowing all-powerful, perfect deity who created the universe and still rules it today...." Evangelism is not in itself a religion; it's a term that applies to people of many denominations who share a similar worldview.

[33] In Congress, July 4, 1776, The Declaration of Independence: "...We hold these truths to be self –evident, that all men are created equal, that they are endowed by their Creator with certain unalienable Rights, that among these are Life Liberty, and the pursuit of Happiness. That, to secure

these rights, Governments are instituted among Men, deriving their just Powers from the consent of the governed."

The First Amendment to the Constitution as part of ten amendments know as the Bill of Rights ratified in 1791: "Congress shall make no law respecting an establishment of religion, or prohibiting the free exercise thereof; or abridging the freedom of speech, or of the press; or the right of the people peaceably to assemble, and to petition the government for a redress of grievances."

[34] Bauer was a domestic policy adviser to President Reagan and ran for president in 2000.

[35] *The Christian Science Monitor,* April 25, 2005, "Military channel reports for duty," by Randy Dotinga.

Chapter Nine

[36] The major conservative think tanks are the Heritage Foundation, the Manhattan Institute, the American Enterprise Institute (AEI), the Hoover Institute and the Cato Institute (which tends to be more libertarian). Donald Rumsfeld and Condoleezza Rice are both Hoover veterans, and Dick Cheney and his wife have long been associated with AEI. Edwin Feulner, the President of Heritage, is quoted as saying, "If people are policy, then the think tanks are becoming America's shadow government."

[37] The History of Colonial Williamsburg can be found at: www.history.org/Foundation/cwhistory.cfm

[38] The British Civil War was actually a series of armed conflicts between Parliamentarians and Royalists over the absolute power of King Charles I. The Parliamentarians defeated Charles II (his son) at the Battle of Worcester on September 3, 1651, ending the monopoly of the Church of England on Christian worship in England and establishing a precedent that the king could not govern without the consent of Parliament and the people. Charles 1 was executed and Charles II exiled.

[39] The UK has a Bill of Rights; it was an Act of Parliament in 1689 that established Parliament as the primary governing body of the country. They also have the Magna Carta (1215), which was a set of baronial stipulations

forced upon the king. In its final version it included the term "Any Freemen," of which there weren't many – but it formed the later basis of rule by law. The founders also used it as a model for The Bill of Rights. Research at: The Magna Carta www.archives.gov

[40] By 1776 the population of the colonies had reached 2.5 million, about one third the population of Britain.

[41] Can be found at Northern Profits from Slavery: www.slavenorth. com/profits.htm

[42] Thomas Friedman refers to the foresight of Marx and Engels in his best-selling book *The World is Flat*.

[43] Colonial Government: www.usgennet.org/usa.topic/colonial

[44] The French and Indian War: www.philaprintshop.com

[45] The colonial women had boycotted the tea imported by the East Indian Company for six years.

[46] One has to wonder if dumping a Wal-Mart truck in Boston Harbor would work as well to preserve American jobs and protect American local merchants. Of course we'd have to get some guys to dress up as Indians and incur the wrath of America's open market profiteers.

[47] Research at: www.u-s-history.com

[48] Research at: www.usconstitution.net

[49] The articles changed the designation of the colonies to states.

[50] When the war ended exactly is confusing (communications were extremely slow). In November of 1782 the British agreed to American Independence and made a preliminary accord with America. In January of 1783 they signed the preliminary peace treaty, with France and Spain; on April 14th, the governor of New Jersey issued a proclamation that ended formal hostilities. Congress ratified The Treaty of Paris on January 14, 1784 and the Revolutionary War officially ended. Research at: www.doublegv. com

[51] Today it is just the opposite. The federal government takes the lion's share of tax dollars and, under the Bush administration, the states are left to beg (usually unsuccessfully) for support of vital domestic programs.

[52] In the United States, early federal bankruptcy laws were temporary responses to bad economic conditions. The first modern laws were enacted

in 1898, and during the economic upheaval of the Great Depression during the 1930s, and were substantially revamped in 1978.

Research at: www.bankruptcylawfirms.com/History-Bankruptcy In 2005, under the Bush administration, bankruptcy relief for middle-income people was eliminated for many and additional shelters provided for the wealthy.

[53] Research at: Shays' Rebellion: www.sjchs-history.org/Shays.

[54] Research at: The History Place: www.historyplace.com/unitedstates/revolution/rev-nation.htm

[55] The Bill of Rights is the first 10 amendments to the Constitution—they were ratified in 1791.

[56] The only mention of a form of government is in Article IV, Section 4: The United States shall guarantee to every State in this Union a Republican Form of Government, and shall protect each of them against Invasion; and on Application of the Legislature, or of the Executive (when the Legislature cannot be convened) against domestic Violence.

Chapter Ten

[57] De facto racial segregation is still a factor today despite civil rights laws to the contrary. Economic factors, "white flight" from central cities, often illegal discrimination by homeowners, real estate agents, and lending institutions have created segregated neighborhoods and consequently segregated schools, and other public and private institutions.

[58] Laws prohibiting interracial marriage (otherwise know as miscegenation laws) were so deeply embedded in U.S. history that they would have to be considered America's longest-lasting form of legal race discrimination. They lasted far longer than either slavery or school segregation. All told, miscegenation laws were in effect for nearly three centuries, from 1664 until 1967... http://www.hnn.us/articles/4708.html

[59] From the 1880s into the 1960s, a majority of Americans states enforced segregation through "Jim Crow" laws (so called after a black character in minstrel shows). From Delaware to California, and from North Dakota to Texas, many states (and cities, too) could impose legal punishments on people for consorting with members of another race. The most common types of laws forbade intermarriage and ordered business owners and public institutions to keep their black and white clientele

separated. Martin Luther King Jr., Jim Crow Laws www.nps.gov/malu/ documents/jim_crow_laws

[60] Carpetbaggers: Northerners who moved south after the Civil War were called "carpetbaggers" by critics who claimed they carried all their possessions in one bag (luggage made of carpeting). Houghton Mifflin

[61] CNN. Com – Senate apologizes for not outlawing lynching.

[62] Sicilian Culture – www.sicilianculture.com

[63] The Dred Scott decision by the U. S. Supreme Court is infamous. The Court ruled that all people of African ancestry –slaves as well as those who were free—could never become citizens of the United States and therefore could not sue in federal court. The court also ruled that the federal government did not have the power to prohibit slavery in its territories. Dred Scott www.pbs.org

[64] As we have seen, the removal of a president from office requires two steps: (1) a formal accusation, or impeachment, by the House of Representatives, and (2) a trial and conviction by the Senate. Impeachment requires a majority vote of the House; conviction is more difficult, requiring a two-thirds vote by the Senate. Impeachment History – www.infoplease. com/spot/impeach.

[65] The U.S. Congress passed the Kansas-Nebraska Act on May 30, 1854. It allowed people in the territories of Kansas and Nebraska to decide for themselves whether to allow slavery within their borders. The Act served to repeal the Missouri Compromise of 1820, which prohibited slavery north of latitude $36^0 30'$. The History Place www.historyplace.com

[66] Stan Klos www.famousamericans.net

[67] Communications and travel at the end of the Civil War were very limited, yet it's difficult to understand why Congress would not have reconvened in special session sooner.

[68] Houghton Mifflin www.college.hmco.com

[69] U S Constitution www.usconstitution.com/CivilRightsAct1866

[70] "African American History," Microsoft® Encarta® Online Encyclopedia 2005

[71] Alabama Department of Archives & History. KKK – www. alabamamoments.state.al.us/sec28det

[72] Lessons for Iraq From Gettysburg – www.washingtonpost.com/wp-dyn/content/article/2005/05/03

[73] "African American History," Microsoft® Encarta® Online Encyclopedia 2005

[74] "Congress of the United States," Microsoft® Encarta® Online Encyclopedia 2005

[75] Johnson launched affirmative action to compensate for past racial injustices and discrimination.

[76] MSN Money - No Kidding: U.S. taxes are a bargain: www.moneycentral.msn.com

Chapter Eleven

[77] Houghton Mifflin college.hmco.com: Robber Barons—derogatory term used to describe big business in the late 19th century who used ruthless, unscrupulous, and sometimes illegal means to build monopolies and develop great economic power. Ten percent of American businessmen controlled over 90 percent of U.S. wealth. Industrial leaders Andrew Carnegie, John D. Rockefeller, and Cornelius Vanderbilt were called robber barons, as well as bankers Jay Gould and J. Pierpont Morgan.

[78] Buzz Flash interview, September 11, 2003. Paul Krugman is a columnist on the Op-Ed Page of *The New York Times* and a professor of economics and international affairs at Princeton University. He has written many hundreds of papers and 18 books. *The Great Unraveling,* a collection of his columns, was the latest.

[79] "Capitalism," Microsoft ® Encarta ® Online Encyclopedia 2005

[80] "Smith, Adam (economist)," Microsoft ® Encarta ® Online Encyclopedia 2005

[81] In the 1920s and 30s the Communist Party made concerted efforts to infiltrate U.S. unions but failed to gain support. The tremendous labor unrest that existed prior to the Roosevelt administration was defused by legislation favorable to labor.

[82] The American Experience: www.pbs.org/wgbh/amex/carnegie/revenge.

[83] "In an era, when the earth is gradually being divided up among states, some of which embrace almost entire continents [like the United

States], we cannot speak of a world power in connection with a formation whose political mother country is limited to the absurd area of five hundred thousand square kilometers." – Adolf Hitler, *Mein Kampf*

[84] One of the most amusing Yiddish words is *chutzpah* (silent "c"), meaning an inordinate amount of gall, brass, or nerve. The classic example of someone with chutzpah is the guy who murders his mother, then throws himself on the mercy of the court because he's an orphan. - La.essortment. com/Yiddish words

[85] In regard to the gold discovery, Horace Greeley wrote in the *New York Tribune,* "Fortune lies upon the surface of the earth as plentiful as the mud in our streets..."

[86] Child Labor Microsoft® Encarta® Online Encyclopedia 2005

[87] Research at: USINFO.SATE.GOV

[88] The *Grapes of Wrath* was also made into a film of the same name directed by John Ford and starring a young Henry Fonda. The film realistically depicts the socioeconomic impact of the Great Depression and a mid-30s drought upon one representative family.

[89] Research at: www.reapinc.org/History Selected dates in labor history are available as well.

[90] The American Experience pbs.org/wgbh/amex/wilson/portrait

[91] The Civil War prompted the first income tax in the U.S. in 1861; it was a flat three-percent tax on all income over $800. Later it was modified to include a graduated tax. Congress repealed the income tax in 1872. In 1894, as part of a high tariff bill, Congress enacted a two-percent tax on income over $4,000. The tax was immediately struck down by a five-to-four decision of the Supreme Court. A surprise Constitutional amendment passed Congress in 1909 as a political fluke that backfired on the Republicans and was ratified overwhelmingly by the state legislatures on February 25, 1913. It is the 16th Amendment to the U.S. Constitution.

[92] Biography of Woodrow Wilson www.whitehouse.gov

[93] Yellow dog contracts stipulated that, as a condition of employment, the worker agreed not to join a union.

[94] Economics www.wsu.edu.8080

[95] Krugman's articles can be found at The Unofficial Paul Krugman Web Page www.pkarchive.org/economy/ForRicher   www.nytimes.com/2005/06/10krugman

[96] Union Member Summary: www.bls.gov/news.release/union2.nr0

[97] Income Inequality in the United States, 1913-1998 by Thomas Piketty and Emmanuel Saez (2001).

1Norquist is president of Americans for Tax Reform. ATR is responsible for the Taxpayer Protection Pledge, which asks all candidates for federal and state offices to commit themselves in writing to oppose all tax increases. Here's the really frightening news: according to ATR's website, as of 2005, President George W. Bush, 222 House members, and 46 Senators have taken the pledge. On the state level, six governors and 1247 state legislators have also taken the pledge. In New Hampshire all four of our Congressional delegation have pledged, as have seven state senators out 24 and 78 House members out of 400. I received the pledges from Norquist when I ran for the state Senate and threw them in the garbage where they belonged.

Chapter Twelve

[98] The strategy was first described and named by David Stockman, President Reagan's director of the Office of Management and Budget.

[99] Sen. John McCain claims many in the service are now "draftees" because of involuntary extended tours of duty. Others look at the tens of thousands of dollars paid for reenlistment bonuses and enlistment incentives as making today's troops "mercenaries." While Bush talks of the "Coalition of the Willing," few Americans know of the "Brotherhood of the Extremely Well Paid," mercenaries working for private security firms in Iraq. Estimates of their number run from 5,000 to 15,000. One of the largest is Blackwater Security Consulting based in Moyock, NC. It's said to have over 450 guards working in Iraq, making it larger than many national contingents that form the coalition.

[100] "Discretionary" programs are those whose funding is determined by the 13 annual appropriations bills. The term excludes entitlements, such as Medicare or veterans' pensions.

[101] Washingtonpost.com February 9, 2005

[102] Thomas Friedman, "Too Much Pork and Too Little Sugar," *New York Times,* August 5, 2005.

[103] Congressional Budget Office Summer Report August 2005

[104] Business.telegraph www.telegraph.co.uk/money/main.jhtml

[105] Budgetary and Economic Terms www.cbo.gov

[106] Millennium BillionFund www.buillionfund.com

[107] Nicholas D. Kristof, *A Glide Path to Ruin*: "President Bush has excoriated the 'death tax,' as he calls the estate tax. But his profligacy will leave every American child facing a 'birth tax' of about $150,000. That's right: every American child arrives owing that much, partly to babies in China and Japan. No wonder babies cry."

[108] National Debt Graph www.zfacts.com/p/318p.html

[109] The interest rate of 5.5 percent that I used in my example hasn't been seen since the early 1960s. During the peak of inflation (1979-1982), mortgage rates climbed to over 18 percent.

[110] Institute on Taxation and Economic Policy Tax Model, July 2005

[111] www.brillig.com/debt_clock

[112] See Chapter 11.

[113] Federal Insurance Contribution Act (FICA) tax is a United States tax levied in an equal amount on employees and employers to fund old age, survivors, and disability insurance portion of the Social Security system and the hospital portion (Medicare). For 2005, the Social Security portion is 6.2 percent of wages up to $90,000 (this limit goes up each year). The Medicare portion is 1.45 percent with no limit.

[114] These securities may include regular Treasury bills, notes, and bonds that you or I might buy (called "public issues"), or ones that are issued only to the trust funds (called "special issues"). Since 1981 the Treasury has invested trust fund assets only in special issues.

[115] Research at www.ssa.gov/OACT/ACT/part5.html

[116] Research at www.ssa.gov/pressoffice/pr/trustee05-pr.html

[117] CBO - Off-budget surpluses comprise surpluses in the Social Security trust funds as well as the net cash flow of the Postal Service. Postal Service outlays were −$2.7 billion in 2005 and total outlays 2006-2015 are projected to be -$46 billion.

[118] The Congressional Budget Process, An Explanation, Revised December 1998

[119] Brookings Institute, "Can the U.S. Government Live Within Its Means? Lessons from Abroad," June 2005 www.brookings.edu/comm/policybriefs/pb141.html

[120] An explanation in part from a *New York Times* editorial on July 24, 2005 titled "A Deficit Disorder": "With much ado, the White House recently announced that windfall tax revenues in the first half of 2005 would probably reduce this year's federal budget deficit to $333 billion, a $79 billion drop from last year.

"That would be a truly hopeful development if the administration planned to use the unexpected improvement as a starting point for continuing deficit reduction. But no. The White House sees the deficit drop as an opportunity to continue the same policies that caused the red ink in the first place. Specifically, the administration is promoting the deficit's decline as evidence that tax cuts spur investment and in so doing increase revenue; ergo, tax cutting should continue, particularly for stock- and bondholders.

"A big problem with the administration's reasoning is that much of this year's bolstered tax revenue is due to the expiration of one of the tax cuts from President Bush's first term. From late 2001 through 2004, taxes were lower than they otherwise would have been because a temporary tax break allowed business to quickly write off purchases of new equipment. Starting this year, purchases must be deducted more gradually, a change that has increased corporate tax payments in 2005.

"Other tax revenue boosters are one-shot deals. A law enacted last year and valid only in 2005 allows companies to bring hundreds of billions of dollars in untaxed foreign profit back into the United States at a special low rate of 5.25 percent, compared with the normal corporate rate of 35 percent. That is inflating corporate tax receipts this year, but is expected to reduce tax revenue over time, since companies will take advantage of the break in 2005 rather than repatriating profits at a higher rate later on."

[121] CBPP August 16, 2005 report.

[122] "Greenspan admits tax cut error," by Michael Gawenda, Washington **[Post?]**, March 17, 2005

[123] House Budget Committee Democratic Caucus, April 26, 2005, John M. Spratt, Jr., ranking Democratic member.

[124] Rep. Henry Waxman, Ranking Member Committee on Government Reform, U.S. House of Representatives – Fact Sheet July 2005

[125] "A Costly Windfall for the Wealthiest Americans" www.cbpp.org/5-25-00tax.htm

[126] Center on Budget and Policy Priorities June 9, 2005

[127] Nicknamed "the Oracle of Omaha", Buffett has amassed an enormous fortune from astute investments though his company Berkshire Hathaway, of which he holds about 38 percent as of 2005. With an estimated net worth of $44 billion, he is ranked by *Forbes* as the second-richest person in the world, behind Bill Gates.

[128] An import certificate is a means by which a government has legal control of the amount and internal channeling of imports.

Chapter Thirteen

[129] Japan is still a fierce trade competitor and buys some T-bills, but not to the extent that China is buying them.

[130] Farrar, Strauss and Giroux, New York, 2005.

[131] Robert B. Reich was U.S. Secretary of Labor in the Clinton administration, and co-founder of the *American Prospect* magazine, from the October issue of which this is adopted.

Chapter Fourteen

[132] On September 24, 2005, Lester M. Crawford, the commissioner of food and drugs, resigned suddenly; he had been under fire for more than a year by consumer advocates and scientists inside and outside the agency, who claimed scientific decisions were being warped by politics.

[133] "All the President's Friends," by Paul Krugman, *New York Times,* September 12, 2005

[134] "Starving the Beast"

[135] The Progress Report September 22, 2005 progress@americanprogr essiveaction.org

[136] "Many Contracts for Storm Work Raise Questions," by Eric Lipton and Ron Nixon, *New York Times* September 25, 2005.

[137] The quote appeared in a *New York Times* op-ed by Thomas Friedman titled "Singapore and Katrina," September 14, 2005.

[138] I speak of it and the deregulation of the Savings & Loans in my memoir, *A Good Stick*, available through AuthorHouse www.authorhouse. com/BookStore/SearchCatalog.aspx

[139] The PBGC was created by the 1974 Employee Retirement Income Security Act (ERISA) to guarantee and protect pension benefits in private traditional pension plans known as defined benefit plans, the type that promise to pay a specific monthly benefit at retirement. http://edworkforce. house.gov/issues/108th/workforce/pension/9040... September 4, 2003

[140] "Bankruptcies: The threat to your pension," by Steve Hargraves, CNN/Money staff writer

[141] Interest only mortgages allow your payments to cover interest only for a period of time, usually the first three to 10 years. Option or flex-payment Adjustable Rate Mortgages allow you to choose what to pay every month: the standard principal and interest, only interest or a minimum that's less than what's needed to cover the interest. Forty-year fixed is like the 15 or 30 but takes forever to pay off. A piggyback is a traditional mortgage and a home-equity loan; it can leave you with little or no equity. A no-doc or low doc lets you borrow without proving you meet the income requirements and you pay higher interest.

[142] The airlines serve about 550 commercial airports but carry many, many more passengers. In 2000, the airlines provided 516.1 billion passenger-miles – the railroads only 5.5 billion. (CBO September 2003)

[143] The federal government essentially owns Amtrak. The Secretary of Transportation appoints Amtrak's management and its board of directors.

[144] Enron's CEO, Ken Lay, now under indictment for the scandal was a great Texas buddy of, you guessed it, President Bush.

[145] Under unlimited homestead exemptions in half-dozen states, "fat cats who go into bankruptcy don't lose their mansions," Senator Ted

Kennedy, author of two amendments to the bill that failed, is quoted as saying. "Where is the fairness in this bill?"

[146] One popular loophole is the creation of an "asset protection trust," which is worth doing only for the wealthy. New York Democratic Senator Charles Schumer introduced an amendment that would have limited the exemption on such trusts. It failed in the Senate; 54 Republicans and 2 Democrats voted against it.

[147] Term used by Paul Krugman in his March 8, 2005 *New York Times* op-ed column.

[148] Public Law No: 109-002

[149] "Senate Approves Measure to Curb Big Class Actions," by Stephen Labaton, *New York Times,* February 11, 2005.

[150] National Conference of State Legislatures Medical Malpractice Tort Reform, July 25, 2005.

[151] Sheller, Ludwig & Badey: Medical Malpractice www.sheller.com/PracticeGroup.asp/?PracticeGroupID=6

[152] "Evidence Shows Lawsuits Haven't Caused Doctors' Insurance Woes," *Public Citizen,* Congress Watch April 2005.

[153] The index measured the health status of individuals by looking at the amount each country spent on its people's health and at health indicators including life expectancy, infant immunization rates and death rates of mothers and babies.

[154] U.S. Department of Labor www.bls.gov/cps/minwage2004tbls.htm#3

[155] The White House Office of the Press Secretary August 9, 2004

Chapter Fifteen

[156] By J. Larry Brown, Robert Kuttner, and Thomas M. Shapiro, The Institute on Assets and Social Policy for Social Policy and Management at Brandeis University.

[157] Building a Real "Ownership Society" – definitely suggested reading.

[158] US Census 2004, Living below the poverty line: White 25,301,000 – Black 9,000,000

[159] There'll be much more on Bush's failed foreign policy and the administration's decision-making process in chapter 18.

[160] National Coalition on Health Care www.nchc.org/facts/cost/shtml

[161] US Census Bureau

[162] The Federal Government establishes national guidelines but each state (1) establishes its own eligibility standards; (2) determines the type, amount, duration, and scope of services; (3) sets the rate of payments for services; and (4) administers its own program. It's a very complex system in which no two states are the same.

[163] Nursing Home Statistics www.efmoody.com/longterm/nursingstatistics. html

[164] Established by the Medicare Prescription Drug Improvement, and Modernization Act of 2003.

[165] Established with the Medicare Prescription Drug Improvement, and Modernization Act of 2003.

[166] "House GOP Vows Broad Cuts is Spending," *The Washington Post,* October 8, 2005

[167] The NH Center for Public Policy estimates that 17 percent of the cost of private health insurance in NH is due to cost shifting from the state government's underfunding of Medicaid.

[168] On October 18, 2005, the Bush administration approved a sweeping Section 1115 waiver Medicaid plan for Florida. It will limit spending for many of the 2.2 million beneficiaries there and gives private health plans new freedoms to limit benefits. It shifts the traditional Medicaid "defined benefit" plan, to a "defined contribution" plan, under which the state sets a ceiling on spending for each recipient. Other states are watching Florida's experience. South Carolina has developed a similar plan and Georgia and Kentucky are waiting in the wings. Michael O. Leavitt, secretary of HHS, approved the proposal just 16 days after it was formally submitted to him, with strong support from Gov. Jeb Bush (the president's brother). *The New York Times,* October 20, 2005.

[169] U.S. Census 2004 - 9.8 percent of people 65 years or older had incomes below the poverty line.

[170] The Arc of Washington State – www.arcwa.org/social_security.html

[171] What President Bush presented was Reform Model 2 of the Final Report of the President's Commission to Strengthen Social Security (2001).

[172] The 2041 projection is by the Social Security Board of Trustees and considered to be very cautious; the Congressional Budget Office is probably more realistic in projecting that Trust Fund will run out in 2052.

[173] Research at: Center on Budget and Policy Priorities – Policy Brief: Protecting Low-Income Families' Savings, June 21, 2005

[174] Human Rights Disparities between Europe and the United States: Conflicting Approaches to Poverty Prevention and Alleviation of suffering, by William Felice www.du.edu/gsis/hrhw/2005/29-felice-2005.pdf

[175] Research at Welfare: www.newsbatch.com/welfare.html

[176] The state welfare programs almost always placed the duty to provide relief on local governments, with the funding to come from local property taxes; local governments still ultimately retain that responsibility.

[177] Section 1115 waivers are now being promoted by the Bush administration for Medicaid.

[178] The great difference between FDR and LBJ was that FDR stood clear of racial civil rights issues, and because of the Depression won a solid Democratic Party majority in the South. LBJ did not. Subsequently, LBJ's Great Society anti-poverty programs and civil rights initiatives (including voter rights) would be linked by the far right, resulting in the South turning solidly Republican.

[179] *Washington Profile* www.washprofile.org/en/node/2295

[180] NH TANF benefits rank among the highest; the maximum benefit for a family of three is $625; by comparison, Alabama is the lowest at $164; Mississippi $170; Arkansas $204; and Texas $208.

[181] Since 1996 eligibility requirements were increased for food stamps. Now an Able-bodied Adult Without Dependents (ABAWD) must also meet special ABAWD work requirements to receive more than three months of food stamps in a 36-month period.

[182] The Bureau of Labor Statistics (BLS) uses data taken by monthly telephone surveys by the U.S. Census Bureau of about 60,000 homes. Annually BLS combines that data with information from state offices of Unemployment Insurance to further compile regional statistics.

Chapter Sixteen

[183] Public Citizen www.citizen.org/trade/wto

[184] In November 1999, the WTO's Third Ministerial Meeting in Seattle collapsed in the face of unprecedented protests from people and governments around the world.

[185] Unlike a treaty, trade agreements do not require a two-thirds consenting vote of the Senate.

[186] RIA Norvosti – Russia – Talks on WTO membership...

[187] Ross Perot

[188] On October 2, 2005, the California Democratic Party resolved to make cancellation of NAFTA and withdrawal from the WTO its official position.

[189] "Fast Track" is a procedure through which Congress gives the president authority to negotiate trade agreements and provides special rules for considering those agreements. Fast track transfers constitutionally mandated powers of Congress to the Executive Branch.

[190] WTO/The WTO in brief – 3

[191] "The Gulf between Baghdad and Doha," by Sam Vaknin, Ph.D.

[192] The coinage of the term has been claimed for the UK Chancellor of the Exchequer Iain Macleod, who died in 1970.

[193] Comment taken from a Nov. 16, 2005 *New York Times* by Edmund L. Andrews titled, "Low Inflation and Rising Wages Can Coexist, Fed Nominee Says."

[194] By comparison, in the United States the average workweek has increased and many Americans find themselves working almost 24/7 in order to make ends meet. Consequently, Europeans are living longer, healthier lives than Americans. Largely because American working mothers have little time to shop and cook, morbid obesity has become the nation's number one health problem.

[195] Definition of civil service: 1. Those branches of public service that are not legislative, judicial, or military and in which employment is usually based on competitive examination. 2. The entire body of persons employed by the civil branches of a government.

[196] This ranks the United States number two in the world; China ranks number one, with 2.3 million under arms.

[197] In socialist countries the term "privatization" was used to signify the turnover of government owned and operated industries such as coal

and steel. That's not the case in the United States, which has never been a socialist country.

[198] "A Private Obsession" – *New York Times*: http://select.nytimes. com/2005/11/18/opinion/18krugman.html

[199] NEA Charter Schools: www.nea.org/charter/index.html

[200] "Warnings of Privatization" – New York Times: www.nytimes. com/2005/10/16/education/16college.html

[201] Report by the President's Commission on Postal Organization 1967.

[202] "The Demise of the Postal Service," By Murray Comarow, www. cosmos-club.org/journal/2002/comarow.html

[203] It is interesting to note that when Ronald Reagan broke the Air Traffic Controller's strike in 1981 the workers were fired and never allowed to return to work. It took years for airline industry to recover. The labor movement in America never has.

[204] Again, data compliments of Murray Comarow. Comarow was executive director of President Johnson's Commission on Postal Organization in 1967-1968 and executive director of President Nixon's Advisory Council on Executive Organization in 1970-1971.

[205] Center for Policy Alternatives: http://www.stateaction.org/issues/issue. cfm/issue/SentencingReform.xml

[206] In 2004 the National Education Association (NEA) estimated that in U.S. public school (K-12) the total average expenditure per student (local, state and federal) was $8,208; there were about 48 million students enrolled for a total national expenditure of about $395 billion. The average teachers salary was $46,726, slightly higher than the median household income of $44,389.

[207] "No Child Left Behind" falls far short of the mark. For one thing, it applies no national standard, merely requires the states to establish one and annually test against it. Instead of helping those school districts wherein students are not meeting that standard, they are penalized, federal grant money is withheld, and students are allowed to tuition out to other schools, further exacerbating the situation. Not surprisingly, states are lowering their standards to avoid the cuts in funding, and teachers are being instructed to teach to the test and not broader curriculums. In most ways,

the law has been nothing more than a political ploy that has done little to increase the level of education in America's public schools.

[208] Organization for Economic Cooperation and Development, *Education at a Glance: OECD Indicators 2004 (Paris, France, 2004).*

[209] Democratic Staff, Committee on Education and the Workforce, U.S. House of Representatives, *FYI 2006 Bush Budget: Breaks Promises, Underfunds K-12 Funding, and Forces Students to Pay More for College,* Feb.7, 2007. Available at: http://edworkforce.house.gov/democrats/photos/ FY06budgetsummary.pdf.

[210] Robert Reich was secretary of labor in the Clinton administration. His radio broadcast comments can be researched at: http://www.robertreich. org/reich/20050621.asp

[211] U.S. Department of Labor - Research at: http://www.workforcesecurity. doleta.gov/unemploy/tra.asp

[212] "Research at Edge: That Famous Equation and You," by Brian Greene www.edge.org/3rd_culture/greene05/greene05_index.html

Chapter Seventeen

[213] "Energy from Fossil Fuels," *Science*, February 4, 1949

[214] "Nuclear Energy and the Fossil Fuels," by M. King Hubbert, chief consultant (General Geology), Exploration and Production Research Division, Shell Development Company, Publication Number 95, Houston, Texas, June 1956.

[215] The publication can be found on the Council's website, www.acus.org - Robert L. Hirsch is a senior energy program adviser for SAIC. Previous employment included executive positions at the U.S. Atomic Energy Commission, the U.S. Energy Research and Development Administration, Exxon, ARCO, EPRI, and Advanced Power Technologies, Inc. Dr. Hirsch is past chairman of the Board on Energy and Environmental Systems at the National Academies. He has a Ph.D. in engineering and physics from the University of Illinois.

[216] U.S. Department of Energy, Energy Information Administration, *International Energy Outlook* – 2004, February 2004,

[217] Aleklett, K. & Campbell, C.J. *The Peak and Decline of World Oil and Gas Production.* Uppsala University, Sweden. Aspo web site. 2003.

[218] O'Reilly, D.J., chairman and CEO, Chevron corporation, *The Washington Post.* July 25, 2005.

[219] Hirsch, R.I., Bezdek, R. and Wendling, R. *Peaking of World Oils Production: Impacts, Mitigation, and Risk Management.* DOE NETL. February 2005.

[220] Research at http://www.commondreams.org/views05/0503-22.htm "Carter Tried To Stop Bush's Energy Disasters – 28 Years Ago," by Thom Hartmann

[221] President Carter's speech can be found at http://www.pbs.org/wgbh/amex/carter/filmmore/ps_energy.html

[222] No one knows with certainty if such an agreement was actually made, but the results are recorded history.

[223] President Clinton's FY2001 Climate Change Budget, February 3, 2000. http://clinton3.nara.gov/Initiatives/Climate/budgetsummary.html

[224] Under the new plan, a business owner who purchases a $110,000 Hummer H1 in 2003 can now deduct a total of $106,000 in the first year. Research at http://www.taxpayer.net/TCS/whitepapers/SUVtaxcredit.pdf

[225] The Center for American Progress is a Washington, D.C. based nonpartisan research and educational institute dedicated to promoting a strong, just and free America that ensures opportunities for all. Its president and chief executive officer is John Podesta, who served as President Clinton's chief of staff.
Research Securing at http://www.americanprogress.org/site/pp.asp?c=biJ RJ8OVF&b=263962

[226] Plan B $_{2.0}$ is published by W. W. Norton, ISBN 0-393-06162-0 (hardcover)—ISBN 0-393-32831-7 (pbk.)

[227] The world's first nuclear power plant came on line at Obninsk, USSR on June 27, 1954.

[228] Research at: http://www.cns-snc.ca/media/toocheap/toocheap.html

[229] Coal liquefaction has been widely used to make synthetic fuels (oil, gasoline and diesel). The Germans in World War II used it extensively because they were rich in coal and cut off from Middle Eastern oil. The

process can be used today, but so far it is cheaper to use inexpensive crude oil pumped from below the ground.

[230] Greenspirit Strategies   http://www.greenspiritstrategies.com/D151.cfm

[231] Amory Lovins et al. "Winning the Oil Endgame" http://www.oilendgame.com/pdfs/WtOEg_ExecSummary.pdf

[232] Corporate Average Fuel Economy: http://www.ita.doc.gov/td/auto/cafe.html

[233] The first prototype diesel engine, invented by Rudolf Diesel, ran for the first time in Augsburg, Germany on August 10, 1893. It was a single 10-foot iron cylinder with a flywheel that ran on peanut oil. In a 1912 speech, Diesel said, "the use of vegetable oils for engine fuels may seem insignificant today, but such oils may become, in the course of time, as important as petroleum and the coal-tar products of the present time." During the 1920s, diesel engine manufactures altered their engines to use the lower viscosity of the fossil fuel (petrodiesel) rather than vegetable oil, a biomass fuel.

[234] Energy Justice Network http://www.energyjustice.net/naturalgas/

[235] Statement by John E. Shelk before the House Committee on Energy and Commerce Subcommittee on Energy and Air Quality, February 16, 2005.

[236] American Lung Association http://lungaction.org/reports/sota05_protecting.html

[237] Report for Congress U.S. Coal: A Primer on the Major Issues, March 25, 2003

[238] "Annals of Science Butterfly Lessons," by Elizabeth Kolbert, *The New Yorker,* Jan. 9, 2006

[239] "How Global Warming May Cause the Next Ice Age," by Thom Hartmann http://www.commondreams.org/views04/0130-11.htm

[240] "Sago Puts Spotlight On Safety Strategy," by Joby Warrick, *The Washington Post.*

Chapter Eighteen

[241] Projected cost was over $451 billion for Iraq and Afghanistan by the end of 2006. The British Medical Journal *Lancet* estimates 100,000

Iraqi civilians have been killed. Bush put the figure at 30,000, which most observers say is way low.

242 The 9/11 Commission Final Report: http://www.gpoaccess.gov/911/

243 http://www.msnbc.msn.com/id/4595173/   The spelling of Al Qaeda as al Qida is from Clark's testimony.

244 Mr. Paul R. Pillar, a retired C.I.A. veteran who oversaw intelligence assessments about the Middle East from 2000 to 2005 in February 2006, accused the Bush administration of ignoring or distorting the prewar evidence on a broad range of issues related to Iraq in its effort to justify the American invasion of 2003. *Foreign Affairs,* March/April 2006 http://www.foreignaffairs.org/20060301faessay85202/paul-r-pillar/intelligence-policy-and-the-war-in-iraq.html

245 Chomsky: "There Is No War On Terror," by Geov Parrish, printed on January 23, 2006. http://www.alternet.org/story/30487/

246 The War Powers Act http://www.hbci.com/~tgort/wpa.htm

247 White House press release: http://www.whitehouse.gov/news/releases/2002/01/20020129-11.html

248 Iran is a known supporter of terrorist groups, and Hamas has claimed credit for numerous terrorist attacks. Both have vowed to eliminate the State of Israel.

249 The United States now spends as much on defense as the rest of the world combined.

250 Research at: http://www.projectcensored.org/downloads/Global_Dominance_Group.pdf

251 "President Jonah," by Gore Vidal, published on Saturday, January 28, 2006 by TruthDig. http://www.truthdig.com/dig/item/20060124_president_jonah/

252 Later in the war, Germany attacked London with V1 bomb-tipped drones and V2 explosive rockets.

253 Bomber crews suffered the highest percentage of casualties of any branch of the military in WWII.

254 Two days after Hiroshima the Soviet Union declared war on Japan. The Red Army and their Maoist Chinese comrades were attacking across a broad frontier. Surrendering to the United States was a far better alternative than a Sino-Soviet occupation.

[255] Atomic Audit: http://www.brookings.edu/comm/events/19980630.htm

[256] The Rosenbergs were executed on June 19, 1953. Because Ethel Rosenberg was too small for the electric chair, which was built for men and didn't fit properly, it took three charges of electricity to kill her.

[257] Operation Castle: The March 1, 1954 test – codenamed Bravo – exploded with far greater power than predicted. It was a thousand times more powerful than the bomb dropped on Hiroshima. The test on tiny Bikini Atoll in the Marshall Islands contaminated a passing Japanese fishing boat and showered nearby villagers with radioactive ash.

[258] Arms Race http://www.pwc.k12.nf.ca/coldwar/plain/armsrace.html

[259] Research at Wikipedia http://en.wikipedia.org/wiki/Weapons_of_mass_destruction

[260] India and Pakistan tested their first nuclear weapons within days of each other in 1998. They have been at war with each other twice since over the disputed territory of Kashmir. In December of 2001, just months after 9/11, tensions between India and Pakistan grew to full military mobilization and brought the world to its first 21st century nuclear standoff. No one doubted that, threatened with national survival on either side, but particularly in a much smaller Pakistan, nuclear weapons would have been used. It is thought that the withdrawal of Pakistani troops from Tora Bora to the border with India allowed bin Laden to escape into the Pakistani wilderness area.

[261] Nuclear Non-Proliferation Treaty http://www.fas.org/nuke/control/npt/

[262] NTI: Issue Brief: Comprehensive Test Ban Treaty http://www.nti.org/e_research/e3_9a.html

[263] CTBTO Preparatory Commission http://www.ctbto.org/treaty/history.html

[264] NTI: Issue Brief: The Biological Weapons Convention http://www.nti.org/e_research/e3_28a.html

[265] Bush has since appointed Bolton as Ambassador to the United Nations over the objections of many Democratic Senators.

[266] NTI: Issue Brief: First Review Conference of the CWC http://www.nti.org/e_research/e3_33a.html

[267] The Bush administration withdrew from the ABM Treaty because it prohibited an anti-ballistic system and nuclear weapons in space ("Star Wars"). Both would have prevented Bush from picking up on that development first envisioned by Ronald Reagan. Although the collapse of the of the ABM Treaty and START II were major setbacks in the nonproliferation of nuclear weapons, the change in U.S. policy never received much public attention—all eyes were on the war with Iraq.

[268] Ted Turner and Sam Nunn founded the Nuclear Threat Initiative (NTI) in January 2001. Sam Nunn is Co-Chairman & Chief Executive Officer of NTI.

[269] This is the estimate of John Otranto, executive director of Global Care based in Munich, Germany. The estimate was made prior to 1997; the numbers would be higher now.

[270] Research at: www.airpower.maxwell.af.mil/airchronicles/apj/apj97/win97/parrin.html

[271] Research at: http://www.abc.net.au/rn/science/ockham/stories/s510828.htm

[272] http://www.whitehouse.gov/news/releases/2005/10/20051006-3.html

[273] Samuel P. Huntington, "The Clash of Civilizations?" *Foreign Affairs,* Summer 1993, 72/3. http://www.georgetown.edu/faculty/irvinem/CCT510/Sources/Huntington-ClashofCivilizations-1993.html

[274] As an interesting aside, a former Iranian Air Force pilot used to fly copilot for me occasionally. He was quite a character, who referred to himself as Persian rather than Iranian.

[275] Reagan kept his part of the deal by selling missiles to Iran, while at the same time supplying Saddam Hussein with weapons. In many ways Saddam is the monster America created.

[276] Research at http://www.eia.doe.gov/emeu/cabs/afghan.html

[277] Research at: http://www.commondreams.org/views01/1018-10.htm

[278] The Taliban http://www.infoplease.com/spot/taliban.html

[279] Osama bin Laden and "al Qaeda" http://www.culteducation.com/binladen.html

[280] Saudi Arabia http://www.state.gov/g/drl/rls/irf/2004/35507.htm

[281] Jihad is an Arabic word that means, "striving in the way of God." This striving can take a number of forms, including the daily inner struggle

to be a better person. However, jihad is often used to refer to an armed struggle fought in defense of Islam. www.pbs.org/wggh/pages/frontline/teach/alqaeda/glossary.html

[282] Research at PBS Frontline http://www.pbs.org/wgbh/pages/frontline/shows/binladen/who/bio.html and http://www.pbs.org/wgbh/pages/frontline/shows/saudi/etc/cron.html

[283] Carl von Clausewitz (1780-1831). In the early 1800s, von Clausewitz, a Prussian who fought against Napoleon and then later became the president of the Prussian Kriegsakademie (War Academy), started notes on his theories of warfare. Before they were completed, he died of cholera while observing the Polish Revolution of 1830. His works were finally compiled and published by his wife. Many consider Clausewitz to be one of the major theorists on warfare.

[284] Transcript of speech at http://www.whitehouse.gov/news/releases/2006/01/print/20060110-1.html

[285] In 2006, Afghanistan produced an estimated 4,100 tons of opium, the main ingredient in heroin, about 87 percent of the world's supply.

[286] While the Vietnam War was a terrible, ill-advised tragedy, the peace is working out pretty well. The United States lifted its trade embargo in 1994, and exchanged ambassadors in 1997. Trade between the United States and Vietnam was over $6.4 billion in 2004.

[287] *The New York Times,* Cheney Warns of 'Consequences' for Iran on Nuclear Issue, March 8, 2006.

http://www.nytimes.com/2006/03/08/international/08diplo.html

[288] Nuclear Madness by Bob Herbert, *New York Times* March 6, 2006

[289] As of the spring of 2006, Abramoff was under federal indictment for various improprieties. DeLay, under indictment in the State of Texas for campaign finance law violations, was forced to resign as House majority leader and later dropped out of his reelection race. Conditions in the Marianas remain basically unchanged.

Chapter Nineteen

[290] As majority leader, Tom DeLay prided himself as being called "the hammer." On April 3, 2006 DeLay announced that he would withdraw from his race for reelection and leave Congress within months. This came

after news that a key former DeLay aide pleaded guilty to conspiracy and agreed to cooperate with the ongoing federal investigation of DeLay's money-for-influence machine.

[291] The number of U.S. troops in Iraq was increased by about 10,000 in 2006 due to the increased violence and attacks upon American forces.

[292] The Latino vote swung key states for the Republicans in 2004. If the Republicans are viewed as anti-Latino, it could cost them dearly in 2006 – 2008.

[293] Former disgraced Speaker of the House Newt Gingrich, when asked in an interview with Time.com about the sorry situation of his own party and the prospects for Democratic gains, suggested that Democrats could make the case against Republican corruption and incompetence with a single slogan: "Had enough?"

[294] The progressive think tanks or research and analysis groups have been end noted throughout the book.

Printed in the United States
68022LVS00004B/16